Futebol
THE BRAZILIAN WAY OF LIFE

Futebol

THE BRAZILIAN WAY OF LIFE

ALEX BELLOS

BLOOMSBURY

First published 2002

Copyright © 2002 by Alex Bellos

The moral right of the author has been asserted

Bloomsbury Publishing Plc,
38 Soho Square, London W1D 3HB

A CIP catalogue record for this book
is available from the British Library

ISBN 0 7475 5403 X

10 9 8 7 6 5 4 3

Typeset by Palimpsest Book Production Ltd,
Polmont, Stirlingshire

Printed by Clays Ltd, St Ives plc

For Ella

CONTENTS

COLOMBIA
Bogotá

VENEZUELA
Caracas

GUYANA
Georgetown

SURINAME
Paramaribo

FRENCH GUYANA
Cayenne

ECUADOR
Quito

PERU
Lima

BOLIVIA
La Paz

BRAZIL
Brasília

PARAGUAY
Asunción

CHILE
Santiago

URUGUAY
Montevideo

ARGENTINA
Buenos Aires

EQUATOR

THE AMAZON RIVER

TROPIC OF CAPRICORN

SOUTH
AMERICA

INTRODUCTION

Football arrived in Brazil in 1894. The 'violent British sport' did unexpectedly well. Within decades it was the strongest symbol of Brazilian identity. The national team, as we all know, has won more World Cups than anyone else. The country has also produced Pelé, the greatest player of all time. More than that, Brazilians invented a flamboyant, thrilling and graceful style that has set an unattainable benchmark for the rest of the world. Britons call it the 'beautiful game'. Brazilians call it 'futebol-arte', or *art-football*. Whichever term you choose, nothing in international sport has quite the same allure.

I arrived in Brazil in 1998. I didn't do badly, either. I became a foreign correspondent. It was a job I'd always coveted and, journalistically speaking, Brazil is irresistible. The country is vast and colourful and diverse. Among its 170 million population there are more blacks than any other country except Nigeria, more Japanese than anywhere outside Japan, as well as 350,000 indigenous Indians, including maybe a dozen tribes who have not yet been contacted. Brazil is the world's leading producer of orange juice, coffee and sugar. It is also an industrialised nation, curiously one of the world's leading aeroplane-makers, and it has an impressive artistic heritage, especially in music and dance.

And, of course, they've got an awful lot of football.

Soon after I arrived I went to see the national team play. It was at the Maracanã, the spiritual home of Brazilian – *ergo* world – football. When the players filed on to the pitch, we jumped and cheered. The noise was like an electric storm, a rousing chorus of firecrackers, drumming and syncopated chants. It crystallised what I already knew; that the romance of Brazilian football is much more than the 'beautiful game'. We love Brazil because of the spectacle. Because their fans are so exuberantly happy. Because we know their stars by their first names – as if they are personal friends. Because the national team conveys a utopian racial harmony. Because of the iconic golden yellow on their shirts.

We love Brazil because they are *Braziiiiiiiiil*.

As a sports fan, I immediately took an interest in the domestic leagues. I read the sports pages, adopted a club and regularly went to matches. Following football is perhaps the most efficient way to integrate into Brazilian society.

As a journalist, I became increasingly fascinated with how football influences the way of life. And if football reflects culture, which I think it does, then what is it about Brazil that makes its footballers and its fans so . . . well . . . *Brazilian*.

That's what this book is about.

I first wanted to know how a British game brought over a little over a century ago could shape so strongly the destiny of a tropical nation. How could something as apparently benign as a team sport become the greatest unifying factor of the world's fifth-largest country? What do Brazilians mean when they say, with jingoistic pride, that they live in the 'football country'?

If football is the world's most popular sport, and if Brazil is football's most successful nation, then the consequences of such a reputation must be far-reaching and unique. No other country is branded by a single sport, I believe, to the extent that Brazil is by football.

The research took me a year. I flew, within the country's borders, the equivalent of the circumference of the world. I interviewed hundreds of people. First, the usual suspects: current and former players, club bosses, referees, scouts, journalists, historians and fans. Then, when I really wanted to get under the country's skin: priests, politicians, transvestites, musicians, judges, anthropologists, indian tribes and beauty queens. I also interviewed a man who makes a living performing keepie-uppies with ball bearings, rodeo stars who play football with bulls, a fan who is so peculiar-looking that he sells advertising space on his shirt and I discovered a secret plot involving Sócrates and Libya's Colonel Muammar al-Gadaffi.

I was not interested in 'facts', like results or team line-ups. Brazil is not big on facts anyway; it is a country built on stories, myths and Chinese whispers. The written word is not – yet – as trusted as the spoken one. (One of the country's more infuriating customs, especially if you are a journalist.) I was interested in people's lives and the tales they told.

The result, I hope, is a contemporary portrait of Latin America's largest country seen through its passion for football.

Brazil is the country where funeral directors offer coffins with club crests, where offshore oil rigs are equipped with five-a-side pitches and where a football club can get you elected to parliament.

I started my research in mid-2000, exactly half a century after the World Cup was held in Brazil and thirty years after Brazil won, so spectacularly, the title for the third time. It was a convenient starting point for reflection on the legacy of 'futebol-arte'.

I claim no responsibility, but within weeks Brazilian football was plunging into its most serious crisis ever. The national team lost a sequence of matches and Congress began two wide-ranging investigations into the sport.

The situation got worse and worse. Brazil kept on losing and Congressmen were shedding light upon a nasty and corrupt underworld. For a moment the unthinkable – that

Brazil would fail to qualify for the 2002 World Cup – was a real possibility.

I understand the crisis as a reflection of more general tensions. Since the 1950s, when Pelé started playing, Brazil has gone from an overwhelmingly rural and illiterate country to an urban and literate one. It has passed through two decades of dictatorship and is learning, sometimes uncomfortably, about how to create a new society.

Meanwhile, the world is different. Football is also different. The only constant seems to be the magic we still invest in Brazil's golden yellow shirts.

I followed the parliamentary investigations closely. I flew to Brasília to see the hearings. I was there when Ronaldo was called to give evidence. He was being asked to explain to Congressmen why Brazil were *only* second best in the 1998 World Cup.

'There are many truths,' the footballer told his interrogators. He said he would give 'his truth', and that he hoped it pleased them. But whether or not it was the '*true* truth' – well, that was up to them.

I immediately scribbled this down in my notebook. I thought it was the most unintentionally observant comment any footballer has ever made.

Brazil has many 'truths'. This book is my search for the '*true* truth' of Brazilian football. I hope it pleases you.

Alex Bellos
Rio de Janeiro
November 2001

Chapter One

THE MATCH AT THE END OF THE WORLD

From his window in the village of Toftir, Marcelo Marcolino looks out on to a snowy hill-face shrouded in a sombre mist. He complains that it is always the same, that the icy bleakness is never softened by a rainbow or a clear sky. Outside, the freezing wind is remorseless. The streets are deserted. Marcelo does not like to leave his house anyway; he spends most of his day watching satellite television in languages he does not understand.

Marcelo always wanted to be a footballer. It was his dream ever since his childhood in Copacabana. Maybe for Flamengo, his favourite club in Rio de Janeiro. Even for their rivals, Fluminense, where his father had once played. He never imagined he would end up plying his trade in the dour north Atlantic, where the average summer temperature is almost ten degrees lower than the Brazilian winter. Where he once travelled to an away game by fishing boat.

The Faroe Islands are halfway between Scotland and Iceland. They were probably first discovered by the Irish monk St Brendan, who sailed past them in the early sixth century. St Brendan was looking for *Hy-Brazil*, the mythical Isle of the Blessed and for some scholars the ancient origin of the name Brazil. One and a half millennia later the Faroes have been discovered by tropical travellers coming in the other direction. They have found their own bitter paradise.

Marcelo first heard of the Faroes when the offer from Toftir's B68 came through. He picked up his visa at the Danish consulate in Rio de Janeiro. They told him to bring a coat. It was not enough. Arriving in Copenhagen to change planes, he felt his first gust of chilly air. 'Oh my God,' he thought, 'I want to go home.' B68 welcomed him at the airport on Vágar Island, in the west of the archipelago, the only location blessed with a runway's worth of flat land. Marcelo was then driven to Toftir, which involves a ferry and an hour-long drive along the islands' jagged contours. He noticed that the treeless Faroe scenery was covered in white. It was the first time he had seen snow.

Even by Faroese terms, Toftir is small and remote. The village's population is 1,000 – about a twentieth the size of the capital, Tórshavn. Toftir is a settlement of a few hundred homes along a windswept coastal road. The houses are unfussy cubes with neat roofs. Toftir has no cinema or restaurant or pub. It has a fish market, a fish factory and a church. And a football club with three Brazilians.

When I arrived at Marcelo's house, at lunchtime, he was fast asleep. Now, ten minutes later, he is up, pacing around with the energy of a hyperactive child. 'This house is my prison,' he says. 'It's difficult. I am used to another culture: beach, beers, women. Here people don't have lives. You don't go out.'

Marcelo, who is twenty-nine, looks the part. His hair was a skinhead but he has allowed a few millimetres' growth for warmth. His black skin is lighter than it usually is in Brazil, a consequence of Toftir's sunless days. He stands elegantly upright and speaks looking down his nose, throwing his arms about and puffing his chest. He has cocky eyes and he likes the sound of his loud voice. His warm exuberance seems undiminished by the inclemency of his new surroundings.

I ask if he goes out on weekends.

'Not any more,' he replies. 'It takes an hour by bus to get to Tórshavn, and there's nothing much to do there anyway. We used to get invited to parties, but parties here are more like . . . *death-watches*.'

He realises that he has got carried away with his criticisms. He calms down and changes his tone.

'But I am happy. I don't complain. I am here because I am a professional and because I have the opportunity to make money. I would never be earning what I am now in Brazil.'

B68 only train for two hours a day. During the morning their international striker works at the Toftir fish market. He lugs crates laden with cod and monkfish out of small fishing boats and on to the quays. It is not obligatory, but the B68 president strongly encourages it. As well he might. B68's president is in charge of unloading fish at the Toftir fish market. There are lots of fish in the sea. He needs all the hands he can get.

Marcelo, who is not the sort of man given to hard work, tries to do as little as possible. He tells me that he sees his role as scoring goals. Elegant, *Brazilian* goals. He may be in the Faroe Islands, but he has not lost his sense of national pride.

He suddenly disappears to fetch a silver trophy from his room. He shows it to me boastfully: 'It's for Best Forward in the Faroese League 2000. Last season our top scorer got sixteen goals. I got fifteen. But he got a bucket-load of goals from penalties. I'm so much better than him but he's a mate of the coach.'

Marcelo likes being a big tropical fish in a small northern sea. 'I'm the king around here,' he says. 'There's no one here who can do what I can do.'

He also knows that he is living his dream, despite the miserable reality. Every Brazilian wants to play in Europe.

'When I go back to Rio people treat me differently,' he brags. 'It's like I'm royalty. People realise you are an important person. No one else from my neighbourhood has played in Europe. If you say you play for a small local club, people make fun of you, as if the team is nothing. Brazilians respect

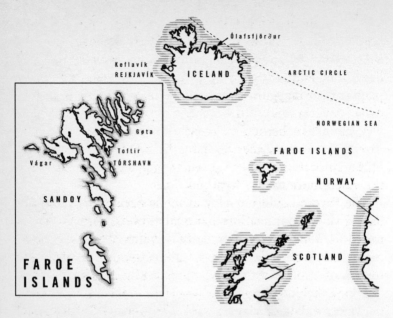

you more if you are playing in Europe. People see you with different eyes.'

He pauses again and adds: 'I will be able to tell my grandchildren that I was someone.'

Unless you listen to Radio Four's shipping forecast or import cod there is little reason to be aware of the Faroes, an autonomous part of Denmark with a population of 47,000. The isolated islands have one of Europe's smallest football leagues and the national side is one of the continent's feeblest. A 1–0 victory against Luxembourg provoked national euphoria.

I meet Niclas Davidsen, B68's president. He has the two-dimensional aura of a cardboard cut-out. His hands are always in his pockets because of the cold. When he speaks he whispers, without appearing to move his lips. A ruddy, wind-chiselled complexion is offset only by the warmth of his ginger beard and fine blue eyes. He invites me into his house. We sit in his living room, which has a picture of Rio's Sugar Loaf Mountain on the wall.

Niclas tells me that B68 are a pioneering club. He puts on a video to show me why. The story begins on 12 September 1990, a day that, trumpets the commentary, 'will linger long in the memory of the Faroese'. The Faroe Islands, playing their inaugural international match in Sweden, overcame Austria 1–0. When the team returned they were welcomed like heroes, in scenes more reminiscent of the 'streets of South America than the staid north Atlantic'. Niclas appears transfixed, even though he must have seen the video more than a hundred times.

The Faroes could not play at home because they did not have a venue that met international requirements. So Niclas raised £1.3 million to upgrade B68's pitch. It was a complicated task. Toftir has no flat land. Engineers needed fifty tonnes of explosive to blow up the hilly knuckle of rock that rises behind the village. For a year labourers worked ten hours a day, six days a week until remote Toftir gained the Faroes' national stadium, which has a capacity of eight times its population.

The video ends. Niclas looks at me. Then, he says, all B68 needed was some good players.

Help came in the form of an Icelandic friend, Páll Guðlaugsson, who used to coach the Faroese national team. Páll called Niclas and said he was flying to Rio to sign up some Brazilians. Did Niclas want in on the deal?

Few things warm the cold extremities of a Faroese football fan quite like the suggestion of a Brazilian putting on the club shirt. 'Symbolically it is very strong to have Brazilians,' says Niclas. 'And Páll told me that many Brazilians were desperate to leave.' The price of fish was high. B68 had money in the bank. Niclas called his Icelandic buddy and asked for four.

In March 1999 Marcelo Marcolino, Messias Pereira, Marlon Jorge and Lúcio de Oliveira arrived in Toftir. Two other Brazilians flew in with them, hired by GÍ, another mediocre team from another out-of-the-way village with 1,000 people, a church and a fish factory.

They were not the only Brazilians travelling abroad that
year. In 1999 more than 650 completed international transfers. They spread themselves widely, joining clubs not only
in the world's most competitive leagues but also, among
others, in Armenia, Senegal, China and Jamaica. In 2000
the exodus continued apace, with transfers to sixty-six countries, including Lebanon, Vietnam, Australia and Haiti.
About 5,000 Brazilians play professionally in foreign climes,
according to the Brazilian Football Confederation. This is
about four times the number of the country's diplomats. In
many ways the footballing diaspora is a parallel diplomatic
service; the sportsmen are cultural ambassadors as well as
economic migrants. They are public figures wherever they
go, promoting their nation's footballing heritage.

Toftir received its Brazilian legion with great excitement.
Schoolchildren shaved their blond heads to look like the
new recruits. They were the subject of interviews on the
local television and in the local newspapers. But B68's expectations were not immediately fulfilled. Playing on snow was
not the same as playing on sand. The boys from Brazil did
not adapt. Lúcio injured himself and went home. B68
finished the league in seventh place out of ten.

Niclas persevered. The team improved. B68 were third in
the 2000 championship. Marcelo won the Best Forward
trophy and contracts were renewed for 2001.

Niclas admits it was a gamble. 'We only knew Brazilian
players from the television, like Pelé and the national team,'
he says circumspectly. 'But we didn't know if the ones we'd
hired were any good. We now know they are. Especially
Marcelo.'

Third place brought with it a coveted prize – qualification to UEFA's Intertoto Cup. The summer Intertoto may
be derided by strong footballing nations, but for the clubs
on the fringes of Europe it is the peak of international glory.
No Faroese team has ever progressed beyond the first round.
With three Brazilians, however, maybe they could break the
national duck.

*   *   *

The alarm goes off at 6am. Messias Pereira wakes up and reads his five daily psalms. The Bible helps his loneliness. Today is a big day. B68 are playing B71. It could be a duel between American bombers or vitamin complexes. The reality is less dramatic: a Faroese football cup tie.

B71 are based on Sandoy, an island only accessible by boat. Niclas drives us to the early morning ferry. The route takes us through a blizzard, torrential rain and moments of icy-bright sunlight. Every few hundred metres the car negotiates a coastal hairpin bend and we enter a violently different climatic condition.

Marcelo is injured and has stayed at home. The other two Brazilians – Messias and Marlon Jorge – look as if they wish they had too. On the ferry, they sit by themselves, huddling to keep warm. Messias wears a denim jacket with a fake sheepskin collar. Marlon has a green coat. Their Faroese team-mates are in B68's red sports outfits and talk loudly in the cabin lounge.

Messias, aged twenty-eight, is a gentle man. He has a goatee beard that makes him look pious and distinguished. Marlon, aged twenty-four, has thick worry lines on his forehead. He is the smartest of all the Brazilians, and the only one who has mastered enough Faroese to be able to have more than a monosyllabic chat. Marlon lives with his Brazilian wife, Angela, who swapped her job as a bus conductor in Copacabana to salt cod in Toftir's fish factory. It was an exchange she was happy to make, since she likes the status of being a footballer's wife.

Today Marlon is conspicuously quiet. He turns very pale as the ferry starts to roll. He excuses himself and disappears to the deck. It gives me a chance to speak individually with Messias, who is the quietest of B68's three Brazilians. 'Football is my life,' he tells me. 'It's what gives me a living. I consider myself very lucky to be here.' The cold ferry is now lurching from side to side. Rain is splashing against the windows.

'But I also consider myself unlucky that I am not playing somewhere better.'

Messias believes his career has more future in the Faroes than in Brazil, where he and Marlon were playing in the second division of the Rio state league. He was earning about £50 a month. Now he is on several hundred, not including the dockwork. 'I decided to come back this season because here I am playing in the first division and I will get the chance to play in the Intertoto Cup.'

The match between B68 and B71 takes place at the end of the world. Or so it feels. The location is inhospitable and desolate. We are in a valley closed off by rock walls and snowy cloud. About fifty spectators turn up. It is too cold to stand outside and they sit watching from inside their cars.

The game is as moribund as the surroundings. Marlon makes one clever pass that creates B68's first goal. Apart from that the Brazilians do not stand out. Neither does anyone. Messias plays competently but is substituted near the end. He takes it badly and storms to the locker room. 'The pressure is huge because you are Brazilian. You have cost the club a lot. Some players in the team make mistakes but are never taken up on them. When we make the same mistakes it's different.'

B68 win 2–0. They tell me the weather was mild. Once the wind was so strong that the referee ordered all the players to crouch on the ground so they were not blown off the pitch.

During the ferry ride back, I have a chance to speak to B68's Faroese players. I ask Hans Fróði Hansen, a central defender who also plays for the national side, what the Brazilians give the team. He is tall and has floppy blond hair in a red Liverpool FC woollen hat.

Hansen first describes the Brazilians as very positive people. I ask how he knows this since they do not speak Faroese well. He thinks for a moment. 'The few words that they can speak are very positive,' he replies through a big smile.

Hansen explains that Faroese football relies on physical strength. It is good to have the Brazilians because they have a better first touch and technique. But he adds that they are not used to the Faroese way. For him the best thing about the Brazilians is psychological. 'When you think of Brazil you think of samba, smiling and dancing. That is very good for us.'

Hansen, in his perfect Scandinavian English, is expressing a universal sporting truth; that Brazilian football has a unique appeal. It dates back to 1938, although confirmation only came with the triple World Cup triumphs of 1958, 1962 and 1970. Brazil's brilliance was consecrated because, as well as winning, they did it with unrivalled élan. In 1970, the victory was given a boost by colour television, which immortalised Pelé and the yellow shirts on the hitherto black-and-white background of world sport. The impact was so overwhelming that – despite never quite playing like that again – the legacy is still felt all over the world. Even in a freezing cup tie in the Faroe Islands.

Every Brazilian is touched by the magic of the 'beautiful game'. The phrase 'Brazilian footballer' is like the phrases 'French chef' or 'Tibetan monk'. The nationality expresses an authority, an innate vocation for the job – whatever the natural ability. I sense that the Faroese players do not rate Marlon and Messias, even though they like what they represent. I ask the coach, Joannes Jakobsen. He tries to be diplomatic: 'If the Brazilians came fifteen years ago they would be much, much better than us. But we are a very proud people and we are getting better – especially if you consider how few of us there are. Football in the Faroes has changed.'

I enquire how. 'We are not losing as much as we used to,' he replies.

I ask Joannes if he would like to hire more Brazilians. 'I would prefer to buy more Faroese players because it would strengthen the side and weaken the competition. I also think it is difficult for other nationalities to adjust to the way we live.'

He adds: 'But as people they are great.'

As we drive back from the ferry – at the end of a twelve-hour day – I ask Marlon and Messias what they think of the standard of the Faroese players. They are both convinced that they are better than their team-mates – it's just that the Faroese are too ignorant to realise. Once you get them started they don't hold back with other criticisms. The Faroese, they say, just don't understand football. For a start they do not pray before games. They do not practise tactics. And they do not offer bonuses for wins. 'In Brazil we would get a little cash for a win and half that for a draw,' says Marlon. 'Here we get nothing. Where's the incentive?'

Marlon believes that if he was Faroese he would be called up for the national side. He decides that it is one of his ambitions. 'I was told that if you play five seasons in a country you are eligible. You have to have direction. That's what I'll try to do.'

If he ever does naturalise as Faroese he will not be the first of his countrymen to gain a foreign cap. Brazilians have played for Japan, Belgium and Tunisia. Recently, the Peruvian Football Federation asked Esídio, who is HIV-positive, to naturalise. He scored thirty-seven goals for Lima's Universitario in 2000 – the most goals scored in a season in Peruvian history.

But more than the chance of representing some desolate Danish rocks, Marlon's real motivation is the Intertoto fixture, which will be against Belgian club Sporting Lokeren. Maybe there will be scouts watching the match. Maybe he will be able to get a transfer to a serious football nation. The more he thinks about it the more important it becomes.

'The idea is to play really well and then leave for another team that pays more money.'

I ask Niclas what happened to the two Brazilians who were contracted by the other Faroese club, GÍ. He says that one went back to Brazil but the other, Robson, is still living in Gøta, where the team is based. He offers to take me there.

Gøta, which is a twenty-minute drive from Toftir, is even more remote but set in prettier surroundings. It is at the head of a small bay, enclosed by steep slopes.

I knock on Robson's door. He is clearly overjoyed to have a visitor. Robson has a flat, round face with thick eyebrows and dark olive skin. He has the typical features of someone from Paraíba, a small and poor state 1,200 miles north of Rio. The state's inhabitants are the victims of an ingrained racial prejudice in Brazil. They are seen as rural simpletons. I sense that his countrymen at B68 are hardly ever in touch.

Robson shows me into his living room. The house is modest and cosy. On the wall is a black-and-white poster of a naked man cradling a baby. A bowl of apples is on the coffee table. Cartoons are showing on the colour television. Robson sits on his sofa, wearing a baseball cap, jumper and tracksuit trousers.

He takes out a photo album from when he used to be a footballer in Brazil. It is the only link to his past. I look at the fading images of teams, taken by poor quality cameras in too much sunlight. I sense that Robson is almost as mystified by them as I am. He tells me that he used to play in the Paraíba state league with Marcelinho, who now plays for Hertha Berlin. Their similarities end there. Robson never made it as a footballer in the Faroes. He played once for GÍ but was so bad he never played again.

Robson aimed low – and missed. He tries to explain. He had retired from football aged twenty-three and decided on a career change. He had just finished a course training to be a security guard when his former agent called him up. Did he not fancy putting on his football boots one last time? 'I told him that I hadn't played in two years. I was in bad shape. My agent just said: "Well, go and run on the beach."'

GÍ's Brazilian import may have disappointed the team, but the village discovered he was well worth the cost of the transatlantic flight. He started at the fish factory, checking for defective fish and chopping off their heads. Robson was such a reliable, honest worker that he was kept on for the 2000 season. Then he met Anja, a ruddy-cheeked nineteen-year-old. Nine months later Mateus was born.

Anja is tidying the house as I chat with her husband. She speaks a little bit of English. She tells me it is much better than Robson's Faroese. 'He understands a lot but it is very difficult for him to speak,' she says, charitably. I see them converse. He mumbles something in Portuguese. She replies in Faroese. I am oddly moved, since they appear affectionate and contented, despite their fundamental communication difficulties.

'I've been out with blondes before but none as attractive as Anja,' Robson tells me later.

With help from Anja's family the young couple set up home. She is a housewife and he works ten-hour shifts at the fish factory. He earns £230 a week. It is enough for a respectable life. Recently he bought his first car.

Anja is a soft and attentive woman. Her hair is a tawny blond that she keeps back in a ponytail. I ask her what she sees in her husband: 'He is a gentleman. If I asked him to wash the toilet he would. The other boys that I know like to drink and go dancing. Robson doesn't. He likes to go to work and stay at home with the baby. He is a family man.'

Robson knows that had he stayed in Brazil he would have remained poor. In the Faroes he feels like a millionaire. He has all the status symbols that Brazilian footballers strive for – a home, a car, a blond wife and a little baby. 'I got all of this through football,' he says proudly. 'I would never have got all this in Brazil – now I live in a country where it is possible to build yourself a future. I have no doubt that my life is better now. Thank God I am doing well.'

But these words cannot disguise a melancholy that he is desperately alone in a foreign land. He has no friends, apart from his wife, nor any chance of returning to Brazil. He says he thinks about going back but he knows he is deluding himself. Anja's parents do not want them to move there – with good reason. If they did, Robson would never earn a quarter of what he earns now. Robson knows he will stay in the Faroes all his life.

*   *   *

The day I leave the Faroes I need to be at the airport early. Niclas lends Marlon his car to take me there. It is mid-April and snowing. Marlon has just learnt to drive. He zooms down the islands' roads. I ask him to slow down since I have the impression he has little experience of driving in icy conditions. It is not something you are taught when you take your driving test in Rio de Janeiro.

On a straight stretch of road Marlon accelerates and hits fifty miles an hour. He loses control. The car glides over the icy surface. Marlon stamps his foot on the brake. Instead of stopping the car spins and we end up back-to-front in the middle of the carriageway.

He drops me off at the ferry to the airport. It is 1°C and the snow has turned to rain.

'Best of luck for the Intertoto!' I shout as I wave goodbye.

Several months before I travelled to the Faroes I had met Marlon and Marcelo on Copacabana beach. It was so hot that the sweat from my brow dripped on my notebook and dissolved the ink. We sat in our swimming trunks and drank water from green coconuts. Marcelo was wearing sunglasses

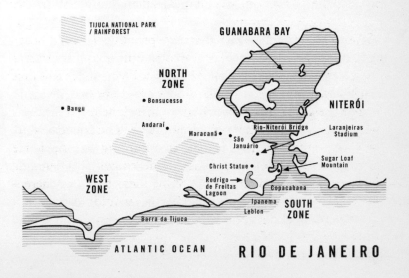

and a gold necklace. He smiled and whistled at women as they passed. They told me that the beach was where they learnt to play football, since they grew up four blocks away.

When Marcelo is back in Toftir, I visit his family. I drive to Copacabana, which is Rio's most densely inhabited neighbourhood. It has four times the population of the Faroes. Four blocks from the beach I take a cobbled street that rises sharply. I follow it until I am well above the Copacabana skyline. Rio is an upside-down city in which the richest live at sea level and the poorest in *favela* hillside shanties. I reach Cabritos Hill and park my car. The favela is an unplanned clutter of simple brick dwellings that spread like a rash across the slope. On the street, children are flying kites and men are sitting around drinking beer. I walk up a narrow alleyway of concrete steps. My presence provokes attention. I pass a plate of rice balancing on a wall, an offering to Afro-Brazilian gods. A neighbour's yard has a fighting cock in a cage. Life in the favela seems as chaotic and precarious as life in Toftir is uneventful and safe.

Marcelo's mum, Maria Nazareth, is waiting for me. Before she invites me in I look at the view. From her house you can see the Sugar Loaf Mountain, Guanabara Bay, Copacabana's tower blocks and the deep blue Atlantic Ocean beyond.

We go in through a gate that has plastic Coke bottles in lines on the top. Maria Nazareth is as thin as a post and has a tough, expressive face. She cackles when she laughs, which she does frequently. Her home is a small box divided into two rooms and a living room. She has a picture of Marcelo posing with a team on one wall. On the opposite she has hung a triangular flag of B68 and the Faroese Football Association. We are joined by Dilma, her daughter, who lives in the same block. Vilma, another daughter, lives next door. Ilma, the eldest daughter, has moved away.

'When Marcelo said he was going we were scared stiff,' says Dilma. 'We didn't know anything about where he was going. We didn't even know where the Faroes were. You see so many things on the TV about footballers being sold to foreign countries, being neglected, going hungry and not even having the money for the journey back.'

Maria de Fátima, Marcelo's sister-in-law, comes in and insists that she bakes me a cake. By now the room is crowded with another five children. One of them, a young boy, tells me that he plays for a football team on the beach. He says that when he grows up he wants be like his uncle and play in Europe.

The Marcolinos are a football family. Maria Nazareth was sixteen when she married her husband, who played professionally for teams in Rio. He never earned enough to leave the favela. Friends said that if his children were half as good as him they would be footballers too. Marcelo started in the junior divisions of Fluminense and Botafogo, two good local clubs. He turned professional at Madureira, a weaker team in the suburbs and then moved to clubs progressively lower in the Brazilian food chain. Until he fell out the bottom and ended up on the other side of the world.

Had Marcelo not inherited his father's ball skills he would be in a job like his Cabritos Hill contemporaries – who are waiters, maids and motorbike couriers; the bottom of the labour market, servicing middle-class Copacabana below. Dilma tells me she works in a bikini factory.

The cake arrives and we eat it with fizzy guarana juice. Maria Nazareth thinks she understands how football works, since both her husband and a son devoted themselves to the game. 'There are so many good players in Brazil that to be a success you need someone behind you. He found himself a backer there in Denmark. He is now a big success there. People love him.'

Maria Nazareth installed her first telephone last year. She says she knows Marcelo's decision to go was the right one since he rings home every week and says: 'Mum, I scored lots of goals.'

Dilma adds: 'He really fought hard to be a footballer. He's happy because he's doing all he ever wanted to do.'

* * *

Two miles from Cabritos Hill is Leblon, one of Rio's wealthiest neighbourhoods. Fábio Menezes lives there with his parents and 420 football shirts.

He invites me in to show me the collection. The shirts are lined up in a long rack. A few with famous autographs have not been washed, which gives his bedroom the fuggy aroma of a jumble sale.

'I bet you can't guess which one this is?' He points to a blue shirt with the initials KSI. He is correct. I am foxed.

'This is Iceland's national strip. It's from when they played against Brazil in Florianópolis. Brazil won 3–0. It was Ronaldo's first match for the national side and he scored a goal.'

He is enjoying impressing me with his knowledge. He selects another strip.

'Now this one is *really* difficult.' Before I have time to choose either a look of perplexity or astonishment, he says: 'South Melbourne. World Club Championships. Last year. Almost impossible to come by.'

I congratulate him on such a rare garment. He shows me some more moderately interesting pieces of malodorous memorabilia. He explains that the collection started because his father is a well-known radio commentator, who was able to get hold of many team shirts from his personal contacts with players. A genuinely fascinating collector's item is an example of the only time the Brazilian national team had advertising sewn on their shirts – 'vs. Chile, in Uberlândia, 1987' – but it somehow seems less surprising than the number of club tops he has from Scandinavia.

Fábio is thirty-two. He is a big man with a pasty face and thinning hair. We leave the flat, in a guarded condominium, and walk to a nearby restaurant. It is one of the coldest days of the Rio winter – a gruelling 15C. Brazilians are wrapped up warmly in jumpers and coats. Except Fábio, who is in a T-shirt, shorts and flip-flops. 'This is the ideal temperature for me,' he says, walking through the evening drizzle without an umbrella. 'I will never be cold again.'

Fábio will go down in history as the man who pushed Brazilian football to its northern extremes. Like the polar explorers who took humankind to new limits, he led his countrymen further north than they had ever been before. He is the agent who first exported Brazilians to Iceland and the Faroes.

We enter the first restaurant we pass, a recently opened establishment offering vegetarian cuisine. We sit down and he tells me how he did it. 'It's easier to place a Brazilian footballer in a team than it is a footballer of any other nationality,' he says. 'There is a worldwide fad for Brazilians. It's sad to say, but it is much easier selling, for example, a crap Brazilian than a brilliant Mexican. The Brazilian gets across the image of happiness, party, carnival. Irrespective of talent, it is very seductive to have a Brazilian in your team.'

Demand, he says, is met by an endless supply. There are about 23,000 professional footballers in Brazil. They play in more than 500 professional clubs. Fábio says that one reason exports have grown is because the internal market has boomed. 'There are more players than ever before because there are more clubs than ever before. The best way to project yourself in Brazil is either to start a church or a football club. Brazil is a dirty country. People use football clubs to serve their own interests.'

Fábio says that even though not every Brazilian is a good player, there are certainly enough successful transfers for Pelé's romantic legacy to survive. He adds: 'It's also economic. Brazilians are cheap labour.' The violent contrast of Rio's cityscapes is mirrored in football. Top players at the best Brazilian clubs earn salaries comparable to colleagues at the richest clubs in Europe. Yet most footballers hardly earn enough to live on. Almost 90 per cent take home less than £100 a month.

Every Friday I buy the football weekly *Placar*. Each issue profiles a Brazilian playing abroad. The section is called 'End of the World'. It is the most gripping read in the magazine, since the stories are an unresolved mix of tragedy and joy. The Brazilians invariably make the same comments, whether they are in Singapore, India, Guatemala or Kazakhstan: they are making more money than they ever did in Brazil, which was too competitive anyway, but they miss their mothers' rice and beans terribly. Fábio says that he is inundated with players desperate to be sold abroad. Many promise to supply forged birth certificates claiming they are younger, hoping this will make them more attractive. No country is too small or too remote or too inhospitable.

I ask Fábio why he decided to become an agent. He said it happened by family accident. In the early 1990s, when he was a law student at Rio's Catholic University, he spent a holiday backpacking round Europe. He paid a visit to a Finnish journalist his father had met when commentating on a Brazil friendly in Helsinki. A year later the Finn called up Fábio in Rio. FC Jazz of Pori, a small town 160 miles from the Finnish capital, wanted to sign a Brazilian player. Could he help?

He thought carefully. Bangu, his favourite team from the Rio suburbs, had an excellent striker called Dionísio. Fábio approached the club. Dionísio was sent to FC Jazz on loan. Fábio earned £1,000, a tidy sum for a hard-up student. Dionísio was a great success. He was transferred to another club, TPV, where he was top scorer and his club became champions of the Finnish league.

Being an international agent seemed easy. It was informal, based on networks of friends. Fábio sold one more player to FC Jazz and once he graduated started to look after players in Rio's second division. His Scandinavian contacts went in the deep freeze for a few years until, in 1998, Iceland called.

It was Páll Guðlaugsson. He had seen FC Jazz in the Intertoto Cup. He thought that the Finnish club's Brazilian gave it an edge. He told Fábio that he wanted a bunch – three for his team, Leiftur, and six for his Faroese friends.

The man from Iceland was buying in bulk. Fábio called around and rustled up some players. Páll flew in and liked what he saw. They shook hands on a deal. Páll invited Fábio to live with the players in Iceland since he spoke English and could act as an interpreter. Fábio flew out. He stayed two and a half years.

'Football opens doors,' he says. 'Even as a law graduate, my prospects to earn money in Iceland were better than in Brazil.'

Leiftur are from Ólafsfjörður, a fishing village of about 1,000 people and situated on the island's northern coast – six hours drive from Reykjavík and only thirty miles south of the Arctic Circle. Thanks to his status as the Brazilian agent, Fábio managed to get a job in the office of a fish-exporting company. During the afternoons he worked in a fish factory to learn Icelandic.

I ask him if it was a happy time.

'Is money happiness?' he replies.

After six months in Ólafsfjörður, another Icelandic team approached him for some Brazilians. Keflavík, a town near Reykjavík, wanted three. Fábio flew to Rio and rounded up some candidates.

'If I had more time I could have got better players. What is very difficult is the cultural level. The intellectual level. The Brazilian mentality is different,' he says. I ask if the problem was the language, the playing style or – perhaps – the Icelandic diet?

'The three guys were sent back after a month,' he says sombrely. 'They were caught stealing watches in the changing rooms.'

Fábio lived in Keflavík for a year and a half. He worked at another fish exporters and on weekends was the most qualified pizza waiter in Iceland. 'I had nothing else to do. My life was work and saving money.'

He appears traumatised by the experience, as if he had been in enforced exile. He repeats that he is never going back again. He never allowed himself to get a girlfriend to warm the cold nights. 'I didn't want to stay there the rest of my life. I'm not crazy. I wouldn't want to bring anyone from there to live here.' Whenever the darkness got to him too much he would go to his coat, where he kept the money he was earning in cash dollars, and count out the notes one by one. 'That was my medicine. It always made me feel better.'

His repressed anger spills over when I mention the Faroese. He describes Niclas Davidsen, the B68 president, as a swindler and his Brazilians as untrustworthy scumbags. When Fábio took his footballers there he had not been told that Faroese tax is 40 per cent. Once the players discovered this they renegotiated their contracts directly with B68, cutting Fábio out of the deal.

'These people – they are nothing,' he spits. 'They will come back and go and live in their favelas and I will not be there to help them.'

I suggest that Fábio is also a con man for selling sub-standard players. It must be difficult to find a Brazilian, like Robson, who was not good enough for a team that is lousy even in Faroese terms.

'If you had a really good player he would never want to go to play in the Faroes. It's as simple as that. Only a really desperate player would want to go there. There is no future.

'But Robson is not *that* bad,' he insists. 'He's certainly good enough to play in the Faroes. He must have been kept out for other reasons. It could be jealousy. Brazilians make people very jealous, you know.'

Fábio has respect for Robson. He tells me how they met. 'Robson's brother has been my hairdresser for years. Robson is a good man. He is honest and loyal. I gave him an opportunity to improve his life.'

Does he not feel a certain responsibility that Robson is now trapped in a foreign land?

'What can I do – I don't think for his dick. But isn't it better him being there than going hungry here? I am happy he has a decent life.'

Our conversation turns to the Intertoto Cup. A week before, B68 played their long-awaited fixture with Sporting Lokeren.

The first leg was in the Faroes. Lokeren is one of the most multinational clubs in Europe. It has players from Guinea, the Ivory Coast, Gambia, Iceland, Yugoslavia and Bosnia. It sent a reserve squad to Toftir of Belgians and Congolese.

On the evening of the match it was cold and windy – typical midsummer Faroese weather. Only about 300 people braved the elements and went to the stadium. Lokeren took the lead after ten minutes. Marcelo equalised on the half-hour. Seven minutes later B68 scored again. For a moment it felt like the Faroese were in reach of a historic victory. But just before the half-time whistle the Belgians drew level.

Sosialurin, the Faroese newspaper, wrote: 'Lokeren fielded a young and inexperienced team, but in the second half it became more and more obvious that they were in much better form than B68's players. In the last twenty minutes there was no air left in the Toftir team, and they could easily have lost by more than 2–4. The marking became loose, and several times the visitors outnumbered the home team when they got counterattacks.'

A week later, B68's squad flew to Brussels, and then took an hour's bus to Lokeren. The three Faroese fans who travelled with the team saw a dull second leg in which both teams were happy to defend. It ended 0–0.

Sporting Lokeren are not a strong team. Not even their first team, which was described as 'dismal' in the British press after they lost in the Intertoto second round to Newcastle United.

I wonder how Marlon and Messias had done. They had not. For both games they were left on the bench.

RORAIMA
Boa Vista

AMAPÁ
Macapá

TOCANTINS
Palmas

PIAUÍ
Teresina

MARANHÃO
São Luís

CEARÁ
Fortaleza

**RIO GRANDE
DO NORTE**
Natal

AMAZONAS
Manaus

PARÁ
Belém

PARAÍBA
João Pessoa

PERNAMBUCO
Recife

ACRE
Rio Branco

MATO GROSSO
Cuiabá

BAHIA
Salvador

ALAGOAS
Maceió

SERGIPE
Aracaju

RONDÔNIA
Porto Velho

DISTRITO FEDERAL
Brasília

GOIÁS
Goiânia

MINAS GERAIS
Belo Horizonte

Ribeirão
Preto

ESPÍRITO SANTO
Vitória

**MATO
GROSSO DO SUL**
Campo Grande

PARANÁ
Curitiba

Santos

RIO DE JANEIRO
Rio de Janeiro

SÃO PAULO
São Paulo

RIO GRANDE DO SUL
Porto Alegre

SANTA CATARINA
Florianópolis

Rio Grande

BRAZIL

Chapter Two

HEROIC FEET

'The Brazilians play [football] as if it were a dance. This is probably the result of the influence of those Brazilians who have African blood or are predominantly African in their culture, for such Brazilians tend to reduce everything to dance, work and play alike.'

Gilberto Freyre
New World in the Tropics, 1959

Football in Brazil has its Year Zero. In 1894 Charles Miller disembarked at the port of Santos with two footballs, one in each hand.

'What is this, Charles?' asked his father, John Miller, who was waiting on the dockside.

'My degree,' he replied.

'*What?*'

'Yes! Your son has graduated in football.'

Miller *fils* was returning to Brazil after spending his school years in Southampton. Miller *père* was a Scottish rail engineer who, like many European immigrants at the end of the nineteenth century, had followed the lucrative smell of Brazilian coffee. John put down track linking Santos to the inland plantations of São Paulo state. He sent his son back to Britain for boarding school, where Charles was such a promising left

Charles Miller

winger that he played for St Mary's, a forerunner of Southampton FC.

Whether or not football was played on Brazilian soil beforehand, Charles is deemed the 'official' progenitor. He can hardly have imagined the role his spherical baggage would have in the country's destiny. The two footballs would later turn him into a national hero, immortalised in a street name in central São Paulo – the Praça Charles Miller. His name also lingers in football terminology: a trick he developed, in which you chip the ball behind your leg, is known as a 'chaleira', a corruption of 'charles'.

Brazil had to wait a few months before Charles's footballs were put to use. With good reason. The British community was midway through the cricket season. In time, however, he set about organising football kickabouts with friends. According to lore the first 'controlled confrontation' between two teams happened on a piece of land where the mules that pulled São Paulo's trams grazed. The participants were expatriate employees from the railway and the gas companies. 'The general feeling was "What a great little sport, what a nice little game,"' reminisced Charles fifty years later. Soon his kickabouts were being noticed. Some were left confused. 'It gives them great satisfaction or fills them with great sorrow when this kind of yellowish bladder enters a rectangle formed by wooden posts,' wrote a journalist in 1896.

In Rio, two hundred miles up the coast, football's arrival was similarly inconspicuous. Oscar Cox, another Anglo-Brazilian, returned with a football from his studies in

Oscar Cox

Lausanne, Switzerland. In 1901 he arranged a game between members of the Rio Cricket and Athletic Association and young well-to-do locals. It was the first time football in Rio spread beyond the Brits. The event passed almost unnoticed. The spectators were made up of the father and sister of a player, two friends and eleven tennis players who stumbled on the game by chance.

Yet the yellowish bladder gained adepts. Fast. Brazil's first football club was founded in 1900 – by a German colony in Rio Grande, near the Uruguayan border. São Paulo inaugurated a local league in 1902. Charles Miller, two years later, wrote in a letter of how enthusiastically Brazilians were taking to the game. 'A week ago I was asked to referee in a match of small boys, twenty a side; but no, they wanted it. I thought, of course, the whole thing would be a muddle, but I found I was very much mistaken . . . even for this match about 1,500 people turned up. No less than 2,000 footballs have been sold here within the last twelve months; nearly every village has a club now.'

Football's European origins helped establish it as the sport of Brazil's white urban elite. Oscar Cox and nineteen friends founded Fluminense, Rio's first club, where matches became glamorous social events. Teams comprised of young students and professionals from the city's best families. Fluminense was a stage to show off cosmopolitanism and refinement. In the stands, women wore the latest fashions and men, impeccably dressed in suits and ties, attached coloured team ribbons to their boaters. They revelled in the Englishness of

Rio players bid farewell to their hosts at São Paulo's Luz train station, after the first matches between teams representing each city, in 1901

it all, cheering players with 'hip hip hurrahs'. The sport was resolutely amateur, in tune with modern European theories of fitness and hygiene.

Brazil, at the turn of the century, was undergoing a period of great social change. The country had only abolished slavery in 1888 – the last place in the Americas to do so. Brazil was also the country that imported more slaves than anywhere else – about 3.5 million, six times more than the United States. Many newly liberated slaves moved into the cities, creating a large impoverished underclass.

Football would only become 'Brazilian' when blacks were able to play at the top level. At first they were excluded from taking part. This did not diminish their curiosity. Unable to enter Fluminense by the front door, they climbed neighbouring rooftops and watched from there. The game, as they discovered, was much more interesting than cricket. And it was simple to copy. All you needed was a ball. If you could not afford it, one could

Blacks on a rooftop sneak a view of Fluminense, in 1905

be improvised inexpensively with, for example, a bundle of socks, an orange or a cloth filled with paper. You didn't need proper kit or even a pitch. The informal game, which could be mastered without a privileged background, spread rapidly among the urban poor. By the 1910s football was Brazil's most popular sport and Rio was believed to have had more football pitches than any other city in South America.

Football was acquiring opposite reputations. It was both the private hobby of the rich and the preferred pastime of gangs of poor youths. Kickabouts became a common sight in Brazilian streets. On their way to Argentina in 1914, Exeter City arrived in Rio. As they were coming ashore they spotted a game of football in progress 'only to discover that . . . they were all niggers. Black as your hat, and most of them playing in bare feet.' Exeter chairman M. J. McGahey sent the dispatch to the *Exeter Express and Echo*. He would have another fright when the tour party passed through Santos. 'If you imagine one of the worst junior grounds you know of, and then take it up and shake it like a carpet and plentifully besprinkle it with stones and pieces of bricks, and then bake the lot in a tropical sun, you will have some remote notion of the ground.'

The first club in Rio to field black players was the Bangu Athletic Club, a team started in 1904 by the British managers of a textile factory in the outlying suburb of Bangu. Factory workers, many of them non-white, were allowed in the team. But Bangu was the exception. Rio's important clubs stayed aristocratic. Bangu was not strong enough to threaten the status quo, and, paradoxically, it buttressed the game's 'amateur ethic' since its players earned their wages as industrial workers.

Slowly, mixed-race players started to filter through to the big clubs. They were made to feel ashamed of their colour. Artur Friedenreich, the son of a German immigrant and a black Brazilian, looked white apart from his frizzy hair. Before matches he tried to flatten his hair as much as he could, covering it in brilliantine and rolling a towel around his head like a turban. He was always the last on the pitch. Most famously, Carlos Alberto, the son of a photographer and the first mulatto to play for Fluminense, whitened his face with rice powder. When his make-up started to come off the opposing fans started to chant 'Rice Powder', which became, and still is, the club's nickname. To this day Fluminense fans throw talc – a cheaper version of the original powder – in the air before big games.

Membership rules at the big clubs were essentially rules to keep the sport as white and upper class as possible. Football provided a justification to reconsolidate theories of white supremacy, which had been thrown into doubt by the abolition of slavery. The insistence on amateurism – which required players to have alternative sources of income – was an effective bar for players from poorer backgrounds.

It took the Portuguese – another discriminated race – to open football up to everyone. Brazil was 'discovered' by Portuguese navigators, and controlled for centuries by Lisbon, yet by the beginning of the twentieth century Brazilians looked to other European countries for cultural guidance. The Portuguese were – and still are – the butt of jokes, a close-knit community of shopowners and merchants.

Vasco da Gama, named after the fifteenth-century navigator,

was Rio's Portuguese club. Vasco broke the big clubs' hegemony because instead of choosing players from among their own, Vasco's directors chose the best footballers from the burgeoning suburban leagues – regardless of background or colour. To get round the rule requiring all athletes to be otherwise employed, the Portuguese community gave them jobs in their shops. In 1923, the first year they were promoted to Rio's first division, Vasco were champions – with a team made up of three blacks, a mulatto and seven working-class whites.

Outraged by this 'fuzzy professionalism', the main clubs set up their own league, excluding Vasco. But Vasco had great popular support. So Vasco were invited back under a set of elaborate conditions that, while not specifically banning black and poor white players, was meant to have that effect. Each player had to know how to sign their name. Vasco, with most of its players illiterate, found a way to jump that hurdle. It sent its squad to reading and writing classes and, if need be, changed their names. A player with a complicated surname would become, simply, 'Silva'. Then the league insisted that each team had to have its own stadium. The Portuguese replied in grandiose style. They clubbed together and built São Januário, the largest stadium in Brazil.

Vasco paved the way for the end of amateurism. When, by the beginning of the 1930s, European clubs had started to contract Latin Americans, professionalism became a necessity to hold on to the country's best players. In 1933, Rio and São Paulo founded professional leagues. Barriers against class and race collapsed. In the inaugural year, the Rio club Bonsucesso fielded a team of eleven blacks. Football, once the preserve of the elite, was finally eclipsed by the masses.

Brazilians play football differently. At least they used to. It does not matter that they might never again. The Brazilian style is like an international trademark, which was registered during the 1958 and 1962 World Cups and given a universal patent in 1970. Its essence is a game in which prodigious individual skills outshine team tactics, where dribbles and flicks are preferred over physical challenges or long-distance passes. Perhaps because of the emphasis on the dribble, which moves one's whole body, Brazilian football is often described in musical terms – in particular as a samba, which is a type of song and a dance. At their best Brazilians are, we like to think, both sportsmen and artists.

It seems that they *always* played differently. Or at least as far back as we can tell. In the early years there were limited occasions for qualitative comparisons, since international games were infrequent. Yet by 1919, after that year's South American Championship, there were glimmers of what would enchant the world half a century later. In an article headlined 'Brazilian Innovation', the journalist Américo R. Netto wrote: 'As opposed to the British school which dictates that the ball be taken by all the forwards right up to the opposition's goal and put in from the closest possible range, the Brazilian school states that shots be taken from any distance, the precision of the shot being worth more than the fact that it is made close to the target. And it further states that the collective advance of the whole forward line is not necessary; it's enough for two or three players to break away with the ball, which, by its devastating speed, completely unexpected, disorientates the entire rival defence.'

Since most Brazilians learnt from informal kickabouts, it was likely that they would play in a way less constrained by rules, tactics or conventions. Since many started playing using bundles of socks, it was also likely that their ball skills would be more highly developed and inventive. Alternatively, one could explain the flashy individualism by pointing to the national trait of showing off in public. Brazil is the country of carnival, not of self-negating uniformity. Archie McLean, a Scottish League forward who moved to

São Paulo in 1912, put it down to irresponsibility: 'There
were great players there, but they were terribly undisci-
plined. Their antics would not have been tolerated in
Scotland. During a game a couple of players tried to find
out who could kick the ball the highest. I soon put a stop
to that sort of thing.'

Some historians have suggested that reliance on the dribble
evolved because of the racism of the game's formative years.
They say that the style was created by black players who
improvised artfulness as a way of self-protection against
whites. If you were black, you would not want to have physical contact with a white player, since this could end in retal-
iation. Blacks had to use guile rather than force to keep the
ball. An interview with Domingos da Guia, the most talented
defender of the 1930s, supports this view: 'When I was still
a kid I was scared to play football, because I often saw black
players, there in Bangu, get whacked on the pitch, just
because they made a foul, or sometimes for something less
than that . . . my elder brother used to tell me: the cat
always falls on his feet . . . aren't you good at dancing? I
was and this helped my football . . . I swung my hips a lot
. . . that short dribble I invented imitating the *miudinho*,
that type of samba.'

There is a revealing parallel here with another Brazilian
invention. Capoeira is a martial art, invented by Angolan
slaves, that was disguised as a dance to fool the slave owners.
In capoeira, the two contestants never make physical contact.
Instead, they taunt each other – usually to music – with
deceptive kicks and trip-ups. The hip-swinging body language
used by a capoeirista is very similar to samba dancers and
Brazilian dribblers.

Whatever the singularities of the Brazilian style really
were, they soon became indistinguishable from the interpretation given to them. In 1933, coincidentally the year
professionalism was introduced, a young sociologist called
Gilberto Freyre published a book that was to mark a water-
shed in the way Brazil was regarded in academic – and

popular – thinking. In *Casa Grande e Senzala* (translated as *The Masters and the Slaves*), Freyre turned racial theory on its head.

Until Freyre, Brazil's racial mixture was seen as a weight around the country's neck. Freyre was the first person to say that its contribution to Brazil was good. Because of the high level of miscegenation – due, he wrote, to the traditional penchant of Portuguese men for dark women and the shortage of Portuguese women during colonial times – Brazil's many races got on in a different way than in other countries. Despite the brutality of the slave era, there was also a unique racial tolerance. Freyre said that the authentic Brazilian was a rich combination of European and African impulses – of, among other qualities, Apollonean rationality and Dionysian malevolence. (Freyre, unsurprisingly, is now regarded by many as as racist as his forebears). In the 1930s, however, his thoughts created a new, pro-mulatto view of national identity – which in football found its most powerful metaphor.

Freyre took the negative and made it positive. He championed playfulness and mischief as national characteristics. The folkloric Rio figure of the 'malandro', a kind of mixed-race artful dodger, was used to embody Freyre's theories. The malandro was a sublimation of whiteness and blackness. In football terms, the malandro took an orderly British game and turned it into a 'dance of irrational surprises'. In 1938, he wrote: 'Our style of playing football contrasts with the Europeans because of a combination of qualities of surprise, malice, astuteness and agility, and at the same time brilliance and individual spontaneity . . . Our passes . . . our dummies, our flourishes with the ball, the touch of dance and subversiveness that marks the Brazilian style . . . seem to show psychologists and sociologists in a very interesting way the roguery and *flamboyance* of the mulatto that today is in every true affirmation of what is Brazilian.'

Sports journalists adapted Freyre's theories, popularising

Exeter City attack Brazil's goal, 1914

the idea that not only was there a Brazilian style but that this style was a proud advertisement for the country's unique racial make-up. This view became the consensus and found its personification in the two outstanding players of the 1930s – Domingos da Guia and Leônidas da Silva.

As football was becoming linked ideologically to national identity, it was also mobilising unprecedented displays of patriotism. When, in 1908, a team of Argentinians came to play in Rio the matches attracted larger crowds than had ever been seen before. In 1914, when Exeter City were on their way back from Argentina, they played a game against an all-star selection of Rio and São Paulo players. The match is considered the debut of the Brazilian national team. About 10,000 spectators saw Brazil win 2–0. Newspapers reported the delirium of the crowd as 'simply indescribable'. In 1919 Rio hosted the South American Championship for the first time. Brazil won and Friedenreich, who scored the only goal of the final game, gained a national prominence that until then no sportsman had ever had. As a measure of the public's interest, his boots were put on display in the window of a city-centre jeweller's.

Football arrived at a time when Brazil, which had only become a republic in 1889, was searching for its own identity. The game's rapid dissemination gave the urban population, lacking in national symbols, a common experience. Football was also seized on by politicians, who saw how it could build national pride. President Getulio Vargas, who came to power in a 1930 rebellion and stayed in power until 1945, used the sport to feed his ideals of nationalism and social harmony. He centralised sport, creating a national council, setting up regional federations and subsidising Brazil's expenses at the 1938 World Cup – to which his daughter accompanied the delegation.

When Brazil travelled to the 1938 World Cup in France, the country was gripped with unparalleled excitement. Journalists invested the nation's hopes in Domingos and Leônidas. Domingos was an athletic defender with such calmness and strength of character that he could dribble his way out of danger. Leônidas was a centreforward whose acrobatic skills earned him the nickname 'Rubber Man'. Brazilians credit Leônidas with inventing the bicycle kick, in which the ball is kicked when the player's body is suspended horizontally in the air.[*]

It was Brazil's third World Cup. In the first two – in 1930 and 1934 – Brazil had failed to pass the first round. The first match in 1938, against Poland, showed how much the South Americans had improved. At 4–4, the game went into extra time. Leônidas was 'simply amazing. He was our

---

[*] In fact, the bicycle kick was invented by a Chilean, Ramon Unzaga Asla, in 1914 – which is why in Spanish-speaking countries the move is called *chilena*. In Brazil, a *chilena* is a back heel, deriving from Chilean-style spurs popular in the south.

Leônidas da Silva

stick of dynamite. He did the impossible. Each time he touched the ball there was an electric current of enthusiasm through the crowd,' wrote a Brazilian reporter. Brazil won 6–5, with Leônidas scoring the winner barefoot, after his boot came off in the swampy turf. 'The shot, strong and unexpected, left everyone in Strasbourg's small stadium open-mouthed,' wrote another witness. 'People were stunned. Europe's sports press, who thought they had already seen every-thing on a football pitch, reacted with fright, confusion and shouts of "bravo!, bravo!, bravo".'

Brazil were knocked out in the semi-finals by Italy, who would be champions, and beat Sweden in the play-off for third place. But even though they were not champions, Brazil were the tournament's real sensations. Leônidas was voted best player. He was the top scorer, with seven goals in four games, and eulogised by the French, who gave him the nick-name *Le Diamant Noir* – the Black Diamond.

When Leônidas returned home he was the most famous man in Brazil. He became the first footballer to endorse a product. A confectionery company, Lacta, launched the Diamante Negro chocolate bar. The Diamante Negro is still around – it is Brazil's second-bestselling chocolate bar and available in another ten countries, including Japan, the United States and Australia.

Leônidas's success was seen not just as good fortune but as a national vindication since he embodied the essence of

Brazil. Football played *à la brésilienne* was already the most potent symbol of nationhood – two decades before Brazil eventually won a World Cup. By the 1930s, there had been attempts to call the sport something less clunkily English than 'foot-ball'. But suggestions – including 'pébol', 'bolapé' (using *pé*, Portuguese for foot) and the Greek-inspired 'balípodo' – did not stick. Instead, Brazilian journalists started to use the transliteration 'futebol'. Futebol was not the game that Charles Miller imported in 1894. Futebol was the sport that was played as a dance; it was the sport that united the country and that showed its greatness. Gilka Machado, held as the greatest poetess of her day, summed up the national feeling in the following poem, written about the 1938 World Cup:

> I salute you
> Heroes of the day
> You made us understand
> In a silent language,
> Writing with your entrancing, winged feet
> An international epopee.
>
> Brazilian souls
> – distant
> overcome the space
> mix with yours,
> follow in your footsteps
> to the rushing ball,
> to the decisive kick
> of the glory of the Fatherland
> (. . .)
> That the Leônidases and the Domingoses
> Fix in the eye of the foreigner
> The miraculous reality
> That is the Brazilian man
> (. . .)

The brains of the Universe
Render themselves, reverent
To your genial feet.

The soul of Brazil
Lays down a kiss
On your heroic feet!

Chapter Three

THE FATEFUL FINAL

'Everywhere has its irremediable national catastrophe, something like a Hiroshima. Our catastrophe, our Hiroshima, was the defeat by Uruguay in 1950.'

Nelson Rodrigues

Every weekday Isaías Ambrósio, a charming seventy-three-year-old with an engaging smile, travels to the Maracanã stadium in Rio de Janeiro where he relives six seconds that happened half a century ago. He leans his tall, hefty frame on a metal rail overlooking the pitch. When he talks his tired body surges forward with purpose. Sweating in the morning sun, he retells the moments that have haunted his life.

'After thirty-three minutes, with only twelve minutes remaining,' he starts. The narration accelerates with the drama of a radio commentator. 'Gigghia takes the ball from the middle of the pitch . . .'

Isaías turns around and points at the grass, which is deserted apart from a few men laying turf. 'And he goes and goes and goes and . . .' Silence. He pauses and takes a breath.

Then, in a sombre tone, slowly, reluctantly, inevitably: 'Goal for the Uruguayans.'

Brazil is not short of footballing glories. They are

somehow not enough. Brazil can shout and cry but it will never win the final of the 1950 World Cup.

A football result has possibly never had such a strong and enduring impact on the emotional life of a nation. 'For me the game is still in the present. The story is not over,' laments Isaías, who helped build the Maracanã in 1948 and is now employed to show visitors around. His daily commentaries are part of an expanding universe of idiosyncratic comings to term with the defeat.

In 1970 Brazil won the World Cup for the third time. The team played with such panache that the final is generally regarded as the highest moment in Brazilian – if not world – football. Its thirtieth anniversary passed barely without trace.

A month later, on 16 July 2000, the highbrow Rio newspaper *Jornal do Brasil* printed the following front page:

Half Century of Nightmare
Zizinho says that Uruguay, winners in 1950, used the tactical system of São Gonçalo's Carioca

The newspaper's story, followed up on three broadsheet pages, declares that the characters involved in the 1950 defeat are still unable to put it behind them. Zizinho, considered Brazil's star player, makes the 'unexpected revelation' that the Uruguayans were using the same tactical system that he had seen in his youth used by Carioca, a small suburban team. 'And we still lost,' he says. Hold the front page!

The Maracanã Tragedy continues to morbidly fascinate Brazilians like no other event. It is so historic that it has its own word: Argentinians, rubbing their hands in glee, call it the *maracanazo*. In Brazil, the match has spawned a thriving literary genre. To coincide with the game's fiftieth anniversary two books were published and a third, from 1986, which contains the entire transcript of the radio commentary, was republished. (Three books about the Maracanã also came out that devote significant sections to 1950.) In 1994 and 1998, two other books on the final appeared. By contrast, the only book in print that I am aware of about the Brazil side of 1970 was published in Britain, in English, and is not available in Brazil.

Roberto daMatta, the influential Brazilian anthropologist, writes seriously that the 1950 game 'is perhaps the greatest tragedy in contemporary Brazilian history. Because it happened collectively and brought a united vision of the loss of a historic opportunity. Because it happened at the beginning of a decade in which Brazil was looking to assert itself as a nation with a great future. The result was a tireless search for explications of, and blame for, the shameful defeat.'

In 1946 Brazil declared a new democratic constitution after more than a decade of dictatorship. Optimism was galvanised by confirmation that in 1950 the country would host the fourth football World Cup, the most important international event to take place within its frontiers. Brazil had first expressed its intention to put on the tournament in 1938. The Second World War forced a twelve-year interruption. With Europe still recuperating from the conflict, Brazil was the only official candidate.

When Brazilians blow their own trumpets they have a tendency to use global superlatives. Size is important since it chimes with a sense of the country's own enormousness. There is even a word for it – 'ufanismo' – an excessive arrogance based on the potential of Brazil's vast resources. To honour the importance of the World Cup and reflect the grandeur of national aspiration, Brazil decided to build the largest stadium in the world.

The Maracanã was conceived as a man-made monument that would be worthy of a place among Rio de Janeiro's other landmarks. Rio boasts the Sugar Loaf Mountain, Copacabana Beach and the Christ statue on Corcovado, a 700m-high granite outcrop adorned by jungle. The new football stadium was to be as audacious and dramatic – a vast concrete ellipse capable of holding 183,000 spectators, 43,000 more than the largest at the time, Hampden Park in Glasgow, and five times the size of the next stadium in Rio, Vasco's São Januário.

Construction started in 1948. More than 10,000 labourers worked on the project like Egyptians building a modern-day pyramid. Most were economic migrants – men like Isaías Ambrósio – to whom the project was the start of a new life as well as a new beginning for the country. The Maracanã fostered a football-inspired patriotism. As building drew to a close workers would test the structure by crowding into the stands to cheer imaginary goals. The stadium was finished in record time. Brazil, so often called the land of the future, could have been excused the thought it was almost there.

'Today Brazil has the biggest and most perfect stadium in the world, dignifying the competence of its people and its evolution in all branches of human activity,' wrote the newspaper *A Noite*. 'Now we have a stage of fantastic proportions in which the whole world can admire our prestige and sporting greatness.' The Maracanã's location at the heart of the city, near the dividing line between the North and South Zones, emphasised football's importance in the hearts of the people. It was surrounded by some of Rio's most traditional neighbourhoods, giving it cultural weight by association. Mário Filho's *Jornal dos Sports*, which had campaigned most loudly for the stadium, said it gave Brazil a new soul, awakening the slumbering giant within. The link with nationhood was explicit. The Maracanã was not only the embodiment of Brazil's sporting ambition but also of the country's place in the modern world.

The city was gearing up for the festival. Posters went up in shops, the post office released commemorative stamps, and, in February, a particularly Brazilian tribute: floats illustrating the World Cup paraded in the Rio carnival. Lamartine Babo, a popular composer, wrote the uplifting *March of the Brazilian Team*, a banner-waving anthem that urged: 'Let's

cheer with faith in our hearts, Let's cheer for Brazil to be champions.'

Of the sixteen countries expected for the World Cup, only thirteen turned up. Brazil insisted on a format that had never been used before and was never used subsequently. There would be no knockout stage. Instead, the winners of each of the four first-round groups would form a final group of four teams. Each country would play every other in the group with the title going to the country that came first.

The opening game was on 24 June at the Maracanã. Flares and fireworks lit the stadium, the military band played and Brazil continued the party by defeating Mexico 4–0. The hosts' next opposition was Switzerland. The game was in São Paulo and Flávio Costa, Brazil's coach, replaced the midfield with three São Paulo players – a common practice to please local fans. The result – a 2–2 draw – was seen as an embarrassing wobble and meant that Brazil had to beat Yugoslavia in Rio to qualify for the final group. Helped, perhaps, by the fact that Yugoslavia's main player, Rajko Mitic, had injured himself on the stairs walking on to the pitch and his head was wrapped in bandages, Brazil won 2–0.

Uruguay, Sweden and Spain joined Brazil as group-winners. Lots were drawn that established the order of

Brazil's adversaries: Sweden, Spain, and then Uruguay. Strictly speaking the Uruguay game was not the World Cup final, it was merely both countries' last game of the final round – even though the results of the previous matches conspired, with unforeseen drama, to make it the decisive game of the championship.

Brazil's first two games earnt them an aura of invincibility. Sweden were demolished 7–1 and the Spanish 6–1. Brazil played a happy, exciting football that left journalists searching for superlatives. A report in Milan's *Gazetta Dello Sport* described Zizinho as Leonardo da Vinci 'creating works of art with his feet on the immense canvas of the Maracanã pitch'.

The cumulative euphoria of the Brazilian fans reached its zenith during the game against Spain. After Brazil's third goal the crowd started waving white handkerchiefs in the air – an 'adios' to the opposition – remembered as one of the strongest images of the tournament. In the second half fans started shouting 'olé', upon which a group began to sing 'Bullfights in Madrid', a popular carnival march. The official supporters' brass band kicked off with the music and the entire stadium joined in. 'The spectacle, which one would have supposed to be merely footballistic, transformed into one of the largest demonstrations of collective singing ever known: it was like the chorus of the fans was a counterpoint to the Brazilians' game,' wrote Jairo Severiano and Zuza Homem de Mello in their history of Brazilian music, *The Song in Time*.

When they went into the final no one doubted that Brazil would fail to be champions of the world.

On paper they were the easy favourites. Even though Uruguay had beaten Bolivia 8–0 in the first round, they were struggling in the final group. Uruguay drew 2–2 with Spain, and had only overcome Sweden 3–2 after scoring two goals in the last fourteen minutes. The results meant that a draw was good enough for Brazil to win the title.

Past form suggested a Brazil victory. Whereas Brazil had

played no European team since 1938, in the same period it had faced Uruguay seventeen times, winning eight, losing five and drawing four. Two months before the World Cup final the teams played three times in Rio. Uruguay won the first and Brazil won the other two. Brazil's confidence was so contagious that the victory was not only predicted but also confirmed in the press before the day of the final. On Saturday 15 July, São Paulo's *Gazeta Esportiva* front-page headline was: 'Tomorrow we will beat Uruguay!' In Rio, the early edition of *O Mundo* printed a picture of the Brazilian players with the words: 'These are the world champions.'

The build-up to the climax was reflected by the steadily increasing size of the Maracanã crowds. Figures showed the opening game was attended by 81,649 paying spectators, which grew to 142,429 against Yugoslavia and 152,772 against Spain. For the final 173,850 entered with a paid ticket – a world record for a sporting event, even excluding the journalists, officials and guests who pushed the actual figure to about 200,000.

Shortly before the match Rio's mayor, Ângelo Mendes de Moraes raised the stakes even further. In fervent tones he urged: 'You, players, who in less than a few hours will be hailed as champions by millions of compatriots! You who have no rivals in the entire hemisphere! You who will overcome any other competitor! You, who I already salute as victors!'

Brazil 1 Uruguay 2
Brazil: Barbosa; Augusto, Juvenal; Bauer, Danilo, Bigode; Friaça, Zizinho, Ademir, Jair da Rosa Pinto, Chico.
Uruguay: Máspoli; M Gonzalez, Tejera; Gambetta, O Varela, R Andrade; Gigghia, J Pérez, Miguez, Schiaffino.
Goals: Friaça 46, Schiaffino 66, Gigghia 79.

Captains Augusto and Obdulio Varela shake hands,
under the eyes of British ref George Reader

The 1950 World Cup final has been discussed, analysed and interpreted so many times, by so many people and for so long that it has ceased to be a game of football and is instead a weave of mythical narratives.

Before the game against Spain, the Brazilian team had transferred its base from an out-of-town hotel to São Januário stadium in the middle of the city. The new location was full of visitors, especially politicians campaigning for October elections. Players remember spending the morning of the game shaking hands and signing autographs. The bus that took the players to the Maracanã had a minor collision. Augusto bumped his forehead.

Uruguay are referred to as the *Celeste* – the Sky-Blues, the colour of their shirts. In Spanish and Portuguese the word has the double meaning 'heavenly'. The suggestion of Divinity is invoked to explain how such a small nation – squashed in between the giants of Argentina and Brazil – has such a glorious sporting history: Uruguay won the football gold in the 1924 and 1928 Olympics and the first World Cup in 1930. Uruguayans are described as fearless defenders of their legacy, protected by the mystique of their sacred shirts. In 1950 the man who most embodied Uruguayan courage was Obdulio Varela, their thirty-three-year-old captain. Obdulio, son of a Spaniard and a black woman, commanded the team from the centre of the midfield.

The Celeste were feeling the pressure. Julio Pérez wet himself during the national anthem. 'I am not ashamed of this,' he said.

The first half was goalless. But in the twenty-eighth minute something happened that changed the panorama of the game. Obdulio hit Bigode, Brazil's left half. The punch – denied afterwards by both players as being more than a sporting tap – nevertheless entered the game's folklore as turning the psychological advantage in Uruguay's favour.

If you ask a Brazilian what his dream is, the answer will probably be to score a goal in a World Cup final at a packed Maracanã. Only one man has ever achieved this. One minute into the second half, Friaça, receiving the ball from Ademir, ran into the box and shot to Máspoli's right. *GOOOOL do Brasil!*

The comeback started in the sixty-sixth minute. Varela to Gigghia. He dribbled past Bigode. Raced down the right wing. Crossed to the mouth of the goal. Schiaffino intercepted, shot cleanly past Barbosa and scored.

A deathly silence descended on the Maracanã.

Even so, with the scores at 1–1, Brazil were still on course for victory.

Until 4.33pm.

Gigghia again dribbled past Bigode and entered the box. Instead of crossing like he had done when he set up the first Uruguayan goal, Gigghia shot immediately to the near post. The angle was tight. Barbosa was caught off guard. He dived to his left but was too late.

'*GOOOOL do Uruguay,*' said Luiz Mendes, narrating

for Rádio Globo, automatically and firmly. He repeated, asking in disbelief: 'Gol do Uruguay?' He answered himself: 'Gol do Uruguay!' He repeated the same three words six more times consecutively, each with a completely different intonation – with various degrees of surprise, resignation and shock.

Football's shrine was as quiet as a tomb. Gigghia said many years later: 'Only three people have, with just one motion, silenced the Maracanã: Frank Sinatra, Pope John Paul II and me.'

'Gigghia's goal was received in silence by all the stadium. But its strength was so great, its impact so violent, that the goal, one simple goal, seemed to divide Brazilian life into two distinct phases: before it and after it,' wrote the sports author João Máximo. Newspapers reported that in Uruguay, three supporters died of excitement hearing the unexpected outcome on the radio. In Rio a fifty-eight-year-old man collapsed at his home.

'When the players needed the Maracanã most, the Maracanã was silent. You can't entrust yourself to a football stadium – that's the lesson that sunk in after 1950,' wrote the songwriter Chico Buarque.

Film footage exists of the Fateful Goal. (The adjective 'fatídico', fateful, has, to all intents and purposes, been copyrighted by 1950. In his Football Dictionary, Haroldo Maranhão gives Fateful Final its own entry.) The camera is behind the Fateful Posts, slightly to the left. Gigghia approaches. When his left foot steps on the line of the box a cloud of white dust rises up. The camera follows the ball into the net but then loses it. Looking for the ball the camera moves back to the post, presupposing that Gigghia had not actually scored, only to go back on itself and find it in the far corner. Barbosa slowly stands up. His posture is heavy, crestfallen.

To Roberto Muylaert, Barbosa's biographer, the black-and-white film is Brazil's Zapruder footage. The goal and the gunshot that killed Kennedy both have 'the same drama

Gigghia runs . . .

. . . shoots . . .

. . . and scores. Barbosa's hell begins

. . . the same movement, rhythm . . . the same precision of an inexorable trajectory . . .' They even share clouds of dust – one from a gun, one from Gigghia's left foot.

Paulo Perdigão writes in *Anatomy of a Defeat*, an obsessive and brilliant biopsy of the game: 'It continues being the most famous goal in the history of Brazilian football . . . because none other transcended its status as a sporting fact . . . converting itself into a historic moment in the life of a nation.'

Second place in a World Cup was Brazil's best-ever result yet it felt like failure. The country never countenanced anything but victory. Loss was unthinkable. 'I was motionless, sitting on a concrete step, watching the sun shine obliquely on the pitch, hearing the silence of the crowd, a silence not even broken by the sobs, in brutal gasps, of the collective orphaning,' grieved the novelist Carlos Heitor Cony. 'Survivors of that cruel afternoon believed they would never again be able to be happy . . . what happened on July 16 1950 deserves a collective monument, like the Tomb of the Unknown Soldier. These are the things that build nations, a people drenched in their own pain.'

Brazilians have a predisposition for colourful melodrama. On this occasion their histrionics were, if not excusable, at least understandable. The Fateful Final is the only time – before or since – that a clear favourite playing in front of a home crowd has lost a World Cup final. Uruguay, Italy, England, West Germany, Argentina and France have all won World Cups in their own countries. Brazil remain the only world champions never to have won as hosts.

Other circumstances help explain the strong emotional impact of the result. It was before the age of television. Almost 10 per cent of Rio's population was in the Maracanã. The match was an intimate and exclusive experience. To upset the largest amount of Brazilians as possible without loss of life, there is probably no more efficient way than creating the largest stadium in the world, filling it to overflowing, and then losing, in the final minutes, to neighbours you had recently beaten, at a sport that is believed to best represent the nation.

As the crowds left the Maracanã only one act of violence was recorded: the granite bust of mayor Ângelo Mendes de Moraes – he who 'saluted the victors' – was knocked over.

Why had Brazil lost? Was it the bump on Augusto's head, the slap on Bigode, the politicians at the São Januário, the excessive confidence or the unbearable pressure of having victory pre-announced? Unable to admit that maybe Uruguay were a better team, or brush off the defeat as a freak result, the idea emerged that it was somehow deserved – that the Brazilians were naturally a defeated people. A victory would have vindicated Brazil's national optimism and euphoria. The defeat reinforced a sense of inferiority and shame.

The writer José Lins do Rego was one of the first to crystallise this view, writing in Monday's *Jornal dos Sports*: 'I saw people leave the Maracanã with their heads hung low, tears in their eyes, speechless, as if they were returning from the funeral of a loved father. I saw a nation defeated – more than that – one without hope. That hurt my heart. All the vibrancy of the first minutes reduced to the ashes of an extinguished fire. And suddenly a greater disappointment, it stuck in my head that we really were a luckless people, a nation deprived of the great joys of victory, always pursued by bad luck, by the meanness of destiny.'

Eight years later Nelson Rodrigues coined the phrase 'stray dog complex' – meaning 'the inferiority with which the Brazilian positions himself, voluntarily, in front of the rest of the world . . . We lost in the most abject fashion for a simple reason: because Obdulio kicked us around as if we were stray dogs.' His phrase is endlessly resuscitated during any national sporting calamity. Brazil's downfall is its lack of moral fibre. The opposition is irrelevant. Brazil is always playing against itself, against its own demons, against the ghosts of the Maracanã. The Fateful Final is a metaphor for all Brazilian defeats.

There was a racist element to recriminations. All three scapegoats – Barbosa, Bigode and the left back, Juvenal, were black – reigniting theories that Brazil's racial mixture was the cause of a national lack of character. Barbosa suffered most. Journalists voted him best goalkeeper of the 1950 World Cup, yet he only played once more for the national team. More than anyone else, Barbosa became the personification of the national tragedy. His shadow still hangs over Brazilian keepers: when Dida played in the 1999 Copa America journalists remarked that he was Brazil's first black first-choice keeper in fifty years.

Barbosa was never allowed to forget 1950. Before he died, virtually penniless, in April 2000 he said that the saddest moment in his life was twenty years after the match. A woman in a shop spotted him. 'Look at him,' she told her son. 'He is the man that made all of Brazil cry.'

To many Barbosa was the victim of the largest injustice in football history. Colleagues shunned him. When, in 1993, he went to visit the Brazil squad's training camp he wasn't allowed in for fear he would bring them bad luck: 'Under Brazilian law the maximum sentence is thirty years,' he always said. 'But my imprisonment has been for fifty.'

According to Roberto Muylaert, in 1963 Barbosa invited friends to a barbecue at his home in north Rio. Only once the guests had arrived did they realise why. The fire was flaming unusually high and was hissing from burning paint. Barbosa wasn't using normal wood. He was burning the Maracanã's posts, reducing to ashes the object that branded his life. Muylaert describes the bonfire as a 'liturgy of purification'. Barbosa was delirious: 'That well-seasoned steak with onion and vinegar sauce that I ate could symbolise Gigghia's leg pumping with the camphor of the game.' If anything is pumping with camphor it is Muylaert's imagination. Rather than revealing football's first instance of cannibalism, however, the succulent literary morsel shows that there is an endless appetite for Fateful Tales.

Brazil's pain is now interpreted as an inevitable rite of

passage. Flávio Costa, the coach, said that Brazil was not psychologically prepared for defeats, because it was a young country with no experience of national tragedies. Since it became a republic in 1889, Brazil had not – barring a few localised skirmishes – been at war with any of its neighbours. It still hasn't. The country has been through political uprisings and passed in and out of dictatorships, but it has very few nationally remembered moments. 'Of all the historical examples of national crises, the World Cup of 1950 is the most beautiful and most glorified. It is a Waterloo of the tropics and its history our Götterdämmerung,' writes Paulo Perdigão. 'The defeat transformed a normal fact into an exceptional narrative: it is a fabulous myth that has been preserved and even grown in the public imagination.'

Britain marks out the twentieth century in blocks divided by the World Wars of 1914–18 and 1939–45. Brazil meters out its recent history in World Cups, since it is during World Cups that Brazil feels most like a nation. Brazil is unique in having participated every time, so it is possible to trace the state of the nation in four-year jumps.

Because 1950 was the start of the unbroken run of World Cups, it is regarded as the beginning of the modern international footballing era. The date, being a round number, is a coherent reference point. It means that no matter how well the national team does, its contemporary history will always begin with the Defeat – just as no amount of Brazilian victories in the Maracanã can mask that it started life as the stage of national humiliation.

Perhaps the greatest irony is that the victorious Uruguayans – who have not won a World Cup since – do not remember the game with quite such importance. A few days before 16 July 2000 I visited the Maracanã. I asked a Uruguayan tour guide, Juan José Olivera, how his compatriots felt about Brazil's obsession with the defeat. 'Young Uruguayans don't really care about the past,' he said. 'They don't talk about the 1950 World Cup. It happened too long ago.'

*   *   *

The crowd at the Maracanã must have contained thousands
of young children since it is easy in Rio to find witnesses
of the event. João Luiz de Albuquerque was eleven years
old in 1950. He remembers sitting behind the Fateful Posts.
'Both goals were scored in my face,' he says, almost outraged
that a child could have been present at moments of such
self-evident horror.

João Luiz is a journalist, broadcaster and Colourful Local
Figure. He lives in a spacious apartment where Ipanema
meets Copacabana. It is cluttered with kitsch *objets d'art*.
A neon bar sign lights a wall and large green sofas are smoth-
ered in cushions. Bossa nova lightly fills the room.

'For me the 1950 defeat was a tragedy,' he asserts. 'I
thought that I was the only person to have experienced it.
I carried the load for many years. It was partly a childish
shame – everyone had said something would happen and it
didn't happen, and nobody explained why. It was only years
later that I discovered there were other people in the stadium
who felt the same as me.'

João Luiz has floppy white hair and speaks in smoothly
diverging sentences. He puts his whisky down and puts his
palms 10cm apart. 'The tragedy was *this* size. But everyone
had a tragedy this size.' He stretches his arms as far apart
as they can go. 'It ended up *this* size.

'I think the defeat took on such big proportions because
it is natural to orchestrate reality – you suffer less if you are
squashed by something huge. It marks you less. I exaggerated my feelings because there was no bigger tragedy. Even
now there are only two dates in the year I remember – my
birthday and July 16.'

In the 1970 World Cup in Mexico, Brazil faced Uruguay
in the semi-finals. It was the first time the teams had faced
each other in the competition since 1950. João Luiz, an
inveterate prankster, called up the Uruguayan Embassy in
Brasília. Posing as a sports reporter, he asked for a number
where he could reach the ambassador once the result was
known. As soon as the final whistle blew on a 3–1 Brazilian

victory João Luiz phoned the ambassador and shouted obscenities down the line. 'I needed to shout the goal that I never shouted in 1950,' he admits, almost cringing with embarrassment.

'I am ashamed of that now. It didn't do anything. It was irresponsible. It did nothing to cure the trauma. It was a fan's reaction, not an intellectual attitude.'

João Luiz subsequently discovered a much cleverer way of laying to rest the ghosts of 1950. He changed the course of history. It started when he was re-watching *Casablanca*. He never liked the film's sad ending, in which Ingrid Bergman gets on a plane leaving Humphrey Bogart behind. So he re-edited it on video, shuffling scenes so that Bogie keeps the girl. The plane still flew, but Bergman returns to the airport. (News of the edit made the pages of *Variety*.)

To make the experience as authentic as possible, however, João Luiz felt he needed a Pathé-style newsreel before the main feature. What event in history did he most want to change?

João Luiz plays me his footage of Brazil winning the 1950 World Cup. Gigghia runs and kicks the ball. But when it passes the post the film spools backwards – making it look like the ball is rebounding off the woodwork. 'Shoots! The post!' says a recognisable voice – Luiz Mendes, who in good humour re-recorded the commentary with a happy ending. The next shot is of Bigode clearing the ball, taken from another match.

'Then I needed to revenge Uruguay, who had caused me so much hurt,' adds João Luiz.

Against Yugoslavia Zizinho had scored a goal with no Yugoslavian in the frame. This became the goal of Brazil's World Cup victory – confirmed by images of the *O Mundo* front page: 'These are the world champions.'

The cleverest moment of João Luiz's inspired montage is the sequence that portrays the Uruguayan team losing. He did not need to search the archives very far for distraught faces. The Uruguayans had burst into tears when they won the World Cup. João Luiz used the same shots to demonstrate the opposite. With a different commentary the tears of joy are utterly convincing as ululations of defeat. The effect accentuates the feeling that the Uruguayans had won by mistake, their tears emphasising the shock, guilt and their own trauma of the hurt they had caused.

Brazil's celebrations culminate with shots of the Rio carnival and a ticker-tape parade in New York. For scenes of national despair in Montevideo he used shots of Eva Peron's funeral in Buenos Aires. 'In my mind Uruguayans and Argentinians are the same – men with big moustaches in overcoats,' says the revisionist editor. The film, perhaps unintentionally, achieves more than a few visual gags. It is a witty and at times moving commentary on the Brazilian obsession with 1950. For its director it had another effect, achieving closure on a childhood trauma. 'The film was six months' worth of psychoanalysis that I never did, that would have taken me ten years, cost a fortune and I would have discovered I hate my mother.'

Another artistic coming to terms with 1950 is 'The Day In Which Brazil Lost The Cup', a short story by Paulo Perdigão. In it the narrator goes back in time to try to change the result. He finds himself behind Barbosa's goal during the second half. When the Fateful Goal approaches he shouts to the goalkeeper. The plan backfires. Barbosa is momentarily distracted and Gigghia scores. Failing to erase the bad memory, the narrator instead becomes its cause. The story was turned into an award-winning short film, which is a minor classic of Brazilian cinema.

Thomaz Soares da Silva, a.k.a. Master Ziza, a.k.a. Zizinho, has been described as the best Brazilian player never to have won a World Cup. He is an important figure in the history of Brazilian football, providing a link between the generation of Leônidas, whom he played with at Flamengo during the early 1940s, and Pelé, whom he played against in the late 1950s. Pelé frequently says that Zizinho was the greatest player he ever saw. Were it not for 1950 maybe both men would be remembered equally. Instead Zizinho is marked by the defeat, whereas Pelé is a symbol of the era of World Cup victories that started in 1958.

Zizinho remembers that he hardly slept in the days following the final. He had been given a two-week holiday by his club, Bangu. 'On the fourth day I called them up and said "I'm coming to train". I couldn't bear staying at home any more. So I went to train. I started playing again and I got over it.'

Zizinho is seventy-nine years old, bright-eyed and street-wise. He grins constantly and speaks a musical Portuguese full of malandro colloquialisms. We are talking in his small apartment one block from the beach in Niterói, across the bay from Rio de Janeiro. I ask him how his contemporaries coped.

'Barbosa died because of it,' he snaps immediately.

'I went on a football roundtable programme and said – "you killed him."'

The press killed him?

'Yes. I say you're to blame. At the end of the game I left the stadium on foot, no one bothered me, people who saw me said only "Man, it didn't work out". But by Tuesday the press were speaking out, giving reasons why we lost.

'They were on top of Barbosa. Always. Not just him, Bigode too. Bigode didn't leave his house. Bigode only went to two places, to my house or to Ademir's house. I would call him up and invite him to a party at my place and promise that no one would talk about football. I said if anyone touched the subject I would chuck them out.

'Bigode left Rio. He went to Minas [Gerais]. He left Minas too because they were pissing him off always going on about the World Cup. Now he's in Espírito Santo.

'Juvenal is in Bahia and never comes back.'

Zizinho said that his temperament helped him deal with the pressure. 'I was never blamed. If I had been I would have answered back. The others were more humble. I answer back to everyone.' He still does. Despite his age, Zizinho is provocative and outspoken. And funny. When Rosaní, his personal assistant, offers to fetch us some coffee, Zizinho winks at me cheekily, as if to say, 'I may be almost eighty, but the ladies still love me!'

Every year in June Zizinho phones his friends and gives them a code. It is to be used to identify themselves when they call him up – to distinguish them from journalists. On 16 July he takes his phone off the hook. 'Otherwise it rings all day, from people all over Brazil, asking why we lost the World Cup.'

On the walls of his apartment are pictures of the football teams he played for and the most treasured mementoes of his career: a sash commemorating Flamengo's three consecutive state titles in 1942, 1943 and 1944 and São Paulo FC's victory in the 1957 São Paulo state championship. He has a poster-sized picture of the 1950 national team, autographed by the players.

It is not immediately obvious where he keeps his World Cup runners-up medal. We find it hidden in a corner of his trophy cabinet. It is the size of a stamp, dirty and black. 'I don't clean it,' he says. 'In Brazil being vice-champion is rubbish. It's better to lose before the final. Losing hurts too much. The only time it's worth being "vice" is vice-president because you get to be president if he dies.'

On reflection he changes his mind. 'In Brazil no one ever kills the president so it's not worth being vice even then.'

After he retired from football Zizinho was, for two decades, a revenue officer in Rio's state administration. His social circle is based around samba musicians rather than football. With an exception: the 1950 Uruguay national team. Their destinies were tied by the game and from that Fateful Friendships grew. 'I had more links with the Uruguayans than the Brazilians,' he admits.

He talks of a telepathic connection with Obdulio Varela. 'I was talking to Ademir once, saying I am thinking about that son-of-a-bitch, why don't we go and see him. Then Ademir went down [to Montevideo] and went to see him to tell him. Obdulio's wife said he was thinking a lot about me too.' Whenever Zizinho was in Uruguay he called the Uruguayan players and whenever they were in Rio they paid him a visit. In the 1970s, Obdulio organised a charity rematch of the 1950 final in Montevideo. Brazil lost by double the amount – 4–2. 'Obdulio told me that the stadium hadn't been so full in years.'

On his bookshelf I spot a virgin copy of Paulo Perdigão's *Anatomy of a Defeat*. I ask him if he has read it? 'No.' He laughs. 'I don't read sad things.

'What's the point? I played that game. I read the book before he even wrote it. I was on the pitch. Look, I'm sure it's a great book. Everyone loved it. But I don't want to feel bitter. So there are a bunch of things that happened that shouldn't have happened. I'm going to want to read about it?'

He continues: 'Do you want to know why we lost?'

He pulls out several sheets of paper on which he has drawn diagrams of football systems. 'Simply because we played WM.' He shows an aerial sketch of a pitch with the ten outfield players joined by a W and a M – the tactical positioning invented by Herbert Chapman at Arsenal in the 1920s.

'The last four games of the World Cup were the first time in my life I played WM. Spain played WM, Sweden played WM, Yugoslavia played WM. The three that played in WM we beat.

'But Uruguay didn't play WM. Uruguay played with one back deep and the other in front. It was a terrible system. But WM is worse.'

Zizinho says he recognised Uruguay's system because he had seen it used before by Carioca, a suburban team that his dad ran in São Gonçalo, near Niterói. One sheet of paper shows this. It is marked up with the names of players from when he was six years old. Reducing the Fateful Final to

the incompatibilities of two tactical systems is Zizinho's way
of demystifying the event – or of avoiding answering more
personal questions.

'I always knew Uruguay played this way, but I never
checked it. Once I was in Uruguay. I called up Máspoli. I
got him in my hotel room. I showed him. I asked him: "How
did you play?"'

'He agreed with me and I made him sign the paper. I said.
"What do you call that system?" He said it was so old no
one remembers the name. "*Es Viejo sistema*,"' says Zizinho
mimicking a thick Spanish accent. 'Their system was crazy
but it wasn't as bad as WM. WM – it's a load of rubbish.
That's why we lost the World Cup.'

Brazil played the 1950 World Cup in white shirts with blue
collars. The colours were not immune from blame. They
were deemed not sufficiently nationalistic. For Rio newspaper *Correio da Manhã* the white strip suffered from a
'psychological and moral lack of symbolism'. With the
support of the Brazilian Sports Confederation, football's
national body, the paper launched an open competition to
devise a strip using all the colours of the Brazilian flag: blue,
white, green and yellow. The national team would use the
winner's design in the 1954 World Cup in Switzerland.

Nineteen-year-old Aldyr Garcia Schlee was working as an
illustrator at the local paper in Pelotas, a town a hundred
miles from the Uruguayan border. Since his job was drawing
pictures for the sports pages, he was familiar with sketching
footballers. He entered the competition for a laugh. 'I was
really scandalised that they were demanding that the four
colours of the national flag had to be used,' he remembers.
'Up to three colours is okay. But four colours is really difficult. No team uses four colours. And the four colours in
the flag are colours that don't go well together. How can
you put yellow and white together on a shirt – what you
get is the national team colours of the Holy See!'

Aldyr and his wife, Marlene, have taken me to their

favourite Pelotas restaurant. La Paisana serves Uruguayan parrillada, traditional cuisine grilled over a wood-fire. Old radios, tango posters and hanging propeller fans conjure images of old Montevideo. Parrillada differs from Brazilian barbecues in that Brazilians spit the meat over a coal-fire, and only cook the flesh. The Uruguayans eat the whole animal. For starters Aldyr orders himself *morrón relleno con sesos*, pepper stuffed with brains, and Marlene chooses *riñón de oveja*, lamb's kidneys.

Aldyr is now sixty-six years old. He looks at least a decade younger than he is. This is partly because his shoulder-length hair has not gone properly grey, and he brushes it back in a way that is uncharacteristically bohemian for a Brazilian living in the rural south. The strongest lines on his face are at the corners of his eyes; he laughs a lot, in a falsetto that is sometimes indistinguishable from tears.

He explains the process of elimination that went through his head. 'White and blue go together – blue with white detailing or vice versa. That was the shorts sorted. What colours are left? Yellow and green – which are the colours most used to denominate the nation anyway. When we tie ribbons in our hair they are yellow and green. So I thought – let's work with yellow and green.'

'I did more than a hundred designs. I did two sashes like an X. I did a V like [Argentinian club side] Vélez Sarsfield. I came to the conclusion that the shirt had to be just yellow. With green it was incoherent. Yellow goes with blue and the socks could be white.'

He painted his version on a piece of paper and his cousin Adolfo sent it to Rio. He says there were three hundred other entrants from all over Brazil, including many professional graphic artists. Aldyr's uniform won – a yellow shirt with green collar and cuffs, blue shorts with a white vertical stripe, and white socks with green and yellow detail. His design was not strictly within the rules. His palette did not have the flag's correct sky-blue. His design used what he had – cobalt blue, a colour which, nevertheless, was faithfully recreated and remains in the uniform until today.

Alberto Lima, of the Judging Commission and the Brazilian Society of Fine Art, said Aldyr's colour distribution was the most 'harmonious'. In second place was Nei Damasceno, who had designed the 1950 World Cup poster. His suggestion was a green shirt, white shorts and yellow socks – 'terribly ugly', quips Aldyr. The thought of Brazil playing in green with yellow socks somehow kills the phrase 'beautiful game'.

As well as a cash prize, the *Correio da Manhã* offered the winner a year's internship as a designer. Aldyr moved to Rio de Janeiro. It should have been a dream time: a golden opportunity to launch a career and a chance to meet his footballing heroes. It was decided that he live with the national squad. He was given quarters in São Januário, where he shared a room with the players Paulinho de Almeida, Salvador, and, later, Dequinha. But the experience was traumatic. 'I was totally disillusioned. The players were a bunch of scoundrels. Only a few had integrity,' he adds.

The shy boy from the provinces was intimidated by the boozing, and the endless lines of women entering the players' rooms for sex. 'I was scared of women. It was a bad time for me'. As soon as he could he returned to his home state, Rio Grande do Sul, where he has lived ever since. Aldyr turned down invitations to design football shirts professionally. He has dabbled only twice since then, both for Pelotas teams. Grêmio Esportivo Brasil used his design for a couple of seasons. The shirt he made for Grêmio Atlético Farroupilha – half red, half green, with a yellow vertical stripe – would not have won any design competition. The team wore it once, lost 4–0, and never wore it again.

Brazil first played in their new strip at the Maracanã on 14 March 1954, a 1–0 victory against Chile. It was only eight years later that Brazil first won the World Cup in yellow. In the 1958 World Cup final, the team faced Sweden, who also have yellow shirts. Having no other kit prepared, Brazil cut off the national emblem from its yellow tops and sewed them on to blue shirts bought at the last minute in Stockholm city centre.

Aldyr's yellow shirts have been so successful that they are possibly the world's most recognisable sporting uniform. One can hardly imagine Brazilian football without them. They are intrinsic to the team's glamour and magic. Yellow is such a strong primary colour that it perfectly synthesised with the flamboyant, flash Brazilian style. More than that, golden yellow adds a warmth and luxuriousness that complements prodigal Brazilian skills. The team colour is so evocative, visually unmistakable and iconic it is almost as if the footballers are personifications of golden statuettes. Aldyr thinks that the yellow gives Brazil 'a touch of the exotic, like something you would expect from Africa'. For Europe, Brazil is exotic enough.

The colour's power also comes from the fact that Brazil is the only major footballing country that uses it. Golden yellow identifies Brazil – around the world and at home. The national football strip, in fact, is a more prevailing symbol than the national flag. The flag – made up of a circle, a diamond and a rectangle concentrically superimposed – was designed for the birth of the republic in 1889. The green represents the forests, the yellow the country's riches, the blue globe with white stars the Rio sky at night. But the flag has the positivist (and embarrassingly outdated) motto 'Order and Progress', and is also tainted by military connotations. When a Brazilian wants to cheer a fellow countryman in another sport he will wear the yellow shirt – because football gives Brazilians a feeling of national identity – citizenship, even – much more than anything else.

Aldyr says it was initially gratifying to see the team run out wearing his creation. He lost interest shortly afterwards, partly because of his bad experiences in Rio. 'When I was younger I owned a shirt that was used by Pelé,' he says. 'But we were burgled and so I didn't have one for a long time. A few years ago I was given a shirt as a present. But the truth is that it was never that important. I never was very proud of it.'

For a man whose best-known work is the strongest symbol of Brazilian identity, it comes as a surprise to learn that Aldyr supports Uruguay. In fact, I should have guessed by his choice of restaurant. His allegiance could not be clearer if he rode a horse around Pelotas in sky-blue jodhpurs singing the national anthem. At his home, a few miles out of Pelotas, a metal plaque with the word Uruguay is visible as soon as you walk in the front door. For good measure he has stuck a Uruguayan flag on the side of his car. Not only is the man responsible for the international image of Brazil unpatriotic, but he shares sympathies with Uruguay: the country that caused the need for his design in the first place.

The following day Aldyr and I drive to Jaguarão, the town on the Brazil–Uruguay border where he was born. The ride takes us two hours. The landscape is flat and green. Cattle

shade themselves from the sun, sitting under pockets of euca-
lyptus trees. It starts to rain heavily so we stop at the only
town en route, Arroio Grande. When we leave, an hour
later, the streets are a foot deep in water.

On the way Aldyr tells me more about his life. He has
been a designer, a journalist, a university professor and is
now a novelist. He also wins competitions. He has won the
Esso Prize, the Brazilian equivalent of the Pulitzer for jour-
nalism, for an investigation into the country's oil resources.
His first book, a collection of short stories called *Contos de
Sempre*, or *Eternal Tales*, won the first Bienal of Brazilian
Literature in 1982. His second book, *Uma Terra Só*, or *Just
One Land*, won the second Bienal in 1984.

Aldyr's fiction is based on the clash between personal and
national identity, exemplified by his own divided loyalties
between Uruguay and Brazil. He was born and brought up
in a frontier town and has never completely resolved to
which side he belongs. He is a Brazilian author, yet he writes
in Spanish. His books are published first in Uruguay, where
they sell well, and then in Brazil, where he is barely known.
His literary universe is the border between the two countries – an essentially artificial line drawn through the homog-
enous landscape of the pampas. Unlike many authors from
the south of Brazil, who are concerned with creating a
regional type, the gaucho cowboy, Aldyr writes about the
contradictions inherent in living on a frontier. 'My writing
is about the other side. It's an attempt to overcome the
dividing line,' he says. Even his name passes frontiers – it
spans three countries: Brazil, Spain and Germany.

We arrive in Jaguarão. The town is made up of well-
preserved squares and cobbled streets. It is clean and happily
provincial. We arrive and cross over the Mauá International
Bridge to Rio Branco, the town on the Uruguayan side. Aldyr
enjoys reminiscing. Even though he was brought up in
Jaguarão, he was moulded by Uruguayan culture. The first
football team he supported was Nacional of Montevideo. 'As
a child we depended almost exclusively on Uruguay. Jaguarão

is closer to Pelotas than Montevideo, but Pelotas didn't have the same resources. We were under Uruguayan control.' A small store has half a roast pig on the counter. Aldyr enjoys showing how barbaric Uruguayans are, although it is an ironic way of praising how much more civilised the country is than Brazil. Uruguayans, not Brazilians, read his books.

The Mauá International Bridge, an elegant stone structure with four turrets at each side, is the defining architectural feature of both towns. Riverboat boss Augusto Schlee transported the cement and steel used in its construction. Three years after its inauguration, in 1931, Augusto's son Aldyr was born. The bridge is at the heart of Aldyr's fiction. It symbolises both the joining of Brazil and Uruguay and their separation. As a young child he made a giant model of the bridge. At his home he has a picture of it on the wall.

We return to Jaguarão and sit in a café in the main square. The sun is low and the buildings glow. Like all Brazilians of his generation, Aldyr has not forgotten about the 1950 World Cup – but for different reasons. He is one of the few Brazilians who believes that Uruguay were worthy world champions. 'The Uruguayan team was fundamentally made up of players from [Montevideo's] Peñarol in 1949, which was an extraordinary team. It was a goal machine. There is no register of any other team which has scored so many goals in one championship. An average of 4.5 goals a game. It was a team that was always destroying opponents. Not even Pelé's Santos did that.

'I am certain today that Uruguay had a team which was better equipped and better organised than Brazil. Even with the disadvantage of not being able to draw and being 1–0 down I believe they had more guts.'

Uruguay used to be a Brazilian province before it fought for independence. It has a population of 3.2 million, a third of the population of Rio Grande do Sul, the Brazilian state to its north. At current rates, there are fifty Brazilians for every Uruguayan. For Aldyr, the Uruguayan victory in 1950 was upsetting but it also reinforced an admiration for the tiny country across the river from home.

In 1995 Aldyr published the collection *Cuentos de Fútbol*, *Football Tales*. (True to form, it was a finalist in the Jabuti Prize, Brazil's version of the Booker). One story is a fantasy of how he used to play football with Gigghia and Míguez. While the two Uruguayans join Peñarol and then the national side, Aldyr returns to Jaguarão. A few years later Aldyr met Gigghia and read him the tale.

'That can't be true?' remarked the footballer. We both chuckle.

On the day of the Fateful Final Aldyr, then aged fifteen, was on Uruguayan soil. He had popped over the Mauá bridge to go the cinema. During one of the matinees the projection stopped, the lights went on and a serious voice said in Spanish: 'Attention. Cine Rio Branco has the pleasure to inform you that the Uruguayans are the world champions.' The audience stood up and sung the national anthem.

The first story in *Football Tales* is about that moment. In order to resolve his conflicting loyalties, the story uses two narratives: of a boy watching the film in the Cine Rio Branco and of a boy watching the match in the Maracanã. The boy in the cinema walks home in silence, hands in his pockets, kicking stones along the bridge. The boy in the stadium writes:

I was crying without knowing why. Crying of emotion, that was obvious: but of a pure emotion that was neither happiness nor sadness, that was neither certainty nor doubt, but that was the whole lot . . . perhaps because I won, perhaps because I lost; I was crying for the innocent magic of that cold afternoon, of that hot afternoon, of that impossible afternoon.

It is a singularly peculiar stroke of fate that a young man already torn between both sides was, in creating the yellow shirt, so explicity involved in the game's aftermath. It is even odder that that same person then became a successful novelist focussing on the relationship between the two sides. Aldyr dismisses winning the shirt competition as an 'accident' and irrelevant in the greater scheme of his life. But in certain ways it still haunts him. 'I like everything about Uruguay,' he says. 'Maybe I say this just to justify myself.' Aldyr's family believes his obsession with Uruguay is irrationally contraire.

Like the Maracanã, the Centenario Stadium in Montevideo was built to host a World Cup. It was the stage for the first tournament, in 1930, which was also won by Uruguay. The stadium was also the largest in the world at the time. My first thought is how much the world changed between 1930 and 1950. I am struck by how small and quaint the Centenario Stadium is. It is set comfortably within a park, compared to the immense concrete, urban Maracanã. It reinforces a sense that Uruguay stole Brazil's World Cup. Uruguay, a smaller and quainter country, already has a monument to its footballing triumph. *It did not need another one.*

Outside the stadium there is a triangle of grass about half the size of a tennis court, which has the sign: '1950 Maracanã Champions Free Space'. It is not well-tended enough to discourage people to walk through it. Which they do. The memorial garden is a well-trodden shortcut between tarmac walkways.

I have come with Aldyr, Marlene and his cousin Adolfo to watch Uruguay vs. Brazil. Marlene had wanted to wear a yellow Brazil top but she could not find the one they have at home. 'That's how much I care about it,' says Aldyr. Marlene, annoyed at her husband's anti-Brazilianness, jokes: 'I wouldn't have worn it anyway. People would accuse me of advertising his product!'

We sit with the Brazilian fans. Aldyr is discreet. He has a Uruguayan badge in the inside lapel of his jacket and a flag he printed from the internet in his pocket. During the

Brazilian national anthem he keeps still and emotionless. He turns ashen-faced during the Uruguayan anthem. Tears drip down the side of his nose. 'It gets to me always. Partly because it reminds me of my childhood but also out of respect, because here I have been accepted as a Uruguayan author.'

Opposite us, the home fans roll out a banner. They pass it above their heads until it covers the upper section of the terraces. The banner has only one thing written on it: '1950'. It seems less a statement of pride than a provocation to the country to whom it still matters.

When the Brazilians run out I ask Aldyr what he feels when he sees the national team wearing his shirt. 'Nothing,' he replies straightaway. 'In fact, I feel guilty. The shirt has been hijacked by the CBF [Brazilian Football Confederation], who sold it to Nike. The shirt is not a symbol of Brazilian citizenship. It is a symbol of corruption and the status quo.' He pauses. 'If the CBF had a different attitude, one which didn't involve stealing, then I would be really happy. I wouldn't feel guilty at all.'

Uruguay win 1–0. Aldyr leaves the stadium to take the overnight bus home. He cannot hide a smile.

The next morning I take a taxi to Las Piedras, a small town ten miles from Montevideo. The drive passes through a rundown industrial area and flat, green countryside. On the outskirts of Las Piedras, we turn left at a McDonalds. A few houses down I knock on a cottage door that I have been told is Alcides Gigghia's address.

A woman answers. She directs me to an alleyway at the side of the house. I follow it. A stairway leads to the flat roof of the building behind. On the roof is a small brick box-home. Even for Las Piedras' modest standards, it is particularly poor. I knock but there is no reply. The neighbour suggests I check out the town market, where Beatriz, his girlfriend, runs a stall.

I recognise Gigghia instantly. The man who scored the most famous goal in Brazilian football is standing behind a table of shirts and jumpers, wrapped up warmly in a sports jacket. His thick black hair is brushed back. He has a small trimmed moustache, just like he did in 1950. The large nose, bent at the bridge, that gave him the childhood nickname 'No-nose' has flattened with age. His sharp blue-grey eyes catch mine. I introduce myself. Did he see yesterday's Uruguay game, I ask. He did. At home with Beatriz. He has not been to the Centenario Stadium for eight years.

Gigghia first says he does not want to speak about 1950. He has spent his life talking about it. We chat by the stall for a few minutes. As we walk to a café I enquire about Beatriz's age. 'She's twenty-eight. I'm seventy-four,' he replies, proudly.

Before I met Gigghia I had been warned that not only does he charge for interviews, but that he only accepts payment in cash dollars. I had also been told that of all the surviving 1950 veterans he is the poorest and most bitter. Yet he does not ask me for money. He answers all my questions. He says he feels neglected by Uruguay, but he says so with good-humoured resignation. 'It's like that for old footballers all over the world.' I do not detect any anger. Once he opens up I feel he enjoys talking about his life.

He takes me through the Fateful Final. The night before, he remembers, several members of the Uruguayan delegation went home, assuming that the team had no chance. But Gigghia believes that Uruguay deserved to win. 'The problem for us was the European teams. There was no TV in those days. We didn't know how to play against what we didn't know. But in South America, we knew all the teams. Brazil were not a surprise. A month before the World Cup we played them three times. We won once, 4–3, and lost the others 2–1 and 1–0. There wasn't much between us.'

A waiter brings us water and miniature glasses of coffee. Gigghia takes me through the six seconds. He took the ball and ran down the right wing. Juvenal and Bigode had no chance of catching him. 'I was too fast,' he says. Barbosa, he adds, did not make a mistake in not covering his left post. 'He did the logical thing. I did the illogical . . . and

I had a little luck. In football you need luck and you need to go after luck.'

He remembers the Maracanã going quiet. 'There really was a silence. It was a complete silence. You could only hear our shouts.' He knew that his goal had won the World Cup before the final whistle. He says that the goal destroyed Brazil's confidence. 'They could not have equalised. They did not react.'

I ask him if he felt bad for having made Brazil suffer. 'I felt a little guilt, but football is like that. In football you win or you lose. Guilt does not come into it. I had achieved what is the greatest dream of any professional footballer.'

After the World Cup Gigghia moved to Italy. He played first at Roma and later won the Scudetta with Milan. He gained four caps for the Italian national side – and scored one goal, against Ireland in Dublin, in a qualifier for the 1958 World Cup. He finished his playing career aged forty-two, in 1970, back in Uruguay.

The Uruguayan government made a few tributes to the Maracanã heroes. Gigghia feels he should have received some financial help. Even the press, he complains, does not value the old champions. The only time he sees the other members of the team is on 16 July every year, when they meet up for a meal in Montevideo. 'We talk about our lives and families. We never talk about football.' Gradually the group number shrinks. Eight of the eleven are left.

Unlike Zizinho, whose home is decorated with football memorabilia, Gigghia has given all his medals and trophies to his son. 'I don't keep anything. You can't live just from memories,' he says. 'In life you live for the moment. When it passes, you forget it.'

But he knows that, unlike Uruguay, Brazil has never forgotten him. In 2000 he was invited to Rio. At the airport's customs check he handed over his passport.

'The girl was twenty-three or twenty-four years old,' he says. 'She took my passport and stared at it.

'I asked: "Is there a problem?"

'She replied: "Are you *the* Gigghia?"'

' "That's me," I said, surprised. The girl was very young. "But 1950 was such a long time ago," I told her.

'She put her hand on her chest and told me: "In Brazil we feel it in our hearts every day."'

Gigghia shrugs and says: 'You know, sometimes I feel like I am Brazil's ghost. I'm always there in their memories.

'In Uruguay we lived the moment. Now it's over.'

Chapter Four

TRIBAL GATHERINGS

Football arrived in Brazil with Charles Miller and his two balls. Or so the official story goes. Well before the first kick-about, however, an Indian tribe was playing a game that consisted of football's most cerebral element. German explorer Max Schmidt was one of the first witnesses. Trudging through the rainforest, he came across a crowd of Pareci Indians playing with a ball made from the rubbery sap of the *mangaba* tree. Two teams were facing each other, bouncing the ball back and forth using only their heads. The game had 'no ceremonial meaning, being just of sporting character', he jotted in his notebook. In 1913 the swash-buckling former US president Theodore Roosevelt journeyed through the Amazon. It is said that he saw nothing on his entire trip that caused him such pleasure as the Pareci's game, which he christened 'headball'. News of the indigenous sport reached Rio de Janeiro, provoking great curiosity. One news-paper suggested it would be interesting to invite the Pareci to Rio: 'Interesting and original. Original, especially – which is already something.' Entering the vigorous debate about whether or not football was too European to be a positive influence in the tropics, 'headball' – if nothing else – was at least authentically Brazilian.

Sixteen Pareci eventually fulfilled journalists' wishes and travelled 1,200 miles from their village to play an exhibition

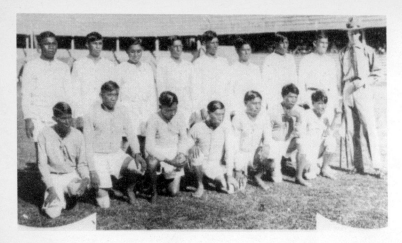

match. The visit, in 1922, was treated like an important sporting event. Fluminense offered their stadium, Rio's largest, which only weeks before had hosted the South American football championship. The Indians slept in tents put up on the pitch. Press coverage fuelled an 'extraordinary interest' in the game, now given its indigenous name, *zicunati*.

The match took place on a Sunday afternoon for maximum attendance. It was staged with the pomp and ceremony of a football international. In front of a packed stadium the Pareci entered the pitch. Dressed in scout uniforms and with their hair brushed to the side, they looked more like Eton schoolboys than Stone Age savages. The absurd scene carried on when they sang, in their own language, their 'national anthem' – upon which the terraces hooted with laughter. After retiring to put on their football kit, they returned as two teams, eight in white tops and seven in blue. The sixteenth member, who had been feeling unwell when the party arrived in Rio, had since died.

The teams stood at either side of a central line. The Indians headed the ball between each other, gaining a point when the opposing side failed to head the ball back – rather like volleyball. Rallies lasted a surprisingly long time. The Pareci jumped, ran and dived, greatly impressing the Brazilians with the speed and agility displayed. As the match progressed, the crowds got the hang of the rules and they started to cheer on the teams – much to the Indians' terror and confusion.

Newspaper reports described the event using football terminology, as if dressing zicunati in football's clothing somehow conferred an urban modernity. On scoring a point the winning team 'shouted between themselves in an extremely original way – like any other goal celebration', noted the *Correio da Manhã*. After two thirty-minute halves the white team narrowly defeated the blues by 21 to 20. 'Zicunati is not at all violent,' wrote one journalist. 'It doesn't even have the fouls and charges common in football. It's a game exclusively for the head.'

O Imparcial devoted its front page to an interview with 'major' Coloisoressê, the Pareci chief.

You must certainly be very tired?
No. This was nothing. It only lasted an hour. Back home we play zicunati every morning from 5am to 11am, and in the afternoon from 1pm to 5pm. It's our favourite pastime . . . Today was strange for us. All this stuff with boots, shirts and shorts – they just get in the way! The turf gets in the way too because it's slippery. Where we come from we have large pitches carefully prepared for zicunati with no grass at all.

The exchange seems less a comment about heading practice in the jungle than a parody of the growing obsession for football in Rio in the 1920s. One wonders, for example, when the Pareci have time for dull chores like hunting and gathering. Unsurprisingly, zicunati did not catch on. The Indians trekked back to their village. About 1,300 Pareci still live near Rondônia-Mato Grosso state border. They carry on making zicunati balls from mangaba latex, and play the sport enthusiastically among themselves.

* * *

The next native contribution to Brazilian football came in 1957, when a player called Índio – Indian – was instrumental in qualifying Brazil for the following year's World Cup. He scored in the first qualifying game (Peru 1–1 in Lima) and was fouled in the second (Peru in Rio), earning a free kick that resulted in the game's only goal.

Índio gained his nickname because he looked like he had stepped out of a Western. In Brazil if you look vaguely Amerindian – having straight hair and dark skin is often more than enough – then it is a moniker you have a good chance of earning. Because miscegenation occurred on such a large scale, there are many, many Índios. More than twenty have been registered as professional footballers at the Brazilian Football Confederation in the last decade.

At least one of them is *genuinely* indigenous. The Índio whose real name is José Sátiro do Nascimento was born in an Indian community where his father is the tribal chief. He is twenty-two years old and a right back at the São Paulo club Corinthians. I watch a morning training session at the club ground, and chat with him afterwards in the dugout.

Índio's life is one of the most remarkable journeys in football. Brazil's Indians are at the bottom of the social ladder – poor and excluded, fearful and distrustful of the outside world. Índio managed to reach the top, becoming the first indigenous player to play not only for a big club but also the national team. 'I never thought I would be a footballer,' he says. It's a cliché but you really believe it. 'I used to work on the harvest. Planting watermelons, that sort of thing. My family had no money for anything. We were always going hungry.'

Dressed in his training gear, Índio looks like any other footballer. His thick, black hair is cut short and lightly flicked. Indian features like delicate oriental eyes, high cheekbones and a strong, triangular nose are not uncommon among Brazilians. Differences are clearest off the pitch. São Paulo, a concrete sprawl of eighteen million souls, does not offer him pleasures. Unlike most successful footballers, who live with their wives and young children, Índio lives alone with his agent. He went to the cinema once and did not like it. 'My life is staying at home and coming to train.' He speaks very fast, in staccato sentences, as if he is reciting a list of prepared statements. He tells me his favourite pastime is going to the shopping mall and eating ice cream. 'Indians don't like cities. We like the bush. It's difficult here.'

As a child growing up in the semi-arid northeast of Brazil, Índio played football with anything circular, even coconuts. 'The green ones don't hurt your feet. We were used to it anyway. I never played football with a proper ball.' His first team was a small amateur side from the settlement where his family were living. The settlement was separated but not isolated from the developed world. In 1995 he was noticed by a scout and sent to Vitória, a first division club in Salvador well known for its youth development work. It was the first time he'd travelled, the first time he saw the sea. 'What a big river,' he thought.

The culture shock was almost too great to bear. He found the food inedible. 'At home we ate snake, all that sort of thing. Anything we could hunt we would eat. Meat, fish, we ate quite a lot of that there – but we ate without spices. At Vitória it was really, really difficult to adapt. The food was very different. I thought it was weird, really strong.' Once he ran away. He laughs. 'I wasn't able to eat that food that they made there any more, I couldn't bear it, I went back home. But Vitória came and got me and took me back.'

Staying in football meant giving up the claim to succeed his father as chief of his tribe. It paid off. In 1996 Vitória's junior team played Corinthians in São Paulo and he was transferred. He made his first-team debut two years later and was called up for the national under-21 side. Índio is now his family's only breadwinner. He supports about forty relatives. 'Where I am from everyone is going hungry. I suffered together with them. I'm not going to let them carry on suffering,' he says. He has housed them in a town 180 miles from São Paulo. 'It's difficult to keep in touch because they don't have a telephone. They don't have money to call me all the time, and I'm in the team hotel a lot.' He used to have a mobile phone, but he broke it because his family called it incessantly on reverse charges.

Índio's promotion to the Corinthians first team coincided with winning the 1998 Brazilian league title, a feat repeated the following year. He played in the team that won the World Club Championship in 2000, but since then has struggled to keep in the side. 'He is inconsistent,' says Fábio Mazzitelli, who covers Corinthians for the sports daily *Lance!*. 'He seems unable to hold a place. Maybe this is something to do with his upbringing – perhaps it shows a lack of confidence.'

Insecurity is not a surprise considering his family's tormented history. Six months before I met Índio I had visited the village where he was born, in Alagoas state. I took a taxi from the capital, Maceió. For the first part of the two-hour journey the fields were full of sugar cane and the air smelled of molasses. The scenery turned more savannah-like until Palmeira dos Índios, where deep greenery reappeared. We entered the town and drove out of it on an uneven track. There were no signs of human activity until the road forked and on the left was a simple brick house.

An elderly woman appeared in a T-shirt and knee-length skirt. I said I was looking for the family of Índio, the footballer. 'He's my grandson,' she replied, and invited me in.

Flora 'Auzilia' Ferreira da Silva is sixty-eight and lives on her own. She sat me on a hard wooden sofa. Her possessions do not stretch to much more than an old television and an antique hi-fi. Indian tribes that have had contact with colonisers for hundreds of years tend to live in homes that copy the way non-Indians live – the main difference is that they are significantly poorer.

A quick glance around the room and I saw no indication that she was related to a famous sportsman – no team poster nor autographed photograph. Several passport photos of her grandchildren were wedged in the frame of a fading colour portrait of her and her daughter. I recognised Índio. The only other image of him was on a badge with a blue border. 'Here's my handsome,' she said clasping it proudly.

Auzilia told me the family's tragic story. Her daughter Josefa married Chief Zezinho, leader of the Xukuru-Cariri. Josefa was fourteen when she had her first child, which died aged two months. Her second also died in infancy. The third, a boy, survived and the fourth was Índio. A feud within the tribe left one man dead and Chief Zezinho accused of his murder. He was forced to leave. Neither he, Josefa or their children have been back since.

XIKRIN DO CATETÉ LAND
Carajás

Águas Belas 1
Paulo Afonso 2

PARECI LAND

XAVANTE LAND

Palmeira los Índios
Salvador

3

TRIBAL LANDS

São Gotardo

Poços de Caldas 4 Rio de Janeiro

São Paulo

1. Xucuru & Cariri flee settlers
2. Índio's family flee tribal feud
3. Índio's family move after more trouble
4. Again on the move for land

The situation of Índio's tribe illustrates the main issue concerning Brazil's Indians – their fight for land. When the Portuguese arrived in 1500 the Xukuru and the Cariri lived on the coast of what now is Pernambuco. With the colonisers' arrival, the Indians settled in jungle near where Auzilia lives today. In the middle of the eighteenth century, pioneers, seeing that the Indians had the best land, set fire to the trees to try to get rid of them. The Indians suffered persecution, slavery and death.

Forced to live in reduced areas and share almost nonexistent resources, the Indians started to fight among themselves. About 2,000 Xukuru-Cariri lived near Palmeira dos Índios. After the bloodbath of 1986, Chief Zezinho began an odyssey looking for a home for his family. He first went to the National Indian Foundation in Brasília, cap in hand. After several changes of address they finally ended up 120 miles away from Palmeira dos Índios, near the town Paulo Afonso, on the banks of the River São Fransisco. They lived there for over a decade until another bloody episode. Índio's brother killed a man in a row over a game of football. The family moved again, 900 miles to the south – helped out by another group of itinerant Indians, the Atikun.

Índio has since relocated his family to Poços de Caldas, on the São Paulo–Minas Gerais border. Having given up hope of being given territory from the government he hopes to buy a large plot of land for the tribe to live on. He says: 'I spend a lot of money on all of them but I won't even get bothered about it. It's my family. I think it is money being put to good use.'

The inconsistency in Índio's game that is pointed out to me costs him his job at Corinthians. A few weeks after I interview him, he is transferred to Goiás, a smaller first division team, based in the savannah city Goiânia. There he asserts his identity further – Goiás already has a player called Índio, so he becomes known by his tribal name, Índio Irakanã.

Índio's emergence is a direct consequence of recent changes to the Brazilian government's Indian policy, I am told by Fernando 'Fedola' Vianna. In 1988, Brazil's constitution recognised for the first time that Indians had rights to the land that they traditionally occupied. 'The Constitution changed the view that Indians should be colonised to an acceptance that Indians should be Indians,' he says. Even if every tribe has not yet won back its land, like the Xukuru-Cariri, the Constitution instilled a sense of solidarity and pride among its indigenous population. 'It meant that Indians were not ashamed to be Indians any more. I wouldn't be surprised if many more Índios appear in the future. Discriminated parts of the population have traditionally found in football a way of climbing through social classes.'

We are speaking in the Instituto Socioambiental, a well-respected Indian rights organisation that is based in a grand colonial house in central São Paulo. Up several flights of a wooden staircase there is an open-plan office full of fashionable young anthropologists in jeans and colourful T-shirts. Fedola has an occupation that is the fruit of conditions found uniquely in Brazil. He is a football ethnographer – a former professional left back turned academic who researches the game among indigenous communities.

Brazil has 216 Indian tribes, and possibly a dozen more who have not yet been discovered. They make up about 350,000 people. They speak about 180 languages. Their villages stretch from the Amazon jungle to the semi-arid northeast and the pampas of the far south. As a 'nation' Brazil's Indians are geographically and linguistically isolated and economically and politically weak. One of the most visible ways in which links between the tribes has been strengthened, says Fedola, has been through sporting events.

In the mid-1990s states with large Indian populations started to hold inter-tribal sporting competitions. The model was copied for the first Indigenous Games in 1996, which united Indians from all over the country. The third Indigenous Games, in 2000, had more than 600 athletes. The games include less well-known sports such as shooting with *zarabatana* blowpipes, running with a *tora* treetrunk and *huka-huka* wrestling. But by far the most popular event is football. In the same way that different tribes speak to each other using Portuguese, their second tongue, football provides a sporting common language.

Top of football's indigenous ranking are the Xavante – a

A Kuikuru Indian flaunts Vasco's strip in bodypaint

tribe of about 10,000 from the state of Mato Grosso. They
are the 'Brazil' of the Indian population, having won football gold at all three Indigenous Games. Fedola's research
focussed on a remote village of 80 Xavante, where he lived
for two months. He discovered that football has such an
intense presence that it shapes the village's internal structure
and external relations. 'Indians in the village play between
themselves, villages play each other and indigenous territories comprised of several villages play other territories,' he

says. 'On match days whole villages squash in the back of a truck to travel to an away game. The village hosting the match also puts on parallel non-football activities, such as feasts and political meetings. Football stimulates this type of social exchange, which otherwise might not go on.' Fedola adds that one of football's strengths is that the tribe believes it may help them integrate into urban Brazilian life.

It is estimated that football reached the Xavante in the 1940s or 1950s. Modern legends surround the tribe's footballing prowess. In the 1970s a team of Xavante visited the Mato Grosso capital, Cuiabá, to play the junior team of a good Cuiabá club. The Indians, 3–0 down at half-time, turned the game around and won 5–3. Years later an Argentine missionary spoke to a member of the defeated team. 'You let them win, didn't you?' he asked. The man replied: 'Not at all. We couldn't keep up.'

Brazilians typecast Indian footballers. A player who constantly attacks in random directions and never defends is said to 'play like an Indian' – although this probably has more to do with Hollywood 'injuns' than indigenous South Americans. Indians are also unfailingly described as tireless and speedy. This stereotype, however, has some scientific backing. In 1997 a team of twenty-five footballing Indians from thirteen tribes underwent tests at São Paulo Federal University's Centre for the Medicine of Physical Activity and Sport. The results showed that the Indians' cardiorespiratory capacity was 10 per cent greater than the average for a professional footballer. In layman's terms, they have more puff. Indians are also stereotyped for not being competitive enough. Fedola believes this prejudice may hold a grain of truth. 'Even though the romantic idea that Indians just play for fun is a myth, I think that the importance they place on victory is less than for us. They say: "we've lost today but tomorrow we'll win."'

In 1996 Fedola visited the Xikrin do Cateté, who live on the southern fringes of the Amazon rainforest. Perhaps he should have guessed something was afoot when he saw one

Xikrin go about his daily life in studded football boots –
Indians are usually barefoot or wear flip-flops. The Xikrin
knew about Fedola's sporting past, and they asked him to
teach them football warm-up exercises. 'I think they already
had an idea what the exercises were, but with me being
there they wanted to know more.' The ex-pro showed them
basic techniques, such as skipping on the spot and making
sideways strides. Fedola gets out of his chair and demon-
strates. They are instantly recognisable moves.

Three months after Fedola's visit the Xikrin performed a
large ritual in the centre of their village, which is surrounded
by a circle of small brick homes. The ceremony began at
dawn. Two flags were raised – one of Brazil and one of the
National Indian Foundation. An Indian read aloud lines
from the Bible in the tribe's native language, Kayapó.

Observing the proceedings was Isabelle Giannini, an
anthropologist who has studied the Xikrin since 1984. She
had seen many similar ceremonies. They customarily involve
two parallel lines of young Indian men wearing feathers and
traditional dress. This time the two lines were dressed in
football kit, each line in a different colour. Strange. The men
started to dance. 'I nearly burst into tears,' says Isabelle.
'They were sprinting in zig-zags, lifting up their right legs
and then their left.' The ritual's dance was a choreography
based on Fedola's excercises.

I ask her if her tears were of sadness. She says not at all.
She says she was overcome with joy. Rather than seeing the
football dance as a denigration of ancient customs by modern
culture, she felt it showed the strength of Indian traditions
to adapt to new realities. 'I thought: "Good on you Indians!
You are here to stay! You will carry on being Indians!"'

She adds: 'The ritual is about understanding the Xikrin's
position in the cosmos. It is about showing that they are in
control of their world. Which is a world that includes football. They appropriated elements from our society and have
incorporated it on their own terms.'

*   *   *

The first Indigenous Games football final ended with a 2–1 win by the Xavante over the Fulniô. The losers claim they were robbed. The Fulniô steamrollered through the opening round with victories of 11–0, 8–0 and 3–1. But the squad had not counted on competing in the swimming, athletics and volleyball too. Unlike the Xavante, who rested for three days before the match, the Fulniô could barely stand up.

In October 2000 I visit the Fulniô, who live about fifty miles from Palmeira dos Índios. Like most Indian groups near Brazil's urban coastal strip, the Fulniô are almost completely assimilated to modern culture. They live in a village of brick homes that is separated from the small town of Águas Belas by a belt of wasteland. The Fulniô village looks like a poor, miniature replica of the adjacent town. Both radiate from a square headed by a Catholic church. But whereas Águas Belas' streets are asphalted and its shops cluttered with clothes and hardware, the Fulniô streets are irregular paths of earth. The only commerce apart from the bakery is craftwork in the Indians' homes.

I arrive at the Fulniô village shortly after sunrise. Homes are empty. Streets are deserted. It has the haunted feel of a defunct film set. I drive around and notice that among the fading pastel-fronted bungalows only three buildings have recently been painted: the local office of the National Indian Foundation, the bakery and the football team, Guarany Esporte Club.

None of the Fulniô have slept in the village that night because we are in the period of the *Ouricouri*, an annual ritual in which the population moves, en masse, to a secret retreat. The hidden camp is three miles from the town, down an orange earth path, shortly beyond a sign that reads: 'Do Not Enter – Danger – Indian Tribe.' Only the Indians know what happens at the Ouricouri. The Fulniô joke, half seriously, that if any non-Indian is found within the gates they will have no option but to kill them. The ritual is the strongest expression left of their traditional culture.

An hour later the square springs to life. An old truck pulls up and a handful of people jump out. Dozens more arrive shortly afterwards in overloaded cars, on motorbikes and on bicycles. The village is suddenly abuzz.

During the Ouricouri, only a few activities are considered important enough to leave the retreat: school, essential errands and football practice.

I make my way to the corner of the central square where Guarany's players are gathering. Someone passes round an ornate wooden pipe stuffed with rolling tobacco. 'Instead of taking a juice in the morning, we smoke this,' he jokes. We walk through the village to the pitch, passing through a rubbish tip. A donkey walks past the goal before Guarany start their practice. The session is eleven-a-side. Ronaldo Cordeiro, the coach, is refereeing barefoot. The others have boots with plastic studs that scrape across the dried earth.

Ronaldo, an intense man with a booming nasal voice, likes to point out Guarany's stars. Several have played professionally for small clubs in the northeast and centrewest. 'He played in Pernambuco. That one was wanted by Flamengo. Many people liked him but he drinks a lot of cachaça*,' he lists as he points around the team.

Essy-a, a twenty-three-year-old attacking midfielder, started his career as a junior at first division Recife side Sport. He then had stints at Olária in Rio de Janeiro, Colo Colo in Ilheus, Bahia, and Anápolis in Goiás – a round trip, as the crow flies, of 3,300 miles. He said he delayed the opportunity to play for a provincial Rio side in the national league until the New Year. 'I prefer to stay here for these months because of the Ouricouri.'

'That's the problem,' interrupts Ronaldo. 'Indians are not equipped to take advantage of these opportunities. We aren't used to being far from home. Indians like to be free. We don't like responsibility. An Indian would always prefer to be messing about here, smoking his pipe.' Ronaldo, who is

---

*cachaça: Brazilian sugar-cane spirit.

forty, is given an air of seniority by a pair of sunglasses attached to his head with string.

The Fulniô are good at football and they know it. The tribe has 3,000 people and three football teams – Guarany, Palmeiras and Juventude. The Fulniô have one-tenth the population of Águas Belas – yet the Indians' teams are much better than the town's clubs. 'We show our superiority through football,' Ronaldo says. 'There used to be a championship between us and them but there hasn't been for a while because there's no point – we always win.'

Afterwards, I check this out and find it to be true. The Fulniô are known around the region as an excellent side. Their reputation is high in the nearest city, Garanhuns, sixty miles away. After the Indians compete in local tournaments, Garanhuns' teams pick off the best players. AGA, one of the city's two professional clubs, has a Fulniô right-winger, reassuringly named Índio. Alfredo Faria, AGA president, praises Índio's stamina with a deferential sigh. 'He runs up and down the field all ninety minutes and then, *after the game*, he runs twenty times around the pitch. Indians' strength is that they have a certain physical vigour. It's in their genes. Ask Mother Nature.'

At the training practice, Ronaldo tells me that the Fulniô are fast. 'We learn about speed when we go hunting chameleons. The Indian has to do things fast because when he hunts he has to bring things back straightaway. Because speed comes from our tradition we don't want to lose it. We also eat strong food. Meat. Fish. And we're used to the hot sun.'

Ronaldo invites me to his home, a brick bungalow with a tiled roof. He has moulded the Guarany crest in cement on the front wall of his house 'because it's a way of it never ending. Guarany changed our community.' The club's initials are in a green circle bordered at each side with an arrow. 'The shield shows both the sporting and the Indian side,' he says. We cannot talk long because he has to get back to the Ouricouri.

I am impressed by the seriousness with which the Fulniô take football. It is not a recent phenomenon. Guarany was founded in 1952. Later, I speak to Blandina Spescha, regional coordinator for the Indian charity Cimi. She agrees that football has become an aspect of the Fulniô's identity: 'Every oppression has a reaction, and many times this reaction is through sport.' Football is particularly empowering because it is the sport most valued in Brazil. Sister Leopoldina de Sousa, a Franciscan nun who lived in the community for two years, adds that football inadvertently strengthens tribal traditions. 'It is a valuable way for the men to demonstrate their masculinity. It really does give them self-confidence,' she says. Football boosts Indian culture in other ways. Fulniô teams confuse non-Indian opposition by shouting commands to each other in their language, Iatê, which in daily life is losing out to Portuguese.

According to Sister Leopoldina, whenever there's a big match on television the Fulniô 'take the day off'. Crowds gather in the few homes that have televisions. Ronaldo has tragic personal experience of the Indians' fervour. 'My brother died of a heart attack when Brazil played Holland [in the 1998 World Cup], and Leonardo's goal was disallowed.'

A peculiar physical trait of some – maybe a dozen – Fulniô footballers is bent legs. Not the ideal sporting profile. But the defect is used to their advantage. One midfielder, swears Ronaldo, is impossible to tackle. His shins skew divergently from his knees, forming a ball-sized gap between his feet when he stands straight. The ball between his feet is protected like an egg in a basket.

A few years after Guarany was founded a young footballer with bent legs emerged in Rio. Manuel Francisco dos Santos – known by his nickname, Garrincha – subsequently became the best-known Brazilian footballer after Pelé.

In the mid-1990s, Garrincha's biographer, Ruy Castro, traced Garrincha's ancestry to the Fulniô. When he arrived in Águas Belas he discovered a tribe with bent legs and a natural talent for football. More than that, the Fulniô chief,

João Francisco dos Santos Filho, shares Garrincha's surname. And some Fulniô have disconcertingly familiar features – Garrincha's full lips, wide nose and jaw-heavy jowl. It was too many similarities to be a coincidence.

Jason Luna da Silva has cropped white hair and a patient, wise face. His legs stand together like an upside-down Y. He is fifty-nine and top striker for Guarany's team of veterans. 'When we heard about Garrincha we were very satisfied,' he says contentedly. For the Fulniô, who previously had no idea of a potential blood relation, the genetic bond was a vindication of a vocation they already knew.

Chapter Five

THE ANGEL WITH BENT LEGS

'Garrincha was the synthesis of the Brazilian: poor, creative and solidary. He was a poor textile worker who with his simplicity and footballing talent filled all of us with happiness.'

João Pedro Stedile
Founder, Landless Movement

In the jungles and forests of Brazil lives a creature called the curupira, protector of the animals and guardian of the trees. 'It is on everyone's tongues that there are certain demons that the Brazilians call '*corupira*', which often attack Indians in the bush, whipping them, hurting them and killing them,' wrote a nervous-sounding scribe in 1560, only sixty years after the Portuguese first landed on South American soil. The curupira is a much-cherished rural myth, especially in the Amazon region. He looks boyish, has red hair and is distinguished by one peculiar physical trait: his feet are back-to-front. When the curupira runs in one direction, his footprints run in the opposite way. The curupira is fast and mischievous. If you try to follow him, you will go the wrong way and be lost in the jungle for ever.

Another of Brazil's popular creations – certainly the most original, according to Monteiro Lobato, pioneer of Brazilian children's fiction – is the saci-pererê. The imp-like saci-pererê

curupira

saci-pererê

has three defining features: he is black, he smokes a pipe and he has just one leg. He is always making a fool of people, freeing horses at night, breaking ears of corn; causing chaos where there is calm. His one leg makes him light and fast. The only way to stop him is to trap him in a whirlwind.

Both of these little monsters have a common characteristic – they use their lower limbs in a cunning way. It is a
valued Brazilian trait. When Chico Buarque sang 'There are
no sins south of the equator' he was describing the Brazilian
anatomy as well as its geography. A samba dancer's gyrating
hips, the feigning swing of a capoerista's kick and a footballer's guile are all trademarks of a national style.

Garrincha was Brazil's most captivating footballer. Like
the curupira and the saci-pererê, he had an uncommon
profile below the waist. He was also crafty, agile and impossible to catch.

When Manuel Francisco dos Santos was born on 28 October,
1933, the midwife noticed that the baby's legs were bent.
His left leg was curved outward and the right leg curved
inward. With proper orthopaedic treatment, his legs could
have been straightened in no time. But this was Pau Grande,
a small town short on medical specialists and shorter on
parents' expectations. Manuel – *Mané* – grew up looking as
if a gust of wind had blown his legs sideways, like in a
cartoon, leaving the limbs disfigured in parallel curves.

Pau Grande might only be forty-five miles from Rio de
Janeiro but in the 1940s it was another world – a countryside paradise, nestling in mountains and surrounded by
rivers, waterfalls and forests. Mané was a sweet child. As
small as a wren, a *garrincha*, said his big sister Rosa, and
the nickname stuck. Later he would be compared to a little
bird for the way he flew past defenders. During his childhood he had a different relation to his feathered friends –
he liked to kill them. Garrincha spent his youth hunting,
fishing, fornicating and playing football. He showed an intu-
itive talent for all four.

Because of his distinctive lineament, Garrincha was able
to move in unpredictable directions. He also possessed an
exceptional ability to accelerate. Combining both, he developed an unbeatable dribble, and was soon the best player
in town. Aged fourteen, he started work at the local textile

factory, as everyone did in Pau Grande. But Garrincha was
an appalling employee. He was sacked for laziness and only
reinstated because the president of the factory football club
– Esporte Clube Pau Grande – wanted him in the team.

Garrincha was simple, carefree and unambitious. Football,
he thought, was not to be taken too seriously. When Brazil
lost the World Cup in 1950 he found it silly that people
were upset. He had gone fishing rather than listen to the
final on the radio. Reluctantly, he went for trials at big Rio
clubs. At Vasco he was told to go home because he had not
brought any boots. At Fluminense he left before the end to
catch the last train home. A few years later, aged nineteen,
Garrincha made it to Botafogo – and only because he was
almost dragged there by an ex-Botafogo player who had
seen him play.

On the second day of his trial Garrincha was put on the
right wing against Nilton Santos, Botafogo's left back. Nilton
Santos was also a member of the national side. Garrincha
dribbled him as if it was a Pau Grande kickabout, and in
one move passed the ball between his legs – something that
no one had ever done. 'I think it's a good idea to contract
this guy,' muttered the defender afterwards. 'Better him with
us than against us.'

In his first full game for Botafogo, two months later,
Garrincha scored three goals. He was always positioned on
the outside right and his style was always the same, based
around the dribble, yet the predictability did not make him
less effective. He would tirelessly dummy one way and then
the other, darting off in one direction and then coming to
an abrupt halt, only to dart off again in another. He could
dribble out of the tightest situation, like a footballing
Houdini. 'His entire body was unbalanced, bent to the right,
so that logically he ought to fall every time he tried to run.
And yet this anti-athlete, this man who challenged physi-
ology, was straight like a plumb line and fell only when
toppled. On the contrary, it was he who unbalanced other
players,' wrote the newspaper *Jornal do Brasil*.

Garrincha's legs

Botafogo's coach tried to teach him to dribble less. He put a chair on the pitch and told him to consider it as a reference from where to cross the ball. Garrincha approached the chair – and dribbled it, sliding the ball between its legs. Asking Garrincha to reduce his dribbles was like asking Carmen Miranda to take the fruit off her head. A referee once threatened to send him off for dribbling a player *too much*.

Garrincha seemed to play for the fun of it. He relished fooling defenders with his skilful moves, taunting them like a champion toreador taunts a bull. Garrincha, according to legend, was one of the origins of the popular Latin American terrace chant 'olé!'. It started when on tour with Botafogo. His duel with the Argentinian defender Vairo had the crowds shouting 'olé!' for the way he daintily skipped over Vairo's stampede-like charges. Garrincha's 'olés!' turned into guffaws when on one occasion he deliberately forgot the ball and carried on running. Vairo followed the player without realising the ball was left behind.

Garrincha was the player, said the playwright Nelson Rodrigues, who taught the fans to laugh. His onpitch clowning is perhaps best illustrated by the occasion when, faced with an open goal, he preferred to carry on dribbling. Garrincha passed three players and then beat the goalkeeper. But instead of scoring, he waited for a defender to run back. Garrincha swerved his body and the defender had to grasp the post so as not to fall over. He then walked into the goal with the ball. He flicked it up, put it under his arm and sauntered back to the centre spot.

The match was a friendly between Brazil and Fiorentina of Italy, Brazil's last fixture before the 1958 World Cup finals in Sweden. When Garrincha scored, the stadium was silent apart from the shouts of his team-mates. In anger. They were terrified that such irresponsibility in a competitive game would cost them dear.

Garrincha had first played for his country in 1955. A year before, at the World Cup in Switzerland, Brazil were knocked out 4–2 by Hungary in a hard-fought match remembered as the Battle of Berne. Two Brazilians and a Hungarian were sent off, and it descended into a players' brawl. Hungary's Ferenc Puskas thumped Pinheiro, a Brazilian fullback, in the head with a bottle.

By 1958 Brazil were feeling the pressure of their unfulfilled potential. The country had still not won a World Cup. Both 1950 and 1954 had been lost by emotional frailty at the crucial moment – first against courageous Uruguayans and then against violent Hungarians. In 1958 the coaching staff introduced a psychologist to make sure the team was mentally prepared. Tests gave pseudo-scientific backing to Garrincha's playfulness. His aggression level was zero and he had below-average intelligence – his score was not even enough to become a bus driver. (In the same tests, Pelé was judged to be 'obviously infantile', lacking the sense of responsibility needed for team spirit. But he had an excuse. He was only seventeen.)

Brazil left nothing to chance. The squad was based in Hindas, a resort near Gothenburg. Knowing his countrymen's priapic tendencies, the team doctor insisted that the hotel's twenty-eight female staff were replaced with men. His fear of players' distractions had even led him to ask the local nudist colony, visible from the window, to insist on clothes.

Garrincha did not play in the first two games, a 3–0 win over Austria and a goalless draw with England. Neither did Pelé. The third match was against the USSR. It was the era of the Sputnik satellite. Cold-war propaganda fuelled a fear of the Soviets' 'scientific' approach. Vicente Feola, the coach, shook up the team sheet and dispatched his secret weapons.

From the kick-off, Garrincha fired himself like a missile into the Soviet defence. After forty seconds of dribble after mesmerising dribble, he shot at the post. Before sixty seconds, Pelé also hit the woodwork, from a Garrincha pass. The onslaught of the opening three minutes, ending with a goal by Vavá, showed an audaciousness and skill that had not been seen before in international football. They are considered by many as Brazilian football's greatest three minutes of all time.

The game, which ended 2–0, marked the beginning of Brazilian football's golden partnership. With Pelé and Garrincha playing together, the national team *never* lost a match.

Newspapers reported that Pelé and Garrincha were only picked because there was a player rebellion. A commission of Brazil's players allegedly went to the coach and pressured him to choose them. The story is so evocative that, even though it was denied by the players afterwards, it is firmly established in football lore. The myth conveys the idea that in a Brazilian team the coach is redundant – that the 'beautiful game' emerged from the players themselves, in spite of the coach's wishes, as if it was a divine phenomenon with an immaculate birth.

The Soviet game was also the moment that Brazil darkened. Pelé was black, Garrincha of mixed black and Indian blood. The team that started against Austria had one black player, Didi. By the time Brazil reached the final they fielded three blacks and two mixed-race players – the first fully multiracial team to win a World Cup.

Brazil knocked out Wales and France on the way to meet Sweden in the final. Brazil won 5–2, their first two goals identical moves created by Garrincha – he slalomed up the right wing, and Vavá converted the crosses. *The Times* described Sweden as 'bewildered by a brand of football craft beyond the understanding of many' and added that Garrincha's marker was 'as lonely as a mountain wind. Garrincha . . . was beyond control and that was that.'

Bellini, the captain, was presented with the Jules Rimet trophy. Brazil's photographers – perhaps because they were shorter than the strapping Swedish pressmen, or perhaps because they were further behind in the scrum – shouted: 'Lift it higher!' So he held the cup above his head, inventing the gesture that subsequently became the internationally imitated sign for sporting victories.

The World Cup consecrated the man with bent legs. 'He is considered a retard,' wrote Nelson Rodrigues, 'but Garrincha proved in the World Cup that we are the retarded ones – because we think, we rationalise. Next to him, next to the prodigous instantaneity of his reflexes, we are luggards, bovines, hippopotamuses.' The poet Paulo Mendes Campos compared him to an artistic genius: 'Like a poet touched by an angel, like a composer following a melody that fell from the sky, like a dancer hooked to a rhythm, Garrincha plays football by pure inspiration and magic; unsuffering, unreserved and unplanned.' In one game for Botafogo, Garrincha kept on dribbling a defender until the ball went off the pitch and they carried on their cat-and-mouse chase on the adjacent track. The referee refused to stop play – as if the beauty of his dribbling justified suspending the rules.

Garrincha was the turf's idiot savant. Anecdotes about his country hick simplicity are as plentiful as those about his footballing brilliance. Many were embellished by Sandro Moreyra, a journalist and close friend. Such as the story that he always gave defenders the interchangeable and anonymous sobriquet *João*, John, because it did not matter who marked him. Or the time the Brazil coach was explaining match tactics to the squad. He saw that Garrincha was paying him no attention, preferring to read a Donald Duck cartoon. 'You,' he said in resignation, 'will do what ever you want.' He did and Brazil won the match.

Brazil took almost the same team to the 1962 World Cup, in Chile, as it had done to Sweden. Pelé, still only twenty-one, had by then established himself as the most complete forward in the world. In 1961 he scored 111 goals in 75 appearances. But he limped off in the second World Cup game and missed the rest. Most of the other Brazilians were veterans, in the twilight of their playing careers. Except Garrincha. Perhaps only Maradona, in 1986, has so single-handedly – no pun intended – won a country the World Cup.

Garrincha's importance to the team was so great that after he was sent off in the semi-final – for cheekily kneeing a Chilean defender in the bum – Brazil moved mountains for him not to be suspended for the final. The linesman who saw the incident mysteriously left Chile the following morning. The president of Peru even intervened, asking the Peruvian referee not to blame Garrincha in his match report. Garrincha was exonerated and played, albeit under a different set of adverse circumstances: a 39°C fever and aspirin.

Later in 1962 Garrincha lived his most glorious moment in domestic football – Botafogo's second consecutive state championship. It was also the beginning of the end.

Garrincha's bent legs had been his strength. They were now his weakness. The way his tibia met his femur meant that each time he swivelled his body the cartilage was wrecked in between, a problem even without the violence inflicted by a sporting life. He was first told he needed to have an operation in 1959 but he decided against it. His faith healer in Pau Grande had told him that if he went through with it he would never play again.

While there was a romance in being a free spirit on the pitch, Garrincha's friends started to worry about his naiveté off it. They suggested he employ a financial adviser. Two bank reps went to his home in Pau Grande and were shocked to discover money rotting in cupboards, behind furniture and in fruit bowls. His house was a slum. The two-times World Cup winner was living in the same conditions as a poor factory worker.

Botafogo had taken advantage of Garrincha's ingenuousness. They always made him sign blank contracts, which they filled in with salaries as low as they could get away with. They also promised him money which they never paid. Garrincha was the club's main selling-point, yet he did not even earn as much as his team-mates. When he complained, the fans turned against him, accusing him of being mercenary and individualistic.

There was another complication: women. Garrincha had married aged eighteen – before he signed with Botafogo. His wife, Nair, was a plain-looking factory girl whose pregnancy forced the wedding. Uneducated and unaspiring, she excelled in only one activity: daughters. Nair bore him eight in little more than a decade. While he commuted to Rio, she stayed in Pau Grande.

Footballers womanise. In this respect, Garrincha was world-class.* As well as his children with Nair, he had two

---

* After his bent legs, the most commented-upon part of Garrincha's anatomy was his penis. In 1959 a song with the chorus 'Mané, who was born in Pau Grande' was banned since it was too similar to 'Mané, who

with an old Pau Grande girlfriend he maintained in Rio and another in Sweden with a local girl when Botafogo were on tour. He also had an affair with an actress who was the vice-president's ex-lover. And then he met Elza Soares.

In Elza, Garrincha found a kindred spirit. She was a well-known samba singer, who, like himself, came from a humble background. Yet the timing was unfortunate. Their love affair coincided with Garrincha's demands at Botafogo for higher wages. When the affair became public it was taken as proof that he was selfish and money-grabbing. Elza was portrayed as a savvy showbiz star and marriage-wrecker. Public mood swung against the couple. For their own safety, Garrincha's financial adviser hid them temporarily in a secret plot of land in Rio's rural periphery.

Yet Garrincha and Elza stayed together. For the 1960s they were Brazil's emblematic couple. In their image Brazil was the country of improvisation and musicality, of triumph through adversity. They were the country's top talents in the country's favourite things – football and samba.

Elza had a tragic upbringing in one of Rio's favela slums. She was raped aged twelve and, because she was pregnant, forced to marry the rapist. Her first three children died in childbirth and she had four more before she was twenty-five. Yet Elza found a way out thanks to her phenomenal voice. Aged eighteen, she won a radio competition, which led to a singing career. When she met Garrincha she was already an established star and had sung with Louis Armstrong.

By 1963 Garrincha's knee was in such a bad way that he

---

was born with a *pau grande*' – Brazilian slang for 'big dick'. A debate about the size of Garrincha's sexual organ ended up in the courts after Ruy Castro, his biographer, was sued for libel for writing that the footballer's penis was 25cm long. The judge ruled in Castro's favour: 'It should be noted that it is a matter of pride, at least in this country, to have a large member . . . Yet size and potency should not be confused. Brazilians dream of having both.'

was hardly able to play two games in a row. Splintered cartilage caused it to swell with liquid, so that it needed to be
regularly perforated and drained. Doctors who saw it were
amazed that he was still playing football. But both the athlete
and the club were happy to delay an operation – Botafogo
needed him to guarantee gate receipts and Garrincha knew
that by taking time off he would be put in a weaker negotiating position. He eventually had the operation, in 1964,
but was never the same player again.

Garrincha was called up for the 1966 World Cup in
England. He was well past his prime, but who would leave
out the star from four years before? On 12 July at Goodison
Park, Liverpool, he played with Pelé for the last time.
Coincidentally, the opposition was the same as the first:
Bulgaria. The score, 2–0. Hungary beat Brazil 3–1 in the
second match – the first time Brazil had lost with Garrincha
in the side. And the last. His international career ended there,
after fifty-two victories and seven draws. Pelé, who had
missed the Hungary game, returned to meet Eusébio's
Portugal. Again, Brazil lost 3–1, and the champions were
out of the tournament in the first round.

Garrincha liked cars. He drove them badly. He had once
run over his father and had also had an accident with Elza
that knocked teeth out of her mouth. After returning from
England he drove up to Pau Grande with Elza's mother to
see his children. On the way back he hit a lorry at fifty miles
an hour. The car flipped over. Elza's mother died.

The accident triggered a depression. Garrincha tried to
gas himself – one of the first of several suicide attempts. His
football career was over and he had killed the mother of
the woman he loved. It did not help that he had been a
heavy drinker since his teenage years. Through his career he
astounded colleagues by his capacity and desire for booze.
When he hung up his boots, the drinking increased.

Their trajectories had started together – but the distance
between Pelé and Garrincha had never seemed so far. In
1969 Pelé scored his thousandth goal – in Rio, at the

Maracanã. After the goal – scored from a penalty – Pelé rushed into the net, picked up the ball and kissed it. A new footballing milestone had been achieved. Garrincha was not in the stadium. He was not even watching the game on TV or listening to it on the radio. He overheard it by accident in someone else's car.

With neither income nor savings, Garrincha asked the Brazilian Sports Confederation for a loan to buy a house. He was refused. On the same day he disappeared and was found drunk and crying in front of a church in Rio's city centre.

Elza thought that a change of scene might pull him out of it. They moved to Rome. Elza found work as a singer but Garrincha had nothing to do except drink. Too ashamed to ask for cigarettes, he smoked butts picked up off the floor. Eventually he was made 'coffee ambassador' for the Brazilian Coffee Institute. It was not hard work. All he needed to do was turn up at European trade fairs and shake hands by the Brazilian stall. He failed spectacularly.

An Italian in Bologna asked: 'So, this Brazilian coffee – is it really any good?'

Garrincha replied: 'Dunno. Never drink it. But I'll tell you one thing – Brazilian cachaça's fantastic.'

On their return to Brazil Elza had an idea to stop Garrincha drinking: they would have a child. Manuel Garrincha dos Santos Junior – Garrinchinha, *Little Garrincha* – was born on 9 July 1976. But with a baby in the house it got worse. Garrincha started beating her up. Elza moved out, fearing he would turn his violence on to the child. After fifteen years together, their relationship ended.

Garrincha married for the third time. His new wife bore him another daughter, his tenth. But his ways did not change. On 19 January 1983, Garrincha spent the morning out drinking. When he arrived home in the afternoon he felt ill and lay down. An ambulance was called from the local clinic. The doctors did not even recognise him. His body was bloated with alcohol, unrecognisable from the nimble athlete

of his youth. He checked in and then transferred to a psychi-
atric hospital in an alcoholic coma. He died at 6am the
following morning.

He was forty-nine and left thirteen children.

Tragedy pursued him beyond the grave. His son with Elza,
Garrinchinha, died two years later, aged nine. He was being
driven back from playing in a football match when the car
overturned into a river and he drowned. It was on the same
patch of road that Elza's mother had died two decades before.

His other son in Brazil, mothered by his Pau Grande girlfriend Iraci, became a footballer. Neném started at
Fluminense and was transferred to Belenenses in Portugal.
He ended up playing in Switzerland. He also died in a car
accident in 1992, aged twenty-eight.

Two of his eight daughters by Nair died of cancer in their
forties. The others live in Pau Grande and Rio de Janeiro.

Garrincha's only surviving son – from his Swedish adven-
ture – is called Ulf and lives in Halmstad, near Malmö.

José Sérgio Leite Lopes was eleven years old in 1958. He
vividly remembers listening to Brazil vs. the USSR on the
radio. About fifteen family members were sitting down at
their home in Rio. They had made little bets about who
would score first, written on scraps of paper, the way many
Brazilians do before games. 'There really wasn't that much
confidence in the national team,' he says. 'We had only
managed a 0–0 draw against England. The myth about the
Soviets being scientific was very strong. We thought it would
be very difficult to win.'

The game started. Brazil pushed forward immediately.
Three minutes later they had scored. José Sérgio stands up
out of his chair to show the flick that Didi made leading to
Vavá's goal. There is not much space in his office, which is
small and crowded with books and boxes. José Sérgio is
head of anthropology at Rio's federal university. It is somewhat incongruous watching a balding academic with large
glasses swivel his body and stick his leg in the air.

Garrincha flies against the USSR in the 1958 World Cup

'It was an extraordinary feeling. You got this idea of this incredibly attacking game. It was so intense. I don't think I was ever more moved by a few minutes of football in all my life. It was football's turning point.'

Didi was voted best player in the 1958 World Cup. For José Sérgio he was the strongest character in the team, more experienced and more versatile than the other forwards. Pelé was a phenomenon for being so young, but it was Garrincha who had the most popular appeal. 'It was the way Garrincha played. He was the guy who undid defences. He humiliated people. When he had the ball you could not get it off him.'

The anthropology department is situated in the buildings of the National Museum, a grand colonial palace that the Brazilian royal family lived in during the nineteenth century. It is at the top of a hill surrounded by landscaped gardens, lakes and the city zoo. José Sérgio's room looks out on to a quad with a disused fountain, palm trees and surrounded by fading pink walls. A bright red and blue macaw is perched by a cage. 'It used to screech so loudly we couldn't teach,' he says.

As a young boy José Sérgio went to the Maracanã and saw Garrincha play. 'His dribbles were like a one-on-one duel. You really didn't know which way he was going to go. He could quite easily dribble backwards towards his own goal. No one did that. I remember laughing. People really laughed. They rarely laughed at other players.' José Sérgio remembers that Garrincha played with a look of great concentration that reminded him of Buster Keaton. He thinks the comparison is a good one, since Keaton's private life was also ravaged by alcoholism.

When I first arrived in Brazil, conversations with friends, acquaintances and strangers would inevitably turn to football. The first time I heard mention of Garrincha, I heard someone say that he was the best player Brazil had ever produced. What about Pelé? Even though I am too young to have seen Pelé play, I was brought up learning that he was incontrovertibly the world's all-time greatest – as if that fact were one of football's fundamental truths. Perplexed, and suspicious that I was being taken for a ride, I started to ask everyone who they felt was Brazil's best-ever player. The reply, invariably, was Garrincha. Even those born years after he stopped playing preferred him.

I had decided to speak to José Sérgio after reading a long article he wrote in the 1980s on Garrincha's funeral. It went some way to explaining the nature of Brazilians' over-whelming affection for the man the poet Vinícius de Moraes called the 'angel with bent legs'.

At about noon on the day that he died, Garrincha's corpse was taken to the Maracanã. Family, former colleagues and fans arrived there for the wake. A quarrel erupted between his family from his first wife and the third. Then another tricky incident occurred when a Botafogo fan covered the coffin with the club flag. One of Garrincha's nephews objected – since the club was a symbol of how he had been taken advantage of. The argument was only resolved when Nilton Santos, the former Botafogo player, intervened and arranged for a Brazilian flag to be put there too.

Nilton Santos was the defender whom Garrincha humiliated at his Botafogo trial. He had become like a responsible elder brother during Garrincha's career. He insisted that, according to the deceased's wishes, he would be buried in Pau Grande – against the wishes of others who wanted him buried in a newly built mausoleum for professional footballers.

Since it is usual for Brazilian celebrities to be buried at prominent, city-centre cemeteries, the day of Garrincha's funeral provoked unique scenes. His coffin was driven to Pau Grande on a fire engine – the same object that he was paraded on after the World Cup victory in 1958. All along the way mourners gathered on the side of the road, on bridges and in buildings. Many waved flags. The cortege drove along the main road, as it left the city, passing warehouses, industrial plants and housing projects. Nearer Pau Grande the crowds were larger. Extra trains were laid on, which blew whistles when they arrived. The local church was packed to bursting point.

A sign on a tree said: 'Garrincha, you made the world smile and now you make it cry.'

At the cemetery in Raiz da Serra, a few miles away, about 8,000 people had been waiting since early morning – far too many people than it could cater for. Mourners climbed trees, gravestones and neighbouring roofs to be able to get a view. When the fire engine arrived anonymous mourners took the coffin to the grave. But the grave was too small. There was not enough earth to cover the coffin properly. Local people threw grass on top. Once the chaos subsided, the cemetery was left half destroyed.

The reaction to Garrincha's death went far beyond what was expected. José Sérgio says there was a national sense of guilt. 'When someone dies you take stock of all the person's life. Garrincha was identified with the public. He never lost his popular roots. He was also exploited by football so he was the symbol of the majority of Brazilians, who are also exploited.'

Pelé and Garrincha are named in the same breath so often that it is like they are a performing double act, or a brand name of bottled sporting excellence. Together, they sum up an era. Yet Brazilians remember them more for their differences than their similarities. They were unexpectedly opposite characters. They did not even particularly get on. Pelé is known in Brazil as O *Rei*, The King. In 1963, a biographical film was released called *Garrincha, Alegria do Povo* – Joy of the People. The nicknames say it all. Pelé is revered. Garrincha is adored. When they say that Garrincha is the best of all time, they are voting with their hearts.

José Sérgio's argument is that even though both players embody the same generation, they are figures from conflicting epochs. There was no player as amateur in spirit as Garrincha. 'It was a miracle that he stayed in the professional game,' says José Sérgio. 'For him he played for the pure pleasure of playing.' Pelé, on the other hand, was unmitigatedly professional. His life story is well known: Pelé's father was a little-known professional footballer whose career was curtailed by injury. From a young age Pelé set his sights on achieving the glory his dad had been denied. He left home aged fifteen to live at Santos FC's boarding house. He never knew anything but a footballer's life.

Whereas Garrincha indulged in most of the vices available to him, Pelé behaved always as a model player. He led a self-imposed ascetic life, concentrating on training and self-improvement. Pelé learned from others and improved over time. Garrincha was unteachable. Pelé had an athlete's perfect body. Garrincha looked like he should not be able to walk straight. When Garrincha was still stuffing his wages into a fruit bowl, Pelé had registered his name as a trademark, employed a manager, invested money in business projects and advertised products – one of the few players to do so at that time. During the 1970s, a survey showed that Pelé was the second-most recognised brand name in Europe after Coca-Cola.

Garrincha demonstrated, quite spectacularly, that there is

Pelé and Garrincha
in Santos and
Botafogo colours

no safety net in Brazilian society – while Pelé, unlike almost
all his peers, found a career beyond football. Garrincha only
ever thought of the short term. Pelé was – and is – always
making plans. Garrincha argued with the establishment. Pelé
became the establishment.

One of the most noticeable aspects when reading books
and articles on Garrincha's life is that there are virtually no
interviews with him. He rarely expressed an opinion. He
comes across as a man without a voice. In this way he *was*
like a silent movie star. Re-watching the little footage there
is of him, you really are reminded of Buster Keaton. For a
start, the images are in black-and-white and, in the trans-
ference from film to TV, slightly speeded up. Garrincha makes
his darting runs, swaying his body in an almost slapstick
way. It is very comical the way he repeats the same move

again and again – like a determined child that never learns.

Pelé, on the other hand, has strong convictions. When he scored his thousandth goal, regarded as his crowning moment in Brazil – since his World Cup victories took place abroad and his club successes were too partisan to cause unanimous joy – Pelé was surrounded by journalists wanting a comment. Instead of thanking his family – which was what was expected – or his coach, or even the goalkeeper, he said: 'Let us protect the needy little children . . . for the love of God, the Brazilian people can't forget the children.'

Journalists laughed. Footballers were not meant to say that sort of thing.

Pelé never stopped talking. He even has a (frequently parodied) catchphrase: 'Entende?', meaning 'Geddit?'. After Pelé retired from the New York Cosmos in 1977 he became a businessman, running his own sports marketing company. In 1993, he stood above the parapet and accused Brazilian football of being corrupt – which led to an eight-year feud with the Brazilian head of FIFA, João Havelange. Between 1995 and 1998, he was Brazil's Extraordinary Minister for Sport. He could have spent the time shaking businessmen's hands, making after-dinner speeches to visiting dignitaries and opening factories. He didn't. He tried to make a difference, drafting ambitious legislation to make football administration more ethical. (His critics, however, claimed he was only interested in 'modernising' so his company could have a larger piece of the cake.) He also writes a weekly football column and he has his own show on cable television. Pelé is so driven and ambitious, one of his friends told me, that he believes he is God both on and off the pitch.

Unlike the rest of the world, Brazil has lived with Pelé for more than two decades since he retired from professional football. They judge him as a businessman, a politician and a journalist, not just as a footballer. It is a complicated and controversial legacy. Garrincha is no longer around to tarnish his own myth.

Even though Pelé helped Brazil win three World Cups, more

than anyone else as a player, he was never the team's one outstanding member – unlike Garrincha in 1962. There is a sense that Pelé belongs more to global heritage than he does to Brazil's. He is an international reference point, and one who is simple to understand: a poor black man who became the best in the world through dedication and skill. In Brazil, perhaps unfairly, he is not a black role model. It is partly because Brazil, despite its racial mixture, does not have a black movement of any visibility. It's also because Pelé's current and ex-wife are white. Garrincha, on the other hand, married black.

It is not that Brazilians dislike Pelé. Far from it. In 1999 his Mercedes was stopped at traffic lights in São Paulo. Two armed men approached the car. On realising who was inside they apologised, hid their guns and went away. Few people – including footballers – command such respect. A year later in Rio, a similar incident occurred to Romário. The robbers took his Mercedes, mobile phone and Romário was made to walk home.

But while Brazilians put Pelé on a pedestal, they do not *love* him the way they love Garrincha. It is more than the fact that tragic figures are naturally more appealing, since they are more human, although this probably helped. It is because Pelé does not reflect national desires. Pelé, above everything else, symbolises winning. Garrincha symbolises playing for playing's sake. Brazil is not a country of winners. It is a country of a people who like to have fun.

The week in August 2001 that Pelé announces a contract with Coca-Cola – pushing his annual earnings from sponsorships to £18 million a year, according to Brazil's main financial newspaper – I go to see Elza Soares in concert.

She may have lost her wealth and her prominence, but Elza has lost none of her glamour. I see her at the Teatro Rival, a cabaret-style venue in the centre of Rio. When she comes on stage she is wearing a lilac silk dress and scarf with a large lilac bracelet. She is standing in red platform high heels. Elza later slips into a second outfit – a slinky yellow and black sequin dress that barely reaches her knees. It would be risqué for a woman half her age, but Elza is at least seventy years old.

The theatre is full, with a crowd that is a peculiar mix of middle-aged white couples, darker-skinned samba aficionados and gay men. During the 1980s Elza became a cult figure in the gay community, who in a certain way identified with her struggle.

Someone in the crowd shouts: 'We love you.'

Elza can still put on a terrific show. She performs samba standards and modern popular Brazilian songs. There is an authentic rawness to her voice. She sings and skats; gutsy and powerfully soprano. In Elza you can hear echoes of the twentieth century's greatest divas: Ella Fitzgerald, Edith Piaf and Billie Holliday.

She begins 'O Meu Guri', *My Boy*, a song by Chico Buarque that could have been written in answer to Pelé's cry to the 'little children'. It is about a woman in a favela whose son is murdered. Elza performs it like a torch song. Her voice fills the theatre. As the tragic story unfolds, teardrops start to move down her cheeks. It is terrifyingly convincing. I feel that everyone in the audience believes she is really crying those tears. The beauty of the song and the power of delivery are overwhelming. It is impossible not to think of the husband and son that she lost.

Modernity has bypassed Pau Grande. This is not a bad thing. The town is geographically isolated, enclosed on three sides by mountains thick with atlantic rainforest. The air feels divinely fresh. The cobbled streets and neatly planned homes are a legacy of the English, who ran the factory and built houses for their workers. You could almost call Pau Grande quaint – an adjective rarely aired in Brazil, and certainly never in connection with Rio's dirty, chaotic suburbs and satellite towns that I drove through before I arrived. The original factory still survives, although it now produces soft drinks instead of textiles.

I park my car by the Mané Garrincha Stadium, the first reference to Pau Grande's most famous son. His painted name above the entrance gate is faded, blemished and stained. Inside there is a grass pitch surrounded by a fence. Some children are messing about. One mishits the ball and it bounces on to the water tank, breaking a pipe. A bar at the back of the terraces has a wall of pictures and trophies. Garrincha is recognisable, dressed in the black-and-white stripes of both Pau Grande and Botafogo. The memorabilia is neither well-arranged nor particularly extravagant. It could be a club bar anywhere in the world.

A teenager arriving for training tells me that about five years ago a mural tribute to Garrincha was painted around the inside of the perimeter wall. 'It was really pretty,' he says. 'But one of his daughters got drunk and smashed it up with a hammer.'

By the stadium there is a patch of grass where a horse is grazing. A plinth makes the bold claim 'Fundamental Stone – Mané Garrincha Museum'. The museum was never built.

I ask a group of teenagers where Garrincha's family lives. They direct me to a house two blocks away. José Mário is sitting in his kitchen alone, drinking beer. He was married to Edenir, Garrincha and Nair's second daughter, who died of cancer in 1997. He says that all of Garrincha's daughters have left Pau Grande. He is very uncooperative and starts mentioning lawyers

'You journalists just write lies about him. Garrincha was the happiest man I ever knew.'

Beyond the factory, Pau Grande – which cannot have a population of more than a few thousand – rises steeply. I follow signs to Bar Mané Garrincha. Its location by a brook, in lush green forest, makes up for the functional building, which is a breeze-block hut with a painted caricature of a footballer on the front. The bar is run by Mazinho, Garrincha's nephew. He refuses to speak to me.

'We've given interviews for eighteen years and no one has ever given anything in return.'

Through asking around I manage to locate Rosa, Garrincha's elder sister. She is seventy-five and lives with her husband in a small one-bedroom home. They both worked at the factory and retired decades ago. They have never owned a phone and even if they could afford it would not be able to install one – since the lines have not yet reached that side of Pau Grande.

Rosa has nothing left referring to her brother, not even a photo on the wall. 'I had magazines, portraits, sashes, but people ask me for things. I gave everything away.'

She is pretty sure at least one of Garrincha's daughters still lives in Pau Grande. I leave and ask some more neighbours. One person tells me to go to the villa. I drive backwards and forwards down the same stretch of road looking for the villa until I realise it is a long building at the top of a stone path.

The villa is a bungalow with six rooms like student digs. Five people are sitting drinking beer out of plastic cups. One is the spitting image of Nair.

I approach her and introduce myself. She looks terrified. After a few tense seconds, she says her name is Nenel and she is Garrincha and Nair's second-youngest daughter. She remembers making her father coffee in the morning. Her real name is Terezinha but she prefers Nenel – that is the nickname he had for her.

Nenel grins a lot, revealing a hairlip and a smile of decaying teeth. She has big eyes, a long chin and ungroomed hair. The wretchedness of her home is shocking even without knowing who her father was. She lives in a room, no bigger than 2m by 2m, together with her twenty-two-year-old son. It has an old single bed, a big red fridge (full of beer) and a sink. A small TV is on, broadcasting an afternoon football match, although no one is paying it any attention.

I ask her if she has ever read Garrincha's biography. She says she's never seen it. From the way she replies I suspect she could not read a page of any book.

Her drinking buddies are about her age, and are a good-natured bunch – I assume not unrelated to the amount of beer they are consuming. Nenel used to work at the textile factory until it shut. She then had occasional work as a maid. I ask if she likes living in Pau Grande, without realising that she knows nothing else. Nenel lives ten miles from the beach. Yet she has never been.

It is a short drive to Raiz da Serra. The large Catholic graveyard is beautifully landscaped on the side of a hill, stacked full of stone and marble tombs.

At the summit stands a tall memorial stone with the words:

Garrincha
Joy of Pau Grande
Joy of Magé[*]
Joy of Brazil
Joy of the World.

And on a plaque underneath:

He was a sweet child
He spoke with the birds

The memorial is dated 1985, three years after Garrincha's death. Neither the largest nor best-positioned in the cemetery, it seems as much a tribute by Magé's mayor, Renato Cozzolino, to himself as it is to the deceased. Both of their names are as prominent.

Garrincha's gravestone is fifty yards away, down the hill, among the other graves. It is a simple slab marked with his name and dates. There are no flowers or any evidence that it has been cleaned recently. It is most conspicuous for its unobtrusiveness.

---

[*]The electoral district of which Pau Grande is part.

The grave is overshadowed by a much larger, white tomb-stone next to it. A pink porcelain vase and a plant pot with plastic yellow roses sit on top. I read the inscription. Miguel Campos was born a year before Garrincha. He died, aged twenty-five, in 1957. 'You will be missed by your mother, brothers and colleagues at Vila Atletico Clube,' it says. VAC's crest is in a metal plaque on the side of the tomb.

The comparison reinforces the private tragedy behind Garrincha's public success. The grave of an unknown foot-baller who played for an obscure local team is grander and better-looked after than the grave of the man whose dribbles twice won Brazil the World Cup.

faroe kings

Top: Anja, Robson and baby Mateus outside their home in Gøta. Right: Messias Pereira, Marlon Jorge, Marcelo Marcolino and B68 president Niclas Davidsen in their club uniforms. Behind them is Toftir.

prodigal sun

Back in Rio, Marcelo Marcolino kisses the trophy he won as Best Forward in the Faroese League. He is together with his mother and family, on the roof of their brick shanty overlooking Copacabana.

Zizinho
Brazil 1950 World Cup Final

Alcides Gigghia
Uruguay 1950 World Cup Final

cartoon strip

Top: The sketches Aldyr Garcia Schlee drew before he designed the Brazilian football kit. Near right: The first and fourth figures digitally restored to their original 1953 colours. Far right: Aldyr and Marlene in the Centenario Stadium, Montevideo, to watch Uruguay vs. Brazil. Previous page: The Maracanã stadium, Rio de Janeiro.

a bird's life

Top right: The Fulniô village square at Águas Belas during the **Ouricouri**. Top left: The stadium of Esporte Clube Pau Grande, Garrincha's first club, now named in his honour. Bottom right: The first – and last – stone of the Garrincha museum. Bottom left: Nenel, Garrincha's daughter, in the room which is her home. Left page: Brazil's two most famous footballers two months before Garrincha's death.

good hair day

Top: Cotton Bud relaxes with two admirers at the 1998 World Cup in Paris. Middle: A younger Cotton Bud in Italy in 1990. Bottom: Guilhermino, one of Fluminense's symbol-fans. He covered himself and his fans with talcum powder for decades.

feathered friends

Top: Big Carl and his favourite British journalist, during the 2001 carnival. Middle: The Hawks at a football stadium with one of their smaller banners. Bottom: The opening float in the Hawks' 2001 parade.

knees up buttons down

Top: Footvolley on Copacabana beach, in view of the Sugar Loaf Mountain. Middle: Marcelo Coutinho practising free kicks in the Button Office. Bottom: Paulinho Figueiredo dictating the conversation at his private society pitch.

men and girls (and those inbetween)

Clockwise from top: Zaguinha arrives at the end of the São Paulo carnival parade without the ball having hit the ground. Milene Domingues sweating out her marriage with Ronaldo (second right), with a little help from Vampeta (far left). Roza FC penetrate the heterosexual opposition. Claudia Magalhães hard at work.

sour times

After a close shave with the pupunha tree, a dribble around the jackfruit tree, the young ecoball striker collided with the mango tree. He was sent off by the referee and ordered to suck a lime. 'The more you suck the sicker you get,' he complained. 'It affects your game.'

Chapter Six

CARNIVAL WITH A TWIST

Ivaldo is fifty-six and a retired military policeman. With his black army crop, bushy white moustache and thick glasses, he looks like exactly the sort of officer who would pull you over for a minor traffic offence. He is, indeed, endowed with a laudable vindictive streak. When I meet him he is yelling a tirade of abuse. His neck muscles are taut and spittle is collecting in the corner of his mouth.

We are in Ilha do Retiro, the home ground of Recife club Sport. Ivaldo is standing at the front of the terraces, directly behind the visiting team's dugout. He is shouting non-stop obscenities at the visiting coach and players. It is difficult to make out what he is saying since he is accompanied by an unbearable noise. He has brought along an antique radio, which is rested on the waist-high wall in front of him. It is blaring at full volume. Like his own utterances, the radio is aimed at the visting team's bench. For the ninety minutes he never turns around to watch the football and only moves from his position when Sport score – to hold the radio above his head like a trophy and dance in a circle.

Ivaldo is dressed up in full Sport kit and has a sign hanging fom his neck with the name Zé do Rádio, or *Joe Radio*. It is his alter ego. 'I am the only fan in the world who doesn't watch the match,' he boasts as the game is about to start. 'I just swear. Anything. Whatever comes into my head. But

I am educated. After the match I go and apologise. It is all done in the spirit of playfulness. My ruse is part of folklore now. Someone even wanted to swap a car for my radio. But I'd never sell up. You can't get radios like these any more.' He has channelled his aggression into a big joke.

Joe's radio is a forty-year-old General Electric, cased in a black leather cover and with a handle like a suitcase. He used to bring it to games to listen to the live commentary, as is common practice in Brazil. But it weighs several kilos – far too heavy to hold in one hand by his ear. So he took it and rested it on the wall that separates the terrace from the pitch. 'I didn't put it there deliberately because of the noise. It was only afterwards I discovered that the noise really bothered the team,' he says. A policeman asked him to remove it. But Joe was a policeman too, and a stubborn one at that. He knew that radios were allowed in the stadium. Keeping his cumbersome General Electric on the pitch-side wall became a matter of principle.

A famous coach once complained that Joe Radio's aural assaults made it impossible to communicate with his team. He tells me proudly that he has a certificate proclaiming him 'the most irritating fan in Brazil'.

There are other colourful characters at Ilha do Retiro. Fifty yards from Joe Radio I meet Dona Miriquinha. She is seventy-five and is dressed from head to toe in Sport's colours: black and red. She has never worn any other colour for twenty-five years. This time she has on a red bandana and a long red shirt with black lapels. She is quietly dancing around a red and black umbrella, like a starlet from a silent movie.

In England, characters like Joe Radio or Dona Miriquinha would be regarded as at best eccentric and at worst certifiable. In Brazil they are considered role models. Fans who exaggerate their passion are known as torcedores-símbolo – *symbol fans* – as if they are ambassadors for the passion and irreverence that everyone else feels.

Behind Dona Miriquinha is a brass band. They are playing

a jazzy tune that they improvise for the length of the match. Sport's mascot is a lion and I see lion cuddly-toys and men in lion masks. It is like a family day out. I see many children, women and old people among the crowd, which is almost entirely dressed in black and red. As the game progresses the fans sing and jump up and down. Brazilians are naturally demonstrative people; never more so than when they are watching a game of football. They are loyal to the dictionary definition – the Brazilian Portuguese word for 'to support' is 'torcer', which means 'to bend or twist'. Its origin is related to the physical action involved. A supporter, a 'torcedor', is someone who bends and twists for his team.

This is what we expect. The exuberance and happiness of Brazilian fans is part of their football heritage. They are an all-singing, all-dancing mixture of races, sexes and ages. They are loud and colourful and *always* up for the party. Brazilians, the cliché dictates, have taken carnival to the football terraces.

It has also happened the other way around.

In 1931 Rio gained its first sports daily, *Mundo Esportivo*. Issue number one coincided with the finals of the Rio state football championship. In what was either an embarrassing lack of foresight or the inevitable teething problems of a new journalistic genre, there were no sporting events to write about for issue two. *Mundo Esportivo* had to look elsewhere to fill its pages.

At carnival time, Rio's black communities used to parade spontaneously through the city. There was already an informal competitiveness between the groups that took part. *Mundo Esportivo* seized the opportunity and turned the phenomenon into a fully-fledged tournament. The paper invented a list of categories and appointed a committee to judge them.

The event was so successful that it has been repeated every year since. It grew until it became the highlight of the festivities. Rio's world-famous carnival procession is, in fact, a

hotly-disputed contest invented by ingenious football
writers.

Mundo Esportivo was less durable. The paper shut down
after eight months.

Mário Filho, the editor of *Mundo Esportivo*, was responsible not only for making carnival competitive but also for
making football matches carnivalesque. He was the first
person to encourage fans to turn the terraces into part of
the spectacle. In 1934, when he was in charge of sport at
O Globo, he launched a competition between supporters of
Flamengo and Fluminense. He encouraged fans to bring
drums, instruments, coloured streamers and fireworks to
matches – with the winner the side that put on the most
exhilarating display. Mário Filho's motivations were not
especially philanthropic – he did so because it increased
general interest in football, generated more copy and sold
more papers.

He was uniquely placed to do this. Although only twenty-
six years old at the time, Mário Filho was already the most
influential sports journalist in Brazil. As a teenager he had
started working for his father, a sensationalist press baron.
Mário Filho, the precocious son, was made literary editor,
sports editor and general manager. His father gave him free
reign and he had begun to merge the jobs – bringing a business mind and a literary bent to the sports pages. Instead
of just printing match reports, he experimented in hyping
games, profiling players and creating a new, chatty journalistic style.

The match between Flamengo and Fluminense that had
the supporters' competition he coined the 'Fla-Flu'. *O
Globo*'s pages spent all week building up to the game. It
was such a success that more and more Fla-Flus were organised – the game is now Brazil's most famous local derby.
The colourful exuberance of Brazilian football supporters
may have happened without the help of Mário Filho. Yet
he kicked it off.

Mário Filho blurred the line between journalist, novelist and businessman. He wrote about football matches in epic terms, creating a romantic mythology of players, clubs and games. The Fla-Flu he immortalised with most passion was the so-called Fla-Flu da Lagoa, or *Lagoon Fla-Flu*, which is worth mentioning for no other reason than it is a wonderful tale. It was the final match of the 1941 championship, played by Rio's Rodrigo de Freitas Lagoon. Fla needed to win. For Flu a draw was good enough. With six minutes left, Fla brought scores level to 2–2. From that point whenever Fluminense gained possession of the ball, they whacked it into the lagoon. The ball had to be brought back, but as soon as it was Fluminense kicked it into the lagoon again. Flamengo put its rowing crews in the water to catch the balls. Each time the ball left the pitch the time-keeper stopped his watch. The six minutes dragged on until it got dark. Yet Flu held out and the championship was theirs.

Mário Filho had red hair and thick red eyebrows. He chainsmoked cigars and also puffed a pipe, which gave him the aura of a grandee. He became the grand homme of Rio sport, as famous as the sportsmen he was writing about and at least as influential as the club bosses. He was increasingly ambitious – both in his literary and entrepreneurial aspirations. He was the loudest campaigner for the construction of the Maracanã (which was given his name posthumously, in 1966). And he created the first ever transatlantic club competition, the Copa Rio, in 1951 and 1952, with top football clubs from South America and Europe. He was also taken seriously as a writer. Of his many books the most impressive is *O Negro no Futebol Brasileiro*, or *The Black Man in Brazilian Football*, a social history that in its day was considered one of the most original and significant works ever written in the country.

In his short story 'Carnaval na Primavera', or 'Carnival at Springtime', Mário Filho wrote that there was such a loud explosion at the start of the 1944 Rio state final that the duty policemen fell to the ground as if following war self-defence procedures. The bang was the result of a dynamite bomb made by the head of the Flamengo fans, Jayme de Carvalho. It was already common by the 1940s to salute your team with small gunpowder rockets. Jayme went one step further. He lit a bomb. It went off covering the stadium with smoke and destroying the grass where it landed on the touchline. At the end of the match, which Flamengo won, Jayme led an impromptu procession of Flamengo fans dancing and singing through the streets of Rio.

Jayme de Carvalho picked up from where Mário Filho left off. Once he was on the scene there was no need to encourage fans to be carnivalesque. He would take care of that himself. Jayme was a low-level state functionary, a job as anonymous as it was possible to get. Yet on the terraces he was a celebrity. He was always over the top. He dressed up in club colours and brought flags and banners. Since this type of merchandising was not commercially available, Jayme's wife Laura would spend her weekdays dyeing cloth red and black and sewing the material together.

In 1942 Jayme formed the Charanga, which means out-of-tune-band, made up of friends playing brass instruments on the terraces. It was the first time organised music accompanied a team, and proved such a success that the idea spread all over country. Now a football match in Brazil without music is unthinkable. Flamengo began to sponsor the Charanga and even paid Jayme's expenses to travel with the team to a championship in Argentina.

Jayme was elected leader of the Brazilian fans during the 1950 World Cup. The Charanga provided the musical accompaniment to the spontaneous rendition of 'Bullfights in Madrid' during Brazil vs. Spain, which was one of the best-remembered moments of the tournament.

With Jayme's help, throughout the 1940s the behaviour of Brazilian fans established itself as creative and theatrical. In São Paulo crowds would hold up different coloured cards to form an image visible at a distance – a technique that was popularised internationally decades later at the 1976 Moscow Olympics. Brazil were streets ahead of the rest of the world. In 1948, when Southampton toured Brazil, a dispatch in the *Southern Daily Echo* reported on a firework display during the half-time period. 'What a queer idea!' it said. When I interviewed the veteran commentator Luiz Mendes, he told me that in 1949 he went to Europe for the first time. He covered Scotland vs. England at Hampden Park. 'I was very surprised,' he told me earnestly. 'Because none of the fans were in fancy dress.'

The Brazilian urge to dress up – which turns football terraces into carnivalesque blocks of colour – seems to be especially powerful because beneath the clothes there are few countries as racially diverse or socially unequal. Brazil has more blacks than any country outside Africa, more Japanese than any country outside Japan, as well as its indigenous Indians and large communities of northern Europeans, southern Europeans, Arabs and Jews. According to the United Nations in 2001, Brazil has the world's fourth most unfair distribution of wealth after Swaziland, South Africa and Nicaragua. The richest 20 per cent live comparably to countries in Europe; the poorest 20 per cent comparably to countries in Africa.

Wearing a uniform – such as a Flamengo shirt or a carnival costume – is a way of denying differences of race and class. In a crowd of people dressed in the same strip, it is easier to forget the violent differences that mark day-to-day life. Since football is the strongest symbol of national identity, wearing a football strip asserts a utopian Brazilianness. Brazil feels like a country that works. Is it any wonder they put on a good show?

The practice of making a song and dance on the terraces fosters a more general inclusiveness. It makes the fan part of the wider event, blurring the traditional division between spectator and spectacle. Which is exactly like carnival, where just by showing up you are taking part.

The current equivalent of Jayme de Carvalho is Claudio

Ribeiro. Apart from Pelé, he is probably the world's best-known black Brazilian face. He is the hyperactive, drumming lunatic with the ever-expanding afro that TV pictures always home in on during Brazil's World Cup games. (Once the cameramen are bored with the beautiful women.) In one gurning paroxysm of delight, his face sums up uncontrolled, happy, *Brazilian* exuberance.

I meet him where he has worked for thirty years – a street stall at a busy intersection in the centre of São Paulo. Coincidentally, the spot is celebrated in the opening line of 'Sampa', a well-known song by Caetano Veloso: 'Something makes my heart skip a beat, when São João and Ipiranga avenues meet.' The address may once have been romantic. Now it is more likely to provoke a cardiac arrest. The avenues are now chaotic and dirty thoroughfares bordering on the city's main red-light area.

Claudio is better known as Cotonete, or *Cotton Bud*, for obvious reasons. When I meet him it is raining and his hair is sheltering in an orange woolly hat. Today he looks like someone with half a pumpkin on his head rather than a walking advert for Johnson & Johnson. He is wearing a yellow Brazil shirt and is leaning on a wooden cabinet.

Cotton Bud tells me his life story as he runs around selling parking vouchers and helping find parking spaces. Before he appointed himself the national team's fan leader, football had already branded his life. He is from Erechim, a small town in the southern state of Rio Grande do Sul. When he was nine, his father – a long-distance lorry driver – took him on a trip to São Paulo. They went to see Corinthians vs. São Paulo. As the stadium was emptying father and son lost each other in the crowd. They did not find each other again. Cotton Bud started living on the streets. 'I sent my dad a card three years later to say I was still alive. But I never went back.'

When Cotton Bud opens his mouth you can see that he has almost no teeth. His smile is like a baby child's. He lost his teeth in a car crash, he says, where three of the four passengers died. 'Dentists have offered to fix my mouth but I want to stay how I am. It's me.'

As a teenager, Cotton Bud went hungry and lived on the fringes of the law. He spent time in a young offender's institution and, aged seventeen, started living in a hostel. He found himself through football – through Corinthians. He started his own supporters club – Explosão Coração Corintiano, or *Corinthian Heart Explosion* – which at its peak had 30,000 members.

Cotton Bud found his true vocation in 1978. He was doing some work in a toy shop when the father of the owner fell ill. There was a spare ticket for the World Cup in Argentina. Cotton Bud was the lucky recipient. He packed his drum and travelled to Buenos Aires.

'The World Cup's just the best. It's the most beautiful thing in the world,' he says. In Argentina he commanded the Brazilian fans' chanting and drumming, and discovered that the way he looked and behaved made him a walking photo opportunity. 'It's the hair – people love it. It's big enough already and often I put a wig on top.'

After the experience in 1978 he decided that he had to go again in 1982. He has been to every World Cup since. Cotton Bud only affords it because he gets sponsorship. He is a Professional Fan. 'Companies know that I will be on the television a lot and in newspapers, so they give me clothes and plane tickets in exchange for a logo on my Brazil shirt.'

Cotton Bud says that he never leaves Brazil with valid tickets for the games. Yet his celebrity status opens doors. 'Brazilians aren't mugs,' he says. 'There's always a way.' He gives an example of how he always lands on his feet: in Paris in 1998 he gave a lecture to about 700 students.

As we chat I sense that not only does Cotton Bud's cotton bud attract attention but so do his actions. He tells me he has been arrested twice – once for punching a Moroccan ('he stole my drum') and once for throwing washing powder in a public fountain.

I can see that Cotton Bud is one of life's agitators. He is unable to keep still. It makes him a difficult interviewee. As he darts off to park someone's car he tells me that he bases his life around four-year cycles. 'I never got married because of football,' he adds. 'There is not enough time.'

On 14 October 1997, Corinthians played Santos away. The match was tense, offensive and violent. Two Corinthians players were sent off and three received yellow cards. Seventeen minutes from the end Santos' defender, Jean, headed in the game's only goal.

As the final whistle blew, many Corinthians fans were conspicuous by their absence. Usually in defeats they stayed behind to jeer their team. Even the club's management thought it was odd, since the club had been receiving threats if performances did not improve.

At forty minutes past midnight the Corinthians team bus started the forty-mile drive home. Military police escorted the team to the edge of Santos. The coach, unaccompanied, then took the motorway. The road climbs dramatically from sea level to an altitude of 1,000m, through tunnels and up a ridge thick with forest.

During the drive the Corinthians security supervisor noticed a black car following the delegation. The car, containing four people, cut provocatively into the side of the bus and its four passengers taunted those on board. Then it disappeared.

Suddenly a lorry in front of the bus breaked sharply. The Corinthians driver managed to switch lanes, narrowly avoiding a head-on collision. He was forced to stop immediately afterwards. There was a roadblock. An old white bus was parked perpendicularly across the lanes.

Several Corinthians fans were on the tarmac. At first it looked like an accident. Then the real motive became clear. The fans were ambushing the team they support.

They ran towards the Corinthians bus. Someone inside shouted: 'Shut the curtains, it's the supporters.' One of the security guards shut the curtains and everyone crouched down as the fans threw sticks and stones.

The first stone shattered the front window. The fans smashed the bodywork and broke its lights. They surrounded the coach and rocked it to and fro, as a hailstorm of objects were thrown. The team feared for their lives.

The driver was hurt. He had an injury to his left eyebrow. A fan had a crowbar and was trying to lever open the door. A security guard managed to push the attacker away. Several in the coach recognised one of the fans: Metaleiro, or *Heavy Metaller*. He was the president of the Gaviões da Fiel, the *Hawks of the Faithful*, which is the largest of Corinthians' many independent supporters clubs. They begged Metaleiro to stop the attack. It worked. The white bus filled up and drove away.

A few hours later, when the team coach was back at the club, Metaleiro turned up. He asked if anyone was injured.

He added: 'Did you like the fright?'

A month later the São Paulo Attorney's Office published a report on the incident. It described the ambush as one of a 'trajectory of acts of violence, disorder and depredation of the Hawks of the Faithful in which the above fact is simply the apex of a sad *curriculum vitae*.

'What is most repugnant is the fact that the victim in this case is not the enemy. Very much to the contrary. It is the players themselves, who find in the supporters clubs the determination and courage that they need to play their football.'

The Hawks of the Faithful have 56,000 paid-up members, which makes them Brazil's largest supporters' club. They are also the only one that requires you to attend a lecture on its ideology before joining. I decide to attend to find out the nature of its politics – are they against right-wingers, or just left backs?

The lecture is held fortnightly at the Hawks' headquarters in central São Paulo. The building is like a youth club.

A mural on the front wall has the Corinthians insignia –
an anchor and two crossed oars – with the phrase 'You
Are My World'. At the entrance there is a shop, Hawk
Mania, which sells merchandising. Tough-looking men
with large hawk tattoos on their arms or backs play five-a-
side football in an indoor hall. The Hawks' motto 'Loyalty,
Humility, Conduct' is painted in large lettering on the
wall.

When I arrive, on a hot summer Saturday afternoon, I
am directed upstairs. Together with about fifty boys in their
teens and early twenties, I enter a room crammed with old
photos, trophies and fancy-dress costumes. Before the talk
starts the room is silent apart from the intermittent zoom
of cars driving by on the dual carriageway outside. It feels
like being back at school.

Eduardo, in a light-green T-shirt, stands up and begins.

'The year was 1969,' he says seriously. 'Corinthians were
in a bad situation. We had the most supporters, but we were
the butt of jokes. We had gone fifteen years without winning
anything.'

The boys look serious. For them it must sound like ancient
history.

Eduardo carries on: 'Brazil was also in a difficult situation.
It was the military dictatorship. If you wanted to speak out
you had to think twice. Wadih Helu had been Corinthians'
president for many years. This really bothered us. But there
was nothing we could do about it. So about half a dozen fans
decided to form a pressure group to try to remove him.

'We had to have a cool name. To capture the moment.
Many options arose. When the name "Hawk" came up
everyone liked it. The hawk is the bird that flies the highest
and sees the furthest.'

Eduardo, who is twenty-five, lectures with heartfelt conviction. He scrunches his eyebrows and purposefully moves his
arms. It strikes me that Eduardo is the sort of person who
in Britain would be a left-wing activist, spending his weekends on marches or picketing McDonalds. Since Brazilian

politics is largely devoid of ideological debate, he channels his energy into football.

After his speech, Eduardo sits down. Sérgio stands up. Sérgio is almost twice Eduardo's age and has been a Hawk for twenty-two years. His delivery reminds me of a paternal headmaster.

'We eat, breathe and sleep Corinthians here. The Hawks shirt is our second skin. But remember – your family must come first. Don't stop taking rice and beans back to your family in order to finance your monthly payments.' This does not sound like a joke. The room is overwhelmingly black and mixed-race, and poor – except for Eduardo and Sérgio, who are white and middle class.

Sérgio says: 'There are Hawks who are hairdressers and there are Hawks who are High Court judges. We will never end! We will carry our banners to Hell!'

Sérgio asks if any of the new recruits would like to say anything. One person stands up. He says his name is Evaldo and he is twenty-three years old. He has wanted to be a Hawk since he was five. 'I never came before because of the violence,' he says. 'I was worried. What if I left a stadium in a Hawks shirt and I was alone? But I want to be part of this supporters club. I cry when Corinthians lose, I really care. It was important to come here today. I can see how this group has a fundament. You have taught me that the Hawks shirt has a strong meaning.'

Sérgio says he is pleased that someone has brought up the issue of violence – so he can dismiss their fears. He says the Hawks are peaceful. 'We are not stupid. We are all good people. Our love is for Corinthians.

'The only player who was ever hit was Viola. And that was because he kicked the Corinthians shirt. The shirt is our lives, it is our skin. Remember – footballers will come and go but Corinthians will be here for ever.'

To bring the hour-long lecture to a close Eduardo gestures to stand up for the Corinthians anthem. He starts a clap, joined in enthusiastically by his young charges. Everyone knows the words. It reminds me of young socialists singing the Red Flag.

> *Hail Corinthians*
> *Champion of champions*
> *Eternally*
> *In our hearts*
> *Hail Corinthians*
> *Of a thousand glories*
> *You are the pride*
> *Of the sportsmen of Brazil*
> *Your past is a banner*
> *Your present is a lesson*
> *You figure among the first*
> *Of our British sport*
> *Great Corinthians*
> *Always flying high*
> *In Brazil*
> *You're the club that's most Brazilian*

After the lecture I have a chance to have a more detailed chat with Eduardo. We leave the lecture room and walk along the corridor to the presidential suite. It is air-conditioned and brightly lit. Coming from the stuffy heat it is like walking into a fridge. The suite has a desk, a couple of cabinets, a sofa and a table. Eduardo asks me not to use his surname. He says that he would suffer discrimination at work if anyone found out he was a Hawk.

I ask him what happened to Viola. 'It was in 1988,' he replies. 'Viola was playing for Corinthians. He was substituted. He took his shirt off in anger and kicked it. So he was sent off. The fans were really agitated – so one of them went into the changing rooms and punched him.' He adds in mitigation: 'Only *one* person.'

It is episodes like this that have contributed to the Hawks' reputation as Brazil's hooligan equivalents. At matches they are Corinthians' most fanatical fans. They have a banner that is so heavy it takes three hundred people to carry it and when unrolled is 100m long and 40m deep. They chant the loudest and their drumming is the most awesome. Yet they are a menacing presence. The Hawks are feared by everyone – even Corinthians itself.

Eduardo and I discuss a more recent incident. Six months previously, a hundred Hawks turned up at Corinthians' ground to protest against the team's elimination from the Libertadores Cup. They brought eggs to throw at players they thought were responsible. The demo turned nasty. When the striker Edílson left the stadium he had no alternative but to walk through the crowd. As he did so the fans attacked him.

Edílson said that because of the assault he would never play for Corinthians again. Shortly afterwards he transferred to Flamengo.

'OK, so I think we went over the top,' replies Eduardo. 'But we always pressurised the club. Edílson was looking for an excuse to leave Corinthians. He knew the Hawks were waiting outside so he decided to go straight through them.'

Eduardo is not a thug, although he does a good job in defending thuggery. He relates everything to the Hawks' origins. The group was founded to stand up for fans' rights. He says it should never lose sight of its independence or militancy. 'Sometimes I think that our pressure hinders rather than helps – but that is the fault of the club's directors and the players. We really shouldn't have so much influence. We don't want to run Corinthians, we just want to be able to express our opinion.'

A few months later, I visit the Hawks to speak to their current president, Dentinho, or *Little Tooth*. We sit again in the bright and chilly presidential suite. Dentinho is a slight man with a permanently worried expression on his face, which might have something to do with the fact that he has a job as a taxi-driver. São Paulo is one of the most congested cities in the world.

Dentinho sees the the Hawks' role at Corinthians like a consumer pressure group – if the product, i.e. the club, sucks, then they complain, often using physical force. 'The strength of the Hawks is that we are a big parallel power within Corinthians. The players know the strength we have. When a player has a problem, or when a new, young player arrives, they always get in touch with us to ask how they will be treated.'

Less generous comparisons would describe the Hawks as a secret police, an austere nanny, a short-tempered lover or a vigilante praetorian guard. I ask if it is normal to storm into the changing rooms and hound players. 'We go there when a player is not fulfilling his obligations – then yes, we go in there and call him to account. That's our job. But we don't "invade" the changing rooms. If we're there it means that someone has let us in. If a security guard lets us in it means he respects us.'

He adds: 'Our members are always calling us, saying that they saw such-and-such a player in such-and-such a place.' The sightings are to warn that a player is stepping out of line, such as drinking, or dating a woman who is not his wife. 'A player uses his body in his job. A player has the right to go drinking or enjoy the nightlife, but not before a game. He needs to be professional.'

The majority of Corinthians' players have bodyguards – to protect them from being pestered by Hawks. They are most scared of the fans who love them the most.

It is not just the players who are intimidated. The Corinthians directors are often hostage to the Hawks' demands. Sometimes they call to ask for approval on new players or coaches. Oswaldo de Oliveira, the coach who won state, national and world titles with Corinthians, was sacked on the Hawks' insistence. 'The directors can't handle the pressure,' Oswaldo told me a year later. 'The club called up later and apologised.'

I ask Dentinho if he regrets any of the violence. 'There are certain situations where we should have thought twice.

But lots of times people blame us and neglect their responsibilities.' When I mention the 1997 ambush he dismisses it.
'It was nothing to do with us.'

During the early 1970s Corinthians fans found that the
Hawks fulfilled a social as well as a political need. The years
were the most bleak of the military dictatorship. The group
provided a great excuse for people with a common interest
to socialise. In 1976, the Hawks founded their own samba
bloco – the name given to the percussion-led musical troupes
that get together at carnival time. It was a way for the Hawks
to keep on meeting over the bank-holiday carnival period.
And it made sense – the Hawks already had a ready-made
band of percussionists; the ones that cheered Corinthians on
the terraces.

The *bloco* grew until it became an *escola* – a samba school
– which is the largest type of samba conglomeration. 'School'
is a misleading translation – samba schools are not educational establishments. They are large fraternities whose principal function is to parade at carnival. In São Paulo – as in
Rio – the main carnival procession is a competition between
the city's fourteen best samba schools. The Hawks' samba
school grew until it was one of the largest in São Paulo. It
won the title in 1995 and 1999.

The Hawks' parade is a megaproduction involving 4,700
people in fancy dress. To take part you do not need to be
a member of the supporters' club. You do not even need to
be a Corinthians fan – although almost everyone is. I decide
to parade with them in the carnival of 2001. In order to
choose my costume I visit the headquarters during a
rehearsal, on a balmy Sunday night in January.

I am one of the first to arrive. In the hall a man is lining
up drums. He has a hawk tattoo on his arm and a scar mark
on the left side of his face. I introduce myself. His name is
Pantchinho. He explains that he is the leader of the *bateria*,
the 300-piece percussion section. He is twenty-five, and is
friendly and soft-spoken. Like many involved in the Hawks'

parade, Pantchinho only became involved in carnival through being a football fan. As a teenage Hawk, he learnt how to drum on the terraces. He still goes to matches but he hardly has time any more. For the three months before carnival he holds rehearsals six days a week.

Most of Rio and São Paulo's main samba schools are community-based. Only the Hawks originate from a football supporters' club. 'We don't restrict ourselves geographically. We attract people from everywhere,' says Rodiney, one of the men reponsible for the costumes. He is setting up a mannequin on the balcony. 'At the Hawks you are representing your samba school but you are also representing your football team. It's like you are part of your team. Like you are a football player.'

He adds: 'The parade is a spectacle, but it is also a competition. It's all about adrenalin – look, I'm getting goosepimples just thinking about it. Corinthians is synonymous with fanaticism.'

Each samba school has a different theme for its parade. This year, the Hawks have chosen the Big Bang, spelt out as 'Myths and Magics in the Triumphal Odyssey of Creation'. Rodiney has finished assembling his costume. It has a blue helmet, a blue shoulder-piece and blue tunic scattered with apple-sized white bubbles. 'It's Water,' he says. Soon the other elements arrive – Earth, Wind and Fire.

Next to Rodiney is Carlão, *Big Carl*. He is a large man and speaks in basso profundo monosyllables. He was one of the original Hawks in the early 1970s. Carlão seems to best represent the contrast of macho football fans fussing over brightly coloured felt, feathers and sequins. He is responsible for the 150 people who will be dressed as Fire. The costume costs me £70.

The second time I see Carlão is in February, on carnival Saturday. I go to the workshop where he has contracted the costumes to be made. It is underneath one of São Paulo's many flyovers. Flimsy planks mark out a room. On wooden tables workers are rushing to finish in time. Carlão says he has not slept in days. His voice is deeper and he is more monosyllabic than usual. A tropical storm starts and the whole place darkens. Water starts pouring through holes in the ceiling, splashing within metres of the worktops. I take my costume and drive away, down a street that is about 2ft high in water.

The weather has cleared when I arrive at the Hawks' headquarters in the evening. On the wall opposite someone has painted a huge hawk and a drum, with the words 'Uma Torcida Que Samba', or '*The Fans That Samba*'. Like going to a match, the atmosphere is tense with an excitement that we are about to do battle.

I am wearing red espadrilles and red jodhpurs with yellow ribbons trailing from the hem. The costume's central section is a metal-framed shoulder-piece with hanging red felt. For good measure I have a detachable red flame with purple feathers that will eventually be attached to my back like a giant wing. As I and several other Fires carefully negotiate our way on to a bus, we look like exotic butterflies squashing into a tupperware box.

The parade takes place in the sambadrome, which is an avenue about a kilometre long bordered by stands on either side. It takes us about an hour to drive there because, this being São Paulo, the traffic is bottlenecked all the way. The buses are shaking with football chants. 'Hey, driver – why don't you fly,' we shout, whacking the ceiling for rhythm. 'Corinthians fans aren't afraid to die.'

I have a chance to speak to my friendly Fires. They are evenly divided between men and women, and mostly young white professionals in their twenties. None are card-carrying Hawks members but they try to parade with the samba school every year. 'There is more energy here,' one says. 'We have two badges. Samba and football. The other schools just have one badge.'

At the sambadrome our floats are already in line back-stage. Women are craned on to the podiums in outfits as minimal as mine is elaborate. Like footsoldiers we gather in our positions. There are several Hawk helpers dressed in white, whose job is to make sure that everything proceeds smoothly. And to make sure we look ecstatically happy. *Gulp!* I've never felt so scared.

Pantchinho leads in the drummers. The volume is colossal. A vocalist sings the Hawks' song, which is accompanied by a miniature *cavaquinho* guitar and belted out from speakers the length of the sambadrome.

Our first float enters the arena. It is decorated in. black and silver. It has a six-metre-high hawk whose wings surround a globe. The globe supports a podium with a gyrating, bikini-clad woman. Behind her there are eight more podiums and eight more women. At the back of the float there is a ten-metre-high podium, another woman, and if you really look hard, the Corinthians crest.

The chorus rings out:

> *I bring love and hope*
> *To this triumphal odyssey*
> *Fly, hawk, party for the people*
> *Burst forth at carnival time*

When I step into the stadium the thrill is euphoric. My eyes well up. I understand what Rodiney meant about feeling like a football player. The stands look like a football stadium. People are waving flags and balloons in Corinthians colours – black and white. The jubilation is contagious. On both sides there are banners the length of the sambadrome saying Hawks of the Faithful. Our vocalist is drowned out because it seems that everyone in the crowd is singing along too.

When we sing 'Fly, hawk' we all stretch our arms out, and turn from side to side as if we are flying too. It strikes me that the football experience has come full circle. With the Hawks, the football fan is no longer a spectator. He is the spectacle. The Hawks are the football fans that have their own fans.

The parade lasts about an hour. I almost do not recognise Eduardo at the end. He is in a snazzy white suit, the uniform given to the Hawks' senior members. He is very worried. The penultimate float broke its axle as it was moving into the sambadrome and had to be left behind. He hopes it will not cost them in the judging. Last year one of the introductory dancers dropped a part of his costume. The Hawks were docked a point and they lost the championship by half a point – the winners had 199.5 and they had 199.

Voting takes place at the sambadrome three days later. Judges give marks out of ten on various aspects of the parade. About 3,000 Hawks turn up – by far the largest contingent of any of the fourteen competing samba schools. But the Hawks only achieve third place. Their supporters start to fight. Riot police move in and fire plastic bullets and tear gas.

Corinthians were named after the English amateur team Corinthians, which toured Brazil in 1910. They are the only one of São Paulo's big clubs that was founded by the working class. Corinthians are known as the team of the masses – the Timão, the *Big Team*, a word that embodies their deep-rooted popular support.

Likewise, the Hawks of the Faithful were founded in opposition to the elite who ran the club. 'They were the humble people who turned against the institution. It was an urban uprising that included the idea of political thought. When they talk about having an ideology, they are not stupid. They are right,' argues Luiz Henrique de Toledo, who is an anthropologist and a leading authority on football supporters.

The Hawks' emergence, says Toledo, cannot be disassociated from the social context of the late 1960s and early 1970s. With civil liberties curtailed because of the dictatorship, football was one of the only spaces where Brazilians could express a political voice. People with few citizen's rights could, within groups like the Hawks, at least affirm their rights as fans.

We are sitting in an ice-cream café off the Avenida Paulista, an aggressively affluent valley of business skyscrapers that could be New York. Toledo, who has a young face and a goatee, says that the Hawks were the first supporters club to organise themselves independently of the team. All supporters clubs now follow the Hawks model. Football clubs usually have several, based around different networks of friends or even criteria including gender, sexuality or age. To be a member of São Caetano's Blue Walking Stick, for example, you need to be over sixty-five, rheumatic and have false teeth.

During the 1970s and 1980s, supporters clubs like the Hawks became focal points for delinquence. It was partly because São Paulo was expanding faster than it could cope with, attracting typically urban social problems. Toledo suggests that perhaps the thuggery was an inevitable consequence of an organisation founded out of a desire for confrontation. I can tell he respects the Hawks. He argues that they are different from hooligans in other countries. Usually, he says, groups of hooligans operate covertly. The Hawks wear their logo T-shirts with pride. They have a very strong presence in the city. 'The Hawks revitalised the São Paulo carnival,' he says. 'They brought a competitive spirit – and they also brought numbers. This was very visible the year they won.'

Toledo goes further in his praises. He believes that the Hawks strengthen democracy. 'They are against apathy in general. They provoke their members to see society differently. The person in the organised supporters group has a political appetite. He might have started because he likes football but once he is part of it he sees the world as political.'

To me, the Hawks are a good metaphor for what I see as one of Brazil's most striking contradictions. Brazilians are a happy, creative, excessively friendly people, yet – because of the country's social problems – they live with levels of murder and violent crime almost equivalent to a country in civil war. The Hawks combine these two extremes; they are a magnet for both awe-inspiring beauty and premeditated brutality.

During the 1980s and 1990s violence between supporters clubs became a public issue. The straw that broke the camel's back came in August 1995, when rioting broke out at the Pacaembu stadium during a match between Palmeiras' and São Paulo's youth teams. The toll was more than a hundred injuries and the coma and subsequent death of a young São Paulo fan. In the aftermath, all supporters clubs were banned from the state's stadiums. Members are allowed to attend matches – but cannot wear T-shirts or bring banners that refer to the organisations.

The two supporters clubs involved at the Pacaembu – Palmeiras' Mancha Verde, or *Green Streak*, and São Paulo's Independente, or *Independent* – were both shut down after legal action by the State Attorney Fernando Capez.

Capez's scruffy and underfunded offices are five minutes walk down the Avenida Paulista. He looks oddly out of place in them. Capez is thirty-six years old, tall, preppy and clubbable. He speaks loudly and quickly – as if he is in a fast-paced city firm.

After his success with Green Streak and Independent he has turned his attentions to the Hawks.

'They're testing me, they're testing me,' he says. 'They stop traffic in the street, they break doors, they smash up cars, they fight at stadiums, they invade the federation's building. I've called them in here. I don't want to close them down unless it's absolutely necessary. I've already told them that. So then what do they do?'

He gets out a blank piece of paper and draws a plan of the motorway where the Hawks assaulted the Corinthians bus. 'They say they didn't do it. That's a lie. They put their bus in front of the Corinthians bus. It was almost a tragic accident. Everyone got out and they used sticks and stones.

'So I entered a petition to have them closed down. I will be sad to see them extinct. There is a happy side to them.

But they judge themselves above the law. They say: "We put on the party, everyone likes us, so we can do what we like. We have been going for thirty years, some lousy attorney can't shut us down."'

Judges voted 2–1 in Capez's favour. The process is currently in appeal. He does not believe the Hawks' appeal will be successful. I ask what will happen if they lose. What about the samba school? 'I will confiscate all their funds. I will close down their lovely headquarters. They will have to find another base, find a new name and start all over again.'

He says that the Hawks are the most difficult fans to take on because of the popularity of their samba school. 'During carnival no one wants to stop them. But then if there is a violent episode everyone comes to me to have them shut down. There is this ambiguity. It's Jekyll and Hyde. When the beautiful side is apparent I am a detestable person. But when the ugly side shows I am the person everyone runs to. I am both hated and loved.'

The problem with the Hawks, he adds, is that they lack a leader of social standing. 'Metaleiro is a good kid. He's just stupid. Dentinho is honest, a worker. But within their number there are bandits.'

He realises that doing away with the Hawks won't stop football violence. But he is neither a politician nor a social worker. 'When violence is institutionalised, when it is in a gang, you have to break the gang. You don't stop the violence, you pulverise it. The police have to do the second part.' He sighs. In Brazil the police are neither well-trained nor well-equipped to fulfil their part of the bargain.

At the end of the interview I ask Capez if he likes football. 'I love it,' he says. I ask what team he supports. 'Look, I've something to show you.' He stands up and goes to a metal cupboard. He pulls out a big wooden engraving. He says that he cannot hang it on the wall, much as he would like to. It is the Corinthians shield with his name at the bottom.

'Do you think I am happy closing down the Hawks?'
He stares at me for a slow second.

'But you have to look at the safety of the population.
Justice has to be dispassionate.'

Chapter Seven

MY LITTLE TONY

The backlands of northeastern Brazil are widely known for their dusty, sun-scorched landscape and for their centuries-old tradition of improvisational poetry. When I arrive in Brejinho I approach two troubadour types and ask them to compose an ode to the local football stadium. They oblige immediately. The men strum their guitars. One begins with the following verse:

> *We're from a humble town a long way away*
> *The place is so small; it's with reason I say*
> *That our pride, our Big Tony, lights up our day.*

The slow strumming continues and the second man joins in, again following strict rules of rhyme and meter:

> *Big Tony's really huge, it's got all you need:*
> *Changing rooms, floodlights and grass*
> *that's grown from seed.*
> *When you see it you think: 'perfection indeed'.*

Brejinho is three hundred miles from the coast. When it rains, it is possible to eke out a living planting rice, beans and corn. When it does not – and it often does not – the people go hungry. In 1993, Brejinho suffered the worst drought in memory. With no harvest, families were forced to eat cactus. Desperate measures were sought to avert starvation. In scenes reminiscent of an African famine, crates of cereals were trucked into the town. Yet amid the hardship, 1993 was special. Work began on Big Tony, the most costly project in the town's history.

Brejinho has a population of 3,000. About 4,000 others live in the surrounding rural area. Its stadium was planned with a capacity of 10,000.

'Do you think Brejinho will stay with its current population?' asks João Pedro, the mayor who built it. 'I didn't do something just for the present. I did something that would last for a long time. The people wanted a stadium more than anything. I promised that one day I would build it for them. And I did.'

I am speaking to João Pedro as he gently rocks in his chair, under a chestnut tree on the pavement outside his house. His voice is slow and hoarse. Sunglasses shade his eyes. His close-cropped white hair and full moustache make him look like a retired military general.

The stadium's inauguration was the peak of João Pedro's career in public life. He remembers it clearly. The state's political chief turned up, as did the president of the electricity company from Recife, the state capital. 'I was very moved because many people were present. And everyone who was there liked it,' he says. Dignitaries feasted on a grand barbecue. A bull was slaughtered especially.

I walk towards the stadium, which is named after João Pedro's late son-in-law, Dr Antônio Alves de Lima, giving it the nickname *Tonhão*, or Big Tony. Brejinho is a simple town of cobbled streets surrounded by hills covered in cactus and giant rocks. When I first see Big Tony I stop and stare: The painted white stadium looks like an ocean liner beached in a dried-up lake.

The stadium is resplendent with the trappings of sporting sophistication. A three-metre-high wall in clean white paint encloses the ground. It has four ticket booths and three separate changing rooms: for the home side, the visitors and the referee. The pitch is of a professional size and has the only green grass for dozens of miles. A curved bar is built into the structure. There is floodlighting, terracing and even a concrete box kitted out for radio commentators.

I enter and sit down on the terraces with João Vilarim, Brejinho's sports secretary, a position that I am surprised is provided for in such a tiny, impoverished place. For a few minutes we watch local teenagers kicking a ball about. Then he tells me: 'We used to feel ashamed because we didn't have a proper stadium. Every town has to have one. We asked and asked and asked. Finally the mayor came to his senses.' My eyes wander to outside the stadium. The land is a dusty light brown. Outside a woman walks by barefoot, balancing a green plastic bucket on her head.

> We're from the land where football is played
> Upcountry, where great strikers are made
> All who come by try to make the grade.

During the 1970s the military regime built mega-stadiums in many of Brazil's largest cities, a populist policy and one which increased feelings of local and national pride. By 1978, according to the *Guinness Book of Records*, Brazil had twenty-seven with a capacity of at least 45,000 and five that held more than 100,000 – more giant stadiums than any other footballing nation. To be blessed with a 'football landmark' became important for a town's self-respect.

In the same way that Rio is unimaginable without the Maracanã, Brejinho is unimaginable without Big Tony. It is part of the city's soul and a reference point throughout the region.

Brejinho's inhabitants like being from the small town with the big stadium. They do not complain, for example, that the town does not have a public market – a venture that would attract commerce and help alleviate the unrelenting misery of daily life. To residents João Pedro had the right priorities. The vast cost was money well-spent. The young town – it was founded in 1963 – needed to affirm its existence with a football shrine.

No one seems to whisper that the ticket booths have only been used once since it opened, that the radio cabin is entered an average of once a year and that the floodlights are about as powerful as a battery torch. Nor does anyone question the logic of the perimeter wall. The thousands of bricks and the breeze blocks used took up the lion's share of the budget. Yet if every match except one has been free of charge, what purpose is there keeping people out?

João Pedro asks me. 'Isn't every stadium walled?' Before I can reply, he tells me the answer: 'Stadiums are always walled.'

In the bakery opposite João Pedro's house, the sales boy agrees. 'A stadium without a wall would be really ugly and weird. It wouldn't really be a stadium any more.'

Food and jobs alone do not win elections round here. As the defining legacy of his mayorship, Big Tony helped assure João Pedro's other son-in-law to electoral success. José Vanderlei was the only mayoral candidate in Pernambuco in the 2000 elections to stand unopposed.

Vanderlei lives in a brand-new house at the highest point of the town. He looks less fearsomely authoritarian than his father-in-law does. When he talks his dark eyes, scrunched forehead and pudgy features often break out into a cheeky smile.

'Some people say we should have built a public market instead. But a politician depends on the demands of the people. We don't just do what *we* want. We do things for the people. The same person who wants the public market, after the market he wants leisure facilities too. Football is important here, just as it is important all over the world. The stadium brings people together.'

He defends the money João Pedro spent, saying that at least it showed that João Pedro did not pocket the money himself. 'OK, so we spent £50,000. Another mayor might have done nothing and the £50,000 disappeared.'

In Vanderlei's manifesto he pledged to finish the stadium to its original designs. He wants to complete the terraces' current capacity from 3,000 to 10,000, build an artesian well to irrigate the turf and install fencing around the pitch – so pitch invasions are impossible. The total cost will be about £30,000. 'Take your house,' he says. 'Don't you always want to make improvements?'

At the time of the stadium's inauguration Brejinho had two football clubs. Sport Centre Brejinho United, known by its acronym Ceub, which was financially backed by the mayor's office and consequently the town's official team. Its rival was Juventus, named after the Turin club side, and run by the disaffected Ceub player Arlindo Formiga.

Arlindo owns Brejinho's only nightclub, Night Commotion. He is the danceteria's factotum. Every week he drives the six miles to a music shop in the nearest large town to rent about twenty CDs – mostly of regional folk music – for 35p each. On Fridays and Sundays, the only evenings Night Commotion opens, he DJs all night.

One hundred metres from João Pedro's rocking chair, on the same street, is Arlindo's front door. When I arrive he looks at me suspiciously. He spent the morning shooting rare birds and thinks I have come to arrest him.

Whether it was his innate sense of motivating the public, his rivalry against Ceub, or simply his passion for football, Arlindo built Juventus into a potent local force. The team was unique in the town in having an organised supporters club. Juventus was for a while the most popular team in Brejinho.

'We called our team Juventus because we had a vote and it won out over Arsenal,' says Arlindo. He fetches blue and white banners with slogans like 'Juventos – The Most Loved' and 'Juventos – Animal'. His spelling is not much better than his sense of colour. Juventus of Turin play in black and white stripes. I ask Arlindo why he chose blue and white. 'Doesn't the Italian Juventus play in those colours?' he replies, a little confused.

Arlindo Formiga (left) and his Juventus supporters

To increase Juventus' glamour he painted Coca-Cola on the front of their strips – not because there was any financial backing, which there would never be in Brejinho, but because the soft drink company sponsored the national team.

Big Tony would have been the perfect stage for a Ceub vs. Juventus local derby. When he tells me that it never happened, I am astonished.

'I don't know what it's like in there,' Arlindo tells me. 'I've never been.'

Arlindo, aged fifty-two, used to be a local councillor. He did himself no favours by opposing João Pedro, a politician who in the tradition of backwoods politics ruled unforgivingly over dissent. 'João Pedro asked a cousin of mine to tell me I was banned. Whoever opposes him never gets to play at Big Tony.'

Where did Juventus play? For several years the team made do with a dirt pitch *opposite* the new stadium, on the other side of the one road that passes through the town. The two Brejinho teams only ever played each other in tournaments away from home. Then, in 1999, the owner of Juventus'

pitch sold the plot and Juventus ceased to exist. Arlindo
sold the posts, the net, the substitutes' bench, four sets of
shirts, twelve pairs of football boots and two balls. All he
has left is the supporters' banners.

He is left with a bitter taste in his toothless mouth. 'The
stadium belongs to the people. It's not private. But they say
it's theirs, so what can I do?' His pride stopped him begging
for permission. 'If you came to my house and on the first
day I sent you away, would you come back? I will never
enter a place from where I have been expelled.'

João Pedro was a classic despotic local chief who received
favours from his representatives in federal government in
exchange for guaranteeing electoral support. João Pedro
played the role *par excellence*. He boasts that Brejinho
always has the highest rate of support in Pernambuco for
the state's right-wing congressman. The payback has been
generous. Thanks to the congressman's influence in Brasília,
in 1998 the Sports Ministry built Brejinho – already endowed
with the best facilities in the region – a brand-new indoor
sports centre.

The town is still without a public market.

I will always sing to the sound of my guitar
That our stadium has admirers near and far
Big Tony is a stage for every football star.

Chapter Eight

CARS, GIRLS AND KEEPING IT UP

Walter Lacet, Flamengo's Number 4, takes possession in his own half. The car dominates the ball with its front left wheel. It accelerates towards the oncoming goal. Nought to thirty in sixty metres. As Lacet approaches the area the angle is tight. He attempts a sharp left. Too late. The car crashes into the side of the post.

'Mmm. It was a wonderful time. God, how I miss it,' yearns Mário Bucich. We are watching a video of automobile football, or autoball, a radical sporting crossbreed from the 1970s played by two teams of cars and a 1.2m-diameter leather ball. Mário talks of his autoball days with the dreamy gaze of a cricketer reminiscing about Sunday afternoons on the village green.

'The referee was always on foot,' he points out softly, proudly. 'And never once did he get run over.'

'Yes he did,' interrupts Ivan Sant'Anna, sitting next to him.

'Sometimes we knocked the ref over,' Ivan adds brusquely, 'but there was never a serious accident in autoball, because the pitch was small. If the pitch were four times the size, full of empty space, then it would have been dangerous. But the size of the pitch limited the speed of the cars.'

We are in the living room of Ivan's eleventh-floor flat in

Rio de Janeiro's nouveau-riche suburb Barra da Tijuca. From the window, you can see beyond nearby malls and tower blocks towards miles of flat land until a lagoon meets a ridge of green mountains. It is a triumph of dramatic land-scape over the immediate urban banality. 'I think autoball has something to do with what you are seeing out there,' says Mário, pointing to the horizon. 'With being free. The Carioca feels free.'*

The video plays on. Ivan serves us coconut water, adding that it is from a very efficient coconut home-delivery service. Autoball is an entertaining spectacle: *It's A Knockout* meets *Demolition Derby*, a mixture of childish fun with adult danger, of absolute simplicity with noisy, dirty, mechanical aggression. Since the ball is so big – twice the height of a car bonnet – the drivers and their machines look exagger-atedly small and childlike, no matter how fast or recklessly they drive. The ball is made of buffalo leather, and it bounces around like a big, heavy balloon as if obeying lunar laws of gravity. The referee runs up and down the touchline, blowing unheard and unheeded whistles and occasionally dislodging the ball from a mass of twisted steel. He's more a glorified traffic warden than a referee, but he gets the surreal thrill of showing a yellow card to a roaring auto-mobile.

Ivan, sixty, and Mário, fifty-seven, have kept in touch since they hung up their driving shoes. Mário, who now works in the solar energy business, is a soft-spoken, well-mannered man whose serene air is accentuated by a profes-sorial white moustache and goatee. I ask what was the worst accident that happened.

'Was it the guy whose car exploded?' says Ivan.

Mário shakes his head: 'No. It was when a spectator was where he shouldn't have been, just behind the touchline, about half a metre lower than the pitch. A driver lost control,

* Carioca: meaning of or from Rio de Janeiro.

spun in a circle and landed on this guy's chest. But I think he only broke an arm, isn't that right?'

Ivan agrees: 'An arm, a collarbone. That's right. The driver was prosecuted. There was a court case. Running someone over is a criminal offence – even if it happens as part of a sporting event. It took five years to come to court.'

'Autoball was exciting,' enthuses Ivan. 'Cars were often flipped over, there were lots of fires. But we were prepared for these things. It wasn't dangerous in the sense that someone could have died, like in a race of Formula Indy. You only risked breaking an arm or a leg, that sort of thing.' For Mário it was good clean fun: 'There was no danger at all. It was a sport. It wasn't a circus show.'

For more than five years autoball was the sport of Rio de Janeiro's young elite, who would buy and trash cars like they were pairs of boots. Autoball acquired rules, a federation and teams endorsed by the five major football clubs, Flamengo, Fluminense, Botafogo, Vasco and América.

It produced its own stars. Ivan scored on his first appearance in 1970 and was subsequently autoball's most prolific striker. 'The other day I was in the fish market, and a man comes up and asks me for an autograph,' says Ivan, slightly mystified that anyone could still remember. 'He said "because you were the best autoball player there ever was".'

Ivan is tall and has a small round head with closely cropped white hair. He is wearing shorts with socks up to his knees. Whereas Mário is reserved, Ivan is loud, direct, domineering and distinctly cavalier. For him, of course autoball wasn't dangerous. When the sport was banned he took up flying acrobatic planes.

His pilot's licence had already come in handy. He and Mário, once 300 miles away in Belo Horizonte for an exhibition match, realised that their cars were in a freight wagon stuck somewhere on the rail line from Rio. Ivan decided to fix the problem. He rented a plane. He flew above the track and followed it back towards Rio.

'He found the train, and then buzzed it three times at the

level of the driver, yelling for the guy to get moving,' says Mário, still in awe of his colleague. 'You ask me what was exciting in autoball – it's memories like that.'

Ivan shrugs: 'I was a pilot. We needed the cars.'

Autoball emerged as a solution for what to do with a 1.2-metre, 12kg ball that had been made by the São Paulo ball factory Drible to commemorate a match of the Brazilian national team. The giant leather orb had stayed in the factory until 1970, when it was lent out for an attempt to create equestrian football. One might have thought polo already fulfilled this need. Not so. In the town of Taubaté the horses were expected to, most unBrazilianly, hoof the ball. 'The game would have been a success – the stadium was full,' wrote O Globo, 'except that the horses were scared to death of the ball, and one of the few to risk a kick broke his leg.'

The buffalo-skinned supersphere ended up in the hands of Mário Tourinho, former member of the Competitive Drivers Association and for two decades team medic of América Football Club. Mário had dreamt up autoball by accident. He was driving along Copacabana and a ball came flying towards his windscreen. Instead of averting the collision he charged into it. Thwack! The ball bounced back like a 'perfect kick'. Eureka! He saw at once that his two passions could be merged into a unique new sport.

Mário was a surgeon. It could be argued that he behaved so as to create new clients. Yet he believed that autoball, despite its violence, was a good way to relax drivers' nerves: 'It's a necessary therapy in today's age, when stress is creating a great human mass of neuroses,' he said. Years later, Mário underlined his position as football's most controversial medic when he performed Garrincha's long-awaited knee operation.

The first autoball match took place on 19 September 1970 – three months after Brazil won the World Cup in Mexico – during the half-time period of a game between Flamengo and Madureira. Luiz Mendes, the radio commentator, remembers that about ten cars drove on to a side pitch and

Autoball player shows off control technique

started driving into each other. The match, however, entered
football folklore for something else. Twenty-six minutes into
the second half Ubirajara Alcântara, Flamengo's goalkeeper,
booted the ball upfield. In the air it was carried by a gust
of wind and bounced straight into the opposing net. Never
before or since has a keeper in Brazil scored from his area.
Autoball was the most crackpot development of the year,
yet its launch was overshadowed by a goal kick.

The sport gradually evolved its practical procedures.
Depending on the size of the pitch, autoball could be three-,
four-, five- or even six-a-side. The cars were old Fords,
Chevrolets, Volkswagens and Renaults. Rules were kept
simple. They followed the spirit of football, with the modi-
fications that reversing was only allowed off the ball, goalkeeper cars were not permitted to save using the side of their
vehicles and there were no throw-ins or corner kicks.
Scorelines were high, such as 9–6 or 7–5.

The first matches were between a team in yellow 'shirts'
and a team in red. But there were teething problems; the

cars were old and broke down, technique was poor and the turnouts were low. The following year, in 1971, Mário Tourinho organised an exhibition game on Copacabana's Atlantic Avenue, the most glamorous stage for a sporting event after the Maracanã.

The road was closed. Crowds gathered. Ivan turned up in a brand-new Alfa Romeo. He asked his colleagues not to bump into him. Another player had the same request. He had rented a car to take part. 'We all took a lot of care not to squash his car,' says Mário Bucich. 'The rental shop should have loved it – the car hardly added mileage and returned scratchless.'

'It was in the middle of the road, it was crazy. But seriously, no one ran into anyone,' swears Ivan.

To raise the sport's profile its enthusiasts approached Rio's football clubs for permission to have teams play under their colours. In 1973 the first Carioca Championship began with fortnightly games between Fluminense, Vasco, Flamengo and América. It lasted six months. The following year América made way for Botafogo.

The cars were painted in team colours and, like team shirts, featured a number and the club emblem. They were fitted inside with a pole from the floor to the ceiling, to make sure the roof would not cave in if they overturned. Different cars had different uses and required different techniques. If a Volkswagen Beetle hit the ball, the curved bonnet would lob the ball in the air – enabling other cars to 'head' the ball with their windscreens or roofs. Cars with square bonnets could be used for penalties and for passes along the ground. Specialist repairmen were on hand. In case of a breakdown 'the mechanics, nicknamed "masseurs", [rush] on to the field with levers, wrenches, and hammers to see if the car can be kept running,' wrote one newspaper in 1975. 'Doctor' Castro, a masseur, surpassed himself when he managed to fix a car that twenty minutes beforehand had caught fire.

Autoball required skill, courage and deep pockets. Ivan, then a partner in a financial broker's, bankrolled his hobby personally. 'It was a very expensive sport. I spent lots of money, say US$3,000 a time,' he estimates. 'You needed to buy a car almost every game. We bought taxis. You had to customise the car. Some people liked even to have two or three cars per game. It really wrecked the clutch, so you had to swap the car a lot.'

There is a certain unavoidable logic to the emergence of autoball, since it suited Brazilian traits of playfulness, reckless driving and wanton destruction. It also combined the two mainstream sports of which Brazil boasts the best international record: football and motor racing. Brazil is the only country to have won the football World Cup four times. Brazilian drivers have won the Formula One championship eight times – more than the drivers of any other nationality. Autoball coincided both with Brazil's post-1970 World Cup honeymoon and with the triumphs of Brazil's first Formula One champion, Émerson Fittipaldi, in 1972 and 1974. Brazil was the best in the world in racing cars and kicking balls. Why not capitalise?

As the mechanics got better, the cars became stronger and with practice the players learnt new tricks. (There were hardly any training sessions. It was too expensive.) Some players preferred less subtle touches. 'Scorning the required crash helmet, his black flight suit unzipped to show his chest hair, [Walter] Lacet gunned around the field with the kind of revved up machismo that seems a prerequisite for autoball. When the ball got pinned between two cars, he would wheel off to the far end of the field and then come roaring back at full speed until the opposing driver backed off the ball. If he did not retreat, mechanics armed with sledgehammers were called in to disentangle the wreckage and, if necessary, provide substitute cars,' wrote US magazine *Time*.

Booking a good pitch was always tricky, since a game of autoball trashed the grass. Fluminense allowed the sport at its Laranjeiras stadium during returfing. Crowds were anything from 4,000 to 15,000. Seventy years before,

Laranjeiras had been the birthplace of football in Rio, where the young sportsmen were white members of the city's elite. Autoball was also a hobby for the young rich. Almost all the players were stockbrokers flush with cash (apart from one cab driver 'obviously venting pent-up aggressions').

Like Marcos de Mendonça, who kept goal for Fluminense between 1914 and 1922 and became an eminent historian, the autoball class also became public figures of some distinction. Walter Lacet is one of the top executives at Brazil's second-largest channel, SBT. Ronaldo Cezar Coelho was one of the founders of the Brazilian Social Democratic Party, together with President Fernando Henrique Cardoso, and he has been elected a congressman three times.

Ivan Sant'Anna is a character as colourful as the sports he played. He lived life large and he knows how to spin a yarn. After thirty-seven years in financial markets he became a successful storyteller, first with a financial thriller, *Rapine*, and then with *Black Box*, an account of three real-life air crashes. During the early 1970s, when he seemingly had more money than he knew what to do with, he spent a fortune travelling to sports events. Between 1970 and 1977 he saw every single game that Fluminense played. 'I saw maybe a hundred games a year. I can remember sometimes I left on Sunday to go to Manaus, I would come back and work, then on Wednesday I would go to Bahia, and at the end of the week I would be in Buenos Aires.

'The furthest I went was Sarajevo. I went to almost all the countries in Africa.' He pauses to list the countries the Fluminense caravan passed through: 'Botswana, Malawi, Burundi, Lesotho, Tanzania. I travelled with them, I stayed in the same hotels. By the end I was almost part of the team. Then, in 1977, I lost all my money and stopped. But for the period 1970–77 I have the impression that I was the biggest football fan that there has ever been in this country.' His feat is probably unequalled in the world due to the large number of matches, the distances involved in the national league and the unpredictability of what might happen. Once, when he was living in Belo Horizonte he came to Rio to see Fluminense play Vasco. The game was abandoned after ten minutes in the second half when the perimeter fencing caved in. The following day, back in Belo Horizonte, he read that the remaining half hour would be played in the evening. He went to the airport but there were no seats left. So he chartered his own plane. He just made it to the game. His team lost 2–1.

Autoball's image of conspicuous consumption and innate sense of waste reflected the economic confidence of the era. Between 1969 and 1973 – the darkest years of military rule – Brazil experienced its 'economic miracle'. GDP rose almost 12 per cent a year. The state borrowed huge sums for grandiose projects like the Trans-Amazon Highway, an ill-fated plan that opened up huge parts of virgin rainforest to colonisation. 'The country felt rich but it was an illusion,' says Mário with bittersweet nostalgia. 'We were getting further and further into debt. In that day to be rich was wonderful. Now things are a lot more difficult.' Autoball, which was almost the private sport of the Rio bourse, can be seen as one of the last extravagances of Rio de Janeiro before it started to lose its power as a financial centre. One by one the banks and big companies moved to São Paulo until, in 2000, trading on Rio's stock market shut down completely.

Autoball came to an end not because of the danger or the expense, but because the government banned all motor sports in the light of the 1974 world energy crisis. The phenomenon reflected an era of accelerated Brazilian excess that spluttered and ran out of gas. 'The four or five years in which there was autoball was an interesting time. It got good publicity,' says Ivan. 'If it hadn't been banned, and it had managed to be played on a big pitch, then maybe it would be known now all around the world. It would be a very exciting sport, much more than car racing. But it needed a fatal accident. This was my premonition – the sport would only be a success if people died.'

*   *   *

Signs that football was destined to overstep its sporting parameters and permeate Brazilian cultural life in more subtle ways were evident even at the start of the twentieth century. The 'violent British sport' had barely taken off its swaddling clothes when children started to play football-inspired tiddlywinks using thick buttons ripped from their coats. They placed two teams of eleven buttons each on a smooth tabletop, and flicked them to ricochet a tiny ball into a miniature net. The result, button football, has survived until today.

Marcelo Coutinho sets up a button football demonstration in his shop, the Button Office, on the top floor of a busy mall in Rio's North Zone. The pitch is a green felt board half the size of a table tennis table. Ground markings are lovingly detailed with white paint. Button football's great strength is that it offers sporting glory to fans physically predisposed to staying at home. Marcelo's body has the generous shape of someone who cannot remember the last time he kicked a ball. But give him a button and his fingers become Pelé's dancing legs. He places a button 20cm from the goal. One flick – *pfutt!* – and the ball flies into the net. *Goooooal.* The goalkeeper, an inanimate domino-sized wedge, never stood a chance.

'Sometimes there's no space to play proper football, or you can't play well. So you play with your buttons instead,' explains Marcelo, whose goatee beard and cropped dark hair is speckled with grey. The Button Office is the only shop in Brazil dedicated exclusively to the sport. Thousands of colourful buttons are stuck on the wall. Men that walk past seem unable to resist ogling, a feeling conspicuously absent in their female partners. The objects of their affection are so marvellously uncomplicated that they seem to have been teleported from a forgotten age. Football buttons are only one small step up the toy evolutionary ladder from coat buttons. They have not sprouted human forms to become like Subbuteo figurines or incorporated holograms or flashing parts. The buttons look like painted poker chips.

The Bangu reserves

Marcelo's Vasco all-stars

Modernity has brought them more sophisticated finishing, embossed lettering and a wider variation of colours – but nothing can disguise what they really are: humble plastic discs.

Marcelo keeps his teams of buttons in custom-made wooden boxes, called 'changing rooms'. He also travels with a first-aid kit that includes furniture polish, liquid silicone cleaner, towels, several types of wax, a cleaning block covered in felt and headache pills. Enthusiasts have several sides they develop, sometimes over decades. Marcelo takes out the champion team he played with from 1984 to 1987 and lines them up: Pelé at right back, Falcão in central defence and Zico, Cruyff and Beckenbauer on the substitute's bench. 'What other team in the world has Cruyff and Beckenbauer in the reserves?' he boasts.

Button football is deeply rooted in the Brazilian psyche. The game's simplicity provided a fantastic canvas for romanticism. Button players – 'buttonistas' – give their buttons the names of players and keep lists of which button is leading scorer. Team colours can also be freely chosen. Marcelo's all-star international team plays in the red and white of Rio club Bangu.

Pelé, Cruyff and Beckenbauer started off in the Bangu first team but had missed a few easy shots. Of course, it was Marcelo who had missed the shots by misflicking those buttons, but the inner game of button football demanded that the stars make way for other talent. 'It's superstition, a psychological thing,' explains Marcelo. 'In reality, all the buttons are exactly the same.' Pelé, he says, was going through a terrible phase up front, so he was substituted. 'But Pelé is Pelé, he can play in any position. He managed to find a way back into the first team, improvising at right back. The shake-up worked and the Bangu defence stabilised, becoming one of the best in Rio.' Marcelo then changed his colours. He formed a squad made up of friends and family, in the blue of Portugal's Porto. His wife, Mônica, was on the right midfield and his son, Bruno, centreforward. For a while he fielded buttons named after historical freedom-fighters: Zapata, Castro and Guevara in midfield, offering service to Gandhi and Mandela up front. Marcelo's current team is an all-star Vasco side, although he took the nepotistic liberty of signing Bruno, Porto's child prodigy.

Button football is similar to Subbuteo in that both are miniature versions of football played on tabletops. Yet button football predates both Subbuteo, created by Waddingtons in 1947, and its precursor Newfooty, created by a Liverpudlian family in 1929. Geraldo Décourt, the first man to try and regularise button football, wrote in his autobiography that he started playing in 1920, when he was about nine. In 1930 Décourt published the first official rule-book, calling it Foot-Ball Celotex since the wooden surface of the tables was imported by the Celotex Company of Chicago.

Button football emerged independently of the toy industry and has managed to stay outside it. Buttons are made by men like Adriano Moutinho, whose thick moustache, shoulder-length black hair and pot belly make him look more like a boozy Hell's Angel than a local craftsman. Adriano, aged forty-four, is a die-hard buttonista who spends eight hours a day at home in a Rio suburb carving buttons out of plastic on his lathe. Some are beautifully adorned works of art, using combinations of materials, miniature shields and coconut husks.

The disorganisation that has been button football's strength has also meant that the sport has become comically riven by factions. Three versions dominate – based respectively in the states of Bahia, Rio and São Paulo. Bahian rules demand a tiny plastic disc as a ball and allow one flick each go. Rio rules have a felt ball and three flicks each are allowed, whereas Paulista rules require a smaller table, a felt ball and twelve flicks. The differences may sound pedantic but the rivalry is intense. In order to cool tempers, sports magazine *Placar* printed The Buttonista's Ten Commandments. Number one: 'There are no bad rules, just different options and tastes.'

After decades of bickering the three sides agreed to call a truce in the mid-1980s. A delegation including members of each ruling faction travelled to Brasília to lobby the government for recognition. On 29 September 1988, the National Sports Council published in a resolution that 'table football' was, de facto, a sport – due to the large number of practitioners and the fact that national championships already existed. It was allegedly demonstrated that the buttonista walks the equivalent of 3.5 kilometres per match, 'physical force' being a prerequisite for approval. A national 'table football' confederation was founded with a revolving presidency between the three modalities.

The incapacity to regularise the rules, however – there are established variations in Maranhão and Rio Grande do Sul, as well as some dangerous renegades who prefer to use a tiny cube as a ball – has left the sport virtually unmarketable. With the advent of computer games, some fear for button football's survival. 'I understand people's concerns with the demise of the Spix's macaw and the golden lion tamarin monkey. But what I'm worried about is the death of button football,' wrote broadcaster and columnist José Trajano in the daily sportspaper *Lance!* in 2001.

Reports of button football's demise are exaggerated. Some of Brazil's top clubs – including Internacional of Porto Alegre and Corinthians of São Paulo – have button departments. Button footballers must wear the club's football kit and play with buttons in club colours when they compete in local leagues. The game is mentioned in pop songs and many celebrities – even professional footballers – make a point of expressing their love for it. By investing in the Button Office, Marcelo has put his money where his heart is. For him button football is as Brazilian as samba. 'Every child comes into contact with button football. It is ingrained in our society.'

Button football reduced the game to a tabletop. So did nail-ball, which is also on sale at the Button Office. In nailball, players flick a coin between two teams of eleven nails hammered into a board. In fact, given any surface area, no matter how inconvenient, it is a good bet that the Brazilians have invented a sport for it that involves kicking a ball. Ecoball, played in the rainforest capital Macapá, prioritises environmentalism in equatorial surroundings: football played on a pitch dotted with trees. If you hit a treetrunk you are sent off temporarily – to suck a lime. Footpenalty, invented in Porto Alegre, uses half a pitch and one goal. 'Footpenalty arose from the necessity to find something to do when one side doesn't show up,' says the founder, Sidnei Oliveira, aged forty-seven.

The difficulty of maintaining full-sized grass football pitches in a tropical, developing country – the cost, the climate and the lack of urban space – has led to the sport being adapted to whichever terrain is available. The incessant modification of football is also the result of a society which is not hung up about changing rules. A hallmark of Brazilian popular culture is inclusion. Carnival is a way of letting barriers between classes drop. Religion is malleable to allow almost any type of belief. Likewise, no one is excluded from appropriating football to suit their quirks or practical needs.

The prodigal son of football's Brazilian offspring is futsal, which has been so successful that it is estimated to be the most practised game in the country – more than football itself. Futsal is five-a-side indoor football played on a basketball-sized court, with twenty minutes each half and a small ball. Players need to be very fast, versatile and have great domination of the ball. Futsal looks like a cross between ice-hockey and football. The ball, which rarely bounces, is passed around like a spherical puck. The game is eulogised as having nurtured several of the most gifted Brazilian footballers, such as Rivelino and Zico. It is regarded as an incubator of the Brazilian soul.

The idea of kicking a ball around a basketball court was first had by a Uruguayan, Juan Carlos Ceriani, at the Montevideo YMCA in the 1930s. But it took his Brazilian colleagues at the São Paulo YMCA to formalise the game into a sport. Since a regular football was too bouncy, the Brazilians experimented with smaller balls weighted with sawdust, cork and horsehair. Futebol de salão, or 'drawing-room football', as it was known before the abbreviation futsal stuck, was nicknamed the 'sport of the heavy ball'.

The first futsal federation was founded in Rio in 1954. Before 1959, when the different state federations unified their rules, futsal spawned some of the oddest practices of any contact sport. In some games, futsal players were not allowed to speak. Any utterance would result in a foul. Fans too, for a short period, were not allowed to make any noise. But the silliest rule stipulated that players were not allowed to play the ball while a hand was touching the floor. This meant that if someone was knocked over, or tripped up, he would avoiding using his hand for support – since this would rule him out of play. Players twisted their bodies to try and land on their backs, fronts, shoulders and heads. The rule was reportedly abolished when a medical paper showed that, due to the large number of broken arms and dislocated shoulders, futsal was the most dangerous sport in Brazil.

In 1971, the International Federation of Futebol de Salão, or Fifusa, was set up in São Paulo. In 1989 the sport was taken over by FIFA, coining the name futsal and splitting with Fifusa. Since then futsal has flourished worldwide. More than 160 countries applied to enter the 2000 World Championship.

In Brazil a professional league has existed since 1996, although a grey professionalism has existed since the 1960s when the best players would be paid hefty 'expenses'. Now, the top futsal players earn as much as some footballers. Manoel Tobias, Brazil's best-paid futsal athlete, is estimated to have an annual income well in excess of £100,000. The sport has grown like a jungle weed. The Brazilian Futsal Confederation (CBFS) has registered about 160,000 new players since 1991 to play in amateur leagues.

'Futsal is the sport now that gives most *alegria* – happiness – to Brazilians,' says Vicente Figueiredo, the author of *The History of Futebol de Salão*. Brazil dominates the world scene. 'Out of thirty-eight international competitions, Brazil has won thirty-five.'

A peculiarity of Brazilian futsal is the dominance of Ceará, a state in the northeast better known for untouched beaches, cowboys, Catholic pilgrims and droughts. Its capital, Fortaleza, is the only one of Brazil's eight largest cities that does not have at least two football teams that regularly play in the top division. Perhaps because of this, Ceará has put its energies into futsal. Ceará is the state with the largest number of victories in futsal's Brazil Cup. 'I think futsal fitted us like a glove. The Cearense is irreverent, he's not interested in tactical systems, he likes messing about,' adds Vicente Figueiredo. 'Here people are more interested in futsal than football. All the big futsal clubs in Brazil always have a Cearense in the team.'

Futsal is the football derivative that is played indoors. On weekends, in Rio de Janeiro, it is possible to find people playing football outdoors twenty-four hours a day. In the traditional neighbourhood of Flamengo, a park of artificial pitches run by the city council stays busy well after midnight. It is the only time when men employed in evening jobs such as waiters, security guards and doormen can play in their own leagues. Demand is so great that some people queue overnight to make sure they are allocated a pitch.

At 6.15am on Saturday morning at the far end of Barra da Tijuca, where Rio is expanding into a coastal marshland and moneyed cariocas live in spacious gated condominiums, the first men arrive for the kickabout at Paulinho Figueiredo's place. By 6.45am fourteen names are down, two goalkeepers have arrived, and two eight-a-side teams are formed.

Paulinho, aged fifty-seven, has not only built a half-size football pitch for himself and his mates but a club house with jacuzzi, sauna, massage table, showers, and barbecue. Three full-time staff toil to keep the grass a perfect emerald green. Sixty men – including architects, engineers, businessmen, bankers and a military colonel – pay £400 a year to be associates. Except the six goalkeepers. They are exempt from the annual fee. Even among the Brazilian well-to-do, no one likes to stay in goal.

At 8am the sun is rising and the temperature approaches 30 degrees C. Paulinho's house is the last building in the condominium and surrounded by lush green. In the quiet distance – beyond an untouched lagoon – you can make out the beach road. A match starts. The average age is about fifty. Sliding tackles are banned because of the fragility of ageing bones. Yet the standard is high. The men run, shout, sweat. Football here is taken seriously. Saturday mornings are a sacred time.

The game is another Brazilian innovation: 'society football', football for the upper class. The game's roots date back to the 1950s, a decade which smiled kindly on Rio's bourgeoisie. It was a time of political freedom and rich cultural activity, sweetened with the national pride of winning the World Cup for the first time. The word 'society', pronounced as in English but written *soçaite* to respect Portuguese spelling rules, was used to characterise glamorous leisure activities. It was fashionable for landlords with large premises to set up small grass pitches for friends. You need money to keep grass in tropical Rio de Janeiro. The posh kickabouts became known as *futebol soçaite*.

Society football is about status. Paulinho's pitch is true to the word's origins. His father, General João Figueiredo, was Brazilian president between 1979 and 1985, the last dictator of the military regime. Paulinho's kickabouts started in 1977 at a society pitch belonging to Lídeo Toledo, doctor for Botafogo and the Brazilian national team. 'It was just a group of friends,' Luíz Vinhaes, a founder member, tells me after the football has stopped. 'But Paulinho was the son of the president. Many people wanted to lick his arse . . . so our group got bigger and bigger.' One member lent them a well-located piece of land in Barra da Tijuca. With astute political timing, the minute Figueredo left the presidency the man asked for his land back. 'Then Paulinho decided to put a pitch here, so we came here.'

By 11am, the men are drinking beer from ice-cold cans and the smell of charred steak from the barbecue wafts over the pitch. For the men and the boys (sons may attend, but not wives or daughters) these kickabouts act as social cement. That's generally true for Brazilians of every class; the only real difference here is the wealth of the participants, who could clearly afford any indulgence. Well-heeled and well-to-do they may be, but as Brazilians, they prefer football.

Since the club is made up of rich, influential men, it inevitably becomes a forum for doing business. 'We chat and swap ideas. It gets you introductions to people who might be useful. Even if there are no politicians here, there are people who have the ear of politicians, people who can get you to see the mayor. Things work out,' says Sérgio Vitor, owner of a video company. When Lúcio Macedo, who runs a marketing business, organised an end-of-year party at Paulinho's, he managed to get a bank to sponsor it, giving £2,000 for a marquee, a barbecue and a carnival samba group. Pictures made *Caras*, the Brazilian version of *Hello!*.

More than the media, the status of Paulinho's club brings members into contact with celebrity footballers. Branco, part of the 1994 World Cup-winning team, and Jairzinho, who scored in every game in the 1970 World Cup, are regulars. Paulinho's mates live out childhood fantasies. 'It's a wonderful thing to do,' says Lúcio, 'to play football on a Saturday morning and pass the ball to a world champion.'

I finally speak to Paulinho. He is slimmer than most of the others, wearing tight olive green swimming trunks. He looks much younger than fifty-seven – partly because of his short dark hair, but mainly because of an incessant grin that reveals a childish gap between his two front teeth. He is a great host and has a mastery for charm and football small talk that must have been perfected through a lifetime of Brazilian society parties. Our conversation is so effortless and pleasant that as soon as it is over I cannot remember what we spoke about.

In São Paulo, society football emerged in the mansions of the richest neighbourhood, Morumbi, but took a different turn in the 1980s. As the city's population expanded, common land that had been used for football became scarcer and scarcer. Seven-a-side society football required less space than full-sized pitches. It began to proliferate for people of all classes, its expansion aided by the accessibility of synthetic turf. Nowadays society football is used to describe any small, outdoor grass or synthetic pitch. Society football pitches now outnumber full-sized pitches in Greater São Paulo.

Brazilians will play football wherever they can. In the central Amazon, three hours by boat upriver from Manaus, I saw a futsal pitch on stilts as part of a luxury hotel complex. Activities included fishing for piranhas, sailing to see Indian tribes and five-a-side kickabouts. Elsewhere in the Amazon football is played knee-deep in water, as if submerged goalposts are only a minor inconvenience. Workers on many of Brazil's offshore oil rigs play on small football pitches enclosed by fencing.

The most obvious example of Brazilians adapting football to suit their marine surroundings happened on the beaches of Rio de Janeiro in the 1920s. Beach football grew so fast that when mayor Henrique Dodsworth tried to ban it in the 1930s, he received a petition with 50,000 names on it and changed his mind.

The 1950s and 1960s were beach football's heyday. Teams based at different patches of Copacabana and Ipanema attracted professionals from the game's grass cousin – and in return produced top players, like Paulo Cesar Caju, who played for Olympique de Marseille and the Brazilian national team. Walk down the beach today, however, and beach football played with eleven men has almost disappeared. The game lost force because as beaches became more crowded it was harder to mark out space, and also because of violence between fans and assaults on referees.

The football that is played nowadays is Beach Soccer, a compact version invented in the early 1990s for television and promoted worldwide by sports marketing group Octagon. The aggressive organisation has filtered down and every few hundred yards along Copacabana and Ipanema children are training in Beach Soccer teams. The five-a-side sport has three periods of twelve minutes each, so with ad-breaks, preview and wrap a game fits perfectly into an hour-long programme. 'In one hour of a Beach Soccer game there are on average 14.7 goals. In the 1998 football World Cup there were 1.8. This makes Beach Soccer a very interesting spectacle,' explains Fúlvio Danilas, vice-director of Beach Soccer Worldwide. Beach Soccer was developed in conjunction with Globo, Brazil's main television channel. Viewing figures have already reached eighty million. Octagon is hoping the sport will eventually follow beach volleyball into the Olympic Games.

To play beach soccer you do not need to be by the sea.

In the inland states of Amazonas, Mato Grosso do Sul and Goiás it is played on sandy riverbanks. Rio's state government has paid for four Beach Soccer pitches to be installed in the city's suburbs. It is considered fairer for poor children than proper football because it does not require boots.

Beach football also suffered because too many stray footballs hit too many sunbathers. In the early 1960s football on Copacabana was banned until 2pm. In order to get round the legislation, a bunch of lads from in front of Constante Ramos Street migrated about 100m to a beach volleyball court in front of Bolívar Street. Famous volleyball players hung out at Bolívar. The Constante Ramos crew started to do football practice there, knowing that they couldn't get banned because then the volleyball players would have to get banned too. And the volleyballers were too well known for that. The result was a sporting hybrid: footvolley.

When you stroll up and down the beach at Rio, which a lot of people do, there are many good reasons to stop and stare. The sky. The landscape. The seascape. The beautiful bodies. But the most spectacular sight is footvolley. It is two-a-side volleyball played only with one's feet, chest and head. The skills needed are breathtaking. Because the smash is almost a physical impossibility, rallies go on for longer than they do in volleyball. It is not a sport which requires brute force so many women play, their main disadvantage being only that they have less flexibility killing a ball with their chests.

Rio's beaches are the city's cultural laboratory. They shape its fashions, its language and its laid-back way of life. There is a sense that footvolley has distilled the essence of Rio – flash, flamboyant, and performed in swimming trucks. The city looks towards the beach and the beach is a stage for footvolley.

Footvolley is also associated with macho rebelliousness. Almir, Brazilian football's original hardman, was one of the sport's pioneers. Almir was Pelé's substitute at Santos and also played in Rio for Vasco and Flamengo. Better known for his fighting, he broke two players' legs and then – in one of the frankest interviews ever given by a player – admitted taking drugs when Santos won the 1963 World Club championship against AC Milan. He was shot dead in a brawl in a Copacabana bar in 1973. A footvolley match was arranged as a tribute.

Edmundo, nicknamed Animal for his violent temper, plays footvolley in Ipanema whenever he has the weekend off – and sometimes when he doesn't. The piece of skill he showed at Vasco that was the highlight of the 2000 World Club Championship was a move you see a hundred times on the beach on Saturdays. With his back to Silvestre he chipped the ball delicately over the Manchester United defender's head and then ran to intercept it and score.

The most famous footvolley aficionado is Romário. When he moved to Flamengo from Barcelona he asked for two sand pitches to be installed – one at the club and the other at its training ground. The club obliged. He has even appeared on a soap opera, playing himself playing footvolley. Romário's influence has been important for the sport's growth. Crioulo, president of the Rio Footvolley Association, estimates that there are 5,000 who play the game regularly in Rio. 'There are now as many footvolley courts in Rio as there are beach volleyball courts. The kids prefer to play with their feet.'

Brazilian beach culture is now unimaginable without football. Other communities have also incorporated the sport into their way of life. Football is so tied to the notion of Brazilian identity that it has become a way for social groups to assert their own Brazilianness. In Rio Grande do Sul, Brazil's southernmost state, the ultra-conservative Centre of Gaucho Tradition organises football tournaments where players must wear *bombachas* – local riding breeches buttoned at the ankle and wide above the knee.

Some types of football have harder challenges than awkward trousers. Blind football was developed in Brazil's institutions for the visually impaired. 'The lads would mess about, then rules developed as different institutions played each other,' says Ulísses de Araújo, national coordinator of blind football. The game is played on a futsal court with five players a side. The goalkeeper is sighted and can orient the four outfield players. The coach on the touchline and a 'caller' behind the opposing goal can also shout instructions. Brazil has won the first two blind football World Cups, in Brazil and Spain. The country has fifty-six teams, covering almost every state.

Brazil has the world's largest commercial cattle herd. In a cross-species spirit of inclusion, even the bulls get a chance. In the rodeos of rural central and south Brazil a football pitch is improvised, members of the crowd are chosen to make two five-a-side teams, and then a bull is released into the arena. 'Footbull is a real crowd-pleaser,' says former rodeo champion Gilberto Mega. 'The bull doesn't go after the ball, he goes after the players. It's not that dangerous because you don't use a hardcore bull. You put a light one in. If you put a dangerous bull in someone could easily get killed.' Emílio Carlos dos Santos, director of Brazil's largest rodeo at Barretos, near São Paulo, adds that the bull must be really bad-tempered. 'It's no fun if the bull just stands there. Sometimes the bull even goes after the ref.'

To see an equally ridiculous spectacle I drive one Sunday in February 2001 to a kickabout pitch on the periphery of Rio. Roza FC, Brazil's only transvestite football club, are playing their annual game against a team of local married men. When Brazil coach Emerson Leão took over the national squad in 2000, his first comment was that he wanted his players to be 'ballerinas' of the beautiful game. He need have looked no further than Roza.

Caroline looks fabulous in skintight jeans but falls over as soon as she touches the ball. After conducting a first-aid examination it is happily reported she has not broken her fingernail extensions. The referee is Laura de Vison, wearing a red plastic dress and knee-high boots. She is a twenty-stone silicone-enhanced club performer whose star trick usually involves lollipops, not whistles. Vison is creative in her interpretation of the rules. 'Penalty! No chatting up the centreforward!' she orders after Roza's first threatening attack.

Beneath the camp slapstick there is a serious point. Playing football is a way for the transvestites to feel included in Brazilian life, which despite the temporary transgressions of carnival remains fundamentally homophobic. For Roza's captain, Kaika Sabatela, a thirty-six-year-old drag queen squeezed into a shocking-pink sequin hotpant catsuit, football is a symbol of political freedom. 'We work, we pay our taxes and we like watching football – why shouldn't we be allowed to play the game?'

What Brazilians value most in football is innate skill rather than team tactics. The purest form of this skill is encapsulated in ball-juggling. Forget adapting football to new terrain, Brazilians have adapted it to where there is no terrain at all. Milene Domingues didn't need a team or any type of pitch to show off her talent. When she was seventeen she kicked the ball in the air a record-breaking 55,187 times over a period of nine hours and six minutes without it touching the floor. It was a meticulously planned challenge; she was trained by Moraci Santana, the Brazil fitness coach at the 1994 World Cup. Preparation included learning how to eat and urinate without dropping the ball. (You duck your head and catch the ball at the back of your neck.) Milene became an adolescent pin-up, a national celebrity, revered unanimously as the Keepie-Uppie Queen. A giant poster of her kicking a ball in the air was on the side of a building on the motorway out of Rio de Janeiro for several years.

Milene, who grew up in a lower-middle-class family in São Paulo, played kickabouts as a child with her elder brothers. After the 1994 World Cup there was a fad for women's football. She joined a club. When the momentum fizzled out she was left holding the ball. Or rather, kicking the ball. Repeatedly. Without it hitting the ground. She was soon performing during half-time at football matches, giving demonstrations and available for cocktail parties, weddings and bar mitzvahs. Business events could book nothing more chic than the pretty blonde teenager tap-tap-tapping a football in the air.

With a certain amount of inevitability Milene married Brazil's male football prodigy, Ronaldo, in 1999. She became a particularly unconventional footballer's wife not simply because she could enjoy kickabouts with her husband but because her close-to-body ball control was better than his. Not bad, considering he was twice voted FIFA Footballer of the Year. It is an endearing football marriage. When I interview her in 2001, Ronaldo approaches us and nags: 'Come on love. We're all waiting for you.' His mates are playing football and she is needed on the right wing.

Becoming Mrs Ronaldo established Milene as Brazilian football's first lady while heralding her abdication from the ball-juggling throne. It unleashed a scramble for the crown. Milene had unwittingly created a title to which there were pretenders. 'I'm the Keepie-Uppie Queen now,' asserts twenty-year-old Claudia Magalhães. Claudia's personal best is 25,184 in four hours and twenty-five minutes. In the south of Brazil, however, opinion differs. Claudia Martini, aged twenty, of Caxias do Sul, claims her record is 41,788 in seven hours and five minutes. Yet both should watch their backs: the Ball Girl, aka Gilliane Xavier Fernandes Gonçalves, aged ten, is a mini-celebrity in the inland agricultural capital, Goiânia. The Ball Girl (current record 190) can be seen during the half-times of first division team Goiás' home games. She already has two sponsorship contracts and a manager.

Like Milene, Claudia Magalhães is from São Paulo. The similarities don't end there. They both have blond shoulder-length hair, are slightly built and have honest-looking pretty faces. It's as if Keepie-Uppie Queens have to be a certain physical type. Claudia has a contract with the São Paulo Football Federation to perform during half-time at games in the state championship. Which she probably wouldn't if she looked like Sócrates.

For Claudia, there is more grace and charm in a woman ball-juggling than a man. Men are better equipped for contact sports. A young Brazilian boy with ball skills will be able to put them to use in youth football, futsal or beach football leagues. With less opportunities for competitive action, but still wanting to demonstrate footballing ability, the girls have become parading mascots.

Brazil's cottage industry of keepie-uppie professionals is not a female ghetto. 'I'm not a pretty girl. I'm old, ugly and poor,' laments Zaguinha, aged forty-nine. 'So I had to invent new ways of doing things.' More than any other ball-juggler Zaguinha has turned his vocation into an art form. He has formalised twenty-three different keepie-uppie tricks. 'This is the Romário,' he says, kicking the ball up using the top of his toes and skipping with his feet, in an instantly recognisable action of the eponymous striker. He moves into a Marcelinho Carioca, named after another Brazilian player. He chips the ball so it hits the inside of his foot and is given some spin, and he passes the ball from one foot to the other. 'The last one I invented is called the World Challenge.' He kicks the ball so it is about to fall behind him and then kicks it back using his heel.

Zaguinha's real name is Manoel da Silva. It is the Portuguese equivalent of John Smith, one of the most anonymous names it is possible to have. In many ways Zaguinha is the universal Brazilian. His story of creativity through adversity reflects the circumstances of the country and the resourcefulness of its citizens. That he is valuing nothing more than playfulness and ball skills makes him the personification of the national passion. More than anyone else I met I felt he best encapsulated football and Brazil.

Zaguinha was always good at knocking a ball around. But his father died when he was thirteen and he worked as a farm hand to look after his family. He ended up with a job digging holes for the council of a small town near the

Paraguayan border. In his early thirties he experimented in trying keepie-uppies using a snooker ball. He perfected his technique and moved on to other spherical – or vaguely spherical – objects like onions, beetroot and pineapple.

In 1994 he was watching television and he heard Silvia Popovic, a Brazilian Oprah Winfrey, tell viewers to 'Follow Your Dreams'. He packed his bags, travelled 450 miles to São Paulo, and made his way to the central square. It was the World Cup and there was a huge outdoor TV screen. He started ball-juggling and crowds gathered round him. He appeared on TV a few times and spent the next four years earning money doing keepie-uppie demonstrations on the street.

Zaguinha, a widower and grandfather of four, is now sponsored by sports manufacturer DalPonte. He wears DalPonte clothes, and carries a DalPonte ball in a string bag the way an executive would carry a briefcase or a mechanic a box of tools. In a leather purse he keeps his money and a set of ball bearings. His record with a 2mm ball bearing, the smallest, is 502. The technique is to keep his left foot on the ground and with his right leg bent move the foot up and down like it is controlled by a puppet string. 'There's a way of hitting everything,' he says.

Of the keepie-uppie coterie, Zaguinha performs more tricks and with more different objects than anyone else. He also performs in more unconventional places. He paraded through the São Paulo sambadrome during carnival without the ball falling and he competed in São Paulo's annual New Year's Eve run. He managed the 15km in two and a half hours. He considered it a training exercise and let the ball drop ten times.

In Rio, only one man is not impressed by Zaguinha. 'Ach! He is young,' dismisses Jankel Schor. 'He has age on his side.' Jankel is seventy-four, Zaguinha's senior by a quarter of a century. Jankel believes he is the oldest footballer in the world. He recently received a laminate from the Maracanã stadium giving him access to the pitch as a 'Sportsman in Activity' –

a unique version of an OAP bus pass. Hundreds of thousands of Brazilians have seen Jankel demonstrate his keepie-uppie skills – first at Vasco's São Januário stadium and now, during almost every big game, at the Maracanã.

Jankel's trajectory is very different from his colleagues, yet not less authentically Brazilian. His family are Russian Jews from Moscow; Jankel Schor is a name as undisguisably Jewish and East European as pickled cucumber. The Schors arrived in Rio in 1933, capitalists escaping communism, when Jankel was five years old. He was offered a contract by Vasco in the 1940s. 'My dad never let me sign it. He was a very radical Jew, very religious. He had very traditional opinions, he thought that if I became professional I would turn into a bum.' Jankel still seems angry at his father's intransigence. He has, in the jargon, not entirely achieved closure. When he tells the story his sunken eyes carry the weight of lost opportunity.

Jankel's father sold schmutter on the streets. Jankel built up a chain of five shops selling children's furniture, but handed them to his son who expanded too quickly and lost the lot. Jankel now walks the street, selling shirts from a holdall, to pay his health insurance.

All his adult life Jankel played football within Rio's Jewish community. With age he retired from playing matches and concentrated on practising keepie-uppies, until he was spotted on the beach and invited by Eurico Miranda, then vice-president of Vasco, to perform at the São Januário. It has given him a new lease of life. His trademark is to walk into stadiums with the ball balanced on his head, like a circus seal. 'No one my age can do that,' he says proudly. 'I consider myself a phenomenon.'

'I don't have time to train. But if I did train for a week, I could keep the ball up for two hours. What I'm lacking isn't technique, it is fitness.' Jankel is a battler still. 'No one is left from my era. I am a survivor. If I had the time to train I would go far.'

I estimate that there are at least twenty 'keepie-uppie

professionals' in Brazil. The most unexpected is the Man
With The Crutches. One of his legs ends just below the knee.
Using the thigh and knee of his injured leg he can keep the
ball in the air. Neither age nor gender are barriers in Brazil
to footballing prominence. Nor is physical disability. Half a
leg is good enough.

The Man With The Crutches is a mythical figure. I had
seen him several times over three years. At the Maracanã
he would walk with his crutches from one side of the turf
to the other and back again, bouncing the ball on his stump.
He always received huge applause. But no one at the stadium
ever knew his name, or how to get hold of him.

After a six-month absence, he appeared at the Maracanã
in March 2001 during half-time at the Guanabara Cup final,
the first stage of the Rio championship. I ran to catch him
as he walked out of the stadium in the opening minutes of
the second half. He was wearing a Brazil shirt with Pelé
marked on the back. He is tall, mulatto, and has long,
straggly black hair.

He told me his name was Fernando Sousa de Araújo, that
he was thirty-eight, born in Pernambuco, and that he lost
his leg when he was run over by a car in 1984. At the time
he was a professional with the Rio club América. He has
no home. He has spent the last fifteen years travelling Brazil,
going from stadium to stadium, surviving on the goodwill
of people he meets on the way. He seems a little shaken that
a journalist is asking him questions. 'Is it a good life?' I ask.

'Yeah, it's healthy, it's happy,' he replies somewhat reluctantly. And he hops along the Maracanã car park and disappears into the terraces.

Juazeiro do Norte ●

Olinda ●
Atalaia ●

Salvador
Lençóis ● →○

Site of first Mass
in Brazil, April 26 1500 ●

Nova Iguaçu
● Jardim   Aparecida
São Paulo ○ ↘
Praia
Grande   Rio de Janeiro

RELIGIOUS SITES

Chapter Nine

FROGS AND MIRACLES

'In football, as in everything else, no Brazilian can exist without a charm around his neck, without his saints and his set of vows – in a word, without his personal and non-transferable God.'

Nelson Rodrigues

Father Edu was desperate to get in touch with Ronaldo. Did I know the footballer personally? Could I find his telephone number? Could I put a message in the *Guardian*? Father Edu told me that Ronaldo had been put under a curse. He told me matter-of-factly, as if there was nothing more natural in the world, as if he was a doctor diagnosing someone with a common cold. The explanation was simple. Romário had acquired bad spirits from having too much sex. Ronaldo, younger, spiritually weaker, more susceptible, had caught the spirits when the two strikers partnered each other during Brazil's 1998 World Cup preparations. Of course Ronaldo would flop in the tournament. His health scare was neither epilepsy nor illness. The cause was evil spirits. It was obvious. Father Edu had even predicted it. And look – afterwards Ronaldo had failed to return to form. The spirits were still there, stubborn. Exorcism was the only hope. But for this Father Edu needed the footballer's permission. He did not need Ronaldo to travel to his official residence in Olinda. All he needed was to speak to the striker on the phone. Was I sure I could not get hold of him?

I visited Father Edu in February 1999. My taxi had dropped me off in Olinda's old town, an area of well-preserved colonial architecture, full of restaurants and galleries. Olinda was one of Brazil's first cities, built on the wealth of the surrounding sugar plantations. Next door to the imposing sixteenth-century Sé do Salvador church, on a steeply sloping cobbled street, is Iemanjá Palace. It is an unassuming building despite its grand name. The most distinctive feature was ruminating in the car park: an anxious-looking grey bull, secured with a rope around its horns and jaw.

Father Edu was sitting behind a table in the palace's main hall, receiving visitors. He is an exotic fifty-nine-year-old: short, tubby, with dyed cherry-blond hair and smelling of sweet perfume. His diction was as warm and quiet as a purring cat, both monotonously earnest and extravagantly camp. Instead of saying 'no' he exhaled 'nonononononono . . .' until he slowly ran out of breath. Like most Brazilians, he could not resist a chat about football. Only he saw the game in a different dimension. Once we had established Ronaldo's perilous predicament, conversation moved on to the real reason of my visit: Náutico, a football club from the neighbouring city, Recife. Father Edu was hours away from sacrificing the animal tied in the car park. 'To this day Náutico owe Exu a bull and until they pay it they will continue with the bad karma,' he said. Simple. Náutico must pay up, or be rubbish for ever.

Exu is a powerful, greedy, short-tempered and occasionally benevolent deity from Candomblé, an Afro-Brazilian religion that emerged from the superimposition of Catholicism on African cults. Slaves were baptised on arrival. They gained a new religion while keeping their own, which created a correspondence between Catholic saints and African gods. Figures are hard to find, but perhaps seventy million Brazilians have an affinity with Candomblé and its variants. The religions have neither dogma nor a central authority. Afro-Brazilian priests, like Father Edu, give spiritual guidance in their own temples, which can be anything from a small house to a community hall.

Father Edu had first humoured the gods in 1962. Náutico's centreforward asked the young priest for some help. Father Edu conducted ceremonies in which he incorporated one of Candomblé's more extrovert entities – the spirit of Zé Pilantra, a bohemian smartarse more than a little partial to booze and cigars. The ritual used up litres of cachaça and appeared to work. Between 1963 and 1966 Náutico won the Pernambuco state championship four times.

Náutico is the club of the Recife upper classes. Some of its white, Catholic directors objected to the influence a black priest was having within its walls. Father Edu was booted out. The team started to lose. Náutico returned to ask for his help. This time they promised him a bull if Náutico won the 1967 championship. The title came but the bull never did. The following year Father Edu insisted that Náutico fulfil their side of the deal. On the day of the state final a bull arrived. But without a crucial part: the animal had been neutered. The gods would not be amused. Still, Náutico won – making them 'hexa-champions', the first team to win the state championship six times in a row. But there was a price to pay.

After the glorious 1960s the club went through three decades of mediocrity, winning the state championship only four times. Their last title was in 1989. The team had tried everything to get out of its rut. When teams feel powerless they often search for mystical excuses. Maybe it was the debt to Father Edu. Some Náutico directors thought it safest to bring him a bull. Thirty-one years late, the club decided to settle its score. This time Father Edu decided to upgrade the ceremony. Instead of indulging Zé Pilantra, the recipient would be Exu, the most demanding deity, and the one most closely associated with the Christian Devil.

I could see that preparations for the ceremony were almost complete. Neatly arranged on the floor of Iemanjá Palace were twelve bottles of cachaça, a bottle of whisky, palm oil, manioc flour, cigars, peppers, honey, onions and salt. Night drew closer. Father Edu prepared to change out of his red armless vest and into religious garb: a baggy white T-shirt, white trousers and a knee-length black and red cape. He sharpened his knife.

To many people the sacrifice was a harmless piece of fun, a picturesque example of Brazilian folk culture and of the extremes to which a passion for football can stretch. Not everyone saw it that way. News of the ceremony had spread through Brazil. One and a half thousand miles away, in São Paulo, it reached the desk of an animal protection group. Shortly afterwards the Pernambuco Secretary of Public Security received a fax, quoting a one-year-old law that banned cruelty to animals. Police were dispatched.

The showdown at Iemanjá Palace was a clash of cultures and generations. Father Edu, surprised, irritated, playing innocent. 'I've always killed bulls at my temples,' he pleaded. In vain. The police didn't budge. On their side was the letter of the law; modern, humanitarian, *First World* Brazil. Father Edu was obliged to cancel the ceremony. But he informed Náutico's directors that since they had fulfilled their part of the bargain, they could be confident the club's fortunes would improve. He made the bold statement: 'Even without the sacrifice, the debt is paid and the team is no longer at risk.'

Father Edu had lost on the night. Náutico were victorious. The team improved. In 2001 at last they won the state championship. I telephoned Father Edu and instantly recognise his syrupy tones. The subject quickly left Náutico and turns to more general football topics. And Ronaldo, did I still not have his telephone number? The striker was recovering from a severe knee injury. More evidence, if it was ended, of the persistence of malevolent spirits. Father Edu reiterated his track record and insisted: 'All I need is his permission and I can undo the spell.'

Vasco da Gama were victims of the most famous curse in Brazilian football. Twice. It dates back to Arubinha and his frog. He might never have had a frog, and he might never have buried it under the pitch at Vasco's São Januário stadium. That is beside the point. The Curse of Arubinha's Frog existed and was taken seriously.

One rainy December evening in 1937 Vasco were due to play Andaraí, a much weaker team. On the way to the game Vasco's convoy crashed into a refuse truck. With Vasco's players held up by the collision, Andaraí's players waited at the ground, sodden and cold. Andaraí could have claimed the points but agreed that the game would take place when Vasco eventually showed up. Andaraí only asked that, in a similar spirit of sportsmanship, Vasco would not abuse their goodwill.

The game started and the gentleman's agreement was instantly forgotten. Vasco knocked in the goals. At half-time they were five up. After ninety minutes, 12–0. Arubinha, on the Andaraí bench, knelt down on the grass, clasped his hands together and looked towards the sky: 'If there is a God in heaven, Vasco must go without the championship for twelve years.' One year for every goal.

Rumour spread that Arubinha had confirmed the curse by burying a frog under the São Januário turf. Frogs, guardians of the rain, are routine vehicles in Brazil for transmitting spells. Vasco's directors laughed. A few years later they did not see the funny side. The club had not won the championship since Arubinha's malediction. Worse, it had the strongest squad in Rio and with the 1943 title in its grasp had lost 6–2 to Flamengo. Vasco asked for advice. A former player with a spiritual calling took a stick around the pitch that – he said – would locate any frogs or frog-like remnants. *Nada*.

The following year Vasco again had a knockout team.

Again they lost the state title to Flamengo. They had one option left. A tractor dug up the entire pitch. Frogless. Vasco fans starting doing sums. If the curse was valid from 1937 it would last until 1949. However, maybe it could be backdated to 1934 – their last championship – and be over in 1946. Vasco's directors begged Arubinha: please, tell us where the frog is? Arubinha said he never buried one and promised the curse would be over. Vasco were champions, unbeaten, in 1945.

Father Santana remembers the next time Vasco had a disturbingly long run without winning the Rio de Janeiro state title. After victory in 1958, the affliction of Arubinha's amphibian reappeared. The drought of victories lasted twelve years. Twelve. Confirmation the curse was true. Father Santana knows because he was the chief exorcist in 1970. 'Vasco were going through a really bad phase. It was necessary to do something,' he says.

Few figures have combined sport and spirituality with as much élan as Vasco's legendary masseur. I had first seen him at a match at São Januário. He walked out of the tunnel with the team looking like Ving Rhames, a huge black man with a bald head and a purposeful stride. He was wearing a white overcoat and carrying a sports bag. Fans cheered the names of the players, one by one, standard practice before games in Brazil. Then a twelfth name: 'San-ta-na, San-ta-na'. He laid out a Vasco banner in front on him, kneeled down and kissed it. He picked up the banner and shook it at the adoring crowd. 'How many goats have you killed today?' one voice shouted above the applause.

Father Santana has twin duties at Vasco – relaxing the players' muscles and pampering the Afro-Brazilian gods, the *orixás*. Only the former is an official function – and he has good credentials, having been Brazil's masseur in the 1962 and 1966 World Cups. The latter role is self-appointed and resoundingly endorsed by the supporters. For decades he has been a much-loved fixture at Vasco games, energetically spurring the team on from the sidelines. 'Rare is the club whose masseur is not a specialist in black magic,' wrote *Realidade* magazine in 1966. Father Santana shows it still goes with the job.

'To get rid of Arubinha's curse,' he explains, 'we organised a ceremony at São Januário.' He assembled about twenty friends. They arrived at nighttime, with candles, food and animals. 'We sat on the pitch and prayed and made our offerings.' The mediums among them entered a state in which spiritual entities entered their bodies. They threw seashells on the ground. The shells' pattern contained messages. 'We were told to do several things. We even buried a wooden cross behind one of the goals,' he adds. At 5am the work was done. Vasco were 1970 champions. 'Since that day Vasco have only improved.'

Father Santana lives in a small mews house in a lower-middle-class area between São Januário and the Maracanã. When I meet him he is wearing a white monogrammed polo top and is sunk deep into a comfy chair. There is nothing in the room that suggests I have entered the temple of a holy man. For a start, he looks as hard as nails. He was a teenage boxer and despite his age – he is sixty-seven – has kept a pugilist's beefy sense of presence. His skin colour is at the blackest end of Brazil's rainbow shades.

His name is Eduardo Santana and he is not a priest, although he earned the nickname because he was always organising rituals and he had a spiritual demeanour. During our conversation he comes across as a quiet and gentle man – very different from his effervescent appearances on the touchline. He is easygoing and accommodating. He is also very funny, sticking his tiny tongue out when he smiles. He likes being called Father: 'With a title you get treated with more respect.'

Father Santana plays up to his role as Vasco's black guru. Encouraged by the radio commentator Washington Rodrigues, he once ran on to the pitch after Vasco won a championship and lit twenty-four candles on the centre circle. He told journalists he was thanking the gods. Yet behind the stunts there is a serious belief. He goes to the Catumbi cemetery with his wife, Carmen, on the eve of important games. 'Just us and the spirits,' he says. They light a few candles, leave a few offerings. As he gets older and his physical condition declines, he has slowed down on the rites. Spiritual work, he says, should only be done when the body is healthy.

The mystique around Father Santana transcends football. He is the best-known Afro-Brazilian spiritual figure in Rio. His exuberant antics express a joy of life that reflects positively on the city's African heritage. Rio paid tribute. In 1991 he was declared the Black King of carnival, a sovereign title created for him and enshrined in law. His duties include watching the processions from the royal box. The Black King is, clarifies the historian Hiram Araújo, 'an intermediary between man and the orixás' – able to invoke 'the magic entity whose powers permit the carnival to proceed in peace and happiness'. This is a man you want on your team.

Father Santana describes himself as a spiritualist – which is a concise way of being vague. Spiritualism was introduced to Brazil in the nineteenth century by Allan Kardec, a Frenchman who thought that enlightenment could be achieved by communicating with souls of the dead. Kardec's ideas did not excite the French. In Brazil, however, they took off among the middle classes as a respectable type of Christianity and also mixed with Candomblé to form a new religion, Umbanda. Father Santana is elastic about which doctrine he follows. He likes Christian Kardecism, Umbanda and Catholicism too. No problem. A characteristic of syncretic Brazilian forms of worship is to experiment with many beliefs and take what you like best.

Many Brazilians dismiss *macumba* – the generic term for Umbanda and Candomblé-type rituals – as witchcraft. A Vasco coach once said that, whereas he was speaking to God, Father Santana was conversing with the Devil. Father Santana quite liked the comparison. 'You can't both pray for the same thing. You pray to different sides and you both meet at the end of the road.'

We look through a box of old newspaper clippings. A photo falls out that looks like a group of sheikhs at a business convention. The crowd of people are in white Arab robes and keffiyehs. All the men have moustaches and Arab skin except one, who is black and sitting in the front row. A blue pen has marked the odd-man-out, just in case you are particularly short-sighted.

The snap is from Father Santana's years as masseur to the Kuwaiti national side. The back row, he points out, are the ministers of the Kuwaiti government, the men sitting down are the players and, there in the front, you-know-who. Father Santana accommodated the cultural differences of living in the Gulf spectacularly. When the Emir told him that he wanted a massage too, but that non-Muslims were forbidden from touching the royal legs, Father Santana converted and changed his name to Ahmed.

I see the official certificate, in English: 'Mr Eduard [sic] Santana, holder of a Brazilian passport, appeared before the court of first instance, legal authentication department . . . declared that he is Christian Catholic and was inspired by Islam and pronounced in front of us the confessions of Faith by saying "I bear witness by saying that there is but one God Allah and Jesus Christ Son of Mary is the servant and apostle of Allah . . . I am totally absolved from all religions different from the religion of Islam."'

It reads like a bigamist declaring a vow of fidelity. Father Santana is a Latin lover of spiritual promiscuity. For him to rigidly swear himself to a new faith is both entirely natural – one more system to experiment – and self-contradictory. It is a comic misalignment of two opposite approaches. Religion in Brazil is a pick-n-mix of whatever takes your fancy, not a way to define yourself against other beliefs.

Ahmed Santana enjoyed life as a Muslim. He learnt a lot. He made a pilgrimage to 'that big stone'. He added to his repertoire of sacrifices the skills required to kill a camel.

Sport has been linked with worship at least since the Olympic Games of ancient Greece and, in the Americas, the ball games of the Aztec and Maya civilisations. Football in Brazil gained a mystical side early on in its development. Father Santana is merely a recent illustration of a colourful tradition that goes back at least to 1932. Mário Filho writes of a macumba ritual in his book of that year's Copa Rio Branco, in which Brazil unexpectedly beat the World Cup holders Uruguay in Montevideo. Oscarinho, a player and active medium, 'unburdened' Leônidas's legs on the eve of the game. Leônidas notched both goals in the victory. Oscarinho did the same ceremony four days later on Jarbas, before a game against club side Peñarol. Brazil won 1–0. Guess who scored?

Brazilian footballers have got up to all sorts of macumba to win games. Bathing boots in water – to quench the thirst of their saint – is distinctly ordinary. As is washing feet and pouring the dirty water on opponents' pitches. The most colourful accounts come from Bahia, the spiritual home of black Brazil, a state where Candomblé temples outnumber churches. Paulo Amaral, Brazil's physio in the 1958 and 1962 World Cups remembers a final of the Bahian state championship in which the players before the match placed themselves round the four edges of the pitch. They all had water in their mouths and were each holding an *acarajé* bean fritter. They spat out the water and threw the food on the ground.

One of the best known dictums in Brazilian football states: '*If macumba works, then the Bahian championship would end in a draw.*'

Nothing riles Father Nílson, Corinthians' former Candomblé priest, more than hearing those words. 'It is said that macumba doesn't win games,' he declares. 'We have proved this wrong.'

He explains.

In January 2000 Vasco played Corinthians in the final of the first World Club Championship. The match was a duel between two of the largest clubs in Brazil. It was a symbolic contest between Rio and São Paulo, the two metropolises whose rivalry shaped the country. Beyond the terrestrial plane another battle was fought. The clubs were competing for the favours of the orixás.

The final ended in a 0–0 deadlock. Penalties were to decide the title. Corinthians converted four out of five. With Vasco on three out of four, Edmundo, one of Vasco's star players, stepped up to pull scores level. He shot wide.

'Exu was paid for stopping Edmundo's goal,' says Father Nílson. He makes it sound so obvious. 'You pay Exu to be your slave. We paid him with a lot of *farofa* manioc powder and juicy steak cooked with onions – he likes to eat well – cigars and cachaça. This was put by the train line just as you enter Lençóis. Thanks to him we won the title.'

Lençóis is not in São Paulo, which is where you might expect it to be considering its importance to Corinthians. Lençóis is Father Nílson's home town, set among a paradisiacal stretch of waterfalls and green mountainous ridges, eight hundred miles north in central Bahia. Father Nílson uses Lençóis as a retreat to soak up its mystical forces.

But if you think that flying to Bahia and preparing a sumptuous banquet is enough to win the World Club Championship, you are very much mistaken. As well as returning to Lençóis, Father Nílson also drove from his home in São Paulo to Praia Grande, a beach on the coast near Santos. 'The sea has infinite strength,' he says. Each of the five ceremonies at Praia Grande involved pushing a wooden boat out to sea laden with food, candles, champagne and whisky. Sometimes the cargo would include items purloined from the Corinthians players' kit bags. The sessions each took three days and three nights. Most of Father Nílson's time was spent fishing, playing cards and swimming in the water. The hardest part was abstaining from meat, a necessary part of the ritual. 'This is very difficult for me because I love meat. But for Corinthians – I'll do anything.'

Meeting Father Nílson is a disorienting experience. When

I arrive at his mother's house in São Paulo he sits me down at the kitchen table. He is wearing a black T-shirt with a white collar, Corinthians colours, and his face looks tired and unshaven. His dark eyes make constant contact. He takes out his own tape-recorder, switches it on and, sounding like a chat-show host, begins: 'It is a pleasure to have you here and I wish you success . . .' I double-take. Who is doing the interview here?

'Macumba does win games – or if it doesn't win them it helps,' he reasons. 'If you are spiritually well you will do well.' The argument in its soberest form is hardly voodoo: macumba may not work if you do not believe in it, but if you do believe in it – and many do – it will at least give you the confidence to play better. For Father Nílson there is an added sense that human beings are manipulated by divine forces which need to be assuaged. Our conversation feels like a New Age therapy session. His world is full of African gods, Catholic saints, interconnected forces, spirits and vibrations.

Father Nílson reminds me of Father Edu. He has a similarly pungent aroma and although he does not reach Edu's level of camp he is warmly intense. Like Edu, he is a proper priest who entered the football milieu circumstantially. 'Before it happened I never thought I would work for a football club. It never came into my head. I think it was decided by God. Now I live for football.'

Or did. In 2000 Father Nílson was sacked from Corinthians after eighteen years' service. He has interpreted his dismissal as a decision of the gods, so he can eventually make a glorious return. His departure marked the start of the worst run in Corinthians' history. The World Club Champions lost nine games in succession. Then, he says, he heard a message on his answer machine asking him to restart his rituals. He did three. Corinthians won six times in a row. 'Coincidence?' he exclaims.

Father Nílson was invited to work for Corinthians in 1982 by Vicente Matheus, the club's then president. Actually, by his wife. Marlene Matheus had been to Father Nílson's temple in the outskirts of São Paulo for some spiritual guidance. He then worked at Corinthians' Parque São Jorge stadium, earning £200 a month, a moderate sum, about four times the minimum wage. For a while he even had his own office. He was an administrative functionary, although the club now denies he was ever an employee. 'All this stuff is very undercover,' says José Eduardo Savóia, a journalist who covers Corinthians. 'No one at the club would ever admit to having a macumba priest because it would be devaluing the work of the coach and the players.'

The Matheuses were larger-than-life characters who had already dabbled in the supernatural. In 1976, after twenty-two years of having never won the São Paulo state championship, Vicente granted a request for a macumba ceremony at Parque São Jorge. What harm would it do? Things couldn't get any worse. The spiritual emergency team was an all-star affair, including Olinda's Father Edu and an anonymous young padre, Miranilson Carvalho Santos, a.k.a. Father Nílson. The holy men took spades and picks to dig up the turf – and discovered human teeth, a femur and a frog. A frog! The following year Corinthians were champions.

'Coincidence?'

During his time at Corinthians Father Nílson describes himself as having been the club's 'spiritual caretaker'. He says: 'I learnt a lot from them and they learnt a lot from me. It was a good marriage. We learnt that Corinthians was a mystical team and that Father Nílson was part of that mysticism.' His real purpose was, he says, to promote black Brazilian culture. He held daily group sessions and counselled players individually. In defeat he told stories of black slaves. 'We would show that the orixás were "chained" too – but they didn't have to be beaten. It was a type of positive brain-washing.'

After we have chatted for an hour Father Nílson is a lot more relaxed than he was when he started. He seems flattered when I ask him what perfume he is wearing. 'Avon's *Touch of Love*,' he gushes. 'I use it every day. It brings out a positive radiation.'

By now he is almost flirtatiously open with his thoughts. He tells me that when I walked in he knew the interview would be good. I was not wearing any lilac. He *haaates* lilac. The colour terrifies him. His voice drops: 'If you had turned up in lilac I would have taken a clove of garlic and grasped it under the table.'

Fear of lilac, he tells me, is not a religious conviction. It is one of his superstitions. He has so many that I wonder how he leads a normal life. Some are not uncommon in Brazil. He puts his right foot on the floor first when he gets out of bed and he always enters and exits a building from the same door. But others are almost deliberately perverse. He always sits to the left of whoever he is with. If he sees an ambulance when driving he parks his car for fifteen minutes, because ambulances are loaded with suffering. If he sees a funeral cortege he immediately turns off down a side street. 'I'm genuinely pissed off with missing the start of games because of this sort of thing,' he moans.

Football is a fertile ground for superstitions because of its ritualised nature and because of the mellifluous influence of Lady Luck. Brazilians, already predisposed to irrational beliefs, have turned football superstitions into a badge of their fanaticism. During the World Cup in 1998, shortly after I moved to Rio, I was surprised to find few people in bars cheering on the national side. Most were at home watching with their families. When I asked one of my few acquaintances whether I could watch at her house I was told that, unfortunately, since I had missed the first match it would be impossible. Superstition dictated that at every match the exact same people must be present. Outsiders were not welcome. Or maybe it was the kindest way to brush me off.

I have since learnt that the only time it is socially acceptable not to wash an item of clothing – Brazilians are obsessively hygienic, shower several times a day and take their toothbrushes to work – is when it is your lucky shirt or piece of underwear. These garments must be worn during every match throughout a competition. While a football supporter may mock himself for always driving to the stadium in the same car, with the same friends, buying the same beer, sitting in the same place and wearing the same shirt, he does so because it makes him an authentic fan, not an eccentric one.

Footballers all over the world have their own superstitions although few are as self-defeating as the Brazilian who refused to enter the centre circle. He told his coach: 'If I go in there, I'll break my leg.'

The most superstitious man in Brazilian football was Carlito Rocha. Like fans that insist on keeping the same routines, Carlito's basic rule was that everything that happened on a day in which Botafogo won should not be changed. This was particularly relevant to the team because Carlito, during the 1940s and 1950s, was Botafogo's president. Match days became ever more complicated procedures. Once when the team bus was stopped going the wrong way up a one-way street, Carlito refused to let the driver go into reverse and ordered the players to walk to the Maracanã on foot. 'Our team does not go backwards,' he said.

On arriving at an away ground he used to spread a kilo of sugar on the walls. He would prepare the team food personally and clean his hands in the hair of the nearest player. Each defender had a little piece of paper put in his boots with the name of the man he had to mark – so they would be on top of them before the game started. The fancy embroidered curtains at Botafogo's club house were tied up in knots for all games, symbolising tying up the opposition. Carlito had so many lucky charms that he ordered a giant gold safety pin to be made to hang them all from.

Yet the greatest of Carlito's talismans would woof very loudly if you approached it with a sharp needle. Biriba, a black-and-white crossbreed, was effectively the team's

Carlito Rocha and Biriba

twelfth man. He made his debut by accident in 1948 at a match of Botafogo's reserves against Bonsucesso. During one of Botafogo's attacks, the ball came flying to Bonsucesso's goalkeeper. So did the scruffy mutt. In the confusion the keeper messed up and the ball went in. The referee said the goal stood.

Biriba was a stray taken in that day by Macaé, a reserve. From then on Macaé was ordered to bring his companion to every match. Carlito used the lucky dog for more than superstitious purposes. He would let it loose on the pitch when Botafogo needed to cool the game down, in order to break the rhythm of the opposition. Botafogo's players never lent a hand in chasing the dog off, leaving it to the other team and the referee. By the time the game restarted, Botafogo had regained the psychological advantage.

Biriba was more than a mascot. He was paid the same bonuses as the first-team players and Macaé became a kept man. The club chef cooked the dog the best cuts of meat.

It is said that the Botafogo doorman even had to taste Biriba's food first since it could have been poisoned. Botafogo's rivals had good reason to do so. The team was improving with the hound on its side. One club threatened to kidnap him. Carlito ordered Biriba and Macaé to sleep together in the club building.

Before one important game Biriba peed on a player's leg. Since Botafogo won the match, Carlito's predictable logic demanded that before each match Biriba should pee on the same leg. It cannot be conclusively proved that the ritual urination had no effect. Botafogo won the state championship in 1948.

Prophetic dreams also had their place at Botafogo. One night in 1945 the sports journalist Geraldo Romualdo da Silva had a premonition. He dreamt Botafogo would tie the match due to take place the following day. In order not to contaminate the atmosphere with bad luck, he stayed away from the team hotel on the day of the game. The result was worse than predicted. Botafogo lost. From then on it was crucial that the pressman never have another similar dream. Botafogo directors made sure that on Friday nights he had the best table at the Urca casino. When that was over men were sent to chat with him until it was time for work. For the length of the championship, he never slept on weekends.

Carlito and Biriba helped earn Botafogo the fame of Brazil's most superstitious club. It is a reputation it still carries today, and one that has no chance of disappearing if bizarrely coincidental events continue to occur, like the match of 29 April 2001. On that day Vasco beat Botafogo 7–0. Nothing strange so far, except that seven is a traditionally mystical number and seven goals is a traditionally humiliating scoreline. Newspapers pointed out that the previous time Botafogo let in seven goals was on 29 April 1994 – exactly seven years before. On both occasions the seventh goal was scored by the player in the number seven shirt. If that isn't spooky enough, both happened on the twenty-ninth, and what is nine minus two? The daily O Dia's headline two days later had an explanation: 'Uranus is to blame.' Dé, the coach, was more preacher-like: 'Seven is God's number, because he created the world in seven days. It's in the Bible. If he's putting me through this it's because he will compensate me in the future. Today's humiliated will be exalted tomorrow.' Gosh.

Another prime number that should have its own entry in the encyclopaedia of Brazilian football is 13. Ever since Mário Zagallo married on 13 June, the day of St Anthony of Padua, it has been his lucky number. Zagallo is the most decorated World Cup footballer of all time. Talent, surely? He attributes his success to St Anthony. He won his first World Cup, as a player, in 1958, and his fourth, as assistant coach, in 1994. The sum of 5+8, and 9+4 is 13. (Let's forget medals as a player in 1962 and coach in 1970). He always wears an item of clothing with the number 13, he lives on the thirteenth floor and his cars have plates ending in 13. (Let's also forget that in 1999 he was sacked by Portuguesa after 13 games). In 2001 he coached Flamengo to the Rio state championship title. After the final's second leg at the Maracanã, press and fans invaded the pitch to surround the sixty-nine-year-old veteran. Zagallo took a figurine of St Anthony out of his pocket and held it in front of them. The final scoreline was 1–3.

To rational Europeans, Brazilian superstitions are hard to swallow. They need to be taken in their context. Brazilian oral culture is so rich in old wives' tales that faith in a number is quite a considered decision. A cherished folk ritual is the *simpatia*, or 'affinity'. In most newspaper kiosks there are several magazines full of simpatias, mostly collected from readers. In a thirty-six-page booklet I bought in São Paulo, I noted the following simple recipe:

How to marry a rich man
Take two onions, three cloves of garlic, and two sprigs of parsley. Put on a white plate. Squash the ingredients until you have a paste and add a pinch of salt. Write

the name of a man you want to marry on a piece of
white paper. Put the paper on the well-seasoned paste.
Leave the plate in the open air over night. Throw everything in the bin.

Another booklet had more male-oriented advice:

Success in betting on sporting events
Buy a rabbit paw. Put it in your pillowcase for seven
nights. Afterwards, take it to a forest with a green pen
and a piece of white paper. Write your name and address
on the paper and roll the paw in it. Bury everything in
front of a big tree that is in blossom. Then ask the
forest spirits to help your luck grow like the tree. Say
thank you and leave without looking back. Bet as you
usually do, but don't exaggerate.

Another common custom is to pray to a Catholic saint asking
for some help, making a vow that if the request is granted
then you will perform a specified task as thanks. It is called
'paying for promises', a religious version of buying something on a credit card. You make the promise, and if the
saint obliges, you pay for it later – usually by making a
pilgrimage to a holy site. Frequently you leave a gift, an 'ex-
voto', that in some way represents what the promise
achieved. If you prayed for a car, for example, you would
most likely bring a model car or a picture of yourself in
front of it. This practice is not unique to Brazil, but Brazil
seems to have embraced the concept with medieval fervour.
It forms the basis for one of Brazil's most successful films,
O *Pagador de Promessas*, The Given Word, which won the
1962 Palme D'Or at Cannes. The film told the story of a
rural worker who expresses his gratitude for the miraculous
recovery of his donkey by walking to Salvador burdened –
like Jesus – with a wooden cross on his shoulder.

Didi, inventor of the *dry leaf* free kick, so called because
it fell in unpredictable directions, paid a very public promise.

In 1957 he promised Our Lord of Bonfim that if Botafogo won the Rio state championship he would walk in his match clothes from the Maracanã to Botafogo's club house. About 5,000 fans accompanied him on the five-mile journey. 'When I arrived I was without my boots, socks, shirt and shorts,' he said. 'I ended up in just my Y-fronts, Botafogo fans took everything from me on the way.' The following year Didi was voted best player in Brazil's victorious 1958 World Cup side. He did not walk back from Stockholm.

In October 2000 I travel to Juazeiro do Norte, a religious town in the northeastern interior. The blisteringly hot, rugged surroundings are Biblical enough even without the 350,000 pilgrims who are there too. The narrow streets are crammed with stalls selling religious trinkets and many people are in black cassocks. Almost everyone is wearing a cheap straw hat.

Juazeiro is a pilgrimage site because it was the home of Padre Cicero,[*] the local priest until he died in 1934. He allegedly performed a miracle, in 1899, when during communion a lay nun's mouth filled with the blood of Christ. On a hill overlooking the town is a 25m-high statue of the cleric, his staff in his left hand, his hat in his right and a strongly pious expression on his face. Brazilians claim it is the third-largest statue of a person in the world, after the Christ in Rio de Janeiro and the Statue of Liberty in New York.

The cult of worship has turned Padre Cicero's former house into a shrine. Inside, crowds of pilgrims head past his original clothes, chinaware, confessional and lectern to his small wooden bed, touching the mattress to soak up its Divine power. They press any possession – hats, bags, even glasses – against the bed to charge it up with spiritual energy.

The bed is also where pilgrims place ex-votos. Each gift is payment for a miracle that Padre Cicero is believed to

[*]I am describing Catholic priests using their Portuguese title, 'padre', to avoid confusion with Candomblé priests.

have granted. I see flowers, dolls, wooden heads, photographs and cassocks. So many objects are deposited that a man sits by the bed stuffing them into a plastic bag almost as soon as they touch the mattress. The ex-votos are then displayed in the Room of Miracles. To enter it is a wonderfully uplifting experience. The walls are covered in photographs of people. All the eyes that stare at you represent a happy story, a personal triumph of faith. There are stacks of shelves full of domestic utensils, model animals and clothes. Hanging in the middle something catches my eye: a St Etienne away shirt.

I approach the silver garment. 'Thank you, Padre Cicero, for the blessings and graces I received,' says a scribbled note sellotaped to the chest. It was signed by the footballer Aloisio, who played for Flamengo and Goiás before transferring to St Etienne in 1999. (He later moved to Paris St Germain.) Adjacent to the note is a picture of the midfielder; he has a shaved head, an earring in his left ear and a toothy smirk.

Aloisio is from a small town in Alagoas, a northeastern state whose economy is based on huge, unmechanised sugar estates that have changed very little in a hundred years. I was determined to discover the footballer's story. A few weeks later I tracked down his mother, Maria da Silva. She told me why she had taken the shirt three hundred miles to Juazeiro in a truck. 'It was to thank Padre Cicero for fixing it for my son to play in Europe.'

Maybe Padre Cicero has a dark sense of humour. Shortly after Mrs da Silva made her pilgrimage, disaster struck. Aloisio ruptured his left-knee ligaments. He would not play for at least a year. Mrs da Silva did not lose faith. Quite the opposite. She ordered a sculptor in Atalaia, her home town, to carve a wooden leg, symbolising the recuperating limb, and returned to Juazeiro. It is not uncommon to take wooden body parts to religious shrines. A church at Canindé, two hundred miles from Juazeiro, receives about 30,000 a year – which pilgrims heap in a giant pile. Most limbs are hand

made. But Mrs da Silva was the mother of a famous footballer. No expense was spared. This time she drove to
Juazeiro in the car that her son bought with his European
earnings. St Etienne had a more practical solution: Aloisio
received the best medical attention money could buy.

Juazeiro attracts about two million pilgrims a year.
Hundreds of thousands of devotees arrive every October in
Belém, at the mouth of the Amazon, for the Cirio de Nazaré,
a religious festival in which participants scrum to touch a
1,200ft rope. At Easter, the world's largest Passion Play takes
place in the world's largest outdoor theatre at New Jerusalem
in Pernambuco. Padre Marcelo Rossi, a young priest who
incorporates aerobics routines into Mass, plays venues bigger
than stadiums. These grandiose celebrations are social as
well as spiritual – they let Brazil express its identity as a
country of deep-rooted faith.

The Patroness of Brazil is Our Lady of Aparecida, which
means 'the appeared one', in reference to a terracotta stat-
uette of the Virgin Mary that was found in a fisherman's
net in 1717. As soon as it was retrieved, the barren River
Paraíba suddenly filled with fish, the first of many miracles
attributed to the figurine. Our Lady appeared conveniently
halfway between Rio and São Paulo and the motorway that
now links Brazil's two largest cities passes within metres of
the National Shrine. It is a giant red-brick basilica whose
white cupola gives it the look of a nuclear power station.
As befits its status as the holiest Catholic site in Brazil, the
complex makes no economies of scale. Each weekend
100,000 drop by.

Brazilians consider Our Lady of Aparecida their queen.
Since the eighteenth century She has been dressed in a velvet
blue mantle. You could say She is wearing Brazil's away strip.
In Stockholm for the 1958 World Cup, panic struck the
national side when they were told they were not able to wear
their lucky yellow shirts for the final. The mood only changed
when Paulo Machado de Carvalho, head of the delegation,
entered the changing room. He shouted exultantly: 'Blue is

the colour of Our Lady! The heavens are sending us a message!' The blue of the away shirts, which had been a problem in the superstitious players' minds, was turned into a talisman.

Our Lady of Aparecida is the Mother of all promisees. I choose to visit Her on the Saturday following the victories of Corinthians and Flamengo in the 2001 São Paulo and Rio championships. Both were unexpected triumphs. I reasoned that if any Corinthians or Flamengo fans had made Her promises relating to that match then it was as good a moment as any for them to pay up. I park my car in Section C of Gospels, by the Pilgrim Support Centre shopping mall, and follow signs to the National Shrine.

Like Father Cicero's house, Our Lady of Aparecida has a Room of Miracles to display ex-votos. The chamber is the size of a village hall. It feels like a museum. Glass cabinets are full of model buses, tractors, ships, boats, planes and cows. They are made out of wood, metal and plastic. Some are professionally done, others are primitively home-made. There are guitars, drums, brass instruments, bicycles, crash helmets, precious stones, crockery, sewing machines and irons. A singed Bible has an explanatory note: 'the only thing that survived a fire'. There are boxes for orthopaedic instruments and hospital equipment – discarded after Our Lady's miraculous cures. Crutches are stacked on a shelf. A box is full of clumps of hair. A common promise is to grow your hair for several years and then cut it in the Room of Miracles.

Thousands of photos cover the walls, the ceiling and upright beams, each image representing a miracle that Our Lady is understood to have granted. One wall looks more like a sports bar than a church basement. It is covered in pictures of hundreds of football teams. I see posters of well-known sides, including the 1994 World Cup champions, Corinthians, Palmeiras and Botafogo and also snaps of local teams and anonymous players. Next to the wall is a cabinet of sports trophies that would make any athlete proud. A glass locker of football shirts is so full that it looks like the window display of a sports clothing shop. I count about seventy shirts pinned up and a similar number folded in piles.

Ex-votos reflect personal worries and anxieties. Entering the Room of Miracles is like entering the mind of contemporary Brazil. A brief look around and you can judge the main areas of national concern: health, family, job – and football.

I read a book of pilgrims' depositions. A picture of a guilty-looking little girl catches my eye, who, I read, swallowed three keys. 'In despair, her family made many prayers to Our Lady of Aparecida that nothing serious would occur. After seven days of suffering, Karla discharged the keys. In December 2000 her grandparents came to the National Shrine to register the fact and pay thanks for her kindness.' Karla, who looks about two, is pictured waving the keys in her hand.

When pilgrims enter the Room of Miracles to pay their promises they may register them at a desk run by Sister Maria do Carmo Rosa. I approach and ask if any football-related ex-votos have arrived recently. Gislaine de Oliveira, one of Sister Maria's young staff, smiles. My reasoning is correct. She tells me that yesterday the uncle of Kléber, the Corinthians left back, had brought in his team shirt. 'He said he came to thank Our Lady for the title,' she says. 'Kléber couldn't come personally because he is grounded in preparation for [the semi-finals of the Brazilian Cup].'

The girls who work behind the desk are used to seeing famous players. In fact, coming to Our Lady is almost a standard ritual for the winning of any title in any sport. I am allowed to open the sports locker. I find a Flamengo shirt signed by Romário and a Brazil shirt signed by all the members of the 1999 Copa America. There are also the yellow running shoes of Sanderlei Parrela, who was fourth in the 400m at the Sydney Olympics, and Ayrton Senna's driving gloves. I doubt there is a more diverse collection of sporting memorabilia in Brazil.

Most gifts, however, are brought by fans. It is striking to

think that someone prays with the same intensity for their team to win as they do to be cured from a brain tumour. When I arrive, at 11am, I have just missed a man in his late thirties who registered a pair of black Umbro football boots covered in mud.

Sister Maria takes out a plastic bag in which she has put the football shirts that arrived in the last fortnight. She lays seven out on the desk. Two are Corinthians, one is Corinthians' fan group Hawks of the Faithful, one is from Ponte Preta, an unfancied São Paulo team having their best spell in years, and one is from São Paulo FC. One is from an orange amateur team that has about twenty names signed on it and the last is an anonymous purple goalkeeper shirt. 'They just keep on coming,' she says.

After hours of waiting I feel I should have made a promise to Our Lady myself. I want to see someone arriving with a gift related to football. Hundreds of people are arriving, but all for different reasons. I see a man come with his niece's hair, a man who gave up smoking handing over a packet of cigarettes, a man giving a guitar and a woman with so many wax limbs she could almost make a person. 'The leg is for my sister-in-law, the foot for my brother-in-law, the lungs for my cousin, the head for another cousin and the heart for my husband,' says Nilza Bombonatti Danelon. 'I take advantage of coming once and I do them all together.'

Then a scruffy child arrives and puts his white baseball cap on the desk in front of the women. The cap has the emblem of the football club Coritiba. He is fourteen-year-old Leanderson da Silva. A week before he was living on the streets of Curitiba, a state capital south of São Paulo. He was given lodging by an educational foundation, who are on a group trip to Aparecida. They asked him if he wanted to give something to Our Lady to ask for her help.

'I'm giving my cap so I can play football better,' he says.

Padre Antonio Carlos Barreiro, casually dressed in slacks and a white striped T-shirt, speaks to me before dashing to take the 4pm Mass. We are sitting on the sofa of the priests' lounge. Padre Barreiro is responsible for the Room of Miracles and seems as interested in my knowledge as I am in his. 'The reality is that there is very little research about the gifts,' he begins. 'Although the Room of Miracles is the second most visited place in the Shrine after the altar, and visits are increasing. We are about to enlarge it.'

He says that the majority of the pilgrims are poor and feel abandoned by society. The large number of gifts relating to the body shows the failing of public health services. 'We are now noticing a lot of houses. This shows that in Brazil it is a great challenge to buy your own house. When people finally have their own house they bring a model of it or a photo here. The gifts paint an anthropological portrait of Brazil.'

Padre Barreiro estimates that about twenty football shirts are brought each month. 'We notice it more when teams get promoted or they win a championship. A large proportion believe that their praying helped the team win.' Most shirts come from Corinthians fans because, he says, they have the strongest support among the poorer classes.

He adds that entire teams sometimes arrive. 'Always small teams. I guess they are passing on the motorway and stop off. They ask to be blessed.'

Near the Room of Miracles is the National Shrine's bric-a-brac bazaar, where they resell many of the ex-votos. You can buy toys, clothes and sewing machines. Donated wax limbs are also melted down, remoulded and resold. (The bazaar has buttocks and shoulders at 80p each. Throats, intestines, bladders and ovaries are slightly cheaper.) The volume of gifts is so great that the National Shrine also has cellars full of storage.

I ask what happens to the football shirts, since I fancy buying one. He tells me: 'No can do'. He says strict rules dictate where the football shirts go. Any gift from a famous sportsperson is kept in the cabinet in the Room of Miracles. Shirts from non-famous people are recycled and handed to the local seminary – for the trainee priests to wear in the seminary's football team.

Before I leave I arrange with Padre Barreiro to produce a questionnaire for pilgrims bringing sports-related ex-votos. I fax him a draft the next day and he kindly makes copies and gives them to Sister Maria in the Room of Miracles. Ten days later I receive the first responses. Seven people have filled in the form – a small number, explains the priest. So many visitors register gifts that his staff do not have the time to always hand out the questionnaire. Many pilgrims do not like to speak about their promises and others are illiterate.

Two are from professional sportsmen. Henrique dos Santos Eliel, a forward at Portuguese first division club Belenenses, brought a pair of football boots and a photo of the club in thanks for playing abroad. Antonio Mesquita Neto took his boxing gown in thanks for winning the W.B.O.'s Latin American light-welterweight belt five months before. The most common ex-voto, however, is a Palmeiras shirt, which make up three of the seven statements. It is initially surprising, since the club has not won a title recently. Bizarrer still, the miracle that was granted was victory in the semi-final of last year's Libertadores Cup. Then the reason becomes clear. In three days Palmeiras play the semi-final of this year's Libertadores. Like cardholders who pay their Visa bill on the last day of the month, the pilgrims are rushing to pay last year's spiritual debts lest the interest accrued affect this year's performance. It was not quite enough. Palmeiras drew both legs 2–2 and lost on penalties.

The remaining two ex-votos are Corinthians shirts. I suspect Divine intervention. One of the pilgrims is from the São Paulo neighbourhood Belém, which is the Portuguese for 'Bethlehem'. Sergeant Maia of the Belém Fire Station gave the shirt he wore when he saw Corinthians win the 2000 World Club Championship. A few days later I happen to be visiting São Paulo. I call Sergeant Maia and spend the morning with him. He is very happy to see me because he believes it is a sign that Corinthians will win the Brazilian Cup the following weekend. (They don't.)

I had assumed that pilgrims were generally dirt-poor and uneducated. Sergeant Maia is neither. He owns a three-bedroom house, drives a VW car and has a fine career in the fire service. Unlike Western Europeans, modernity and progress do not seem to be causing Brazilians to lose their religiosity.

Sergeant Maia is short, stocky and has a neck as thick as a champion pitbull. A man of boundless energy, he is unable to pass a fireman's pole without excitedly sliding down it. On the station shelf are jars stuffed with poisonous tropical snakes. 'I killed all of them,' he boasts. 'I love my profession, I've done loads of big fires, I've saved lots of lives.' He shows me a Corinthians T-shirt. 'I rescued this guy. His first words to me were: "What team do you support?" Then he went out and bought me this shirt.'

Corinthians fans like to think that God supports their club. 'We also think of Our Lady of Aparecida as a Corinthians fan, although we must remember that other teams pray to Her as well.' For the World Club Championship, says Sergeant Maia, She showed her true colours. 'I do not think the victory was totally down to Her, but I think She helped quite a lot – together with God, of course. I believe that had I not asked for it, it could even have not happened – and also if I do not pay the promise then maybe my team could be castigated in another way. You have to pay your promises because if you ask another time you will not be attended to.'

If there was ever a need for a Promisers Anonymous, Sergeant Maia would be the founding member. His life is measured in holy vows. When he was promoted to corporal he donated his soldier's uniform to the National Shrine. He often goes for a month without alcohol after pledging he will not drink if Corinthians win. He makes promises to a whole range of saints, depending on the nature of his request – money matters to St Hedwig, the patron saint of debtors, professional matters to St Expeditus, the military saint, football matters to St George, Corinthians' patron saint, and if all else fails to St Jude, the patron saint of lost causes.

In his wife, Maria Aparecida Franciulli, he found not only Our Lady's name but someone equally devout. Shortly after they married she took her wedding dress to the National Shrine. Once their first child was born they took flowers to another Brazilian saint, Our Lady of the Good Birth. She also shares his fanaticism for football, although she supports Corinthians' archrivals. 'The problem is that I fell in love with the woman,' he laments. 'I did not fall in love with the Palmeiras fan.' The couple's attrition over football overshadows the marriage. It consumes their passion. When Palmeiras lost to Manchester United in the 1999 World Club Championship, Sergeant Maia, the prayerful and responsible fireman, set off fire crackers joyously in the street.

Catholicism in Brazil is as old as the discovery of South America. Four days after Portuguese navigator Pedro Alvares Cabral stumbled across an idyllic coastline on his way to India, on 22 April 1500, he ordered a Mass to be held on the shore. He baptised his discovery the Isle of the True Cross. During Portuguese colonisation, the militant Catholicism of the Iberian peninsula kept religion central to Brazilian life. It was only at the beginning of the republic, in 1889, that the link between Church and state was cut. But already a deep religiosity was part of the Brazilian psyche. Construction of the Christ statue in Rio in 1931 showed that the Church was a strong institution – stronger than the state, at least, which had just been through a revolution. Subsequent governments sought refuge in Catholicism's moral authority. More than 70 per cent of Brazilians are Roman Catholic, making it the world's largest Catholic country.

The Portuguese community, proud of its heritage, has kept conspicuously Catholic. Portuguese social clubs invariably have a small chapel. Vasco da Gama, the colony's most prominent institution, has gone one step further. It has a chapel the size of a church inside its stadium. No club in Portugal has a chapel the size of Vasco's. It is as if Rio's Portuguese – infected by Brazil's sense of enormity – reinvented their own characteristics on a much larger scale. Vasco's chapel dates from the 1950s. When it was founded earth from all the main Portuguese clubs, including Benfica, Sporting and Porto, was brought over and buried underneath.

Our Lady of the Victories is a striking white building with stained-glass windows about twenty metres behind one of São Januário's goals. It can be seen from every point in the stadium since the stands only cover three sides of the pitch. There were plans to move the chapel so seating could go all around but this was vetoed. Our Lady cannot be touched. A new project has been approved that will incorporate it. The structure will be an architectural oddity since not only will it leave a gaping hole for the chapel but there will be a passageway from the chapel that runs directly on to the pitch. Hallowed turf indeed.

José Carlos Lino de Souza used to be a Vasco athlete. He competed in 100m and long-distance races and then fenced foil and sabre. The day he was ordained Padre Lino his colleagues at Rio's São José seminary cheered him with Vasco banners as if he'd won a gold. Padre Lino is now Vasco's priest. It is an evocative image – the spiritual leader of the team whose crest includes a caravel used five hundred years ago by sabre-rattling Catholic colonisers is a champion fencer.

On Saturdays Padre Lino performs his priestly duties at Our Lady of the Victories. I visit one sunny autumn morning. The chapel is tidy and full of flowers. It fits about a hundred people, although only about twenty are inside. The comforting noise of tennis being played outside lightly echoes through the chapel walls. Padre Lino's first appointment is to baptise Thiago Garcia, aged two months and two weeks. The baby's father, Luiz, used to be in charge of banners at Vasco's organised fan group Young Force. He now works for a company that provides the club guaraná soft drinks. To keep numbers down not everyone is allowed to be baptised in the chapel. Luiz enquired and was approved because of his past and present links. 'I'm certain that Thiago will grow up to be a good Vasco fan,' he states proudly, coddling the baby in his arms. Poor child if he doesn't. Next in is Marcela Camargo Pessoa, a swimmer, celebrating her fifteenth birthday. She is dressed in a tangerine ball gown and heavily made up. Her family has paid a cameraman to video the occasion. 'As soon as I arrived here eleven years ago I fell in love with the chapel,' she says. Later, I ask to take a picture and she hugs the plinth under the bronze bust of Vasco da Gama.

In the back chamber, Padre Lino hangs up his white robes, loosens his dog-collar and flicks through *Lance!*, the sports daily. Aged forty-one, he looks the perfect sporting cleric. He is respectably dressed, in trim physical condition, talks with a religious nod and has a relaxed body language. He sees himself as a pioneer. 'The Catholic religion doesn't officially work with sport. I'm trying to do something new. This is my laboratory.'

Padre Lino is down to earth. He admits he is still working out what his role is at Vasco. He learnt the hard way. Edmundo and Romário, Vasco's two strikers, once had a very public falling-out. Father Lino tried to mediate. His efforts blew up in his face. The press's zoom lenses caught him talking to Edmundo during a training session, which embarrassed them both. 'The football player is very different from all other athletes. He comes from a much more difficult social situation. The ones with problems shut themselves off.'

Our Lady of the Victories only functions on Saturdays because during the week Padre Lino attends a parish in the Rio suburbs. But he goes to São Januário for as many matches as possible and is a regular sight in the stand in his collar and tunic. Padre Lino's presence with the team in the changing rooms depends heavily on the coach. When a devout believer is in charge he takes Mass before big games, sits on the subs bench and flies with the delegation to international matches. He has married Vasco players with whom he has formed strong bonds.

Vasco was the club of Portuguese merchants that revolutionised Brazilian football by fielding black players. Padre Lino represents its Portuguese heritage, Father Santana its black. The club is a neat microcosm of Brazil. Both religious spaces happily coexist. 'I respect Father Santana for the figure that he represents. He is very dear to me,' Padre Lino says. 'Vasco has a strong black tradition. We can live together. There is a syncretism here that you see in Brazil as a whole.'

Beyond the protocol the roles are almost identical. 'I think the Masses do help because it gives peace of mind. It certainly doesn't hurt,' comments Padre Lino. He adds: 'Once we were losing 2–0 and at half-time [the coach] asked me to bless the pitch by throwing holy water on it. We turned the match round and won 3–2.' He is not very far from talk of frogs and miracles. The religions are differentiated more along social lines. The Portuguese run the club. 'Father Santana does not have an entrée among the directors the way I do,' adds Padre Lino. 'Father Santana is really restricted to the footballers and the fans.'

On match days Padre Lino drives in from his parish in the Rio suburbs, clips on his dog-collar and enters the changing rooms. He purifies the players with holy water. 'I arrived late on Thursday and the only water I could get in time was a cup of mineral water. I blessed it quickly and threw it on the team,' he says light-heartedly. Most want a mild sprinkle. Some ask for more. Helton, Vasco's goal-keeper, stands upright with his long arms outstretched like the Christ the Redeemer statue. Padre Lino throws water on one hand and then the other. Once in goal Helton says a prayer to each post. 'Generally goalkeepers are the most religious,' he says, adding that keepers' pre-match rituals are so elaborate they should be considered 'true liturgies'.

Goalkeeper in typical pose

Goalkeepers are perhaps excessively godly because they need all the moral support they can get. It is the least glamorous position and the one most blamed when things go wrong. They are in the shadow of Barbosa, who was never forgiven for letting in one goal. Brazilian goalkeepers have been known to kick the posts with their heels, spit on them and kiss them for good luck. None were quite as superstitious as Darci, of Bragantino, who before each match kicked the ball in a circle around the referee. He then kneeled on the ground to pray, pretending to tie his laces. He finished off the ritual tracing his leg along his goal line and kicking a few balls in the opposing net.

Goalkeepers' religiosity reflects Brazilian psychology. The language fans use to describe goalkeepers is itself liturgical. A brilliant outfield player is called a *craque*, a crack player. A brilliant goalkeeper is never a craque. He is referred to as a 'saint'. Great saves are invariably 'miraculous'. It is very common for magazines and television bulletins to superimpose halos on outstanding keepers. It is as if Brazilians do not believe in the concept of goalkeeping

skill. Castilho, who wore Fluminense's number one shirt
from 1947 to 1964, was nicknamed *Leiteria*, slang for Lucky
Man.

> *Saint Taffarel who is in goal*
> *Like a guardian angel*
> *Sweet like honey*
> *Defending our goal, our hope, our happiness*
> *This urge to sing and dance*
> *That comes from you*
> *That comes from your blessed hands*
> *Which defend the last piece of earth*
> *Of the Fatherland.*

This prayer was written by the novelist Carlos Drummond
and printed in the highbrow *Jornal do Brasil* the day after
Brazil beat Holland in the semi-final of the 1998 World Cup.
The game went to penalties and Taffarel's saves sealed the
victory. Penalty shoot-outs, when the outcome depends most
on goalkeepers, are matches' religious epiphanies.

João Leite was known as God's Goalie. At matches he
distributed the Bible to the referee and opposing teams. In
1981 he joined forced with Baltazar, nicknamed God's
Goalscorer, to found the sports movement Athletes of Christ.
João Leite was in the Brazilian national side and Baltazar
would later play for Atletico Madrid, where he broke the
record for number of goals scored during a season. The
Athletes of Christ was a high-profile group that reflected
the emergence of a new religious phenomenon in Brazil –
protestant evangelism.

Evangelicals are currently the most visible religious presence in football. Due to the proselytising nature of their
worship, they are walking propaganda machines. Football
is a great stage to show what God can do. Their hero is
never Pelé. It is always Jesus. They evoke God at all times.
Underneath their football strips they wear vests with religious messages like *100 per cent Jesus* and *God is True*.

Their spare time is spent at Bible readings and they give 10 per cent of their earnings to the Church.

The prominence of evangelicals in football reflects the enormous growth of such churches in the lower classes. In less than thirty years, the evangelical flock has grown from almost zero to more than twenty million. Strongest where social structures are weakest, where crime, unemployment and poverty are highest, evangelism offers an exciting new spiritual life and a break from the past. The believer is told that prayer can bring miraculous cures because you have direct contact with the Holy Spirit. Services are full of ecstasy, singing and exorcising demons.

Evangelicals demonstrate their faith constantly in their daily life. They are typically more disciplined, more saintly and sanctimonious. Regina Novaes, of Rio's Institute for Religious Studies, believes that as football has become more money-oriented and competitive this style of life attracted a disproportionate number of footballers. 'The career of a footballer is very difficult. You need a lot of persistence and help from your family. I think being an evangelical gives them a sense of direction.'

Athletes of Christ, made up of evangelicals from diverse denominations, now number about 7,000. Most are footballers. Many are famous. In the 1994 World Cup six of the Brazil squad were Athletes of Christ: Zinho, Mazinho, Jorginho, Müller, Paulo Sérgio and – no surprises – God's other goalie, Taffarel. Four played in the final. They were accompanied in the US by their own chaplain, ex-Formula One racer Alex Dias Ribeiro, who published a behind-the-scenes account of the cleanest-living men in the competition called: *Who Won The Cup?* The answer: Him Up There.

Müller, who was appearing in his third World Cup, took religion further than his colleagues did. He subsequently founded his own denomination, Pentecostal Life With Christ, for which he built a church in Belo Horizonte costing several hundred thousand pounds.

Rio's chapter of the Athletes of Christ meets on Monday

nights in a Baptist church hall near the Maracanã. The service involves lots of singing accompanied by an electronic keyboard. The sound is an instantly recognisable dirge that one hears wafting from evangelical churches on street corners all over Brazil. On Friday mornings unemployed Athletes of Christ footballers meet at Jorginho's football school on the outskirts of Rio. Successful footballers in Brazil tend to build sports centres in the communities they grew up in. Jorginho's has four synthetic pitches, a bar and his 1994 World Cup number 2 shirt framed in a window.

Evangelicals used to fight against profane activities like football and pop music. They warned against the game, saying footballs were 'the Devil's eggs'. But once they embraced popular culture, membership took off. The Athletes of Christ feel they have a global responsibility. After the kickabout at Jorginho's the thirty footballers sit in a circle of plastic chairs. Edilson, who has returned from the Portuguese club Marítimo, tells his colleagues: 'God is using Brazil in a special way. Brazil is the country that has the best football. Football is a tremendous way to talk about evangelism. We are a very powerful arm of God.' The discussion is very repetitive and self-congratulatory. Sérgio Morales, who played in Saudi Arabia, enters his opinion: 'The best way to evangelise is to do it with your conduct. You don't need to say anything. People will see. You can be put on the bench and still be happy. People start to see that Christ lives with you.' Edilson, aged thirty-two, and Sérgio, aged thirty, have a deep self-assuredness. Evangelicals have a way of talking and listening; an almost menacingly flat expression across their eyes.

Later I speak to Edilson and Sérgio. Evangelicals are often defined by what they left behind. Edilson's story is typical. 'I was almost an alcoholic. I only managed to stop drinking when I accepted Jesus. I was miraculously liberated from it when I became an Athlete of Christ. I had a lot of happiness with football, but not as much as accepting God into my heart.' Miracles are common enough for there to be a real chance of one happening to you. 'A while ago I got a big injury in my knee during training,' explains Sérgio. 'It was very swollen. A former Athlete of Christ did a prayer for me. As soon as it was finished I was instantly cured. You see that the Lord is real. You see He is not a long way away in the sky.'

Many clubs are wary of the Athletes of Christ. Not for theological reasons but because of the fear that a 'born-again' faction could disturb team unity. Grêmio once had more than ten evangelical players. The directors felt the number excessive and they were all transferred.

The Universal Church of the Kingdom of God is the largest evangelical church in Brazil and the most aggressively expansionist. It was started in Rio in 1977 by a preacher, Bishop Edir Macedo. By 1999 it had more than 3.5 million members in more than thirty countries. Bishop Macedo courted controversy by using the profits to buy one of Brazil's main terrestrial television stations. In one memorable broadcast a Universal priest kicked a statue of Our Lady of Aparecida to smithereens because it was a 'false idol'. You would not offend the average Brazilian more if you punched the president in the face. In 2000 Bishop Macedo bought a football club.

Universal FC, which played in the Rio state second division, caused a small revolution. Marcos 'Marquinhos' Antônio da Silva Nunes points to a newspaper cutting: 'Look at those crowds.' He still cannot believe it. 'Teams in the second division don't have supporters. In our opening match, the stadium was full. I was told it holds 15,000 – and there were people who weren't able to get in outside.' On a preparatory tour they attracted 11,000 in Brasília, 45,000 in Salvador and 50,000 in Belo Horizonte. Tickets for Universal's matches, available in churches, sold out.

Marquinhos is neatly dressed in an ironed shirt and carries a black leather briefcase. He looks much younger than thirty-six, which, he likes to say, is testament to his puritanical ideals. We are in Nova Iguaçu, a satellite town of Rio de

Janeiro, in the office of three evangelical politicians. Even though they are from different parties, they operate together. In Congress, state assembly and city council evangelicals form a political bloc.

Universal FC made other innovations. Marquinhos tells me proudly that their fans changed terrace chants. 'Normally you shout "Ref you're blind, *swear word* is the answer".' He cannot bring himself to say a rude word. 'This was changed to "Ref you're blind, *Jesus* is the answer".' The word *terror* was swapped in another chant to *amor*, love. Marquinhos has this smug intensity; a humility that touches on self-righteousness. 'You had a young group of fans and what was surprising was that they didn't fight, they didn't swear and they didn't drink. No one sweared at the ref. Winning or losing – we were happy.'

In the 1970s Marquinhos was a promising left back. He won a Brazil cap at junior level. He had a moderately successful career, peaking at Botafogo. Coaching Universal was an opportunity to bring the Church into his profession. Even though there were only four other Universal members in the team, he says the ethos of the Church filtered through. 'We played cleaner. We had more ingenuity on the ball. These days, non-Christian players go to the ball with wickedness, they don't trust the other player. A footballer from the Church isn't like that. When we played there were fewer fouls. We played with more of a conscience.'

Under Marquinhos' control Universal started the season well. 'Our team was weak physically. We were all skinny and small, but technically we were a good team.' They would speak to God to ask for his help. Not to win, but to deliver them from accidents. Marquinhos knows God is not enough to win in football. 'There is a practical side too. You have to have a team. You have to have talented players.'

Universal's HQ brought in a more experienced coach, Renato Trinidade. It was a bad decision. Universal started to lose. The Brazilian translation for 'If it ain't broke don't fix it', is 'If the team's winning, don't meddle with it'.

Marquinhos quotes this several times and adds: 'He meddled and look what happened. He came at the wrong moment.' He is still angry. For a second he almost loses his cool.

Shortly before the beginning of the 2001 season, the Church decided to close the club down. Marquinhos thinks their priorities went elsewhere. 'I think they should do it again next year. Even if they don't employ me. Universal was the only team that gave a meaning to the second division. No one else had any supporters.'

One other team in Brazil is owned by a church. In Jardim, a town near the Paraguayan border, Reverend Moon founded New Hope in late 1999, which disputes the first division of the Mato Grosso do Sul state championship. Moon arrived in Brazil in 1995 and set about trying to create a world base for his Unification Church. He bought 55,000 hectares around Jardim, a remote and undeveloped area, and built an educational centre that caters for 5,000. 'The movement sees sport as the only way to break barriers of race and religion,' says New Hope's press officer José Rodrigues. The club started with high expectations, poaching three players and the coaching team from the 1999 Mato Grosso do Sul champions, Ubiratan. New Hope was eighth out of seventeen in its first season, endearing itself to locals apprehensive about Moon's motives. 'The club gives the idea that the movement has only brought good things to Jardim,' adds José Rodrigues.

Religion, carnival and football form a Holy Trinity of Brazilian popular culture. Rio de Janeiro is the city of the Christ statue, the sambadrome and the Maracanã. It is common to say that football in Brazil is a religion. I think this is incorrect. Football is not an alternative faith, but a platform for Brazil's religions to express themselves. Before every game – from amateur leagues to the World Cup final – Brazilians say the Lord's Prayer and (except evangelicals) the Hail Mary. Each of Brazil's faiths coexists peacefully,

often in the same person. Footballers can, without fear of
contradiction, light a candle for Our Lady of Aparecida and
leave a bottle of cachaça for Exu. Or wear a cross around
their necks and a sprig of rue behind their ears. Football
reflects the depth and variety of Brazilian faith. Religion too,
has learnt from the sporting spectacle. The Maracanã now
fills to its fullest for religious events. The temple of football
is also the temple of Christ. With or without a frog under
the pitch.

Chapter Ten

THE UNCONFOUNDABLE GOAL

'To see only the ball is to see nothing at all.'
Nelson Rodrigues

The proprietor picks up the phone and introduces himself.

'Mauro Shampoo,' he says, firmly. 'Football player, hairdresser and *man*. I'm the only one in Brazil.'

He adds: 'Would you like to make an appointment?'

Mauro Shampoo is dressed in his football kit. He finishes the call, puts the phone and scissors to one side and starts to kick a ball in the air. He wants to show me that even though he has hung up his boots he has not lost his touch. He manages to juggle the ball in the tiny space between his customers without it falling down.

In his permed prime Mauro Shampoo was captain of Íbis, a club in the first division of the Pernambuco state championship. In the late 1970s, Íbis went for three years without winning a game. The team became known as the Worst in the World. 'It was a great privilege to have that reputation,' he says. 'We even had a fan club in Portugal. When we started to win they sent us angry telegrams.'

While he was a footballer Mauro kept his day job as a hairdresser, hence the nickname Shampoo. It also inspired him to call his wife Pente Fino, or *Toothcomb*, and his children Cream Rinse, Secador and Shampoozinho, or *Dryer* and *Little Shampoo*. Retired from the game, he runs his own salon in Recife. He is a cult figure among local footballers, who regularly drop in for a cut and dry.

Silly nicknames are not exclusive to Brazil's worst players. Dozens of the best have been known by preposterous *noms-de-plume*. The habit started early. In the national team's first match, in 1914, there was a forward called Formiga, or *Ant*. Brazil's attack in the 1930 World Cup was led by Preguinho, or *Little Nail*. The following decades saw the new faces Bigode, Nariz and Boquinha (*Moustache, Nose* and *Little Mouth*) all play for their country. Most inappropriately, the tough-looking captain of Brazil's 1994 World Cup-winning squad was called Dunga. It is the name of Dopey in translations of *Snow White and the Seven Dwarves*.

Brazilians are obsessive nicknamers. It reflects their informal, oral culture. There is a town where so many people have nicknames that the phone directory lists them that way. Cláudio, in Minas Gerais, has 22,000 inhabitants. 'We rarely know people by their real names here,' explains the book's editor. 'If we didn't have a nickname directory, people would hardly use the phone.'

Nicknames may be used by the members of any profession, no matter how high-level. The ex-governor of Piauí state is formally called Mão Santa, *Holy Hand*, and the president of the Rio Football Federation is Caixa D'Água, *Water Tank*. Luis Inácio da Silva, the left-wing presidential candidate in the last three general elections, changed his name by deed poll to include his nickname 'Lula' so as to make it clear on ballot papers who he was.

I raised my eyebrows one lunchtime in April 2001, when the TV sports bulletin announced that Caniggia and Maradona had both scored goals in domestic games. I had thought that Caniggia was playing in Scotland and Maradona had retired years ago. Yet Caniggia had put one away for Rio Branco in the Paraná state championship and Maradona for Ferroviária in Ceará. Both players are Brazilian duplicates, named after the Argentinians for physical similarities;

Caniggia because he used to have long hair and Maradona because he is stocky and short.

Footballers are often nicknamed after other footballers. It makes sense. A boy with outstanding sporting skills is more likely to be called Zico than, say, Zarathustra. In 1990, Argentina knocked Brazil out of the World Cup. (It was a Caniggia goal from a Maradona pass.) The defeated team included Luís Antônio Corrêa da Costa, whose professional name is Müller. He was named after the German striker Gerd Müller. Gerd went to two World Cups, in 1970 and 1974. Not bad, but his namesake went one better – he went in 1986, 1990 and 1994.

The age gap between the Müllers meant that they never faced each other. In Brazil footballers have played against the people who inspired their names. Roma was so called because he reminded friends of Romário, who is thirteen years his senior. In late 2000, they eventually played in the same match, Roma for Flamengo and Rómario for Vasco. Newspapers commented that the younger one played more like Romário than the veteran did.

Sometimes names describe the way the footballer plays, such as Manteiga, *Butter*, whose passes were slick. Pé-de-Valsa, *Waltzing-Foot*, danced for Fluminense and Nasa, who played for Vasco, heads the ball like a rocket. Nicknames also paint a social portrait. In 1919, when the Brazilian national team was made up uniquely of whites and mulattos, they played a Uruguayan team that included a black player, Gradin. He was the first black international to play in Rio. Soon afterwards many black Brazilians were given the nickname Gradim (the 'm' is the Portuguese transliteration). By 1932 a Gradim appeared in the Brazilian national side.

Coming from a European culture very sensitive about racism, I was very struck when I first arrived in Brazil about how common and acceptable it is to refer to someone by their skin-colour. Many footballers' names, were they British, would mobilise the Commission for Racial Equality. There was once a famous player called Escurinho, or *Darky*.

Telefone was so called since telephones used always to be black. Neither Petróleo, *Petrol*, nor Meia Noite, *Midnight*, left any doubt as to their complexions.

Pretinha, which means *Little Black Girl*, played for the women's national team during the 1996 Atlanta Olympics. Her name manages to offend European sensibilities not only of race but also of gender. And what to make of her team-mate Mariléia dos Santos? Ms dos Santos registered herself in the competition under the name Michael Jackson. She was named after the pop star because of a musical gait. When she was put on as a substitute in the third-place play-off, she did *not* moonwalk on to the pitch. Even so, when her name was announced, the crowd erupted in laughter.

Referring to someone by their nationality – or by the nationality that their physical features suggests – is not offensive. You could draw a map of Brazilian immigration just by tracing the names of footballers' international nicknames. Polaca, Mexicano, Paraguaio, Tcheco, Japinha, Chinesinho, Alemão, Somália and Congo (*Polack, Mexican, Paraguayan, Czech, Little Japanese, Little Chinese, German, Somalia and Congo*) were all players. Near the Uruguayan border many are called Castelhano, *Castilian*, just because they speak Spanish.

As well as providing a lesson in world geography, names also sketch a map of Brazil. Many players gain the nickname of the town or state they are from. Brazil is a huge country and internal migration is great. Often a player's home town is the most obvious thing that distinguishes him from his colleagues. In recent years the accepted way of differentiating two players with the same name is to add the home state. When Juninho was transferred back to Brazil after playing at Middlesbrough he became known as Juninho Paulista – *Juninho from São Paulo* – because his team contained another Juninho, who became Juninho Pernambucano – *Juninho from Pernambuco*. The more informal moniker is always preferred, rather than – heaven forbid! – using the Juninhos' surnames.

Brazilians are a very body-conscious people. To call someone *vaidoso*, or vain, is often a compliment, since they are fulfilling their social obligation to be beautiful. Unfortunately for Aírton Beleza, *Aírton Goodlooking*, he won his title for being the opposite. Marciano, *Martian*, was not named ironically. Neither was Medonho, *Frightful*. Tony Adams is lucky he is not Brazilian. Otherwise there could have been two footballers called Cara de Jegue, *Donkey Face*.

Footballers have been nicknamed almost everything. Even numbers. There was a player called 84, one called 109 and another called Duzentos, *Two Hundred*. Animals are well catered for – Piolho, *Lice*, Abelha, *Bee*, and Jacaré, *Alligator*. (Jacaré is less remarkable for his name – the result of a hereditary protuberant chin – than for his status as tennis player Gustavo Kuerten's favourite footballer. When Kuerten won the 1997 French Open he praised Jacaré in interviews. On the back of the recommendation, the footballer was sold from the small club in Kuerten's home town to a big club. He ended up in Portugal, although he returned shortly afterwards. Kuerten is a tennis player, not a talent scout.)

Nicknames increase the theatrical aspect of Brazilian football. They contribute to its romance. Pelé would have played the same had he been known by his real name, Édson Arantes. Yet the word 'Pelé' contains some of his magic. Its simplicity and childishness reflects the purity of his genius. How could Pelé be real if he did not have a real name? Pelé is less a nickname than it is a badge of his greatness, the name of the myth, not of the man.

'Pelé' has no other meaning in Portuguese, which increases the sense that it is an invented international brand name, like Kodak or Compaq. The etymological origin of 'Pelé' is much discussed but still unclear. Édson was known as Dinho at home. When he joined Santos he was called Gasolina, *Gasoline*. Then he became 'Pelé'. Nicknames, like wines, can improve through time.

The use of nicknames also conveys the idea of extended

childhood – of men who have not grown up. Some Brazilians believe this is internalised, creating a low sense of self-esteem.

The writer Luis Fernando Verissimo goes further. He believes that nicknames are a historical relic from the times of slavery. 'The footballer's nickname was less a "stage name" than a name from the slave quarters, a way for him to know his place and his limits,' he writes. Instead of showing equality and inclusiveness, he argues, nicknames reinforce a culture of submission.

Imagine you were faced with a team consisisting of Picolé, Ventilador, Solteiro, Fumanchu, Ferrugem, Gordo, Astronauta, Portuário, Gago, Geada and Santo Cristo (*Lollipop, Ventilator Fan, Single Man, Fu Manchu, Rust, Fatso, Astronaut, Docker, Stutterer, Frost and Holy Christ*) – all of which are or were names of professional players. You probably wouldn't take them seriously. Exactly, thought the radio commentator Édson Leite.

After the 1962 World Cup many players were near retirement. Brazil overhauled its squad. The new team started to lose. Whose fault was it? Édson Leite blamed the nicknames. They were at best childish and at worst embarrassing. Of course a team that sounded like it had been found in a kindergarten playground would be awed in the presence of, for example, Argentina, which had grand, almost pompous-sounding players called Marzolini, Rattín and Onega.

For a brief while Édson Leite ran a campaign to call Pelé, Édson Arantes, and Garrincha, Manuel Francisco. It gained a fair momentum, but eventually failed. There was one major flaw. Nicknames may be puerile but they are often a lot less silly-sounding than players' real names.

Luiz Gustavo Vieira de Castro runs the register at the Brazilian Football Confederation. When I meet him a pile of paper is stacked high on his desk. The forms are applications to inscribe new players. He picks up one arbitrarily and reads it aloud.

'Belziran José de Sousa.

'Bel. Zi. Ran' he repeats, dwelling on each syllable.

'Elerubes Dias da Silva.'

'Ele. Rubes,' he sighs.

'Look – just one of the first seven names is normal.'

'Belziran?' he asks, as if it was a particularly rare species of Amazonian beetle. 'Elerubes?' Luiz Gustavo's mouth curls and he shakes his head.

'Whatever happened to José?' he implores. 'Now there's a good name.'

Luiz Gustavo says that Brazilians' names are increasingly ornate. It saddens him. He feels it is an indication of a lack of education. Made-up names are an embarrassment – not just for the poor soul involved but for the country too. He shows me a list of about 200 professional footballers that prove his point. The roll call goes from Aderoilton and Amisterdan to Wandermilson and Wellijonh.

Whether or not Brazil's culture of naming is the result of ignorance, it is certainly an extension of the creativity applied in other fields. If Brazil changed football it did so only by breaking orthodoxies and rewriting the rules with a playful, elastic flamboyance. The same process produced Tospericagerja.

In 1970 the aforementioned baby was born. He incorporates the first syllable of more than half the team that won that year's World Cup: Tostão, Pelé, Rivelino, Carlos Alberto, Gerson and Jairzinho. Another 1970 child was Jules Rimet de Souza Cruz Soares, named after the World Cup trophy. Jules Rimet proved worthy of the tribute – he became a professional footballer, in the Amazonian state Roraima.

World Cups have left a trail of onomastic devastation. In celebration of victory in 1962, a child was named Gol *(Goal)* Santana Silva. Perhaps Gooooool Santana Silva would have been more accurate. Whenever his mother screamed at him, passers-by must have thought: 'Who scored?' During the 1998 World Cup semi-final penalty shoot-out with Holland, a baby was named Taffarel each time he made a save. Regardless of the tot's sex. First, Bruna Taffarel de Carvalho was born in Brasília. A few minutes later, when the keeper's defence won the match, Igor Taffarel Marques was born in Belo Horizonte.

Zicomengo and Flamozer sound like two Texan cops from a low-budget TV show. They are, no less glamorously, two brothers who incorporate 'Flamengo' with two of its stars from the 1980s, Zico and Mozer. It was the idea of Fransisco Nêgo dos Santos, a night watchman who lives more than 1,000 miles from Rio. Even his daughter, Flamena, could not escape his passion. When Fransisco took his children to meet Zico, he was deeply disillusioned. He said bitterly afterwards: 'Zico treated me like I was a mental retard.'

A conventional Brazilian way to name a child is by creating a hybrid word from the mother and father's name – as if the name is a metaphor for the physical union. Gilmar, for example, is the joining of Gilberto and Maria. Gilmar dos Santos Neves was born in 1930. Gilmar grew up to become Brazil's most successful goalkeeper, winning the 1958 and 1962 World Cups.

Gilmar Luíz Rinaldi, born in 1959, was one of several children named in his honour. As may be expected, the young Gilmar was a hostage to his namesake. 'Whenever I played football I was always put in goal,' he says. 'No one let me play in any other position.' But Gilmar discovered he had a talent. He eventually turned professional and was called up for the national side. In 1994 he won a World Cup-winners medal as Taffarel's reserve. Name had determined nature. Gilmar had *become* his namesake.

First names are especially relevant in Brazilian football since, together with nicknames, that is how footballers are generally known. Brazil and Portugal, its former colonial power, are the only countries in which this is the case – and Portugal much less so, since it is a more traditional, cere-monious society. First-name footballers are a reflection of the informality of Brazilian life. 'The Brazilian contribution to civilisation is cordiality – we gave the world the *cordial man*,' wrote the historian Sérgio Buarque de Holanda. You can call someone by their first name or nickname even in the most official situations. Politicians, doctors, lawyers and teachers are addressed the same way as you address a close friend. In a Brazilian record shop George Benson, George Harrison and George Michael are listed together, under G. (Brazilians are also tireless in using the suffixes '-inho' and '-ão' – meaning 'little' and 'big' – which increases the impression that the country is both excessively intimate and exagerative. In the 1990s many Ronaldos played for the national side. The first three were easy to name: Ronaldão, Ronaldinho and Ronaldo, *Big, Little and Regular-sized Ronaldo*. Easy. But in 1999 another Ronaldinho turned up. What was left? Would he be nicknamed Ronaldinhozinho, *Even Littler Ronaldo*? No. He was first called Ronaldinho Gaúcho, *Little Ronaldo from Rio Grande do Sul*. Then, since he was no longer so little, the original Ronaldinho graduated to Ronaldo (the first Ronaldo was no longer in the squad) and so Ronaldinho Gaúcho became Ronaldinho.)

Using first names was one of the first ways, in the early years of the last century, that Brazilians changed football's conventions. They at first imitated the English expats, whose teams were listed by surname. But it did not stick. How could you distinguish two brothers? The confusion was resolved the Brazilian way. When teams were mixed with Europeans and Brazilians, naming style determined nationality. Sidney Pullen was known as Sidney because he was a Brazilian, albeit of English descent. His team-mate Harry Welfare, born in Liverpool, was always Welfare.

Brazilian football is an international advert for the cordiality of Brazilian life because of its players' names. Calling someone by their first name is a demonstration of intimacy – calling someone by their nickname more so. Brazil feels like a team of close friends; mates from the kickabout at the park. It fosters an affection that no other national team commands. The fan personalises his relationship with Ronaldo by virtue of using his first name, which does not happen when you call someone Beckenbauer, Cruyff, or Keegan.

Because footballers are known by first names and because

Brazilians are imaginative namers, players are a great window on national concerns. One of the most common names for footballers is Donizete. In 2000 there were three Donizetes in the Brazilian first division. It is not a traditional name. Fifty years ago there were no Donizetes. Two centuries ago, however, there was an Italian opera composer called Donizetti. A Brazilian music-lover named his sons Chopin, Mozart, Bellini, Verdi and Donizetti. The latter became a priest who, in the 1950s in São Paulo, became a famous miracle-worker. It spawned a wave of Donizetes. One estimate puts the number at more than a million people.

American culture is a strong inspiration for babies' names, especially Hollywood. Not just film stars but the place itself. Oleúde was a strong club player in the 1990s. He tended, however, to be known by his nickname, Capitão, or *Captain*. Since he was often captain, this was very convenient. How long before Brazilian football does away with proper names all together?

Alain Delon, the French actor, once said: 'It's much more exciting being a football player than being a film star. To be honest, that's really what I wanted to do.' He must be tickled by the success, if not at the spelling, of his South American namesake. For a period in 2001 Allann Delon was highest scorer in the Brazilian league. 'I might not have the actor's eyes, but I'm charismatic and always a success with the ladies,' jokes the twenty-one-year-old, a squat mulatto with thick eyebrows and matty black hair. He was very nearly called Christopher Reeves, but his mother changed her mind – swapping one misspelt film idol for another. 'Can you imagine how weird it would sound "Christopher Reeves shoots into the corner of the net",' he says. 'Allann Delon is much better.'

The cast list of Brazilian Football: The Movie also includes Maicon, who has played for Brazil's youth side. His father paid tribute to Kirk Douglas by naming his son Maicon Douglas, after Kirk's son Michael. The man at the register office wrote it down wrong.

Other celebrities in football boots include Roberto Carlos, the veteran left back, who was so called because his mother liked the *real* Roberto Carlos, who is Brazil's equivalent of Frank Sinatra. The tribute turned out to be especially poignant, since the singer was run over by a train in his youth. In other words: the footballer with one of the most coveted kicks in the game was named after a man with a gammy leg.

Roberto Carlos's music is subtly contained in another footballer: Odvan, who played for the national team in 1998. His mother was so taken by the song O Divã, *The Divan*, that she immortalised it on his birth certificate.

Spelling mistakes due to transliterations are often the result of ignorance, but not always. Brazilians have a relaxed attitude to spelling. It is often used as a device to customise names, rather than as a convention to be obeyed. Less-educated parents tend to prefer the aesthetics of the letters 'w', 'k' and 'y', which are not part of the Portuguese alphabet, and also lovingly run two consonants together. Allann Delon's father could not remember how the Frenchman spelt his name so he added an 'l' and an 'n' for good measure. Registrars are obliged to take down the name that the parent dictates. In 2000, a magazine reported that 'Stephanie' was so popular that a registrar in São Paulo listed seventeen different spellings (from Stefani to Sthephanny) and asked parents to choose by number.

Inconsistent spelling was not one of the major grounds for Congress's football investigations. It could have been. And for a moment it seemed that it was. At the beginning of ex-national coach Wanderley Luxemburgo's testimony, Senator Geraldo Althoff asked him: 'How will you sign your name?'

The senator looked like an exasperated headmaster berating a naughty pupil. He said: 'Will you use a W and a Y or a V and an I?'

It was a simple question, in spite of the accusatorial tone and the humiliating circumstances of the interrogation, but

Luxemburgo could not give a straight answer.

He replied that his signature would be Wanderley and his documents would read Vanderlei. Althoff had the rankled expression of a man at the end of his tether. How could he believe a word the man said if he was in two minds as to his own identity?

Questionable spelling, it seems, comes with the job of national coach. Luxemburgo's predecessor, Mário Zagallo, misspelt his name for almost fifty years.

Zagallo was born Zagallo on 9 August 1931. He became the footballer Zagalo during the 1940s. Zagalo played for Flamengo, Botafogo and the national side. Zagalo won four World Cup-winners medals. Always Zagalo. Never Zagallo.

Then one day, around 1995, the veteran was giving a talk at a São Paulo newspaper. A reporter enquired about his surname. He replied that on his birth certificate it had a double 'l'. The following day the newspaper printed Zagallo.

Gradually other newspapers and TV stations followed suit. Books rewrote his achievements with his 'correct' name. The desire for spelling rigour turned into a self-contradictory mess. For a while Zagallo kept on signing a newspaper column Zagalo, even though the same newspaper in other articles spelt him differently. Zagalo might have been a mistake, yet it was nevertheless his footballing identity. It was doomed to be erased from history.

The episode is less a victory of thoroughness over inaccuracy – or of punctiliousness over common sense – than a demonstration that Brazil is a strongly oral culture. What does it matter to Luxemburgo if he is Wanderley or Vanderlei, or to Zagallo if he is has one 'l' or two? Both names sound the same.

Zagallo's name stands out in another way. He is the only Brazilian forward who has won a World Cup final to be known by his surname. So what? This explains a great deal. The *coup de grâce* of Brazilian naming customs is that you can often identify the position of a footballer depending on how he is known. Goalkeepers tend to be known by their surnames and first names; forwards by their nicknames. Zagallo is the exception that proves the rule.

I compiled a quick list of the Brazilian national team's all-time top scorers. Seven of the first ten are known by their nicknames. In fact, the only surname among the top twenty-five is Rivelino – but this should not really count. First, it sounds like a nickname. Secondly, Rivelino really is a nickname – his real name is Rivellino. Part of the artifice of a Brazilian goalscorer is to have a name that bluffs.

Zagallo was not a flashy left-winger. He did not *deserve* a nickname. He did what was expected, nothing more.

Likewise, Brazilian goalkeepers rarely have nicknames. Of the nine goalkeepers to have had more than twenty national caps, four are known by their surname and four by their first name. Only one is known by his nickname – Dida – and that took eighty years to come about. He won his first cap in 1995.

Defenders also tend not to have nicknames, although the phenomenon is less extreme than for goalkeepers. 'There is always the impression that a defender who uses a nickname does not take responsibility for his actions. Who can trust a defence that has a pseudonym?' asks Luis Fernando Verissimo. 'The ideal defensive line-up should list the defenders with their surname, their parents' name, national insurance number and a telephone number for complaints.'

If referring to someone by their nickname shows intimacy and affection, then Brazilians are fonder of their attackers than of their defenders. Which we know already. And as for goalkeepers? Their surnames reinforce the fact that they are loved less. No wonder they are tormented souls. According to a popular saying: 'The goalkeeper is such a miserable wretch that the grass doesn't even grow where he stands on the pitch.'

The list of unhappy owners of the number one shirt predates Barbosa, who suffered for fifty years after letting in one goal. Jaguaré was Brazil's best keeper in the 1920s

and 1930s. He would catch the ball with one hand and then
spin it on his index finger. He would dribble opponents or
bounce the ball on their heads when their backs were turned.
Jaguaré went to Europe, where he played for Barcelona and
Olympique de Marseille. But he spent all his money as soon
as he earned it. One year after returning to Brazil, in 1940,
he was found dead in a gutter. Castilho, who played for
Fluminense between 1947 and 1964, committed suicide.
Pompéia and Veludo – two other flamboyant Rio goalkeepers from the 1950s, ended up alcoholics.

Brazilian goalkeepers have to find love from other quarters. Pompéia said: 'The goalkeeper likes the ball the most.
Everyone else kicks it. Only the keeper hugs it.' This affection was reciprocated in a delightful children's book written
by Jorge Amado, Brazil's most famous novelist. It tells the
story of a ball who falls in love with a talentless goalkeeper.
The keeper becomes unbeatable since the ball always heads
for his arms, where it is kissed and then warmly held to his
chest. One day, the goalkeeper has to defend a penalty which
he does not want to save. So he runs away, leaving the goal
wide open. But the ball chooses to follow him. They marry
and live happily ever after.

It is not only in Brazilian literature that the ball is considered a real person. Players of a certain generation – when
football was less about force and more about delicacy –
describe the ball as a lady to be courted. 'The ball never hit
me in the shin, never betrayed me,' says Nilton Santos, who
played for the national side between 1949 and 1962. 'If she
was my lover, she was the lover I liked the best.' Didi, Nilton
Santos's team-mate in the 1958 and 1962 World Cups,
opined: 'I always treated her with care. Because if you don't,
she doesn't obey you. I would dominate her and she would
obey me. Sometimes she came and I said: "Hey! My little
girl," . . . I treated her with as much care as I treated my
wife. I had tremendous affection for her. Because she's tough.
If you treat her badly she will break your leg!'

One of the reasons why Brazilians regard a ball as a

woman is semantic. In Portuguese, 'a bola' – the ball – is a feminine noun. (Unlike 'el balón' in Spanish or 'le ballon' in French, which are masculine.) Since Portuguese has no word for 'it', the ball is always described as 'her' or 'she'. In a verbal culture in which there is a tendency to give everything nicknames, it was only a small step until the ball grew human characteristics.

If a player is scared of touching the ball, commentators say he is 'calling the ball "Your Excellency"'. If he is displaying intimacy with the ball, he is 'calling the ball "my darling"'. I cannot imagine that eskimos have as many words for 'snow' as Brazilians do for 'bola', ball. Haroldo Maranhão, in his *Football Dictionary*, lists thirty-seven synonyms:

> Leather balloon, child, girl, doll, chubby one, Maricota, Leonor, pellet, Maria, round one, mate, sphere, kernel-stone, balloon, her, infidel, plum, leather, little round one, baby, pursued one, globe, wart, chestnut, leather sphere, young lady, Guiomar, Margarida, mortadela, little animal, capricious one, deceitful one, demon, tyre, bladder, number five, leather ball.

Five are women's names. Margarida is *Margaret*. It gives a whole new meaning to the phrase: 'Pass the Marge.'

'In Brazil you can call the ball anything,' jokes the radio commentator Washington Rodrigues. 'Except "ball".'

Once before a match between two small Rio teams, Washington took the personification to another extreme. He declined to interview the players. Instead, he interviewed the Margaret. How did she feel to play among two small teams when she had once played with Pelé? Didn't she feel like giving up, throwing in the towel? The interview lasted ten minutes and ended with the ball in tears.

Radio bears a lot of the responsibility for the richness of Brazilian football talk. Radio influenced football more than any other medium. It was the vehicle that turned football into a mass sport by allowing all corners of the country to follow games. Radio was more suited to Brazil than newspapers since the country is so big and large parts of the population were illiterate. Radio grew in parallel with football – the 1950s and 1960s were both the golden age of Brazilian football and the peak of popularity of transmissions.

Radio gave football a language of its own. Right from the earliest sports broadcasts the aim was to create as much excitement as possible rather than clinically describe what was going on. In 1942 Rebelo Júnior, a commentator who started his career narrating horse-races, invented sport's most famous prolonged vowel. A player scored and he shouted 'gooooooal'.

Rebelo Júnior was nicknamed the Man of the Unconfoundable Goal. His unconfoundable 'gooooooal' echoed through history and is now a mark of all Brazilian – and Latin American – radio and television football coverage. His colleagues found that it had advantages. Raul Longas, nicknamed the Man of the Electrifying Goal, wailed like a siren for longer than his peers. There was a reason. He was short-sighted and could not properly see who scored. The extra seconds allowed his sidekick to write down for him the player's name on a piece of paper.

The most listened-to football commentator during the 1940s and 1950s was also the most idiosyncratic and colourful. He is, still, one of the most listened-to Brazilians in the world. Ary Barroso wrote many of Carmen Miranda's most famous songs. He also wrote the light samba 'Aquarela do Brasil', translated as 'Brazil', which is one of the most performed pieces of music of all time. It has been recorded by as diverse artists as Frank Sinatra, Wire, Kate Bush and S'Express.

Ary was a Renaissance man. As well as writing music he was a football commentator, pianist, writer, local councillor and, later, a television-show host. Ary was also a Flamengo fan. It would not be unfair to say that he was a Flamengo

Ary Barroso

fan above all his other roles. In the early 1940s his compositions had made him internationally famous. He flew to Hollywood and was invited to become musical director of Walt Disney Productions. For a composer, there was possibly no higher position in showbusiness. He refused.

'Because don't have Flamengo here,' he explained, ungrammatically.

Ary's love for Flamengo eclipsed any impartiality he might have had as a commentator. Instead of shouting 'goooooal' Ary blew into a plastic mouth organ. It was easy to tell who had scored. If it was Flamengo the mouth organ would squeal repeatedly with joy. He would blow extended flourishes like an excited child. If it was against Flamengo the organ would emit a short, embarrassed 'frrp'.

Ary was entertaining because he was passionate, unpredictable and irresponsible. He once told his audience when a striker was approaching the Flamengo box: 'I'm not even going to look.' Another time the radio fell silent because he had run to the edge of the pitch to celebrate a goal with the team. Yet, his audience was not just Flamengo fans. He was a parody of the general Brazilian assumption that *everything* is motivated by personal interest. In the closing minutes of a match in which Flamengo was losing 6–0, a man arrived at the stadium willing to pay any price to be let in. 'I don't want to see the game,' he told the confused gatekeeper. 'I just want to see Ary Barroso's face.'

Brazilian football authorities allow journalists on the touchline during the match, interviewing players and the referee as they come on and off. This practice was started by Ary Barroso. He was the first broadcaster to put a reporter on the pitch – to get him different angles on the game. This created situations which shocked the English when Southampton travelled to Brazil in 1948. 'The usual radio commentators and photographers refused to be kicked off the field so that the match could start. The radio and press seem to be the deciding factors in this country about the time when a match shall commence!' tut-tutted referee George Reader in a dispatch to the *Southern Daily Echo*.

The importance of radio within football has led to another peculiarly Brazilian phenomenon – the 'radialista'. The radialista is ostensibly a radio broadcaster, yet because the idea is to be as showy as possible they are celebrities in their own right. Many radialistas take advantage of football's prominence to launch themselves in other spheres. Reporting on football matches teaches you skills such as public speaking, thinking on the spot and how to rouse a crowd. The list of politicians, businessmen and lawyers who started their careers commentating on local football matches is a long one. Rio state governor Anthony Garotinho aims to be the first ex-radialista to become Brazilian president.

Radialistas can be anything they want to be. Washington

THE UNCONFOUNDABLE GOAL   243

Rodrigues, the interviewer who reduced a football to tears, jumped to the other side and became coach of Brazil's largest club. It was the equivalent of making Des Lynam coach of Manchester United.

Washington does not look like a sportsman. When I meet him at his radio studio his ample physique is comfortably rested in a chair. He is genial and soft-spoken. Washington's broadcasting style is not the firework variety; he is the most verbally creative of his peers. He has coined more than eighty phrases, of which several have passed into common usage. His style is witty and intimate, for example calling fans in the *geral* standing area Geraldines and those in the *arquibancada* terraces Archibalds.

Washington – like Ary Barroso – is a dyed-in-the-wool Flamengo supporter. He has never hidden it. It is a trademark of his style. When, in 1995, Flamengo were in trouble the club's president – himself an ex-radialista – wondered who could pull them out of the crisis. He asked Washington, even though he had never been a coach, a player or even a linesman before.

'What were Flamengo looking for?' Washington says. 'The club wanted internal peace. They wanted someone who could identify with the fans. I am not a coach, nor do I have pretensions of being one. But everyone knows what football is. We are all football coaches really.'

The radialista was given a four-month contract as coach. 'What did I do?', he asks. 'Tactics is like a buffet. If there are forty plates you eat four or five. You don't eat all forty. I asked all the players to put on the table their ideas about the best way to play. Then I put mine and afterwards we chose the best.'

Washington introduced other unorthodox methods. He was unable to understand games standing on the touchline because he had only ever seen football from his position in the radio cabin. So he asked the Brazilian Football Confederation if he could install a television in the dugout. They were unsure and asked FIFA. FIFA replied that it was unsure, since it had never been asked before. Eventually, it gave him the all-clear. Washington sat in the dugout, watching television instead of watching the players.

He lasted his four-month contract. He did not turn Flamengo into champions, yet he had moderate success. The club must have been happy enough since three years later, when the club was again in difficulties, he was given another four-month contract. In his second stint he helped Flamengo avoid relegation from the first division of the national league.

He adds: 'It was an educative experience. In forty years I didn't learn as much as I learnt in those eight months. I started to see players in a different light, how they are during the week, what their personal lives are like. It made me regret a lot of things I had said or written before. I am really careful now in criticising a coach.'

Football journalism has been the start of many eminent Brazilians' careers. On 5 March 1961, Joelmir Beting was at the Maracanã, reporting on a game between Santos and Fluminense. He saw Pelé take the ball just past the centre line and dribble one, two, three, four, five . . . six players before beating the goalkeeper. It was a work of art. Those present say it was the most wonderful goal he ever scored. But it was before the era of televised games. The dribble would never be seen again.

Joelmir thought that a way to make the goal eternal was to cast it in bronze. He commissioned a plaque that was put up in the stadium the following week, dedicated to 'the most beautiful goal in the history of the Maracanã'. The phrase 'gol de placa' – *goal worthy of a plaque* – entered the lingua franca, and is still the highest compliment in Brazilian football.

Joelmir now has a different plaque. He is a distinguished financial commentator.

Football was also a trampoline for Brazil's Monty-Pythonesque comedy troupe Casseta & Planeta. The humorists started a satirical magazine in the 1970s. Later they were given their own show by Globo, the main TV station. In 1994, Globo asked them to provide daily sketches during the World Cup. During the tournament they broadcast clips from the United States for the lunchtime and evening news bulletins. 'None of the international journalists really knew what was going on,' says Bussunda, one of Casseta & Planeta's comedians. 'Here was a bunch of Brazilians dressed up in ridiculous costumes making complete fools of ourselves wherever the national team went.'

When Brazil won the final – in Los Angeles' Rose Bowl – they filmed a spoof video dressed as Californian hippies singing 'The Age of Romárius', to the tune of the 1960s anthem 'Aquarius'. It was one of their best-received gags. By the end of the World Cup Casseta & Planeta had a celebrity status almost as big as the footballers themselves.

'When we flew back to Brazil it felt like we were champions too,' says Bussunda, whom I meet sitting in his office in Ipanema.

Casseta & Planeta now have a weekly primetime show on Globo. They carry on writing gags based around football. 'Football is a very rich seam. If we were writing just about what goes on on the pitch, then maybe there wouldn't be enough material. But when you are talking about football you are talking about Brazil,' he says.

Bussunda is a TV natural. He makes you laugh just by looking at him. His expression is wonderfully glum and he is blessed with a portly comedy stomach. His obesity is part of his act. The catchline for his weekly articles in the sports newspaper *Lance!* is: 'the columnist who is a ball already'.

Casseta & Planeta is my favourite Brazilian television programme. The satire is no-holds-barred. They send up politicians, personalities and even Globo itself. Sometimes I can't believe what they get away with.

I ask Bussunda whether any of their victims have ever complained? He looks at me with a straight face. 'The only time we ever received external censorship was when we were planning a sketch about Fluminense.'

The incident occurred when Romário was playing for Flamengo, who are Fluminense's arch rivals. Casseta & Planeta invited him on the show and asked him to wear a T-shirt that said, 'Não use drogas. Não torça para o Fluminense'. Literally, this means, 'Don't take drugs. Don't support Fluminense'. But it is a pun on the word 'droga', which also means 'something rubbish'.

Fluminense went to court and obtained an injunction against the broadcast.

'So what did we do?' asks Bussunda. 'We played the interview with Romário right up to the moment he was going to show the T-shirt. Then we cut to images of three goals that had been scored against Fluminense the Sunday before.'

Bussunda did not realise the offence it would cause. His voice is deadly serious. 'I received several threats. I received emails saying that people knew where I lived, that they knew which school my daughter goes to. I was really taken aback. I even had to change telephone numbers.'

He adds: 'In my career it is the one joke I regret. I realised that the joke had hit the wrong target. We wanted to poke fun at the Fluminense directors. But we hurt the fans.'

Bussunda learnt that in Brazil there is only one thing you cannot joke about: a fan's passion for his club.

As well as Ary Barroso and Jorge Amado, football has been part of the public lives of many important cultural figures. Pixinguinha, a black musician who pioneered the use of Afro-Brazilian percussion instruments, wrote the first major composition dedicated to the sport. The song '1x0' was written in 1919 immediately after Brazil won the South American Cup by a goal to nil. The speed and dexterity of the music portrayed the skills of the goalscorer, Friedenreich. More recently, Chico Buarque, who is probably Brazil's most highly respected singer-songwriter, has written songs and articles about football. Chico also owns his own football pitch and amateur football club, where he plays three times a week.

In 1976 the contemporary artist Nelson Leirner was asked to design a trophy for Corinthians. A veteran of artistic 'happenings' during the 1960s, he decided to make a trophy that was a 'performance' rather than an object to keep. He made a Corinthians flag which was 4m by 8m and tied it to helium-filled balloons. The trophy was presented to the club during a match at the Morumbi in São Paulo – it was set free at the beginning of the game and drifted up and away out of the stadium.

Corinthians lost the game and Leirner was accused of causing the team bad luck.

A week later, the flag landed on a farm four hundred miles away. It was taken and put up in a bar in the nearest town. From that moment on the local team lost match after match. Its supporters blamed the flag. Corinthians had gone twenty-two years without winning a title. Perhaps the flag had brought the curse? They began to perform religious rituals to exorcise the bad spirits. Eventually, a television station heard of the story and returned the flag to São Paulo.

Literature and football have been linked since football's early days. In 1930, Preguinho, the *Little Nail*, scored Brazil's first goal in a World Cup. His father, Coelho Neto, was a novelist and founder of the Brazilian Academy of Letters. Coelho Neto was a die-hard Fluminense supporter. He attended games wearing a white suit, straw hat and walking stick. His elegant attire was no guarantee of writerly reserve – in 1916, complaining against a penalty, Coelho Neto led one of Brazil's first pitch invasions.

Despite his love of football, Coelho Neto did not include it in his fiction. Football, though enjoyed by all levels of society, was for many years not deemed serious enough for art. In 1953 it was considered scandalous when it featured in a play. *A Falecida*, *The Deceased Woman*, tells the story of Tuninho, a widower who wastes his wife's burial money on football because he discovers that she had been unfaithful.

The Deceased Woman is by Nelson Rodrigues, Brazil's

Nelson Rodrigues at the Maracanã

greatest playwright. Nelson adored causing offence. Usually
the taboos he broke were more subversive than mentioning
sport. He was obsessed with adultery and incest. Between
1951 and 1961 he published daily short stories in a Rio
newspaper, almost always about marital infidelity. Nelson
had a wonderful gift for dialogue and a wickedly perverse
sense of humour. He described the hypocrisies of lower-
middle-class Rio like no one before or since.

Nelson was the younger brother of Mário Filho, the
pioneer of Brazilian sports journalism and the man who
conceived the Maracanã. Of their ten other siblings that
survived infancy, all went into journalism. When two of
them started a sports magazine in 1955, Nelson was asked
to lend a helping hand.

Nelson's columns took football-writing into a new dimension. For a start, he made up characters and situations. Perhaps he felt the freedom to do this was because he was not a sportswriter – he was a famous playwright. An equally likely reason was because he was so short-sighted that he could hardly make out the events on the pitch. For example, in order to explain flukish occurences, Nelson said it was the work of the Supernatural de Almeida, a man from the Middle Ages now living in a fetid room in a northern suburb of Rio. The Supernatural is an absurd concept, but his public loved it because it played into their own superstitions. It became part of football's vernacular. Several times I have heard commentators say, when trying to explain an unlucky bounce: 'Look! It's the Supernatural of Almeida!'

Nelson, without intending to, gave Brazilian football its clearest voice. It is a peculiar, if explainable twist of fate that Brazil's two most important football writers were brothers – since Nelson might never have started without Mário Filho's influence. Their styles were very different. Mário Filho's texts were serious opuses. Nelson, on the other hand, articulated the hyperbolic passion of a fan. 'I'm Fluminense, I always was Fluminense. I'd say I was Fluminense in my past lives.' He coined dozens of phrases that seem as relevant now as when he wrote them four decades ago. He described players like Pelé and Garrincha as transcendent icons – which no one had done before. Nelson was the first person to describe Pelé as royalty. 'Racially perfect, invisible mantles appear to hang from his chest,' he said when the player was just seventeen. Pelé, of course, later became known as The King.

When games started to be televised, Nelson was not impressed. 'If the videotape shows it's a penalty then all the worse for the videotape. The videotape is stupid,' he said, famously. Nelson's Luddite comments are often quoted today. Partly this is because he reminds people of the golden years. But also it's because Nelson got it right. Brazilians do not like to be objective about their football. They like it to be halfway between fact and fiction. They like it to be as informal as possible; full of stories, mythologies and inexplicable passion. Football is about Ronaldo and Rivaldo but it is also about Margaret and Tospericagerja and Mauro Shampoo.

Chapter Eleven

NAKED FUTEBOL

No one remembers exactly who was playing or when it was. But we can be sure that the match was a battle of life or death and the team losing 1–0 needed the win like a man needs air to breath. Suddenly, a player kicked the ball with such courage that it missed the goal and landed in a nearby creek. But he was not as courageous as the right back of the losing team. Without half a thought he plunged into the water. The match was all or nothing and he had no time to lose. Two minutes later he returned. His legs were trembling like a young liana. And white, white, white. He was so shaken that he couldn't speak, only point. Everyone ran to the riverbank. There she was. A snake. So calm, so large . . . And the worst of it was that she was lovingly spiralled around the ball. [*]

In order to prepare his football club for the Big Kickabout, Audemir Cruz pays for Erica dos Santos to have a manicure, leg wax and haircut. Audemir is the president of Vila Nova and Erica is the team's beauty queen. He has, as is required, already bought her a bikini and a pair of trainers.

---

[*]excerpts from Manaus newspaper *A Crítica*

Now he is fussing over the final arrangements. When she is ready he takes her in his maroon 1975 Ford to the stadium. Audemir, who is thirty-eight, drives slowly because he is still learning and does not have a licence. They pass slums that clog the sides of small rivers, high-rise blocks and shopping centres. The humid heat gives the sensation of being incubated in cotton wool; the sun is so strong it feels like someone is stretching your skin. At the stadium Audemir hands Erica Vila Nova's team shirt. It is white with green vertical stripes. He wishes her luck. She smiles nervously, says thank you and walks silently backstage.

In the Big Kickabout, the Brazilian rainforest has a football tournament that perfectly reflects its size, exoticism and mystique. It takes place in Manaus, an improbable metropolis a thousand miles up the River Amazon, at the heart of one of the world's last wildernesses. When I visit, in 2000, 522 teams are taking part. That's quite a sum, considering that they are all local sides. But the Big Kickabout's most gargantuan eccentricity is that it is really two tournaments – a football competition and a beauty pageant. Teams are obliged to enter both. While the boys battle on the football field, the girls fight it out on the catwalk.

Audemir has taken Erica to the opening ceremony, in which all the girls must parade. When I arrive, the stadium is filling up. I walk through crowds of men in their team strips and vendors selling beer from polystyrene ice-buckets. Some people are banging drums and shaking tambourines. Others have flags and banners. It's like a crowd waiting for a significant sporting event.

Behind a central stage the beauty queens are almost ready. It is an overwhelming sight. More than five hundred women are dressed in bikini bottoms and football shirts. They are completing their make-up and shining their buttocks and thighs with almond oil. The average height is not much more than 5ft. Most have strong indigenous features, the result of hundreds of years of miscegenation of white Europeans with Indian tribes.

One girl catches my eye. She stands out from the others, having thick, unnaturally bleached blond hair and bright red lipstick. What is most striking about her, however, is her green and white shirt, printed with the word 'Arsenal'. I approach her. She introduces herself as Lady Roberta. I ask if it's her real name. She frowns: 'Of course. Why?' Lady tells me that Arsenal is one of the competition's strongest teams. She had been spotted in the street by one of the team's sponsors: 'He asked me straightaway to be their queen. It's so exciting taking part.'

The temperature has hardly cooled by the time it gets dark. The girls are told to queue up in single file, as the ceremony will shortly begin. The line stretches behind the stage for about 200m. They tie their football shirts in a knot above their tummy buttons so they can show off their hips. Tucked in each bikini bottom is a piece of paper with their competition number.

In front of the contestants is the reigning Kickabout Queen, Kamila Jeniffer. She is wearing a swimsuit, a sash, a sparkling tiara and a preposterously luxurious – and, I presume, uncomfortably hot – blue mantle. Kamila Jeniffer is standing in a buggy. She is driven on to the stage and steps on to a podium. The podium starts to rise. One metre, two, three – and soon she is ten metres higher than the stage.

The Big Kickabout takes itself seriously. Very. I feel like I am watching the opening ceremony of an international gala. Before the girls come on a soprano from the city's phil-harmonic orchestra sings the national anthem. She is accom-panied by a rifle-wielding military escort. An acrobatic dance troupe warms up the crowd. Then the sky explodes with fireworks.

Like orderly schoolgirls out on a country stroll the beauty queens file on to the stage. They walk at a brisk pace, at arm's length apart, coquettishly flicking their hair back when it gets in their way. The crowd is cheering, lighting flares and waving coloured balloons. There are so many girls that there is no time to dawdle or pose. They walk down the catwalk, turn back and then exit. Football shirts have never looked so appealing. It is like a conveyor belt of adolescent fantasy. The parade seems endless. Have you ever seen 522 beauty queens in a row before? Actually, there were only 521. Armandão Maringa Junior, a team of evangelical Christians, refused to allow their queen to wear a bikini. She was exempted on religious grounds.

Once the girls have all been on and off they are allowed back on to dance. Music plays on the sound system as the queens fill the catwalk. Later, a samba band performs. The ceremony turns into a big concert. The tournament is declared officially open, but as yet no ball has been kicked.

The match was being played near a road. A driver passing by lost control of his Beetle and the car went straight on to the pitch. At that very moment the right winger of one of the teams was running directly to the goal. Because his head was down he did not see the approaching vehicle and they went slap-bang into each other. There was a huge crunching sound. His team-mates ran to see whether their colleague was hurt. But to everyone's amazement he wasn't even scratched. In fact, he was so tough the car bonnet was dented. The driver wanted to charge the winger for repair costs! 'This is the first case of a pedestrian running over a car,' joked one of the crowd.

After the opening ceremony there is a seven-day wait until the first weekend of matches. The interim gives me the opportunity to meet Arnaldo Santos, the Big Kickabout coordinator. Arnaldo is a football commentator and has the corresponding syrupy timbre. He is wearing a silky patterned shirt and sitting in his office in Manaus's Olympic sports complex. 'The Big Kickabout is not just about emotion,' he begins. 'It's about *commotion*.' It sounds like a radio jingle and I suspect he has said the phrase many times before.

Now his voice has warmed up he carries on, increasing his speed and professional breathlessness. 'In the first year I ran the competition, the first day was a nightmare. No doubt about it. I've never had a day like that in my life. At 5am a footballer was killed at the bus stop on his way to a game. At 9am a supporter died of a heart attack. In one game both goalkeepers received fractures – one in the collarbone, the other in the rib. There were another four cases of broken legs. Oh my God, I said to myself, how can all this happen at once?'

Arnaldo, as expected, answers himself. It happens because of the numbers involved. He assures me that the Big Kickabout is the largest football tournament in the world. Confirmation, he knows, will only come with a mention in the *Guinness Book of Records*. So he is detailing every statistic. On his desk is a bound and hardbacked annual report, which has a list of all of last year's 1,330 games. The figures are impressive. About 13,000 footballers from Manaus take part. On the opening weekend, 254 matches take place on 40 different pitches. Anyone can enter, which is why it is such a colourful, unpredictable event.

The competition's premise is delightfully self-contradictory. A 'pelada', which I have translated as *kickabout*, is the type of disorganised, improvised football that Brazilians play wherever they have space – on beaches, street corners and open fields. Peladas use anything as a ball, the players are often barefoot and the pitches are usually precarious. Brazilians romanticise their pelada culture as the reason for their dazzling-ball control skills. The Peladão, or *Big Kickabout*, is an attempt to formalise the inherently informal.

'The idea is to keep the games as close to the spirit of peladas as possible,' says Arnaldo. Only one of the pitches has any grass, and few have any markings. 'We have kept the rules to a minimum. For example, there's no offside. Throw-ins can be taken with your feet. And penalties are taken at fifteen paces.'

Arnaldo, who is sixty-two, exudes a seriousness that is accentuated by a distinguished mole above his lip. He has run the Big Kickabout, now in its twenty-eighth year, since 1998. He shows me a thirty-two-page rulebook that includes a disciplinary code with 204 articles. I quickly skim the beginning. Section 1, article 1, reads like a communist manifesto. 'The Big Kickabout has as its aims the social integration of the people through sport, encouraging and bringing to the fore the courage and beauty of Amazonian youth.' Later, on closer reading, I discover paragraphs on the procedure for tropical storms, the punishment for not giving the ball back at the end of games and that queens risk declassification if they wear tinted contact lenses or G-string underwear.

In fact, certain people *are* forbidden from taking part: professional footballers and those who have fallen foul of the disciplinary code. Violence is a problem. Referees have been chased up trees, threatened with knives and attacked by dogs. Already, before the tournament has started, the list of Athletes Banned For Ever includes ninety-three names.

For the tournament to function properly, Arnaldo has developed a formidable organisational structure. All participants have to submit two passport photos and a photocopy of their ID cards. Five staff work full-time processing the information and organising the fixture list. He has also formed a tribunal to judge complaints, made up of eleven lawyers. They have their work cut out. Usually the Kickabout final is delayed by several weeks because of litigation by teams who allege they were unfairly eliminated.

The tournament has the form of the World Cup. It starts with group stages and then becomes a knockout competition. The winning team's prize is £5,000. The Kickabout Queen wins a brand-new car.

We move on to talk about the beauty pageant. All 522 candidates for queen are given a screen test. They must all turn up at the local TV station. Arnaldo mimes what the camera does: 'It starts on the face and then goes down her body to her toes. She turns around and the camera rises up her back. Then we do a close-up. We can do about a hundred girls an hour.'

Each candidate also has her picture taken and sticks it on a detailed form with precise body measurements, hair and eye colour. Arnaldo then takes all the videos back to his house and chooses the best 120, who qualify for the second round.

'We have a standard. The girls have to be beautiful and curvaceous. You see, if we just judged on legs it would be impossible to choose. A characteristic of the girls round here is that they have great legs and bums. Things start to get complicated above the waist.'

The twenty-eight rules of the beauty pageant do not exclude anyone from participating. This year, contestants range from twelve to twenty-eight years old. About forty are mothers, fifty are competing for the second time and twenty-three have already modelled professionally. One is a stripper. Her team were so awed by her performance in Manaus's red-light area that they invited her to be their queen. I think she is the most authentic candidate. In an unfortunate double entendre, the word 'pelada' is also the Portuguese word for 'stark naked'.

The male and female events run concurrently. The first phase of the football tournament has teams arranged in groups of four or three, with the top two qualifying for the next round. The beauty pageant is divided into eight heats of fifteen queens, which are broadcast on local television.

Both competitions carry on side by side. But they are not independent. Far from it. The most idiosyncratic feature of the Big Kickabout – and it was a tough call – is that if your football team gets knocked out, then your queen can have you reinstated.

'This is the way it works,' says Arnaldo. 'The sixteen queens that make it to the last round qualify their teams for a parallel football tournament. The winner of the parallel tournament gets a bye to the Big Kickabout quarter-final. It's really worth having an attractive queen. Look, in 1998 Arsenal were eliminated but got a second chance because they had a winning queen. Arsenal ended up Kickabout champions.'

Manaus, during the end of the nineteenth century and the beginning of the twentieth, was turned by the exportation of rubber into one of the most prosperous cities in the world. The building that best symbolises the era is a neo-classical opera house that was built with iron from Scotland, stone from Italy and tiles from France. A block from the opera house is a two-storey office the Big Kickabout uses as its administrative headquarters. I visit on the morning that the local newspaper prints a list of the girls selected for the second round.

I see my first commotion. A man is shouting and cursing at the administrative staff. He is an Arsenal player. Lady Roberta, his queen, was not on the list. 'This is an outrage. There are girls who qualified who are the size of little potatoes – ours is *tall*. We have never been eliminated in the first round before.'

I ask for Arnaldo and am directed to a back room. He looks nothing like the smooth executive that I met before. He is tired and stressed. There are bags under his eyes. His shirt buttons are almost all undone. He is sat surrounded by pictures of hundreds of queens in swimsuits.

He is going through them one by one, making the final selection. He says he has been up all night watching the videos. 'I can't bear it any longer. We have only chosen 105 so far. I have seen so many that I can't tell the difference between them any more.'

I ask what happened to Lady Roberta? It was a mistake. She had qualified but the fax to the newspaper got jammed. Anyway, he is impatient with people's complaints.

The pressure has put him in a temper: 'People don't realise the work that this involves. It's not a game. It's very organised. Professional football in the state is not as organised as we are.'

Arnaldo, almost shouting now, says that he has just struck a team off today because he discovered it did not bring a queen to the opening ceremony and the excuse was not good enough.

'My decision is final. Last year I banned a candidate because she took her bikini top off when the newspaper photographer asked her. Candidates *have* to have good posture.

'It was a shame – she was an attractive girl.'

He launches on an emotive and self-justificatory defence of the Big Kickabout.

'The tournament is an escape valve. It suffocates social disorder.' His forehead is pumping.

'What sustains this country is the fact that it has football. Football is the shout that comes from the depths of those who hardly live, of people who aren't sure where their next meal will come from. The jubilation of scoring a goal renews the soul.'

When the player arrived the game had already started. He signed the forms and went straight on. The first time he touched the ball he dribbled half the team and scored a goal. Then he ran off into the jungle. No one understood why. Minutes later the police arrived and his haste was immediately explained.

Vila Nova are from São Francisco, a typical working-class neighbourhood of Manaus. Most of the homes are made of wooden planks. The streets have recently been asphalted. There is a mild smell of sewage. You can see that urbanisation is a constant battle against the forces of nature – where residents have not cleared space, thick vegetation grows.

Audemir is a quiet and industrious man. He has a messy

black fringe that almost brushes against his eyebrows. We are sitting with his friends at the local bar, Novo Encontro, which is a simple wooden shack with a big fridge of beer.

'This is where it all began,' he says. 'We realised our area didn't have a team in the Big Kickabout. We thought it should, so we founded one ourselves.'

The Amazon has long attracted migrants seeking fortune. Many ended up in Manaus, the rainforest's largest inland urban centre. It is a city of hope. Novo Encontro means *New Encounter*. Vila Nova means *New Villa*. Audemir chose the name – copied from a professional club in central Brazil – because it chimes with the pervading atmosphere of starting afresh.

Using the official terminology that is *de rigueur* for Kickabout start-ups, Audemir appointed himself Vila Nova's president. He named Maurício Lima, his brother-in-law, vice-president and another brother director of sport. Four other brothers-in-law were involved in the team, which debuted in 1998.

The club is now the focus of community life. 'São Francisco used to be divided into little groups,' says Mauricio. 'People didn't mix. When the team started to play well, everyone got together. We started out with a hundred fans, mostly family, and this reached three hundred at the end.'

It has turned mild-mannered Audemir, who is a bar waiter, into a local celebrity. This year he managed to assemble a squad of twenty-six players. He has also changed the name of the club abbreviations from FC to the much more modern-sounding AA, or Associação Atlética, *Athletical Association*. Vila Nova may be small but its self-image is optimistic and grandiose.

The Big Kickabout's bureaucracy is time-consuming and potentially costly. Audemir spends much of his free time registering players, organising kit and trying to raise money. He has with him a leather file with the details of all his players and letters asking for sponsorship.

And Vila Nova's queen? When the club was starting out, Audemir, again, relied on family. In 1998 it was his niece and in 1999 it was his sister. Neither made it past the first round. Audemir did not expect any different; he had chosen for convenience rather than beauty. Better an ugly queen than no queen at all. This year, the team's local popularity has meant that he has been able to choose a much more glamorous candidate. Erica dos Santos is a local belle; she was spotted taking part in the neighbourhood's folk-dancing festivities.

Not every club in the Big Kickabout is tied, like Vila Nova, to a particular neighbourhood. Because the tournament is free and open to anyone, clubs are formed around a myriad of social circles. A firm of beefy security guards, immigrants from the same jungle village, and a rock band all have their separate teams.

Another, Barra Pesada FC, are overweight. Three months ago one of their players had a heart attack during a game. 'We won the game but we almost lost a friend,' says team member Fernando de Abreu. He knows the team's chances of winning the beauty pageant are slim. 'Our queen – she couldn't be otherwise – is the fattest in the contest.'

I cannot imagine that any other football competition more accurately reflects its surrounding society than the Big Kickabout. The competition *is* the surrounding society. The 13,000 footballers come from all parts of Amazon life. The Big Kickabout is Manaus, in all its wild, sexy, lawless, sprawling enormity.

The team's names are colourful too. As well as Arsenal, there is a team called Manchester. 'We chose it because it's a beautiful name,' says the club president, 'and because we have no money.' Aston Vila, Ajax, Barcelona and Real Madrid are recognisable doppelgangers. El Cabaço Futebol Clube, meaning *Hymen FC*, is an example of the local sense of humour. Colonel Kurtz, if he had been staked out in the Amazon, would surely support Apocalipse Clube.

A day after spending time with Vila Nova I visit a team

at the other end of the financial scale. Unidos da Glória, or *Glória United*, has the set-up of a professional club. It is based in Glória, a traditional neighbourhood of Manaus. The team is sponsored by the Amazon's largest flour company, which means it can pay for a squad of twenty-two players, a proper coach, good quality equipment, transport and a decent amount of beer for afterwards. Glória's 'wardrobe assistant', Fernando Salles, is paid to keep three footballs and the twenty-two sets of socks, boots and shorts in the three-room hut where he lives with thirteen family members.

On the afternoon I arrive there is a barbecue to commemorate the club's eleventh birthday. About two hundred people have turned up. Three large speakers are balanced precariously on each other, blaring out music sung by a man playing a Yamaha organ. The noise makes it impossible to talk.

The power behind Unidos da Glória is Américo Loureiro. He has a stubby nose, thick eyebrows and a necklace with a blue image of the Virgin Mary hanging on his hairy chest. Américo worked in a wood factory for thirty-six years, and was a union leader for twenty-five.

We walk down the street so as to be able to hear ourselves. 'Unidos da Glória are the passion of the neighbourhood. We have more fans than anyone else,' he says. This year he is trying to make up for a poor showing in 1999. 'Last year we waited a long time to look for players. By the time we got round to it, all the best players had already been contracted by other teams.'

He has also put particular thought into Glória's queen. He invited last year's runner-up, Samantha Simões. 'We made her a proposal. It's hard for a girl to refuse. It's like a footballer being asked to play for Flamengo.'

The Amazon is a place of fable and legend, partly because of the influence of indigenous oral Indian culture, and the Big Kickabout has developed a mythical history of its own. This has been helped by raconteurs like Américo who, having been involved in the event since its inception, never miss an opportunity to embellish an anecdote. Usually involving himself. Only the stories don't always have a time or place and the characters don't always have names.

Originally Américo was involved in a team called JAP. He tells me that once there was a side called São José. They were from upstate and invincible in their region. One year they decided to play in the Big Kickabout. They came to Manaus and demanded to be in the same group as JAP. Américo cackles: 'After twenty minutes we were 24–nil up. Even our goalkeeper scored.'

As we are talking Messias Sampaio turns up. His appearance is unexpected good fortune, since I was already planning to speak to him. Messias invented the Big Kickabout in 1973, when he was working as a journalist. Thanks to its prestige he launched a successful political career. He is now leader of the city council.

Messias is here to show solidarity with Glória and Américo, whom he employs as a political aide. He is immensely personable and we sit down on small plastic stools. He has wispy hair, bad teeth and talks eloquently, with a politician's sense of patience and timing.

Manaus's *belle époque* only lasted until an Englishman took the rubber plant to Asia, where it could be cultivated more efficiently. The city then endured half a century of collapse until it flourished for a second time – as the site of the world's most unlikely industrial park. In 1967 Brazil passed a law giving tax breaks to build factories in Manaus. It was, together with projects like the Trans-Amazon Highway, part of the military government's policy to 'colonise' the rainforest. The inducement worked, and the city changed from being a depressed backwater to Brazil's main producer of light electronic goods. (Despite obvious logistical problems, such as the lack of a road or rail link to the south of the country.) The population boomed from 300,000 in 1970 to 1.4 million at the end of the century.

'A huge amount of young people came to Manaus looking for work in the early 1970s,' says Messias. 'But there was an enormous lack of leisure facilities.' Messias was asked by his employers, the local media group Rede Calderaro de Comunicação, to come up with a large promotional event in which the public could participate. An amateur football tournament was the ideal solution. Brazil had won the World Cup for the third time, cementing football's place as the people's passion. Yet Manaus did not have a strong professional scene. The few professional clubs played in the nationally irrelevant Amazonas state league. Messias sensed a demand for competitive football.

He sensed right. The first Kickabout had 188 teams. The second 286 and by the third the number was more than 500. It grew in parallel with the industrial park and the tournament rapidly embedded itself in the fabric of the city. Even though it is still funded by Rede Calderaro – at an annual cost of £200,000 – it is a local institution.

The Kickabout was embraced so enthusiastically because every Brazilian, so the saying goes, sees himself as a footballer. In the Big Kickabout, everyone *can* be a footballer. I think the tournament became enormous for other reasons too. Manaus is so remote and disconnected from Brazil's centres of power that its residents, like English expats on the Spanish coast, feel a need to overexaggerate national characteristics.

After the first Big Kickabout Messias pondered how he could involve women in the event. 'I remembered that there were many female football fans. In fact, there were many *beautiful* female fans. So we wondered how we could mesh these two things.' As he says this he puts his hands together so his fingers link.

'Women's football didn't exist at the time. So in the second year I insisted that every team present a queen. It was a complete success because it characterises the two things that Brazilians like best – football and women.'

For several years the opening ceremony was held in

Manaus's main avenue. Queens paraded on floats, as if it was a fully-blown carnival procession. Messias boasts: 'The Kickabout's beauty pageant is so popular now it's more important than Miss Amazonia!'

The introduction of a beauty contest needs to be understood in a regional context. The Amazon hardly has an event that doesn't include an ambassadorial role for attractive young women. The carnival has its queen, as do the festival days of saints Peter, Anthony and John in June. And each rainforest municipality has a queen tied to its principal agricultural product. Coari has a banana queen, Maués has a guaraná queen, and so on for oranges in Anori, milk in Autazes, açaí in Codajás and cupuaçu in Presidente Figueiredo. It seems only natural that football has one too.

I ask Messias why he decided to let the teams with the prettiest women back into the football competition?

'I did this to make people invest more in their queens, so they took that part seriously. But there was another reason too. Just say that a team is very good and they lose because the referee makes a mistake. The tendency in such cases is to go and beat him up. Football deals in passionate feelings and referees don't have bodyguards. But if the team knows that they might not be knocked out because they still have a queen then they are less likely to turn violent. The queens act like a tranquilliser.'

Messias believes that the strength of the Big Kickabout is that it lets people at the bottom of the social scale act as if they are at the top. To be president of a football team is a mark of respectability. In a society marked by inequalities, the tournament promotes equality. No matter how humble they are, teams mirror the structure of professional clubs. Nine out of ten, for example, have their own coaches. Messias believes, also, that because the rules are so egalitarian it mobilises every section of society. 'Criminality goes down during match days,' he adds 'because everyone is involved.'

We chat about why the competition became so enormous.

Messias believes that Manaus has the most football-obsessed people in Brazil. 'People here have so many obstacles. The dirt pitches, the heat, the rain. And the more obstacles you put up the more the people fight to overcome them.'

Imagine the scene. The procession of the queens was still held in the city centre. The public packed the avenue to see the pretty brunettes pass by. Everything was going perfectly when a beautiful girl started to catch everyone's eye. From what was said she was truly spectacular. Tall and slender like a doll. She did not walk – she glided. From her pointed high heels she looked down on everyone around her. Other contenders were already considering sabotage. 'How about breaking one of her high heels?' thought one machiavellian mind. Suddenly, someone shouted: 'She's not a woman!' Eek! I wonder how many guys were already fantasising erotic thoughts?

Nei Rezende invites me to his family home, which is a wooden hut on stilts. Outside, his father swings gently in a hammock. A black dog is tied to a chain and fast asleep. I climb the steps inside and stand on the uneven floor. I can see it is a sporting household. By one wall is a set of shelves cluttered with medals and trophies. Behind them are posters of football teams and glamour models. The two things that Brazilians like best.

Nei is a Big Kickabout pro. He could have joined one of Manaus's professional clubs, but he turned them down because he earns more playing in the 'amateur' competition. He was signed up for £500, a mobile phone, twenty sacks of cement and 2,000 bricks to build a house. As a professional he would be earning the minimum wage, which is £50 a month. In 1988, the last year for which figures are available, thirty people applied to the Amazonas Football Federation to have their professional status revoked so they could play in the Big Kickabout.

Many of the richest teams are connected to local busi-
nesses. Nei says that some of his friends play for these teams
in exchange for a full-time job. The Big Kickabout, they
realise, offers a more secure future than a career as a professional player.

The Big Kickabout is the best way to make a name for
yourself in Amazonas football. Manaus has more than sixty
neighbourhood leagues. 'All through the year, the main
teams have scouts at the local championships,' says Nei. 'If
anyone stands out they get his telephone number and sign
them up.' It turns the tournament into a shop window of
new players. França, the Big Kickabout's most illustrious
alumnus, reached the national team. França headed the
equaliser in a 1–1 draw against England at Wembley in
May 2000.

Nei hopes that the tournament will launch him too. 'I
stopped studying at primary school. Football is the only
thing I know how to do. My aim this year is to make a
name for myself in the Big Kickabout.'

Manaus has eight professional clubs. Only two, which
play in the national second division, can afford to pay more
than the minimum wage. The rest survive on nothing. To
understand their penury, I visit América FC.

América is based in a garden shed.

The shed is situated across Amadeu Teixeira's patio.
Amadeu, now well into his seventies, is a distinguished-
looking gentleman. He has a narrow, withered face with
sunken blue eyes and slicked back hair. When he
pronounces 'América' it sounds like 'Omega' because he
has no teeth.

He leads me into the team 'headquarters'. It is crowded
with medals, trophies, pictures and sports kits. There is a
banner on the wall that says: 'Amadeu Teixeira: A Football
Legend'. I do not disagree. Football coaches in Brazil are
considered lucky if they last a season. Amadeu was made
coach in 1956. He still is. I would wager that he is the
longest-serving football coach in the world.

América's largest trophy is taller than Amadeu himself. It has three tiers: a model of a footballer stands on what looks like a giant cocktail shaker, which stands on a metal platform supported by four columns. He tells me it is for América's greatest triumph: the 1994 Amazonas state championship. Amadeu won his first, and only, state title after thirty-eight years of trying.

'Continuity is the key,' he mumbles.

Amadeu's longevity seems all the more remarkable considering the lawlessness of Amazonas professional football. Lesser men would have given up decades ago.

'We should have won the state championship several times before,' he claims. 'In the 1970s we played Nacional in the final. Nacional's president was also the state governor. He stood at the side of the pitch shouting to the referee to tell him to red card our players. From what I recall we had two players sent off.

'In another year we played the final against Rodoviária. We were winning when all of a sudden the lights went off. No one knew how to switch them back on. Can you believe that? So a rematch was arranged, which we lost.'

Using a piece of paper to represent a pitch he uses his finger to trace where the ball went when América were in the 1988 final with Rio Negro. 'One of our players kicked the ball into the box. One of their players jumped to head the ball but it bounced in the wrong way into the goal. The linesman ran to the ref and made something up. The goal was then cancelled. The referee was a famous guy who had flown up from Rio especially. Everyone knew that he had lunch with Rio Negro and sat at the table with the president and the players.'

Amadeu was a thirteen-year-old boy when he founded América with his schoolfriends. This is one aspect of his career, however, which is not out of the ordinary. Botafogo of Rio, for example, was founded by fourteen-year-olds. Amadeu had a career as an administrator in the mayor's office, but devoted his spare time to the club. He developed youth teams and even tried out other sports, like cycling, volleyball and basketball.

One day in the 1960s he saw a girl playing football in the street. She was nicknamed Pelé and was as good a dribbler as the boys. It inspired him to develop the idea. He found enough girls to form two teams. But during a training session a legal official turned up. News of his innovation had reached Brasília. The Minister of Education was sending him a message: women playing football was forbidden by law.

Amadeu shows me a newspaper cutting from 1969. 'Up there in the Amazon there's women's football' reads the article, from a São Paulo newspaper, written as if nothing was more amusing and exotic. Four years later, far less controversially, a woman's place in Amazonian football became wearing a bikini and competing for Kickabout Queen.

As well as the professional state league, the Amazonas Football Federation organises the Copa dos Rios, the *Rivers Cup*. It is an amateur tournament between teams representing the state's municipalities. Since Amazonas is three times the size of France and the principal mode of transport is by boat, the competition is perhaps the best example of the lengths Brazilians will go to play football. Referees from Manaus will often spend weeks travelling up rivers to get to matches.

Municipalities invest heavily in the Rivers Cup because it is one of the only ways that distant and isolated communities socialise with each other. 'There is no other cultural activity that integrates the municipalities like the Rivers Cup. It is the only event that really brings them together,' I am told by Fernando Seabra, a manager of the Amazonas Association of Municipalities.

This is not entirely true. The Big Kickabout also involves teams from the remote rainforest. In 2000, ten Amazonas municipalities will have their own kickabout championships (with queens, of course). They will take place in villages and towns stretching to 350 miles from Manaus. The winners of the upstate tournaments play-off for a place in the Big Kickabout's final rounds. If you include all the affiliated competitions, total participation in the Big Kickabout doubles. In 1995, it reached some 30,000 footballers.

The score was getting humiliating. On the goal that made it 4–0 a supporter of the losing team ran on to the pitch wanting to savage the ref. Francisco was on the verge of cuffing the official when, faster than a ray of sunlight, Eurico entered the scene. Eurico was the central defender and as big and tough as a bouncer. Francisco suddenly recoiled. He was not stupid. He kneeled on the ground and pleaded with the ref to save his skin. They all struck a deal. Francisco was a cab driver. He agreed to give the ref a lift home. Two decades later Francisco still drives a cab. Whenever he passes the ref he always stops and offers him a lift. Everyone thinks he's still scared of Eurico.

Amazonas, despite being the second-least densely populated state in Brazil, is paradoxically one of the most urban. Half of its population lives in Manaus. Demographically, it is like an overpopulated island surrounded by an almost empty sea. When I take a taxi to an outlying neighbourhood, where the city is pushing into the rainforest, I am astonished by the monotony that I see from my window. We could be in any poor city in Latin America. For most of its citizens, the Amazon is urban *brown*, not a lush equatorial green.

At 7am, after an hour's drive, my taxi pulls up outside House 16, Street 8, Block 13. It is a small lot of land with a tiny hut, where Paulinho Jorge de Moraes lives with his pet cat. Inside, yellowing posters of Rio de Janeiro football teams are stuck on the walls. Paulinho is the only man to have been part of the Big Kickabout organising committee every year since 1973. When I arrive he is already in his ref's outfit. He has a smile of gold-capped teeth and is wearing gold bracelets, a gold signet ring and chains of gold necklaces with lucky charms. He would not look out of place in a pub in the North East of England.

If one man best symbolises the fantastical nature of the Big Kickabout, then it is Paulinho. His friends advise to discount 30 per cent of what he says as wild fantasy. He claims to be 5ft tall. It is an opportunistic overestimate.

Perhaps the only statement concerning Paulinho that is *not* an exaggeration is that the Big Kickabout has defined his life. It has empowered him with a self-respect and city-wide prestige that would have been otherwise unimaginable.

'Ever since I was *really* small I always wanted to be a referee. My mum was always against it because she thought I would get beat up too much, but with time she got used to it,' says Paulinho, who is fifty-two years old. 'When you are a referee what is important is not size. What is important is an understanding of the rules.'

Paulinho is a fearless disciplinarian. In twenty-seven years of Big Kickabouts he claims to have sent off 5,982 players. I sense that he is less a referee than a one-man war against the regular-sized. 'Normally I'll send off between eighteen and twenty players a weekend. It's much more common for me to send someone off than not.' Everyone needs to be careful when Paulinho is on the pitch. Once, an angry supporter called him 'Bar of Motel Soap' for being bijou and perfectly formed. 'I showed her the red card,' he snaps.

I ask if he has ever suffered violence. Paulinho tells me he has been chased off the pitch by a woman with a broom and given eight stitches when a player punched him in the head. 'The police found him and took him to me and asked me to beat him up,' he adds. 'Now he is one of my best mates.' Another time he sent off a man who was as 'big as a monkey'. The man had to be restrained from invading the pitch and retaliating. But when, that evening, they bumped into each other in a bar they shook hands. Paulinho says: 'He invited me to a brothel, paid for drinks and women to come to my table. It's these memories that makes the Kickabout such a beautiful event.'

Studded boots do not come in sizes small enough so Paulinho wears trainers with his yellow ref's outfit. Everything in his house is petite; instead of a fridge he has a minibar. 'I would like to be buried with my ref's uniform on, with a yellow card in one pocket and a red card in the other,' he says, patting his chest.

I give Paulinho a lift in my taxi as we drive back into town. It is the first Sunday of the competition and 136 games are to be played on forty pitches between 8am and sundown. Paulinho directs the driver to pass several pitches where Kickabout games are taking place. In fact, wherever there is a set of goalposts there is a match underway. Manuas may be surrounded by equatorial jungle, yet all the pitches are dusty rectangles of ochre earth. I see pitches covered in stones, glass and even bones.

Paulinho is not refereeing today. In its initial stages, the Big Kickabout is self-regulated. Each team must supply four officials – a referee, two linesmen and an administrator – whom are then selected to look after games involving other sides. It is in the team's interests to take this seriously since the team is penalised if its refereeing committee does not show up.

I stop off at one pitch to see the procedure all the way through. First to arrive are the officials. The referee has brought the ball, a whistle and a red and yellow card. The two linesmen have their flags, which are made from a beige cloth nailed to a wooden stick. (Once, a referee left the red card at home and improvised with a cigarette packet.) The fourth official sets up a makeshift desk in the shade. He has a piece of paper that he picked up at the Kickabout Headquarters on which to write his report of the game.

A minivan turns up and the first team spills out. I am consistently impressed by how conscientiously the bureaucracy is taken. The president lines up all the shirts on a fence and distributes them to his players. The president, equipped with the team's personalised Kickabout ID cards, then makes sure that each player signs the referee's piece of paper.

The game starts on time. The referee does his job well. He is neither partial nor does he, as is once said to have happened, stop the game so he can relieve his bowels. To encourage good refereeing, in fact, the Big Kickabout provides a parallel competition for teams of the sixteen best referees. The winner of this tournament enters a three-way play-off with the winner of the best sixteen queens' teams and the upstate champion. The overall winner then wins a bye into the Big Kickabout's last sixteen.

After a morning of hopping from pitch to pitch I spend the afternoon with Vila Nova, who are playing their first game. I arrive at the muster point a few hours before kick-off. It is underneath an olive tree near Audemir's house. There is a bench made from a plank that bends when you sit on it. About ten people are milling around.

The atmosphere is tense. Maurício Lima, Audemir's brother-in-law and Vila Nova's vice-president, explains that the preparations have been a disaster. He had designed a new strip. He has just picked them up from the printers, run by a friend. The sponsor's name, Delirium Drinks, is smudged badly on the chest. They will have to use last year's kit instead.

Delirium Drinks is the nightclub where Audemir works. The value of the sponsorship can be seen across the path from the olive tree: a big polystyrene ice-box containing two crates of beer.

News has come through that Erica, Vila Nova's queen, has not made it into the second round. Audemir is frustrated. 'I'm almost against the idea of having a queen,' he grumbles. 'It is just one more expense. We spend more money on our beauty queen than on our players. Teams with money can bankroll a pretty girl. Teams like us have to rely on the strength of our football.' He says the last sentence as if this is somehow unfair for a football competition.

An hour before the game the team walks the mile to the pitch. Friends join in as we pass neighbouring streets. The path follows a canal and then goes through a slum. Maurício says that it is controlled by drug dealers who forbid walking through it at night. It is a community on stilts. The slum is above a brook, which you can see between the wooden slats of the walkways. One of our convoy is singing and beating a drum hanging from around his neck. Vila Nova is the only club to have a gay supporters club, founded by Marcos, a local chef. Marcos and his friends are the *real* Kickabout Queens. They have made green pom-poms and are waving them as we go by.

When we reach the pitch, I recognise Audemir's maroon Ford. He is lifting a tank of water out of the boot. He rests it on a shoulder and carries it towards the touchline. I notice that Audemir, Maurício and the other brothers have a different type of green and white football strip than the players. It is to distinguish the players from the coaching staff. I ask Maurício if any of his family is *not* present. He replies: 'Just my dad. He gets too excited and ends up fighting with the ref.'

Vila Nova's opponents are Unidos da Rua Natal, or *Natal Street United*. Audemir is visibly nervous. Before the kick-off the team puts their arms round each other in a circle. Audemir's voice is shaking for the team talk: 'The symbol of our team is an eagle. It stands for guts, courage, strength, willpower. Remember – there's no such thing as a lost ball.' They recite the Lord's Prayer. To finish they put all their hands together in the centre of the circle and shout: 'Vila Nova!'

The match begins. Vila Nova dominate but the opposition is tougher than expected. Both teams are disciplined. Neither has an obvious weak spot. A Vila Nova player falls and injures his leg. Two of the coaching staff run on with some ice.

The first half ends goalless after twenty-five minutes, as the regulations specify for the first two rounds.

I had heard so many fanciful tales and romantic anecdotes about the Big Kickabout that I had almost begun to doubt them. But a magical-realist script unfolds in front of

my eyes. With ten minutes to go I hear the gay supporters
start to scream. A Vila Nova player has turned up late from
work. He is very good-looking and, before he has entered
the pitch, the supporters are jumping up and down. They
cheer him on: 'Go, sexy! Go!'

The late arrival has no shoes. But he tells Audemir that
he only knows how to play barefoot. He runs on to the
pitch and takes a position in central midfield. Each time he
touches the ball Vila Nova's fans yelp excitedly. His presence changes the balance of play. Vila Nova push forward
constantly. They win several corners. Minutes later the
hunky substitute scores.

Vila Nova win 1–0.

'Great result lads,' says Audemir, shaking everyone's hand
as they walk off. 'For our debut game we did really well.'

Afterwards, the team goes back to Vila Nova's olive tree
for the 'barge', the name given to the obligatory post-match
party. The gay supporters volunteer to be waitresses. They
open the beer bottles and make sure everyone's glass is full.
In the humid night heat the whole neighbourhood is out
celebrating. 'Football is the beginning of everything,' argues
Maurício Lima. 'The rest comes afterwards.'

*The referee caught sight of a treacherous kick and,
without blinking, blew his whistle. Foul. Or maybe
penalty? Well, that's just a detail. The important thing
is that all the players advanced on the ref hungry for
blood. But Manuel wasn't stupid. He had come
prepared. Under his uniform he had concealed a
revolver. With his hand on the gun he threatened to
shoot. 'Who's got enough guts now?' he roared, with
flames coming out of his nostrils. It turned into a
desperate scramble. Players fell over, stumbling on each
other in the mad confusion. It was such a tumult that
no one paid attention to one little detail. His weapon
was a bluff. It was just a little toy, the sort you can
buy for 50p.*

Front-page news: Pretty women and football

I leave Manaus the following day, but am able to keep up with the competition back in Rio. Twice a week *A Crítica*, the Manaus daily, publishes a sixteen-page supplement which I reserve at my local 'international' newspaper shop. (This is not so silly; Manaus is further from Rio than Argentina, Uruguay, Paraguay, Bolivia, Chile and Peru.) The supplement is pure testosterone. On half of its pages is football. On the other are pictures of sexy girls. Over the coming months I read that Vila Nova pass through both group stages without losing a game. They are defeated 3–1 by Central

Park St Antonio in their first game in the knockout round, when there were only forty-five teams left. The Big Kickabout is eventually won by 3B Suprishop, a team run by the owner of an electrical goods superstore of the same name. Samantha Simões of Glória United wins the Kickabout Queen final, which is broadcast on live TV. Lady Roberta, of Arsenal, does not pass her second-round heat.

Chapter Twelve

A GAME OF TWO HEMISPHERES

It is commonly known that the Amazon rainforest shelters many endangered species. Less publicised is that it also harbours one of the world's last remaining pockets of 1980s British electropop. I make this gratifying discovery shortly after I land in Macapá, the sleepy capital of Amapá state. A taxi takes me to the 'best nightclub in town'. The door of Site 500 leads straight on to the dancefloor, which is crammed with a dolled-up young crowd dancing to the Pet Shop Boys and the Human League.

Overcome by nostalgia, I start dancing, even though, at thirty-one, I feel the oldest by about ten years. Apart from a short bald man dancing with a circle of pretty girls. He looks about forty-five and is very English. His complexion is freckly and fair, with a nose almost vertically coming down from his forehead and a tiny mouth. Were it not for the loud music I would have made conversation. Instead, we exchange complicit glances. He slaps my shoulder cordially. I wonder how an Englishman could have ended up in Amapá, which has no tourist industry, or, in fact, any real industry at all. With just 440,000 inhabitants Amapá is the second-least populated state in Brazil, geographically a diamond-shaped extension of the Guyanas, with 90 per cent covered in jungle and no road connection out. I dance for an hour and leave.

I have come to Amapá to visit a football stadium bisected

by the equator. Since the 1970s – when the dictatorship built enormous concrete stadia in Brazil's major cities – the augmentative suffix '-ão', meaning 'big', became a stylistic necessity in naming football grounds. *Zerão*, or Big Zero, is the most poetic. As well as being mildly self-contradictory – how can you have the augmentative of nothing? – it is wonderfully evocative of its location. Zero stands for the line of zero latitude, but it could equally describe what goes on in Amapá. With a name that sounds like a euphemism for the cosmic void, where better to build Big Zero than Nowhere Central, a piece of jungle at the end of the world?

Brazilians are stereotyped for their expressive attitudes towards sex and football. With good reason. What did Britain do on the Greenwich Meridian? It built an observatory, flagging its longitudinal privilege with a global reminder of its punctuality. How did Brazil mark the line of zero latitude?

'It's a real turn-on fucking on the equator,' says José Archangelo, whom I meet two days later on the touchline of Big Zero. We are watching the final of the state championship's first phase. São José, from Macapá in the northern hemisphere, are playing Independente from Santana in the south. He carries on: 'Before the stadium was built there was nothing here – just a clearing in the rainforest and a 50m line of concrete. In those days me and my mates would drive out loads. We'd get pissed, sing songs on the guitar and shag girls.'

He starts thrusting his pelvis up and down, which wobbles his weighty belly. 'The girl would lie on the concrete line and have one leg in either hemisphere. It gave you a real turn-on to think you were fucking on the centre of the world.

'Man, I lost count of the times I did this. We couldn't have sex with virgins because those days if you had sex with a virgin you had to marry her. So we took our maids or picked up girls from brothels. If we couldn't find any we'd use the equator in other ways. We'd get our dicks out and run along it to see who's line of piss went the furthest.'

José is interrupted because a São José player has been hurt. He is the team medic and he scuttles on to the pitch.

Alain Delon
French Actor

Allann Delon
Brazilian Footballer

separated at birth

Mauro Shampoo

Football Player, Hairdresser and Man

Av. Cons. Aguiar, 1880-Lj. 21-Boa Viagem-Recife-PE
Brasil

our fathers

Top: Ministers of the Kuwaiti government stand behind the Kuwaiti national team. Father Santana, masseur and spiritual playboy, is second from the left sitting in the front row. Bottom: São Caetano players César (100 per cent Jesus), Claudecir (God is True), Adhemar (Thank you Jesus) and Wagner (ditto) genuflect after one more goal.

all saints

Top: Wax throats, hands, bladders, breasts (single and double), necks and other limbs on sale at the National Shrine. Middle: Posters of football teams in the Shrine's Room of Miracles. Bottom right: A staff member in the Room of Miracles with donated shirts. Bottom left: Sergeant Maia brandishes his son's 'Impassioned Fan Diploma' issued by the Supreme Court of Corinthian Faithful.

belles of the ball

Top: Beauty queens in their team shirts parade at the opening of the Big Kickabout. Middle: Erica dos Santos models Vila Nova's kit, at home with her mother. Bottom: Lady Roberta, Arsenal's muse, waits backstage with 500 other BK contestants.

red devil

Left: Paulinho Jorge de Moraes, at home with his pet cat, makes the gesture for which he is best known. He has sent off almost 6,000 players in three decades of the Big Kickabout. Below: Vila Nova's gay fan club livens up the wooden shanties on the way to their opening game.

are you experienced?

In 1956 the Soviets put down the Hungarian Uprising, Nasser nationalised the Suez canal and Amadeu Teixeira was made coach of América - a position he holds until today.

a river runs through it

A footmud pitch in the Amazon, off the Macapá esplanade. Near right: A footmud goalkeeper during low tide. Far right: Valdez Almeida's feet.

Carnaval 2001
AS GATINHAS
NUAS DO
SAMBÓDROMO

Intertaras
O SEXO
VIA
INTERNET

Harley-Davidson
PAIXÃO
SOBRE
RODAS

Homem ideal
ELAS
QUEREM É
UM MACHO

A musa
da CPI do
futebol **Renata
Alves** sem cam...
e sem meião

Nº 373 • FEVEREIRO DE 2001 • Revista mensal • Proibida a venda a menores de 18 anos • R$ 7,40

ISSN 0531-9153

9 770531 915005

eft: Renata Alves, football's whistle-blower turned soft-porn centrefold. Top right: Eurico Miranda
riously tries to clear the São Januário pitch. Behind him, the electronic scoreboard reads: 'Thank
ou fans for keeping calm.' (Overleaf: the moment the fencing collapsed.) Bottom right: Arnon de
Mello behind a picture of his father, President Fernando Collor de Mello, and his grandfather,
enator Arnon de Mello.

basic principles

Top: Sócrates, in 1982, urges Brazilians to exercise their rights and 'vote on the 15th'. Middle: The Doctor as he is today. Bottom: Mundica taps latex from a rubber tree, the first step in how to make your own football.

At Big Zero the equator marks the centre line. When the referee tosses the coin he asks the team captains: 'Which hemisphere would you like to start in?' The equator also bisects the one stand, on the west side of the pitch, slicing through the middle of seats, sparing nothing as it circumnavigates the globe. The stand is equipped with a bathroom at either end. If the match is dull, spectators can always spend their time checking that in each sink the water spirals down the plughole in opposite directions.

Fortunately, São José vs. Independente is anything but dull. The match is hard-fought; the referee's hand is never far from his yellow card. It is a symbolic battle between good and evil. In the northern hemisphere are sitting members of São José's supporters club, the 'Diabolic Fans', wearing T-shirts with cartoon devils. In the southern hemisphere, Independente's players have 'Jesus. Yesterday, Today and Forever' printed on the back of their shirts.

About 3,000 spectators fill the stand. Each team is cheered by a musical band. Fans hold transistor radios, listening to the commentary from local broadcasters sat a few metres behind. One Independente supporter has brought his lucky pair of bullhorns.

The stand is neatly painted in yellow and has a capacity of 5,000. From the top you feel like you are on the highest building for hundreds of miles. You can see the Amazon in the far distance, the rainforest canopy and how strikingly Macapá has expanded in recent years. Amapá is Brazil's fastest-growing state. Originally on Macapá's outskirts, Big Zero is now reached by suburbs of simple one-storey homes and asphalt roads. The sky is an ever-changing kaleidoscope of dramatic white, black and blue cloud formations.

Paid for by the Amapá state government, Big Zero was exactly the type of ostentatious project that Brazilian politicians love to fund. It was hoped that the stadium would be a reference point for the city, a potential tourist site and the stage of nationally important games in the years to come. Fernando Collor, the Brazilian president, was guest of honour at the inauguration in 1990. Zico and Paulo César Carpegiani led a side of nationally capped veterans against Amapá's team of seniors.

The stadium was the grandest construction in the state since the Portuguese built a riverside fort in an area which is now central Macapá. The fort, dating from 1782, is in good condition. I somehow doubt that Big Zero will be around in 220 years. The stadium is already a historic relic. It has already started to fall down.

Life in the Amazon is a constant battle against the elements – the heat, the rain and, during September, the wind. Big Zero was so badly planned for the climatic conditions that its roof blew off. The eight concrete roof supports were more sturdy, and they now stick nakedly in the air, as if showing the scoreboard: Nature 1, Big Zero 0, with only a few seconds on the clock.

Joaquim Neto, vice-president of the Amapá Football Federation, says that during September teams prefer to play in the northern hemisphere because of the vicious southerly wind. 'A footballer playing north–south once crossed the ball from a corner, and the strong wind pushed it in the net,' he says.

Joaquim is my guide. He is a gentle man with a white moustache, trusting eyes and an easygoing sense of humour. His day job is in the local government agricultural department. He also has a daily football show on Amapá television.

He tells me that Big Zero holds other surprises. He asks me to look carefully at the floodlights. I see immediately. They are *in front* of the stand. It doesn't matter where you sit, your view of the pitch is always partly obscured by the floodlight posts.

'This must be the only stadium in the world like this,' he says. Joaquim knows it's shameful, but he shrugs his shoulders and makes a feeble excuse. 'It was the first stadium the firm had ever done.'

I watch the second half sitting next to Joaquim and other federation dignitaries. We are sitting on a bench by the touchline. With a few minutes to go, Independente are leading 2–0.

Suddenly, I feel a hand cordially slap my shoulder. The sensation is immediately familiar. It is the middle-aged, English-looking man from the nightclub, dressed in a neat blue shirt. He has the same complicit grin. Before I have time to speak, Joaquim introduces us.

'Alex, meet Senator Sebastião Rocha.'

'Welcome to Amapá,' smiles the state's senior parliamentarian.

We shake hands. I remark, instantly, that I recognise him from the dancefloor.

'Oh yeah?' he replies. 'Site 500 is excellent. Have you been to the club Arena. That's cool too.'

'You must really like house music?' I ask, slightly baffled that a man who spends his weekdays in Brasília, more than 1,000 miles away, spends his weekends clubbing in Macapá.

'I love house music. But I can't dance. I just kind of sway. You should go to Belém. The clubs there are excellent.'

The final whistle blows. As Independente's fans invade the pitch in celebration, Senator Rocha tells me about his life. In his teenage years he played for Independente, which was then an amateur club. He studied medicine and is a professional gynaecologist. In 1998, he became a senator for the left-wing Democratic Workers Party. Despite my image of him surrounded by young girls, and a cordial slap that I now see was as much political campaigning as anything else, I find him sincere.

For Senator Rocha, Big Zero is the victim of political negligence. When it was inaugurated there were promises that stands would be built on all four sides. But they never came and the stadium became a white elephant. Bickering between state and federal government has left Big Zero's fate at an impasse.

'It could be used a lot more. It has great potential. But it wasn't even built properly. Did anyone tell you that the roof fell down?' He shakes his head. He believes that with a little political vision and some federal funds Big Zero could be a major international sporting venue.

'I think we could put on matches between the Brazilian national team and other national teams. Why not? We could have an Olympic village here. Why not? There needs to be dialogue between the state and Brasília.' Judging from his weary tone of voice, however, I feel this a dream in which even he has little faith.

We part company. Independente fans are all around us and he is in demand. 'Maybe I'll see you tonight at Site 500,' he says. 'Sundays there are excellent.'

Joaquim drives me back to my hotel. He switches on the radio. Amapá FM is playing 'I Don't Wanna Dance' by Eddy Grant. I comment that the music reminds me of my youth. Joaquim takes this as a sign to turn the music up to full volume. We can barely hear each other speak.

Amapá stands out in Brazilian football not just for its folkloric stadium. The state has a disproportionately large number of professional clubs – twelve, one for every 37,000 people. At that ratio, the United Kingdom would have more than 1,500 clubs, enough for seventy-five divisions. 'I've always said we have too many teams,' shouts Joaquim as I hear Yazoo sing 'Situation'. 'It's all down to personal vanity. People prefer to have their own team rather than support someone else's.' The teams are all either broke or almost broke. Most players receive the minumum wage – about £50 a month.

We talk about corruption in the local federation. He owes his position as vice-president to the withdrawal of the previous president, who was accused of being part of a national drugs-trafficking ring. The ex-president fled and was temporarily imprisoned. 'His house has more security than the governor's mansion,' says Joaquim.

The previous afternoon we had driven along the Macapá promenade, which, since the Amazon is several miles wide at that point, has the feel of a seaside town. About a hundred metres into the river I noticed two goal posts and a crossbar poking a few centimetres above the surface, as if a football pitch was almost completely submerged.

'That's where they play *futelama*, footmud, when the tide is low,' Joaquim said.

Before I leave Amapá I have a chance to play footmud. Two goal posts about 100m apart have been fixed in the riverbed, forming a decent-sized pitch. During low tide, the water disappears and young men congregate for a kickabout.

On the morning I arrive a treetrunk has been washed up between the posts. Four lads carry it to the side and use it as a subs' bench. I walk to the pitch in my swimming trunks. The riverbed surface – compact mud covered with a thin film of water – is as slippery as oil. I stumble around with a nervous lack of balance. Before I have even touched the ball, I am covered in mud. My favourite move is the sliding tackle – it is possible to skid, foot first, for several metres, splashing everyone nearby with muck. The game is played until the tide returns. You do not stop until the water is up to your knees.

Valdez Almeida is footmud's big fish. Last year he organised the sport's first tournament. Two 'stadiums' were set up in the river – the Surubim (which is a type of fish) and the Catamarã (catamaran), so called because they sound like São Paulo's Morumbi and the Maracanã. Twenty-one teams took part, all named after marine animals. First prize was a water buffalo; the runners-up won a pig.

Leadership comes naturally to Valdez. He lives in Santa Inês, a poor riverside neighbourhood of small box homes and earth streets, where he is president of the residents association. He is impressively active for such a lethargic place. As well as his community duties, he works during the week fixing electricity pylons and he runs marathons.

We are sitting on the riverfront after the footmud is over. Aged twenty-six, Valdez looks like a soldier. His light hair is cropped. He has small eyes and a sportsman's taut features. He exudes an authoritative calmness. He has left-wing, socially concerned views, which have taken him to conferences round

Brazil as a young community leader. When neighbours pass him they come over, shake his hand and say: 'Hello, president.'

When he was younger Valdez was a professional footballer in Macapá. Because of his strong character, he was always team captain. He played many times at Big Zero. Given the choice, he always prefered to start the first half in the northern hemisphere.

'I found that generally we would win and I would score a goal if we started in the north.'

For Valdez the centre line separates not only two halves of a football pitch, but is the symbolic divide of North and South America. He felt more comfortable playing in the north because of what the northern continent represents. 'I have an affinity for North America. It is, how shall I say, further ahead.'

Valdez's admiration for the north is geographically logical if, considering his political beliefs, unexpected. Macapá is almost as close to Miami as it is to Montevideo. Brazil north of the equator contains some of the country's least populated, most backward and poorest land – which by the caprice of its latitude is part of the developed hemisphere.

His respect for the United States has left its mark on his family. It led him to call his son Wallace and his daughter Jhennifer. (Jennifer and its many alternative spellings are the most traditional of the 'American' names poor Brazilians give their daughters, probably because of the success of the TV series *Hart to Hart*). Valdez's spelling mistake was deliberate. In Portuguese, the J of Jennifer is pronounced softly, like the 's' in Erasure. Valdez wanted an authentic English-sounding J like, say, the 'D' in Duran Duran. 'There are so many Jennifers round here that I wanted mine to stand out. So I added an 'h'. '*Jh*'-ennifer. '*Jh*', he emphasises.

By the time I leave Amapá I have learnt that Big Zero is more than just a stadium. It is a fabulous Brazilian folly and a microcosm of the tension between the northern and southern hemispheres.

Chapter Thirteen

TORTOISE IN A TOP HAT

'The problem with Brazilian villains is their lack of consistency. We do not have long-standing villains, stable villains, villains in whose lack of character we can rely . . . And that's the social importance of Eurico Miranda, the most promising new villain to appear in our lifetimes in a long time. A villain conscious of his function . . . disposed not to let us down and to endure. At last, a consistent villain.'

Luis Fernando Verissimo, *O Globo*

Eurico Miranda is alone in the Vasco da Gama president's office. He is sitting slobbishly in a comfy swivel chair, with his feet up on the window ledge. Below him he looks out on to the pitch at Vasco's São Januário stadium, where a match is about to begin. It's a warm Wednesday night in October. About 10,000 home fans are cheering as the team is announced on the loudspeaker. Inside the president's office, however, the atmosphere is eerily devoid of excitement. The crowd's roar can hardly be heard above the purr of the air-conditioning. The room – spacious and marble-floored – is chilly, brightly lit and quiet. Eurico, peering through a gap in the tinted-glass windows, keeps watch with a haughty detatchment. Isolated in his turret, he reminds me of a debauched and lonely king.

Since 1967, when he first joined Vasco's board, Eurico has evolved into the most powerful club director in Brazil. He is the most exaggerated example of a particularly pompous and belligerent breed. Eurico, aged fifty-six, looks like a character from Dickens. When I enter the room he is wearing thick leather braces with his suit trousers. He is considerably overweight, with a barrel stomach overshadowing his skinny legs. Eurico's mouth, which has a sharply defined top lip, is the strongest feature of his face. He cannot smile without looking smug. His grey hair is slicked back and, toadlike, his neck is wider than his head.

For Eurico, the end justifies the means. And the end is always Vasco. In a 1999 match, Vasco were tying 1–1 when the referee sent off three Vasco players. Eurico came down from his presidential perch, invaded the pitch and forced the match to be suspended. Among the other tricks in his ample repertoire is an occasional refusal to let visiting teams warm up. Eurico is loathed by most football fans, but idolised at Vasco because he puts his love for the club above the rules. Vasco fans, called 'Vascainos', do not care that he is rude, confrontational and authoritarian. 'Ethics?' says Eurico. 'That's for philosophers.'

Shortly before the match begins, I hear the door open and the sound of voices fills the room. We are joined by half a dozen men in their twenties. They come in hurriedly, talking loudly, and rush to the window. Two are Eurico's sons – Mário, aged twenty-six, who is head of sports at Vasco, and Euriquinho, or *Little Eurico*, aged twenty-three. Mário is serving a two-year ban from FIFA after a fracas at the World Club Championships. Eurico demanded that Mário be let into the Vasco changing rooms even though he did not have the correct credential. In the ensuing scuffle a FIFA press officer fell down a set of stairs.

Eurico's sons approach their father, slap him on the shoulder and hug him. They then crouch around him. During the game, Eurico behaves like a foulmouthed fan. Each time Vasco's defence has the ball he shouts abuse. He swears continually. Frequently, he gets up and leaves the room for a minute or so. When he passes me he makes friendly conversation: 'I get very tense during games these days,' he says. At half-time he disappears. After the match his sons take me to the changing rooms, which are crowded with players, journalists and other staff. The mood is funereal, since the visiting team equalised 2–2 in the ninetieth minute. I spot Eurico again. He is sitting in a chair surrounded by several other of Vasco's directors, who are humouring him like courtiers. It is a menacing portrait of a man in love with displaying his own power. 'Just like the Godfather,' someone whispers in my ear.

A month later, in November 2000, Vasco holds its three-yearly elections. Eurico is a candidate for president. Like almost all of Brazil's clubs, Vasco is a non-profitmaking organisation governed by its members who choose a ruling council. In practice, this amateuristic structure is hijacked by authoritarian leaders, like Eurico, who climb their way to the top based on personal relationships, patronage and exchanging favours. A club boss is nicknamed a 'cartola', which means 'top hat', a pejorative reference to their lofty origins.

I visit São Januário on election day. When I arrive cars are double parked and inside hundreds of people are milling around. The stadium, built in 1927, is one of Rio's glorious historic buildings. A bronze bust of a bearded Vasco da Gama stands impressively at the entrance. Murals with blue Portuguese tiles portray ocean scenes of caravel fleets. Original metalwork features incorporate the Patée cross, the club symbol, which the navigator had painted on his sails. Inside, almost everyone has a sticker or a T-shirt with Eurico's name. I try to find some opposition supporters, but they are few and far between. I make my way to the indoor sports hall, where the wooden ballot boxes are cordoned off.

Under Vasco's constitution, the election is between slates. The winning slate receives 120 members on the ruling council, and the second slate receives thirty. It is a way of ensuring that the opposition always has a say in club affairs.

Vasco, Rio's first champions to field black players, is proud of its democratic heritage. At this election, however, United Nations monitors would be horrified. Halfway through the afternoon Eurico realises that his slate will win, so he starts a second one. When voting is over, a row of old men – the electoral committee – sit at a long wooden table to count the ballot papers. Gradually the results come through. Eurico's slates have come first and second. This means he has all 150 councillors. He has – against the spirit of the constitution – eliminated the opposition.

When the results are read out, his supporters cheer. Eurico gives an impromptu press conference. Shouting aggressively, he says: 'This proves that the more I am criticised, the more Vasco supporters like me. The people who voted for me are motivated by *paixão* – passion.'

He is smoking a cigar and surrounded by a scrum of well-wishers and tough-looking security men. They all chant the club's war cry: 'Vas-co, Vas-co, Vas-co.'

The next time I meet Eurico is in his cabinet office in Brazil's Congress. Vasco's obstreperous strongman has been a federal deputy, the name given to the 513 members of the lower house of parliament, since 1994. In 1998, Eurico was re-elected with 105,969 votes – one of the highest in the state of Rio de Janeiro.

Eurico used the club to get elected. His campaign slogan was 'the Vascaino votes for a Vascaino'. His staff were from Vasco's supporters club and his posters had the caravel of Vasco's crest. The money for his campaign came mostly from football sources: the Brazilian Football Confederation gave him £15,000 and Ronaldo's two agents gave him £5,000 each. Eurico was accused of organising games with Vasco's junior teams in the interior of the state to raise votes and also of promising a town that he would ensure its football club had a place in the state second division. The town did not even have a football club.

The cabinet offices of Congress's deputies are in a ten-storey block in the centre of Brasília, the modernistic capital city inaugurated in 1960. I sit in Eurico's office for an hour before he turns up. When he arrives he does not have much time – he is not someone who ever has much time – and so he answers my questions rapidly.

Ostensibly Eurico represents the Brazilian Progressive Party, or PPB. You would never know. 'I was elected with the proposal of defending Vasco's interests,' he says. 'I never made any other promises.'

I ask what Vasco's parliamentary interests are. 'I am Vasco in the context of sport,' he replies. 'I'm here to defend football clubs. Our clubs are different from clubs in England. Here, someone's club is the only thing he has. The Brazilian has nothing else. I have to defend this.'

For a moment he sounds altruistic. The reality is more complicated.

While Extraordinary Minister of Sport, between 1995 and 1998, Pelé introduced a bill that aimed to increase transparency in football. Brazilian clubs are governed by the same rules as they were when they were founded in the amateur era. Directors are unpaid and club finances easily hidden from public scrutiny. Eurico, for example, earns nothing for his work at Vasco. Yet like many other cartolas, Eurico has assets that appear incompatible with his official earnings. Eurico lives in a luxury penthouse in a well-to-do area of Rio. He also owns a mansion in Brazil's equivalent of the French Riviera that has a £150,000 yacht at the jetty. Numerous incidents increase suspicion that football bosses are self-serving and negligent with club money, such as the time in 1997 Eurico returned from a Vasco game at the Maracanã with about £30,000 of the gate receipts *in his pocket*. He told police he was ambushed outside his house. The money was never recovered.

Cartolas would not cause so much general disgust if their clubs were also rich. But most clubs are broke. It is almost the norm for players' wages to be paid months in arrears. In 2001 it was revealed that Romário, Vasco's star player, was paying some of his team-mates' wages himself.

During the passage of Pelé's bill through Congress, Eurico was its most vocal opponent. He combined the obstinacy of a fan with an obsessive knowledge of legal detail. His debating style is loutish – as if he is hurling abuse on the terraces. When someone said something he did not agree with he would either laugh loudly or shout, out of turn, 'You know *nada* – nothing.'

Despite the great popular appeal of Pelé's reforms, Eurico's lobby managed to neutralise them. When the bill was approved, in 2000, the so-called 'Pelé Law' only had 11 per cent of the original text left. Pelé said he wanted his name taken off it.

Apart from blocking football legislation, Eurico takes very little interest in politics. He is one of the least active federal deputies. In his first term he proposed two bills, one about footballers' contracts and the other about selling cars. In his second he has proposed nothing. Eurico is assiduous, however, in turning out for congressional votes, in which he always follows his party line. However, he never hides that Vasco is his priority. He asks for meetings not to be held on match days, and has left midway throught important sessions so he can fly back to São Januário.

I ask Eurico if he likes being a politician. It must be very tiring, I suggest, together with his Vasco work. He pauses to think. 'No, I don't really like it. But I need to be here. Things would be a lot worse. We would already have the Pelé Law.'

His place in Congress brings with it another advantage. Elected Brazilian politicians are immune from prosecution. Eurico faces several legal actions which have been suspended because of his parliamentary status. The law was introduced more than a century ago to stop politicians being framed for murders, although it is now used by many as a defence against all sorts of prosecutions. It is not unknown, in fact, for political careers to be based purely on the desire to avoid imprisonment. (In 2001, prosecutions against at least twenty of Eurico's colleagues have been thwarted because of statutory immunity.)

I would not call Eurico charming, yet he is entertaining. Unlike many politicians, especially in Brazil, who are weaselly and endlessly evasive, Eurico at least answers every question with a sharp-tongued repartee. He is coarse and forthright. Even though it is difficult to believe his answers are anything but rhetorical posturing, he has the authenticity of an obsessive, truculent fan. We talk about the fact that journalists constantly criticise him for his authoritarian ways. When I mention Juca Kfouri, who is the most outspoken, he snaps: 'Kfouri is an imbecile. Who is he to say anything? Journalists should only give information. And who is he anyway? He is a zero. Put it this way: who does this person represent? He represents no one.' Eurico never misses an opportunity to pull rank. 'I represent the Vasco nation – more than twenty million people. You are worth who you represent.'

We leave his office together. In the lift, I suggest to him that it was unethical to introduce a second slate halfway through the Vasco election.

'I agree,' he replies with a big grin. 'In fact, I'd go further. I was taking the piss. It was to show my strength.'

Eurico is not the only footballing parliamentarian. The presidents of three other national first division teams – Sport, Santa Cruz and Cruzeiro – have also sat in the lower house in recent years. There are Congressmen who are presidents of smaller teams and Congressmen with positions in state football federations.

Dino Fernandes, a fifty-year-old deputy from Rio, used to play with Flamengo's junior team. He trained on a few occasions with Zico, who later became the club's greatest idol. When Dino was elected in 1998, his first project was a glorified version of what you do on your first day at secondary school. He compiled a survey and sent it to the other 512 deputies. The questionnaire asked: 'Which football team do you support?' Dino's aim was to prove that Flamengo was the most popular team in Congress.

The survey took forty-five days to complete. Those who did not reply Dino telephoned or went to see personally. He had to be careful, since he knew that some people would say they liked Flamengo when really they were just being politically opportune. 'That happened,' he confirms. 'But I would put a little mark in pencil on their form and discount them from the totals.'

Dino had estimated that there would be about a hundred parliamentary Flamengo fans, or 'Flamenguistas'. The result gave him a wonderful surprise. The club was supported by 157 deputies – or 30 per cent of the house – forming a bloc larger than any single party. Vasco limped home second with forty-four. After that came Fluminense, Corinthians and then Botafogo.

In order to commemorate his findings, Dino asked for permission to hold a ceremony in the Chamber. Each of his colleagues who had shown a preference for Flamengo was invited to attend, where they were presented with a diploma, 'Deputy of the Ruby-and-Black Nation', in reference to the club's colours. Dino's eyes almost well up when he recalls the moment: 'It was on the fourteenth of September 2000 at 1400 hours. It was a beautiful party,' he remembers. Current and former presidents of Flamengo were present. 'It was unheard of, to pay respects to a football club in the House. People said it was one of the biggest celebrations there has ever been there. It was packed. People came from all over Brazil.'

Flamengo paid tribute to Dino and rewarded him with the title of Vice-President of External Relations. He was given an office in the club's headquarters in Rio de Janeiro, which is where I meet him. The room is small, but it has a privileged view over the Rodrigo de Freitas Lagoon. Dino is a gentle man whose floppy hair, centre parting and droopy moustache make him look like a character from Asterix.

Congress is made up of seventeen political parties. With

the exception of the left-wing Workers Party, which has an ideology, the parties are effectively just administrative machines. Dino was elected for the PSC. (Parties are known by their acronyms, which seems to reinforce the fact they do not stand for anything.) As soon as he arrived in Brasília he switched to the PSDB. Now, he tells me, he is thinking of jumping ship a second time, to the PTB. 'It's a smaller party. I prefer to be the member of a party where you only need 40,000 votes to be elected. At the PSDB you need a lot more, maybe 70,000.'

Since policies are not especially relevant for party membership, Brazilian politics is more about negotiating personal or corporate interests. It allows for deputies like Eurico, who is representing his personal interest. Eurico, in fact, *is* his interest.

Dino had a serious motive behind his football questionnaire. With such a fairweather attitude to party loyalty, it was natural to look elsewhere to form political allegiances. He wanted to form a bond between the Ruby-and-Black deputies which he could use as a lobbying force. He tells me he has plans to propose serious legislation regarding the social responsibilities of football clubs. 'My political bloc [the PSDB] has about a hundred deputies. With one hundred and fifty more Flamengo deputies we have a lot more chance of passing laws,' he argues. He says that it worked. 'The ceremony was to butter them up. After they received the diplomas the vast majority supported my social project.' He intends to use the Ruby-and-Black caucus for other legislation too. 'Here you can change your party every day if you want to. But you could never change your club. It's a different type of passion.'

The weakness and profusion of political parties is a symptom of the youth of Brazil's democracy. The country was in a military dictatorship from 1964 until 1985. After a transition period, Brazilians in 1989 elected their first leader in almost three decades. President Fernando Collor de Mello was only forty years old, a little-known politician from the tiny northeastern state of Alagoas. His youth, energy and good looks were the symbol of a new Brazil.

Collor was also the first Brazilian president who started public life as the president of a football club. He is a strong example of the deep-rooted promiscuity between football and political power. Running a football club gives you good public visibility and, if the team is successful, lots of votes.

In 1973 and 1974 Collor ran CSA, of the Alagoan capital Maceió. Collor, whose family runs the local television station, radio and newspaper, later became mayor and state governor. 'Being CSA president was decisive for his career,' says the Alagoan political scientist Eduardo Magalhães Junior. 'Collor was a man of the elite. CSA is a team whose supporters are exclusively lower middle or working class. It was fundamental to give him an affinity with the people.'

Collor's presidential term was a disaster. He was unable to tame the economy and, as the press and Congress turned against him, his administration became fatally weakened by corruption scandals. He eventually resigned during impeachment proceedings. Brazil's young face of democracy had turned out to be the face of its corrupt, oligarchical past.

CSA, however, continued to be used as a political launchpad. Its subsequent presidents include Collor's cousin Euclides and Augusto Farias, who have both been elected to Congress. In 1999, CSA's directors voted twenty-three-year-old Arnon de Mello into the club presidency. Arnon is Fernando Collor's son.

In December 2000, I am in Maceió and I visit Arnon in his office. It is in the same building as the family newspaper. Arnon has his father's sporty good looks. He is tall and exudes a well-fed healthiness that is rarely seen in Alagoas. The state is one of Brazil's poorest. More than a third of the population are illiterate and the infant mortality rate is the highest in the country.

Arnon is exactly the sort of person you want to dislike. Born into a provincial dynasty, he is a symbol of Brazil's grotesque inequalities. Between the ages of four and twenty-three he never lived in Maceió – he was brought up in Switzerland and then studied at the University of Chicago. Being president of CSA pays no money, and he can only afford to do it because he is given substantial hand-outs by the family firm.

Yet I am won over by his charm. He is modest and genuinely excited about running a football club. I suggest he must be one of the youngest club presidents in Brazil. 'I am not just the youngest,' he stresses, 'I am the youngest by thirty years.'

Arnon is already showing that he has his father's populist DNA. During the state championship he travels to every upstate game and often sits with the fans. 'If things go bad it's normal to have oranges and cans thrown at me, but if things go well I'm carried on people's shoulders and they call me the best president in Brazil.'

At Chicago he graduated in economics. He says that he's trying to modernise the way clubs are run. 'People say that the only reason I wanted to be in CSA was because I want to be a politician. I think in the past there was a lot of this. I am trying to do something different. I want to leave a club that isn't in debt.'

I ask him if he will enter politics. 'I think the probability is big. My great-grandfather was a politician. My grandfather was a politician. My father was a politician. And I like politics. So I think it's likely. But I'm not in a hurry.'

In the 1970s and 1980s, CSA were in the first division of the national league. In 2000 they should be in the third. But a few weeks before the league is due to start Arnon calls up Eurico Miranda.

'I asked him if he could help put CSA back in the second division,' says Arnon. He imitates Eurico's reply: 'You know how he speaks – "piss" here, "bollocks" there. I didn't know what would happen.'

A few days later, the list of teams competing in division two was announced – including CSA.

*   *   *

In the evening after I interview Eurico in his cabinet, Vasco beat the Argentinian side River Plate 4–1 in the Mercosul Cup. The following morning, I watch how Eurico behaves in Congress. He keeps teasing the other deputies like a self-satisfied schoolboy, showing them four fingers in one hand and one in the other. He has another reason to be smug. After the match he called up the team in Buenos Aires and banned them from giving interviews. It was a way of getting at the press. On television I see images of Vasco's players, including Romário, arriving at the airport with their hands over their mouths.

A few days later I go to São Januário. I watch a match sitting next to Fernando, Vasco's diligent and eternally worried-looking press officer. He explains to me that Eurico was retaliating for what he sees as censorship against him. 'Eurico believes he is the victim,' he says. 'He thinks that Flamengo gets more coverage. He thinks Vasco is treated with a certain disinterest.' He shows me a press release in which it states that José Carlos Araújo, one of Brazil's most esteemed radio commentators, is banned from matches at São Januário.

I suggest that Eurico must be an impossible boss. 'It's his way. He has a very strong temperament. You have to live with it.' But he adds that Eurico is very loyal to his friends and deeply religious. 'Wherever he is in the world with Vasco he has to go to church every Sunday. In Tokyo, Mexico and Australia, he made a point of finding a Catholic church.' Eurico does have a benevolent streak. He used to send retirement money voluntarily to Barbosa, the ex-Vasco goalkeeper who became a national pariah after the 1950 World Cup.

The current incident is not the first time that Vasco has banned journalists from São Januário. It started in 1997, when a letter was sent out saying that the club would not be responsible for the physical security of journalists who had criticised it. In 1999 some reporters only entered São Januário with legal orders and accompanied by policemen.

José Carlos Araújo – whose picture is in the paper narrating a match watching it on television – claims to have been manhandled and had cups of urine thrown at him.

I am not the only one who finds Eurico's censorship a petty and dangerous precedent. The issue spirals out of the sporting arena and reaches Rio's state assembly. Chico Alencar, president of the human rights committee, drafts a motion repudiating Eurico's 'restriction of the free movement of journalists'. The motion is signed by thirty-six state deputies, an absolute majority. However, scenes in the assembly deteriorate. One of the state deputies against the motion is Roberto Dinamite, who played for Vasco and the national team in the 1970s and 1980s. He manages to persuade political allies to remove their signatures.

He tells them: 'The problem is that Chico Alencar is a Flamenguista.'

Latin America has produced many demagogic leaders. A Brazilian version is the 'coronel', or colonel, a local political chieftain – usually nothing to do with the military – who is constantly showing off his power. The coronel is probably a legacy from colonial slave-owners, who used swagger to reinforce segregation. Eurico is football's coronel. He is popular because many people identify with strong public figures. And also because under his command Vasco are successful. Since 1986, when he became vice-president in charge of football, the club has won six state championships, two Brazilian leagues, the South American Libertadores Cup and was runner-up in the World Club Championship.

I do not need to wait long for a gobsmacking example of his authoritarianism. In the semi-final of the Brazilian championship, he sacks his coach, Oswaldo de Oliveira, in the changing room after the game. Eurico says it was the result of an argument about what time training should start the following Monday. 'It was simple. He disagreed with my decision and I sacked him,' says Eurico. 'It wasn't a heavy chat. At Vasco there's a hierarchy, orders exist to be respected. I can't see things escape from between my fingers.' Then Eurico reveals another motive. Once the final whistle had blown, Oswaldo and Cruzeiro's coach had given each other an amicable hug in a spontaneous public gesture of fair play. In Eurico's eyes, the fraternisation was unacceptable.

In 2000 the Brazilian championhip is called the João Havelange Cup, in homage to the Brazilian who was president of FIFA for twenty-four years. Eurico's Vasco make the final, against São Caetano, a team from São Paulo. The title is to be decided over two legs. The first match, in São Paulo, is tied 1–1.

On Saturday 30 December I drive to São Januário for the second leg. It is a glorious midsummer day. The sensation as I approach the stadium is of being a cyclist in the Tour de France. The streets are full of men waving at me, who only open a path for my car when I am almost running them over. This gesticulating army is a common Brazilian scourge: vigilante car park attendants. They find you a space, help you park it and, supposedly, guard it – for however much money they can con from you. It's a wily ruse for making money, and inevitable since São Januário does not have a proper car park – neither, for that matter, does the Maracanã.

São Januário holds about 30,000. It is full to bursting point – entirely with Vasco fans. São Caetano had asked for their allocation but Vasco, in a typical show of bad faith, sold all their tickets to Vascainos. Vasco made a verbal agreement to give São Caetano their fair share, but the Rio club reneged.

Instead of sitting in the press box I decide to watch the match from the terraces. The standing area stretches in a curved dog-leg along two sides of the pitch. I position myself behind the centre line. The crowd is crammed together. Vendors squeeze through selling plastic bottles of mineral water and ice lollies. We are in direct sunlight and many men have stripped off their shirts. It is about 40°C.

Vasco are the favourites. As well as the home advantage they have a line-up that includes Romário and several other stars of the national side. São Caetano reached the final with a team of unknowns, including one player who had spent a year and five months in prison for involvement in a burglary.

The match starts with festive celebrations. The crowd lights flares, waves flags and throws streams of toilet roll cascading in the air. The stadium is shaking with drumming, fireworks and the sound of happy chanting. The game kicks off. In the early minutes São Caetano have the run of play. There midfield is fluent and they create good chances. Only heroic goalkeeping by Vasco's Helton prevents the visitors opening score. After twenty-one minutes Romário is substituted, with a problem in his left thigh. The crowd starts to feel tense. Two minutes later the referee blows his whistle to halt the game. I do not understand why. Within a few seconds word comes through that there has been some problem with the fans. We look to our left. I am given a leg-up to see what has happened. About fifty metres away, at the corner of the stand, I see that the fencing in front of the terraces has twisted over. A mass of fans are piled up behind it.

From my position, it is difficult to see how serious the accident is. Two ambulances drive on to the pitch. Then I hear the buzz of a helicopter. It gets louder and louder until the stadium is drowned in an unbearable noise. The helicopter slowly hovers and lands in the Vasco goal area. A man strapped to a stretcher is hurried on to the helicopter. He looks seriously hurt. I decide to try and get on to the pitch. I leave the terraces, find a side door, show a security man my press card and he lets me through.

The scene is shocking. Much worse than I expected. The grass looks like a war zone. There are dozens of people lying on the ground. I see people on stretchers looking lifeless and others wincing in pain. I am shaken by the horror of what I see. I walk to the perimeter, where the fencing has caved

in. By the time I arrive, everyone has been removed. But
from seeing the number of people on the pitch and the
number left on the terraces, I judge that several hundred
people must have been involved in the crush. About fifteen
metres of the fencing – made of metal bars with spikes – is
lying over a metre-deep trench that divides the terraces from
the pitch. I look at the bottom of the trench. It is filled with
a heap of about fifty pairs of shoes, which fell off as fans
scrambled to safety.

I turn around and see Eurico. He is storming around the
pitch, stepping between the injured and shouting at the
medics. He shows absolute indifference to catastrophe:
'Nothing serious happened. But something could if the game
doesn't continue. I want these fucking ambulances out of
here!'

Eurico is surrounded by his heavies and a trail of journalists. He is wearing a blue shirt, with large sweat patches
under his arms, on his shoulders and on his chest. He is
spitting with rage. He shouts aggressively, pointing his finger
in the air. He shows no respect for the injured or those at
their aid. His only concern is in clearing the pitch so that
the match can restart.

The São Caetano president appears and is promptly
surrounded. He says that it is common sense to cancel the
game. Then the State Civil Defence Secretary, who is also
present, gives the all-clear for the game to proceed. But the
situation is completely out of control. The pitch contains
two helicopters, about ten ambulances and hundreds of journalists, fans and medics. The Vasco and São Caetano players
are sitting by the touchline protected by military police.

It is a tragic, farcical impasse. The situation continues
until the referee finally signals that the game really is over,
about an hour after he halted it temporarily. He leads the
players back into the changing rooms.

The temperature is still almost 40°C.

It emerges that the state governor, Anthony Garotinho,
watching the events on television at home, had called up

São Januário and ordered the end of the match.

Eurico is livid. He starts a slanging match in front of the cameras. 'He's false and incompetent. It was this poof of a governor who called off the game. The bloke's a wimp.'

A few minutes later the Vasco players unexpectedly reappear. They saunter out of the tunnel and head for the halfway line, where the João Havelange Cup is standing on a table. The players hoist up the trophy and, together with Eurico, complete a lap of honour. No one can quite believe the shamelessness or insensitivity, since they have most certainly not won anything. A bunch of young hardmen manhandle journalists out of the way. They shout Vasco's war cry and also: 'Eu-ri-co! Eu-ri-co! Eu-ri-co!'

The statistics come through later: 168 people are injured, two seriously: a man has a cranial wound and five-year-old girl has a perforated abdomen. It is a miracle that no one was crushed to death.

The following day, *Lance!*, the main sports paper, publishes a front-page editorial:

Many people share the blame for yesterday's tragedy at São Januário, but only one is responsible: Eurico Miranda. The cartola, who believes he is the most senior authority in the country, has always been praised by Vasco supporters and criticised by his opponents for putting his club's interests above anything else. No one imagined that he was capable of taking this obsession to the limit of not respecting human lives.

It is New Year's Eve, the last day of the twentieth century. The match resonates with a *fin de siècle* symbolism. The João Havelange final, the most prestigious match in the Brazilian football calendar, has turned into a tragic showcase of incompetence.

Brazil is a continent-sized country. The distance between its most northerly and southerly points is further than the distance between London and Baghdad. There is no rail system and, even today, most intercity roads have only one lane. Before air travel, a national league was a logistical impossibility. For seventy years, Brazilian football developed around state leagues.

The first attempt at a national tournament happened in 1922. It consisted of all-star teams representing seven states. The intention was to bring all the country's best players together in one place, so it was easier to choose players for the national squad. This 'Tournament of States' was for decades considered the national football championship. It grew to include twenty-four states and was held twenty-six times in the following forty-one years.

It was not until 1971 – once Brazil were already three times World Cup-winners – that a national club championship was inaugurated. The competition, which brought the country together through football, fitted the military regime's strategic and ideological objectives of national integration. Almost too well. A place in the league became a powerful tool for political bargaining. The first Brazilian league included twenty teams. The number increased steadily until, in 1979, it included ninety-four clubs. A popular saying stated that where the government was doing badly, a local team was put in the national league, and 'Where it's going well, one goes in as well'.

Political desires to include as many teams as possible for as long as possible caused unfeasibly complicated rules. Concentrate hard and try to understand the system used in 1978: There were seventy-four teams, divided into six groups (A to F). Four had twelve clubs and two had thirteen. Each team in each group played each other once. Who qualified to the second stage? They all did. The six top clubs in each of groups A to F formed four groups of nine (G to J). In these groups the six top clubs proceeded to the third phase. The other teams from the first phase formed six groups (K to P), two with seven and four with six, of which just the winners qualified for the third phase. That makes

twenty-four from G to J and six from K to P. Are you still
with me? Together with the best-placed loser from G to J
and from K to P, these thirty teams formed four new groups
of eight clubs (Q to T). The top two in each group went
forward to the next phase of eight teams, who played a
knockout of quarter-, semi- and then final finals. You can't
help thinking that they only stopped because they were
running out of letters in the alphabet.

Between 1971 and 2001 the format of the Brazilian league
changed every year. Some years were more eccentric than
others. In 1974, one criterion for classification was the
amount of money taken in ticket sales. In 1975, teams gained
an extra point for winning by two or more goals. In 1985
the rules were so perverse that Coritiba were champions
with a negative goal difference. The system – used uncon-
troversially in all the major European countries – in which
every team plays each other once at home and once away,
with the winner the team with the best combined results,
has never been adopted. When there is a league, the best
teams *always* proceed into a knockout stage. Brazilians do
not understand championships without a 'final'.

Constantly changing rules have devalued the league's credibility, which is reflected in low match attendance. In 2000
the average crowd size is only 11,000 per game, a third of
the figure for the 2000–2001 English Premier League. The
crowds in Brazil look exaggeratedly small since stadiums are
generally enormous – six used in 2000 have a capacity of
more then 70,000.

The Brazilian league also suffers because it has to be
squeezed in among everything else. State and regional leagues
did not go quietly when the national league came along.
The big clubs play up to seven tournaments annually – the
state league, the regional league, the national league, the
national cup, the cup of state champions and two South
American cups. The calender is so complicated that some
players go for years without taking a holiday.

Brazil's size also counts against the national league, since it is too expensive for fans to travel to away games. Matches that are not local derbies generally only have one set of fans. This makes the state leagues much more exciting, meaningful tournaments. Low gate receipts and low credibility all through the year are reasons why Brazilian clubs cannot raise the money to hold on to their best players. Most prefer to play in Europe, which devalues the domestic scene even further.

There have been efforts to attract crowds by making football a more dynamic spectacle. Most are inventions by Eduardo José Farah, the São Paulo Football Federation president. Over the last decade he has introduced a three-minute basketball-style 'time-out' in each half and contracted football cheerleaders for the state league. He also experimented with putting two referees on the pitch at the same time – to lessen the number of fouls. (It worked.) Another way he tried to discourage violence was to award a free kick on the fifteenth foul. He has also pioneered the use of a white foam spray that referees use to mark the point from which a free kick should be taken and the line where the defensive wall should stand. (The foam disappears after a few minutes. Some clubs complained that the grass did too.) In 2001 Farah did away with the tie. Matches ending 0–0 resulted in no points for either team. Score draws were settled on penalties with one point for the loser and three for the victor. Tostão, the 1970 World Cup striker who is now a magus-like sports columnist, wrote Farah's no-draw rule was because 'in American football there are no draws. We love copying this North American style, where everything is based on winning and being a millionaire. We copy from them the taste for opulence, consumerism, obsession for practicalities, hypocritical moralism, superheroes and glass skyscrapers. But football and life aren't just made out of winners and losers. The draw is democratic, healthy and solidary. One learns to share.' FIFA agreed and banned Farah from transferring his rules to the regional and national leagues.

The end of the dictatorship did not take the politics out of the national league. It was shaped by a culture of vested interests and it continued that way. In 1996, for example, Fluminense finished second from bottom. The Rio team should have been relegated in 1997. Yet after backroom deals the league was expanded from twenty-four to twenty-six clubs, just so Fluminense could stay up. Eurico led the campaign to save Fluminense. 'Clubs with tradition, fans and investment should not be allowed to be relegated,' he argued. Unfortunately, Fluminense were second bottom again in 1997. This time they could not avoid the drop, and played 1998 in division two. In 1999, they were sent down to division three.

In order to protect the big clubs from unfair eventualities like relegation, in 1999 a new rule was introduced. First division teams would be relegated based on their performance over two years, the reasoning being that big clubs would not be penalised for one irregular season. It was copied from the Argentinian model, which bases its relegation criteria on results over three years.

But the ruse did not work. At the end of the 1999 season Botafogo were staring division two in the face. What could the big clubs do to keep Botafogo up?

Midway through the season, Botafogo had lost a game against São Paulo in which São Paulo fielded a player who had fraudulently altered his birth certificate. Botafogo went to the Sports Supreme Court which – twisting the tournament's original rules – awarded them the points for that game. With these extra points Botafogo rose out the relegation zone at the expense of Gama, a small club from Brasília.

The move, however, only caused more problems. Outraged at the Sports Supreme Court's biased decision, Gama went to a civil court and won the legal right to stay in the first division in 2000. This prompted FIFA, which punishes teams who enter the common justice system, to ban Gama from all affiliated leagues. It put the Brazilian Football Confederation (CBF) in a Catch 22. If it organised a national league, then by law Gama had to be included.

Yet it was forbidden from including Gama by order of FIFA. Less than a month before the beginning of the season no one knew if there would be a national league. In protest, a supporter started a hunger strike in front of the CBF headquarters in Rio.

A group of the biggest clubs devised a solution. They decided to organise a one-off league, called the João Havelange Cup, independently of the CBF. In order to be able to exclude Gama legally, any similarity between the João Havelange Cup and the national league had to be entirely coincidental. So, the 104 teams invited to take part were divided into four divisions, called 'modules', which were named after colours. As if that would fox anyone. Gama went straight back to court and won the legal right to be included in the 'blue module', the thinly disguised first division. When the João Havelange Cup eventually began, the number of teams had climbed to 116, making it the largest competition in Brazilian football history. The blue module had another surprise – Fluminense, hopping all the way up from the third division.

Even by the pitiful standards of previous leagues, the João Havelange Cup was a terribly organised creation. In the blue module, some teams played three more home games than others, a third of games were rescheduled and one team went for a month without playing a game. The knockout stage included teams from every module, which meant that – theoretically – a club which was not in the first division could win the national title. This was, in fact, on course to happen. São Caetano qualified to the knockout stage after they were runners-up in the second division, sorry, yellow module. In many ways the São Januário disaster was the final that the monstrous João Havelange Cup deserved.

When they need to, Brazilians always find a way around the rules. In 1940, two clubs from Rio Grande played each other in the final of a local tournament. The first match was a tie. Three rematches also ended in ties. A creative solution was found: the tournament was declared a draw and the trophy sawn in half.

Laws exist to be subverted. This could be the motto of the Sports Supreme Court, the judicial power of Brazilian football, which will judge whether there will be a rematch of the João Havelange Cup final. Contrary to my ideas of justice, the court is not made up of neutral lawyers. It is divided into three Flamengo fans and two each for Vasco, Botafogo and Fluminense. These nine men are hostages to the teams they support. The system constitutionalises the defence of the large Rio clubs' interests over the common good. Brazilian society is marked by unfairness against the less privileged, and this is reflected in football.

I decide to interview Luiz Zveiter, the court's president and a Botafogo fan. Zveiter's secretary tells me that he will see me on Tuesday. When I call on Tuesday to confirm, she asks me to call the following Tuesday. When I call again to confirm, Zveiter is again not available. We continue this charade for a month. I can tell from the tone of mild surprise when I call, that no effort is being made for my interview. Finally, I ask why Zveiter does not want to see me. His secretary replies: 'He's very busy at the moment. He's running for Grand Master of the masons.'

I remark: 'Isn't there an incompatibility in being a judge and a mason?'

'Why?' she questions. 'You don't make any money from being Grand Master.'

Failing to reach Zveiter, I speak to the sports lawyer Heraldo Panhoca. In his opinion the partisan nature of Brazilian sports justice is a consequence of twenty years of dictatorship. 'When liberty came, there was no control any more. People did not know how to live with this freedom. The Rio group has been using all its interests to keep hegemony over the court's decisions.'

If there is one man who appreciates the relativity of sports justice, it is Eurico Miranda. He describes the tribunal as 'there to be used' as if it was a personal ally, since he knows

that he can use his weight and influence to get results –
which he usually does. Eurico is in favour of disorganisation so long as it favours his club. The Sports Supreme Court
decides that there should be a rematch of the Vasco vs. São
Caetano final. This is a victory for Vasco which, according
to the rules, should have been penalised for the accident.

Eurico's influence in bending justice happens not just in
the tribunals. Zico, the former national team player who
now runs his own small Rio club, says that the state divisions are organised so as to favour Eurico's friends. José
Roberto Wright, a former referee, adds: 'Referees are chosen
for political reasons. They know that if they displease [the
federation president] and Eurico Miranda they will never
referee again.'

One incident which sums up the impotence of small teams
occurred in 1997. Vasco were playing Itaperuna, a small
upstate Rio club. Itaperuna were winning 2–1. Vasco drew
level. 'Our team was playing well, we were going to win.
Then suddenly the ref sent off three of our players. And
every time we approached the Vasco goal we were offside,'
says Paulo Matta, who was Itaperuna's coach.

Matta, who played for Vasco and in Europe when he was
a player, stormed on to the pitch in protest. He took off his
shirt. He took off his shoes. He undid his trousers and took
them off too. He was soon buck naked in the middle of the
pitch.

Matta, who has a sunken face and a tattoo of a football
on his left arm, tells me he was suspended for a year and
two months. He says, as an ironic boast: 'It was the longest
suspension anyone has ever had.' He adds: 'The problem
with referees is that the majority of refs make their living
from it. I'm not saying that he was paid by Vasco to throw
the game but if Vasco wins then he knows he is more likely
to be picked to referee the next Vasco game.'

Eurico Miranda was born in Rio on 7 June 1944, the son
of Portuguese parents. He went to a well-known Jesuit school

although, unlike his middle-class peers, he also spent his youth working behind the counter at his family's chain of bakeries. Eurico studied law at the federal university, and in the 1970s got a job at a Volkswagen car dealer's. Yet wherever he went he caused problems. He left the car dealership under a cloud of allegations of financial impropriety. Brazilian media have also reported that in the 1970s he was sued for 'undue appropriation' of his condominium's funds.

When Eurico was five years old his father first took him to see Vasco. Less than two decades later he was already formally involved at the club, as head of the register. In 1975 he was made director of basketball and in 1986 vice-president responsible for football. Married with four children, he has few friends and few hobbies outside Vasco. When he has time he plays cards and, due to chronic insomnia, spends hours at night piecing together jigsaws.

In the aftermath of the São Januário tragedy, I am taken aback by the vitriol in the media attacks against Eurico – even though he undoubtedly deserves it – because he has been involved in countless controversies before. His behaviour was perhaps shocking, but it was not inconsistent with previous acts. There is a strong sense that the media is gleefully letting out years of pent-up hatred. Eurico becomes a national pariah. He plays the role of pantomime villain perfectly, never apologising nor showing the slightest remorse.

Partly because football is so linked to national identity, and partly because of the seasonal mood of self-reflection, Eurico's vilification prompts a wave of national soul-searching. He is seen as an expression not just of the backwardness of football, but a metaphor for all that is backward about Brazil. He is damned as a relic of the era of the dictatorship – a symbol of power without shame. 'He represents a world of psychological feudalism that has not yet passed, but that wherever it goes, rules, and that we need to free ourselves from,' says the poet Geraldo Carneiro.

Because Eurico is a Congressman, he is protected from

prosecution. Even so, Governor Garotinho starts a criminal legal action for libel and slander and sends it to the Supreme Court, requesting them to lift Eurico's parliamentary immunity. A police investigation is launched into the incident. Public mood is so strong that when the policeman in charge defends Eurico by saying that he was 'evidently traumatised', the officer is summarily sacked.

The cause of the São Januário tragedy is traced back to a scuffle at the back of the terraces. An argument between two Vasco fans about Romário's substitution broke into a fight. The flight of people out of the way caused the crowd to charge forward, which gathered force and became a stampede. The pressure of the crowd on the metal perimeter fence at the front of the terraces was too much and it gave way. Hundreds of people were squashed on top of it. As the days go by, all the injured recover. But Eurico's irresponsibility seems beyond doubt. It appears that he put his own fans' lives at risk by letting the terraces fill to way past their capacity. The antique São Januário was in no condition to hold such an important match.

Eurico denies that the stadium was overcrowded. He claims that he helped the victims for the first few minutes and then, when he saw that they were no longer in any risk, decided that the game should continue – for fear that the terraces would turn violent.

A week later I am in a bar when I bump into a Vascaino friend. I always considered him a moderate – ashamed and embarrassed by Eurico's authoritarian methods. I am stunned by his reaction to the São Januário crush. 'The stadium wasn't overfull,' he says immediately. 'Eurico was right to want to continue the game. There was no further danger to the crowd. The only reason the game was stopped was because TV Globo wanted to broadcast its soap opera.' He explains that in 1992, when two people fell to their deaths at the Maracanã, the match was played. 'And at Heysel too.' My friend repeats the mantra: 'Everyone just wants to get at Vasco.' The horrible thought dawns on me that the events of the São

Januário, rather than turning Vascainos against Eurico, instead strengthened their support for him.

Eurico masterfully turns the episode to his advantage. He plays on people's beliefs that everything is motivated by personal interest. He attacks the media. Eurico claims that Globo put pressure on Governor Garotinho to intervene when it realised that the match's delay would mess up its programming schedule. Eurico's assault on Globo works. Like a dictator declaring war on an outside threat, he unites Vascainos and detracts from the accusations against him. It attracts public sympathy too, since Globo, Brazil's main channel, is as unpopular as he is – possibly more so. Weekday football matches, for example, always start at the prohibitively late time of 9.40pm because Globo dictates that they must follow its evening soap opera.

A fire at Globo's Rio studios, in which a seven-year-old girl almost dies with 40 per cent burns, is seized on by Vascainos as divine justice. 'The spells are turning against the spellmaker,' says Eurico's son Euriquinho. 'The more [Globo] persecutes my dad, the more the idolatry grows.' As if to prove this point Vasco organises a 'hug' around São Januário, in which its fans link arms around the stadium walls. Father Lino, the Vasco priest, holds Mass on the pitch.

The rescheduled final of the 2000 Brazilian league takes place on 18 January 2001 at the Maracanã. It is live on Globo. When Vasco's team appears, viewers cannot quite believe what they are seeing. The players have the logo of the SBT television channel, which is Globo's main rival, prominently on their shirts. Strange. Not only are Vasco not sponsored by SBT, but it is against the law for TV companies to advertise on football kit. It transpires that Eurico ordered the SBT logo to be printed – without even asking SBT's permission. He is sticking two fingers up at Globo. And with style too – since Globo are forced to broadcast their rivals' logo for the duration of the game. He has the last laugh too – since his audacity wins him more support. Only Eurico has the nerve – or lunacy – to attack Globo.

About 60,000 fans are in the Maracanã. São Caetano start well, but the experience and quality of Vasco's players soon shows. Vasco win 3–1 and – with justification, this time – lift the João Havelange Cup. Romário says afterwards: 'I dedicate the title to Eurico. He is Vasco's number-one fan. He treats the club like a son. Fathers always want the best for their sons.'

Vasco's full name is the Vasco da Gama Regatta Club, founded in 1898, on the four-hundredth anniversary of when the Portuguese navigator sailed to India. The club still competes in rowing, and has a base on the banks of the Rodrigo de Freitas Lagoon. The building was chosen for Eurico's presidential inauguration ceremony, four days after the João Havelange victory. Even though he has acted like the president for more than a decade, he was only the veep.

I watch the whole evening's proceedings from the balcony. In the main hall are several hundred people, mostly men in dark suits and ties, who are mingling and, when they recognise a friend, hug each other demonstratively. There is an awesome feeling of male bonding, power and self-importance. The guests are heavyweights from football, politics and the judiciary. The *real* João Havelange is talking to Ricardo Teixeira, the president of the Brazilian Football Confederation. Cesar Maia, the mayor of Rio, is present as are other local and national politicians. The event is a triumphant show of force for a man who only weeks before was the most despised man in the country. He is still courted by the people that matter.

On a stage there is a long wooden bench. Behind it are twenty-two medieval-style chairs with tall backs and no arm rests. When Vasco's dignitaries are called up to their seats, at least twelve judges are named; proof, it seems to me, of Eurico's constant success in the law courts. Eurico is called last, and there are many cheers. Two attractive girls, dressed glamorously, walk on with the João Havelange Cup, an odd-shaped trophy with a gold-coloured football. The crowd

shouts 'Tetracampeão', or '*Four-times champion*', since it is
the fourth time they have won the national league. Eurico
smiles broadly.

Francisco Dornelles, the federal Employment Secretary,
describes Eurico as a 'fascinating person'. He adds: 'He has
a great big heart even if sometimes he's like a tank. He is
a victim of his love for Vasco.' Bernardo Cabral, a senator
from the Amazon region, describes Eurico as a 'jabuti' – an
Amazonian tortoise – and tells the myth of its indestructi-
bility. Trees may fall on it but when they rot the tortoise
moves on. Likewise with the criticisms of Eurico, the criticisms will die and he will continue. Cesar Maia calls Eurico
'our great sporting and political leader – the greatest football boss that this city has had in many years'. He insinu-
ates that Eurico is the club director that every other team
wants. 'Thank you very much for existing. Rio thanks you
very much for having a director like you. I really hope that
all our other clubs discover a talent like yours.'

Eurico finally makes his speech. He talks about how proud
his father would be. He breaks out in tears which are over-
whelmed by clapping.

Eurico describes himself as a David against the Goliath
of the Brazilian establishment. He identifies himself with
Vasco, and compares his struggle against public opinion to
Vasco's struggle in the 1920s against racism.

'Ever since we were founded we were destined to be the
small club among the big ones.'

He rallies the faithful: 'I was elected to defend the interests of Vasco and Vascainos.'

The crowd booms: 'Hear! Hear!'

To cap the absurdity of Eurico's rehabilitation as a demo-
crat, he receives a peculiar tribute one thousand miles away.
Tocantins, a club from Imperatriz, a city in the state
Maranhão, prints a picture of the Vasco president on their
football shirts.

I telephone the president of Tocantins, Justino Oliveira
Filho and ask why. 'Eurico has many injustices against him.

He fights for his ideals,' he says. 'We always saw him as a role model. He is the only director in the whole world whose whole life is his club. You need to confront things the way Eurico does.'

While it is outrageous that a man like Eurico is portayed as a downtrodden freedom-fighter, it is not illogical. Eurico is fighting for more than Vasco, he is fighting for the status quo. And his grand inauguration shows that he is winning. Football is still controlled by old, dictatorial Brazil. By the 'coronels'. But Brazil is changing. For how much longer will – or can – it last?

Chapter Fourteen

WE LOST BECAUSE WE DIDN'T WIN

'I also hope that my truth pleases you, because there are many truths, many truths. It's up to you to decide which is the true truth and analyse it afterwards.'

Ronaldo

On Sunday 12 July 1998, Brazil played France in the World Cup final. The match took place at the Stade de France, in St Denis, Paris. I watched it on television in Rio de Janeiro. Brazilians tend not to watch international matches in public places, preferring instead to stay at home with their families. I was invited to a friend's flat. On the way over I bought a T-shirt from a street-seller with Ronaldo's name on the back. July is Brazilian midwinter. The weather was in the low 20s, grey and drizzly.

Brazil were favourites. Not only were they the title-holders but they also had Ronaldo, aged twenty-one, who had twice been voted FIFA player of the year. If he was the best in the world, then it stood to reason that his team would be the best in the world too. But when I arrived I was told that Ronaldo was not in the starting line-up. Apart from the realisation that I – and a few million others – were wearing shirts that had suddenly lost their relevance, I sensed a changed mood. Brazilians had taken victory for granted. Now there was doubt.

Shortly before the game, the TV commentary announced that Ronaldo would, after all, be playing. We watched the team come out, hand in hand, a gimmick invented four years before to show unity. Ronaldo was indeed included. Yet the relief was momentary. Once the game had started, Brazil played with no sense of purpose. Ronaldo seemed slow and apathetic, his posture downcast. After twenty-seven minutes, Zinedine Zidane headed France into the lead. At the end of the first half, he headed in another. Emmanuel Petit completed the 3–0 scoreline: the heaviest defeat Brazil had ever suffered in a World Cup. When the final whistle blew, some of the women in the room had already stopped watching and – I remember this very strongly – the men were crying. I sensed that the tears were not just for the defeat but for the manner of the defeat. Brazil had not even put up a fight.

Brazil's wanton performance was a mystery. They were unrecognisable from the exciting team of the quarter- and semi-finals. In the postmortem, reports emerged that Ronaldo had felt unwell before the match. We learnt that he had been rushed to a clinic for tests, which explained why Mário Zagallo, the coach, had left him off the first team list. When he returned from the clinic, with the all clear, Zagallo put him back on. The situation's unique circumstances lent itself to fabulous conspiracy theories. Here was the world's most famous sportsman, about to take part in the most important match in his career, when he suddenly, inexplicably fell ill. Was it stress, or epilepsy, or had he, perhaps, been drugged?

Ronaldo, it was confirmed, had experienced some kind of fit in the afternoon of the game. The team doctors were not sure what it was, since the striker had no medical history of fits. The tests, which gave Ronaldo a clean bill of health, also gave no clues. Questions started to be asked about the role of Nike, the sportswear manufacturer, which sponsored both Ronaldo individually and the Brazilian team. Perhaps Nike, since it had invested so much money in him, insisted that

Ronaldo play when medical common sense suggested that he should be left out. It might have been far-fetched – why would Nike risk the life of its poster boy? – but it was the conspiracy theory that stuck.

Nike was a ready-made scapegoat. During the tournament, it had already drawn suspicion about the power it wielded behind the scenes. Its $160-million ten-year contract with Brazil was the largest ever sponsorship deal of a national team. Combined with a general xenophobic distrust of a foreign company, there were worries that for such a large sum the team had surrendered too much control.

As happened in 1950 – the only other time they lost a World Cup final – Brazil discovered that coming second leaves more of an emotional impact than coming first. Within weeks, a lawyer began a civil action in a Rio court demanding explanations about what happened on the day of the defeat. The judge even summonsed Zagallo, although nothing came of the case. Concurrently, the Rio de Janeiro Regional Medical Council started a professional ethics action against Lídio Toledo and Joaquim da Matta, the team medics. Both Zagallo and Ronaldo gave evidence. The medics were eventually unanimously absolved.

Suspicions about Nike refused to go away. The conspiracy theorists felt vindicated when, in January 1999, the contract between Nike and the Brazilian Football Confederation (CBF), was leaked to the press. The contract revealed that Nike *did* have a say in the organisation of matches. The firm had the right to organise up to fifty 'Nike friendlies' in which at least eight first-team regulars must play. One influential journalist called the deal a 'melancholy surrender to the power of money. I understand now the wave of popular feeling that blamed the Brazilian defeat on a commercial deal.'

In Brasília, a little-known Communist Congressman called Aldo Rebelo took on the case. He entered a petition in the House of Deputies – the lower house of Congress – to start

an inquiry into the Nike–CBF contract. He based his argument on the possibility that the contract could have violated
'sovereignty, autonomy and national identity', which are
guaranteed by the Brazilian constitution.

Aldo's petition sat in the queue for a year and a half. The
CBF lobbied hard against its realisation. The inquiry looked
as if it had passed its sell-by date when, in September 2000,
along came Cameroon and Renata Alves.

Renata Alves first reminds me of how beautiful she is on
the telephone before we meet.

'Are you sure you will recognise me?' she asks.

I reply that since she has appeared regularly in newspapers
and on television, I am well acquainted with her appearance.

'Look,' she says anyway. 'You can't miss me. I'm tall and
thin and people say I'm very pretty.'

Her arrival, late, at a ritzy pizza restaurant near Ipanema,
causes the other diners to ogle. We move to a discreet
table. Renata sits down and reassures me: 'I am *very*
famous.'

Renata is, unquestionably, infamous. Her beauty is less
assured. She has a big, broad physique, and concise,
slightly harsh features. Above a birdlike mouth, her
eyebrows are thickly pencilled. She is wearing a gold necklace with an 'R' medallion, gold bracelets, three gold rings
and gold nail polish. Her hair, in a tom-boyish bob, has
golden highlights. We order pizza, which she eats with
Heinz mustard and ketchup. (This is a sign of Brazilian
sophistication. In cheaper venues the mustard and ketchup
are never Heinz.)

Renata, who is in her thirties, used to date the football
coach Wanderley Luxemburgo. She explains, in between
mouthfuls, how they met. 'It was on the Avenida Brasil. He
followed my car. When we both parked I told him to stop
following me. He said he couldn't stop following such a
beautiful woman.' I nod my head as if to say, 'Of course!'

The couple started a relationship – extramarital, on his part – which in 1993 grew from sexual to financial. Luxemburgo employed Renata as his proxy. She would attend auctions and buy him assets such as property, cars and jet-skis. Only she bought so much that it caught the attention of tax investigators. In August 2000, a Rio judge approved a police request to inspect Luxemburgo's private bank accounts on suspicion of tax evasion. The ruling was an issue of great public interest since by that time Luxemburgo was coach of the national football team.

Luxemburgo had inherited the post – the most important in the country, it is often said, next to the Brazilian president – after the 1998 World Cup. Under his command the team won the 1999 Copa América. Yet performances had subsequently deteriorated. Embarrassingly so. In the qualifying group for the 2002 World Cup, Brazil lost to Paraguay and Chile within a month. It was only the second and third time that Brazil had lost a qualifier in the tournament's seventy-year history. Luxemburgo's popularity was in freefall. When news of his alleged financial improprieties broke, the public hooted with *schadenfreude*.

Journalists following up the tax case discovered, to their delight, that Renata was not standing by her ex-man. Quite the opposite. Renata and Luxemburgo had fallen out and she was suing him for about £500,000 in allegedly unpaid wages and commissions. Egged on by the press it was not long before both were venting their spleens in public. She tells me that her intention was never to attack her ex-boss, but she was provoked by his comments about her. 'When I heard him say that he didn't know me, I cried and cried. People told me that I had to stop being a little girl and start to say what I knew.'

And boy, what did she know! Or what she said she knew. Renata opened the lid on football's sleaze like no one before. Her most seriously-taken claim was that Luxemburgo, when he was a club coach, made illegal 'bungs' from buying and selling players. It was assumed that this went on anyway, but Renata's allegations had pressing relevance because of Luxemburgo's position and because she claimed she had proof.

Renata also displayed an innate talent for self-publicity. Luxemburgo, she said, insisted she dress in Palmeiras's football shirt, long white football socks and high heels for sex.

Bombarded by allegations, Luxemburgo flew to the Sydney Olympics. The Olympic gold is the only major football title that eludes Brazil. Had Luxemburgo won it he may have regained public favour. Instead, Brazil were knocked out in the most unexpected and humiliating fashion – in the quarter-finals against Cameroon, who had only nine men on the pitch. A week later Luxemburgo was sacked.

The combined effect of Cameroon and Renata Alves put Brazilian football into an unprecedented crisis. Brazilians were already aware that there was something rotten at the heart of their domestic game. They were barely able to organise a national league, games were played to half-empty stadiums, most clubs were on the verge of bankruptcy and their best footballers played in Europe. Yet while the national team did well these problems could be brushed under the carpet. Now the national team was an international laughing stock. Politicians sensed the climate to act. Within days of Luxemburgo's dismissal, the Senate – the upper house of Congress – launched a high-profile investigation into the state of the game.

The investigation had the status of a Parliamentary Commission of Inquiry (CPI), which is the most serious type of congressional hearing. CPIs have stronger powers of investigation than police, since they can open up bank accounts, tax and telephone records. CPIs had previously concerned themselves with issues such as drug-trafficking, banking corruption and the judiciary. Now, for the first time, football was in the dock.

Renata's accusations were crucial – if not pivotal – in

provoking the Senate's CPI, since they provided a starting point for investigations. She was football's whistle-blower. I can tell Renata has adapted to her public role with brio. She is playing brilliantly the soap-opera role of a wronged woman fighting for justice. 'I am no longer the "ex-secretary" or "ex-lover",' she gloats. 'I am "Renata Alves". I am public property.' She relishes telling me that she has nine lawyers and that she has bought six wigs to disguise herself and sometimes travels in the boot of a car to avoid the press. She is starting up a website – www.renataalves.com.br – on which I later read such indispensable tips such as: 'If you start a new relationship never take your mobile phone to the restaurant. Your ex-boyfriend could call.'

Renata tells me that in the morning she had posed for pictures for a bikini catalogue. She adds that she has been inundated by all the top-shelf magazines. They want to take pictures of her wearing nothing but a Palmeiras top, big white footballers' socks and high heels.

Posing naked is a tried-and-tested way of affirming female celebrity. *Playboy*, regularly the country's biggest-selling monthly magazine, is a traditional showcase for football's muses. Ronaldo's two bizarrely identical ex-girlfriends, for example, launched a career as the 'Ronaldas' by appearing in lesbian clinches in its pages.

I suggest to Renata that she will be doing herself a disservice posing nude since she will lose all her credibility.

'I don't agree,' she replies. 'People who see the photos will think: "Didn't Wanderley choose well."'

The Senate CPI gave Aldo Rebelo the political momentum to resurrect his Nike inquiry, which also had the status of a CPI. Congress had never put football under the spotlight before. Now both the lower and the upper house were doing it at the same time.

Aldo wanted to clear up once and for all what happened on the day of the 1998 World Cup final. To do this his investigating commission voted to call up the main characters surrounding the mystery of Ronaldo's health. First up is Mário Zagallo. I fly to Brasília to watch the events from the touchline.

It gives me an opportunity to meet Aldo, who is rapidly becoming the most popular Latin American Communist after Fidel Castro. We dine together in a silver service Spanish restaurant a few blocks from Congress. On the next table is Pedro Malan, the Brazilian Chancellor of the Exchequer. Aldo very much fulfils the international left-wing aesthetic. He has a thick Stalin-style moustache, he chainsmokes high tar cigarettes and tends to slip into Marxist jargon. Yet he is earnest without being humourless. He smiles often, with a broad grin of perfect teeth. I have the impression of a decent, hardworking and idealistic man.

In 1998, when the Brazil squad returned home after losing in France, Aldo says that he saw a picture in a newspaper of fans waiting at Rio international airport. One held a banner with the Brazilian flag, where in place of the motto 'Order and Progress' was the word 'Nike'. A CBF heavy destroyed the protest. Aldo says this image crystallised his thoughts as to what was going on.

'Of course we gave away sovereignty,' he argues. 'I think that the CBF betrayed the nation, even though I don't think they had that intention.' He believes that the Nike contract debased the national team by forcing it to play an inordinate number of lesser nations purely for the purposes of marketing. 'Disney didn't export Mickey and Donald, but the CBF sold the national team,' he says. 'There is nothing more representative of the country than football. It is an element of our self-respect. You cannot let business destroy the passion.'

Until his CPI was installed, Aldo was better known as the deputy behind a bill to defend the Portuguese language from foreign – particularly American English – words. 'My two battles are part of the same general fight,' says Aldo, puffing on a Marlboro. 'It's a fight for the preservation of national identity in front of the pressure of globalisation. I think you can integrate in the world without accepting [other countries'] cultural standards.'

Aldo talks with a distinctive regional twang. He is from Viçosa, a small town in Alagoas, where his father was a farm hand on a large cattle estate. It was a very poor childhood. Aldo says he grew up playing football with oranges, adding that green ones are best since they are less soft. He is clearly passionate about football. He starts reciting teams from the late 1960s and early 1970s.

'Félix, Oliveira, Galhardo, Assis and Marco Antonio. Denílson and Didi. Cafuringa, Samarone, Flávio and Lula,' he says without pausing for breath. The line-up was Fluminense's from the Roberto Gomes Pedrosa Cup in 1969, which he remembers listening to on the radio. 'For the final match Flávio was injured and Mickey played in his place. He scored the winning goal from his head from a free-kick taken by Denílson.'

Aldo managed to leave Viçosa to study in Maceió, the Alagoan capital. There he became one of the leaders of the anti-dictatorship student movement. He was first elected to Congress in 1989, aged thirty-three. I ask him if he honestly believes that Ronaldo was chosen because of pressure from Nike. He replies: 'It is presumed that Nike preferred their own players to play.' I press him: was there overt pressure to play Ronaldo? 'I am obliged to think this,' he says.

He adds that Nike's presence created a harmful atmosphere within the national team: 'I do not think Nike was the unique cause [of Ronaldo's fit], but I think it helped. I think Ronaldo had more pressure on him than he could cope with.'

I tell Aldo that the appearance of footballers explaining themselves in parliament is particularly comic since most countries would *dream* of reaching the World Cup final, regardless of the scoreline. Aldo breaks into a hearty smile: 'Second place in the World Cup is a complete failure. It's like you are chatting up a girl and she says you are only second in her affections because she prefers someone else.'

On Tuesday, 21 November 2000 – two years, four months and nine days after Brazil lost 3–0 in the Stade de France – Zagallo apppears in front of Aldo's congressional commission. It is one of the most eagerly awaited hearings of the year. Dozens of people cram the neon-lit corridor to queue for a good seat. Few are there for the business in adjacent committee rooms – an investigation into regional funding and one into the occupation of public land in the Amazon.

Zagallo arrives together with Lídio Toledo and Joaquim da Matta. The three men look like country hicks turning up at a city wedding, smartly dressed in different-coloured suits, out-of-place and slightly awed by what is going on around them.

We are let in to the committee room. Zagallo, who has thick glasses and wispy white hair, sits on a raised bench beside Aldo, who is presiding over the hearing. Facing them are several benches of deputies and behind that about fifty members of the press.

In his folksy manner, Zagallo begins the session as if he is an introduced guest on a TV sports show: 'It's a great pleasure to be here . . . I could never shirk an engagement in which the yellow and green is to the fore. I always like to talk about the yellow and green and it couldn't be any other way.'

Suddenly he turns aggressive. He holds up a copy of a sports paper and says that it alleges that he sent a letter to try to stop the investigations taking place. He claims it's a lie.

'I want to see who's got morals round here,' he charges.

The deputies start shouting 'order, order' into their microphones.

'I'm not dishonest, dammit!' responds Zagallo.

Aldo tells him he cannot speak out of turn.

'What's this about? You want me to keep quiet while all this is being said? This is ridiculous.'

Eduardo Campos, a young deputy from Pernambuco, says: 'I am probably half your age, but I am showing many times your equilibrium . . . please don't feel attacked, but don't have the petulance to attack whoever it might be in this house.'

Zagallo's face is bright red – half in anger and half in embarrassment. His aggressive style backfired. He looks completely humiliated. Zagallo, who is sixty-nine, is Brazil's most decorated World Cup footballer. He played in 1958 and 1962, coached in 1974, was assistant coach in 1994 and coached again in 1998. He is the embodiment of Brazil, the talisman of the national team. The deputies are treating him like he is a defendant in a murder trial. The clash of football and political cultures is descending into farce.

Dr Rosinha, a left-wing deputy with a bushy beard, mutters: 'He's not at the touchline of a football pitch where he can shout at the players.'

The confusion about the letter is explained. Zagallo signed a statement for the CBF, denying that Nike had influence over the national team. The statement was used by the CBF in a letter it sent out to lobby against the hearings. But Zagallo's confrontational approach sets the tone. Once the atmosphere calms down, he is very defensive and unhelpful.

He explains his version of events at the Château de Grande Romaine in Lésigny near Paris on 12 July.

Zagallo says that the team had lunch together and then everyone went back to their rooms. He went to his, where he watched a video of France's semi-final against Croatia. He said he heard a commotion going on outside, but assumed it was French fans, so he paid no attention. He then went to sleep until about 5pm. Only when he left his room was he told that Ronaldo had had a funny turn – about three hours after it happened.

In the evening, Ronaldo was sent to the Lilas clinic in Paris. Zagallo went to the Stade de France with the rest of the squad.

Zagallo says that Edmundo was chosen in Ronaldo's place. During the team-talk he says that to motivate the players he told them the story of the 1962 World Cup, when Pelé was forced out through injury but Brazil still won.

About forty minutes before the match Ronaldo turned up at the stadium and, according to Zagallo, started putting on his kit. The tests had revealed nothing. Ronaldo was itching to play. 'Faced with this reaction, I chose Ronaldo,' Zagallo tells the hearing. 'Now, was it his being chosen that caused Brazil to lose? Absolutely not. I think it was the [collective] trauma, created by the atmosphere of what had happened.'

The cross-examination feels more like a glorified post-match press conference. The deputies ask questions like frustrated sports journalists. Zagallo defends his decision by saying: 'If you invert the situation, and I didn't put Ronaldo on and then Brazil lost 3–0, then people would say, "Zagallo is stubborn, he had to put him on, [Ronaldo] was the best player in the world." . . . So I think I would do the same thing again . . . I even asked [Ronaldo] at half-time: "How are you feeling?" [He said] "Zagallo, don't worry I'm feeling fine".'

He justifies his decision by repeatedly referring to the medical tests. 'The [medical] results, I always say, were from a French clinic.' He stresses the word 'French' as if that guarantees its authority. For if it was a *Brazilian* clinic no one would believe it.

After Zagallo speaks for four hours, Lídeo Toledo and Joaquim da Matta are called up together. One of the deputies is a doctor and the conversation becomes very technical.

Toledo and da Matta say they are still unsure of what really happened to Ronaldo. They say it cannot have been any sort of a fit since there were no traces of anything in the tests. They say they have spoken to medics and colleagues about what it could have been and no one knows. Ronaldo's incident, they say, was unique in the history of sports medicine.

Toledo, like Zagallo, defends his decision to let Ronaldo play by stressing that he had been given the all clear. 'The French doctors said he could play. They only asked him one thing – that he didn't score a goal against France.'

He describes the pressure he was under: 'Imagine if I stopped [Ronaldo] playing and Brazil lost. And if afterwards he said: "I didn't play because of Dr Lídio." At that moment I'd have to go and live on the North Pole.'

The first day of evidence, while full of colour, does not appear to be incriminating Nike. All the witnesses deny that the sportswear manufacturer called the shots backstage. We wait anxiously for Edmundo, who appears at the hearing two days later. Edmundo had made leading comments after the final that the Nike contract forced Brazil to play Ronaldo for ninety minutes.

Like a good detective yarn, gradually a full picture is unravelling. Edmundo keeps the hearing gripped as he takes us through his side of the story.

I was in the hotel just after lunch. It's usual for players to go to their rooms and rest. Those who like to sleep sleep, others like to read, others like to listen to music. So, I was in my room. It was one of those rooms linked to another room. There was me and Doriva in one, and Ronaldo and Roberto Carlos in the other. About 3pm, I can't remember the exact time, I was watching television and Roberto came into the room: 'Edmundo! Edmundo! Doriva! Ronaldo's feeling unwell!' And when I saw what it was I despaired, because it was a really strong and shocking scene. And I ran through the whole hotel, hitting all the doors and shouting for everyone, so that the doctors would come as soon as possible. Since the rooms where the doctors and coaching staff were were a little further away, the footballers got there first. I shouted to everyone and returned to the room. When I got there César Sampaio was already administering first aid: he

was unrolling [Ronaldo's] tongue, that sort of thing.
It was César Sampaio and me that took the initiative,
because no one ever knows what to do, whether to do
this or that, before the doctors arrive. And, eventu-
ally, we managed to unroll his tongue, he fell asleep
and the doctors got everyone together and told us:
'Look, we've got a really important game, a World
Cup final, and Ronaldo will wake up and not know
what happened. So, we're not going to say anything
until the time of the game. Let's all go back to our
rooms and rest.' We were to have a snack at about
6pm. We went back to our rooms, we rested, but, you
know what I mean, everyone was worried. My room
was linked, so I saw everything. Every five minutes
someone came and stared, and Ronaldo was there,
sleeping like a baby. When it got to 6pm, snack time,
we were all like we are here, eating. Ronaldo was the
last to arrive. He sat down, didn't speak to anyone,
which wasn't normal, he always messed around. This
time he spoke to nobody. He sat down, with his head
down, and didn't eat anything. He got up and went
towards the football pitch that was at the side of the
restaurant. And Leonardo got up in desperation and
said: 'Doctor, you've got to take this lad for some
tests, I don't know what, he's not well.' That was
when the doctors approached Ronaldo and told him
everything and that they would take him for the tests.
He said: 'No, I've got to play. It's the World Cup
final, I want to play, I want to play' . . . the doctors
told us afterwards that they told him: 'You'll do all
the tests. If you are well, then you'll come back and
play.'

Deputy José Rocha wants more details. He asks: 'When
you got to Ronaldo's room, the horrible scene that you
described, how did you find him? Was he hitting out, or
shaking?'

Edmundo replies: 'Yes. He was hitting out a lot. I don't . . .'

'Lying down?'

'Lying down, and hitting himself with his hands like this, with his teeth . . .'

'Together?'

'Locked together and with his mouth foaming.'

'Foaming?'

'And it was really shocking for me because he is a strong lad. He's big. And doing that with all that strength.'

'His whole body hitting itself?'

'The whole body, yes.'

'And some of your team-mates had to hold down his arms?'

'Yes.'

Deputy José Rocha then asks what time Zagallo arrived.

Edmundo replies: 'I can't be precise, because one building was for the players, and the other was for the coaching staff. But maybe ten, fifteen minutes.'

'Ten minutes, fifteen minutes?' repeats the deputy.

Edmundo agrees: 'Definitely no later than that.'

Aha! The hearing has stumbled on its first cover-up. Zagallo had said he only found out three hours later. Who is lying and why?

I return to Brasília a month and a half later to see Ronaldo's deposition. He is the star witness. The committee room is packed with journalists and public squashing to get a view. Aldo Rebelo has brought his son, Pedro, to ask for an autograph.

Ronaldo is looking very smart in a light-coloured suit and plain blue tie. I need to pinch myself to remind myself of the absurdity of the situation. Here is the world's most famous football player, still only aged twenty-four, having to explain to his own parliament why he lost a football match.

The session starts and the atmosphere is tense. Aldo, explaining the formalities, tells Ronaldo he has a maximum

Ronaldo and Aldo Rebelo in Congress

of twenty minutes to state his case before answering questions.

Ronaldo, grinning, looks at the empty bench in front of him and says: 'Do I, as a witness, have the right to a glass of water?' It's a perfect opener. His cheeky charm wins over his audience immediately.

Ronaldo is smooth and well-prepared. He takes the deputies through 12 July 1998. He had lunch and went to bed for a rest. When he woke up, at about 5pm, he joined his team-mates for the afternoon snack. Leonardo started to tell him that there are more important things in life than a game of football. He did not understand why Leonardo was telling him this. It was only revealed to him after the snack, when the doctors told him that he had suffered from a mysterious fit.

One deputy probes the Zagallo cover-up. He asks if the coach had gone to see him fifteen minutes or three hours after his fit. The deputy camps up his delivery, like he is asking if Colonel Mustard left the lead piping in the conservatory or in the kitchen.

Ronaldo replies confidently: 'I think at that moment there

were more important things to know than if Zagallo had gone to see me or not.' His answer kills that line of enquiry stone dead. The Zagallo cover-up is a red herring.

There is a comic lack of coherence to some of the questioning. Deputy Eduardo Campos asks: 'In the national team's tactical scheme, you had a role . . . This is fact, it was reported at the time in some newspapers, you had a role in marking Zidane . . . or is this . . .'

'Who did? I had a role?' asks Ronaldo.

'Yes. In the tactical scheme, in marking Zidane?'

'Is this really going to help . . . for the CPI?' Ronaldo protests.

'It will. I think it will. Otherwise I wouldn't have asked.'

'OK. I can't remember about Zidane's marker, who had to mark him.'

'You don't remember?'

'You mean at the moment of the goal . . .'

'No,' says the deputy. 'Not at the moment of the goal.'

Ronaldo carries on: '. . . or during the game?'

'During the game.'

'Ah, I don't remember who had to mark . . . Zidane. I also think that whoever should have marked him didn't mark him very well, right?'

Deputy Eduardo Campos jokes back: 'Because two went in, yeah?'

Ronaldo agrees: 'Yeah, right.' The chamber laughs, it seems to me, in nervous relief.

The purpose of the investigation is the Nike–CBF contract. Ronaldo is asked about his own contract with Nike. He says he cannot talk about it because he signed a secrecy clause. The deputies say that he is legally obliged to by the statutes of the hearing.

'I'm not here to defend Nike or the CBF, but I also have my own opinion,' says Ronaldo, now slightly irritated. 'I'm here to try to clarify things and to give my opinion if need be. But . . . I have no doubt that Nike is serious . . . Sincerely, if I was Nike I wouldn't think twice about taking this contract, ripping it up and leaving Brazil, because of all these problems. Because I can't remember in the history of Brazilian football a contract to help Brazilian football grow . . . I can't remember a contract that has had such a big interest from such an important business for Brazilian football. So, the relation that I have with Nike is a very good one, because it really never demanded anything of me, apart from using its boots during games, which is the least I could do, and, preferably, score a few goals with their boots. That's the only thing that Nike have ever asked me for.'

As the hearing draws to a close, several deputies make sycophantic remarks. 'I hope that you get back to playing as soon as possible,' says Sérgio Reis, referring to a knee injury that has kept him out of action for about two years. 'And a request by a fan of the Ruby-and-Black Nation that, when you come back, perhaps you return to our dear Flamengo.'

Deputy Ronaldo Vasconcellos says that Ronaldo's cautious answers are making him more like a defender than a striker.

The footballer disagrees.

Deputy Ronaldo Vasconcellos apologises: 'OK. I don't want to make you feel uncomfortable. Dear Ronaldo, people say a lot of things. Now I want to ask you in an objective manner. I know it's not easy putting it down in a few minutes or seconds: Why, in the opinion of the athlete Ronaldo, did Brazil not win the World Cup in France?'

Ronaldo loses his patience: 'Why didn't we win? Because we let in three goals, because we lost, because . . . I don't know. In football – not just in football, but in sport – you win and you lose. How many times has Brazil won? And no one asked why, or a few people asked, why we won. But you win and you lose. We lost. Be patient. Just because we lost are we going to invent a bunch of mysteries, invent a bunch of stuff?'

'A destiny?' suggests Deputy Ronaldo Vasconcellos.

'Probably,' says Ronaldo.

'Good health to you, sir,' says the deputy, and he switches off his microphone.*

After the defeat against Cameroon, it is thought that the national team has reached rock bottom. Yet the Olympic débâcle is merely a sign of humiliations to come. First, the CBF cannot find a coach willing to replace Luxemburgo. After three weeks under a caretaker, Candinho, it offers the job to the former national goalkeeper Emerson Leão. He continues the downward slide, acquiring a knack for losing to teams which have never previously beaten Brazil – Ecuador, in a World Cup qualifier, and Australia, in the third place play-off of the Confederations Cup. Leão's woeful reign has a correspondingly ignominious end: dismissal in the departure lounge of Tokyo airport. Luiz Felipe Scolari takes over on a wave of popular support – the fourth coach in nine months. Brazil fly to the 2001 Copa América in Colombia with renewed hope. Yet they have further to fall. Scolari's men are knocked out by Honduras. *Honduras?*

Meanwhile, the CPIs are revealing almost comic levels of corruption and incompetence. Hardly a day passes without new accusations. For months the sports pages of Brazilian newspapers look more like the crime pages. The parliamentary investigations are a fitting backdrop for the striking decline of the national team. It is impossible not to see them as influencing each other. The worse the team performs, the more the investigations gather steam. The more dirt the investigations uncover, the more demoralised the team

---

*While this signals the end of the public inquisition into Ronaldo's fit, the press are not convinced and continue to speculate. The most plausible explanation is printed more than a year later, in January 2002. A report in *Lance!* quotes a source close to Ronaldo saying that the striker had an injection in his knee of the common anaesthetic xylocaine ten minutes before the fit, which entered a vain accidentally. It adds that Ronaldo did not tell anyone at the time so as to protect the team medic. Both Ronaldo and Toledo deny the allegation.

becomes. How can footballers wear the national shirt with pride, or supporters cheer them on, if national football is being revealed as rotten to the core? Brazilian football, for the time being, is set on a vicious circle of self-destruction.

In the Senate, Renata Alves's testimony does not disappoint. She says that there used to be a house in Rio nicknamed the 'embassy', where coaches, agents, club directors and members of the CBF met to do deals, pay commissions and even fix matches. She says that Luxemburgo would take money in cash dollars stuffed in a 007-style briefcase. The CPI also receives a fax in which Renata claims that before he went on international flights, Luxemburgo would fill footballs with 'a white powder similar to the drug known as cocaine'. Luxemburgo denies the allegations, and counters the attack by saying that Renata is using the fax as extortion.

The president of the Minas Gerais Football Federation, Elmer Guilherme Ferreira, is questioned about nepotism. He replies that he 'tries to surround himself with people he can trust'. The Minas Gerais Football Federation is revealed to employ twenty-seven of Elmer's relatives, including brothers, cousins, nephews, uncles and his father.

In the House of Deputies, Aldo is casting his net wider than the Nike–CBF contract and has begun to examine the broader issue of commercialisation in football. His CPI, in fact, is becoming the football equivalent of the Untouchables. A delegation flies to Europe to investigate the trafficking of underage players and false passports. They bring back Fabio Faria dos Santos, a sixteen-year-old, who gives moving evidence. He says that he was taken to Belgium by an agent on the promise that he would get a false passport and be negotiated to a team within a fortnight. He was abandoned by the agent and lived clandestinely for eight months, only surviving thanks to handouts from a family of Brazilians he was lucky enough to meet.

Aldo also travels. In Maranhão, a poor state in the northeast, he orders the arrest of the vice-president of the state football federation, who is accused of having a stack of forged birth certificates at his home. It is common in Brazil to adulterate ages because younger players can be sold for more money. A footballer with a false age is called a 'gato' – a *cat*. Aldo discovers a 'supercat' – Rosenílton Torres, who was transferred to Belgium with a document saying he was seven years younger than he is. Aldo describes Maranhão as a 'cat factory' for the ease and frequency of adulterated birth certificates. One tiny club, Americano, sold a hundred players abroad in five years. Americano do not even dispute the state championship, claiming lack of funds.

The picture that is emerging of Brazilian football is that it is a vast, unregulated bazaar of bartering players for personal gain. A modern day slavery – a scramble to sign up the 'rights' to promising youngsters and then make money by selling them to the highest bidder. While a few cartolas and agents are becoming very rich, most clubs are left destitute, most players are impoverished, and the 'beautiful game' lies on the operating table.

(I use the term 'slavery' with reason. Once in Florianópolis I met with Vidomar Porto, who used to be the night watchman at local club Avaí. Vidomar, aged forty-five, was not paid his wages so he sued his employer. The court ordered Avaí to pay up. Only the club was broke. Its only liquid asset was its striker, Claudiomir. So the judge ordered that Claudiomir become Vidomar's property.

But what could a night watchman do with a striker? Vidomar wanted money. So he decided to sell him to another team. 'I telephoned Claudiomir,' Vidomar told me. 'He accepted it well. He knew I didn't have anything against him. We were friends just like we were before.' The pair, accompanied by Vidomar's lawyer, Waldemar Justino, drove up the coast to sell him to Joinville, a rival club.)

Little thought is given to investment on football infrastructure, education or development. There are some exceptions. In Salvador, Unicef runs a one-off scheme that gives 'citizenship' lessons to Vitória's junior teams. Ruy Pavan, the coordinator, says that players are taught about workers' rights, black pride and gender issues. 'The majority of players are poor and black. They are very exposed and not always prepared.' He adds that the teenagers enjoy the classes but are more interested in practical advice. 'They have had such wretched upbringings that they often do not know how to run a bath.'

Several European clubs have links with Brazil. The most directly involved is Internazionale of Milan, which funds football training centres in eight states. They provide sporting materials and teachers for 5,600 nine- to thirteen-year-olds. Children attending these centres, if they are any good, are then attached to Brazilian clubs and when they become adults Inter have first refusal on signing them as pros. It is philanthropic, but does nothing to stop the drain of good players abroad.

In Maceió I visit a club that has very efficiently turned football into an export commodity. Corinthians Alagoano, named after the São Paulo club, was founded in 1991. Four years later the club made its debut in the second division of the Alagoas state league, one of the minor state leagues. Corinthians won promotion in its first year, but abdicated its right to play in division one. Its president, João Feijó, explained that his players were like baby crabs – he wanted to fatten them in the second division and sell them at maximum profit. In the first division, the costs were too high.

After topping the second division again in 1997, Corinthians were unable to avoid the misfortune of promotion, and have played in the first division since 1998. I arrive at their administrative offices, one block from the beach. The building looks more like an insurance broker's than a football club. There is a yellow sofa in reception, a pool out the back and bright-coloured modern art hanging on the walls. The club has no fans nor state titles, yet it is the richest in town.

I am handed a press release, which tells me that the club's principal objective is to 'discover players and launch them in Brazilian and international football'. It includes a list of fifteen players it claims it has produced – five play in Portugal, two in Japan and one each in Italy, Turkey and Russia. Not bad going for a team that is not even ten years old. And not bad too considering Maceió is a football back-water.

Fernando Aguiar, the club's director of football, takes me upstairs. We pass a cabinet full of trophies. He leads me into the Marketing Room. Through the back, like a secret chamber, there is a professional video-editing suite. I am told that every player in the Corinthians squad is made his own 'showreel', compiled with his best performances. Each video is recorded twice – once in Portuguese and once in English.

Fernando explains that the market price for a Brazilian goes up and down depending on the performances of the national team. 'Foreign clubs assume that the best Brazilians play for their country,' he says. 'So if the best players are playing badly, then they assume that the others must be even worse.' After the 1994 World Cup, business boomed. Now, with Brazilian football in crisis, Corinthians' trade is down.

One anecdote concerning Corinthians' president, João Feijó, reinforces just how businesslike the club is run. An old school friend bumped into him and said: 'João, there's this fantastic kid who plays kickabouts near where I live – you should take a look at him.'

João Feijó immediately took out his laptop and typed in the child's name. After a few seconds he said: 'No. He's no good. I have a list of all the best young players in the state and he isn't one of them.'

In its colonial period, Brazil's rural structure was based on huge estates, or 'latifundos', where typically only one crop was grown – such as sugar, cocoa or coffee. Latifundos were based on slavery and upheld the local oligarchies.

Even though there has been some change to break up large properties and diversify crops, in the poorer parts of the country the latifundo system survives almost intact. The first time I came to Alagoas, in 1999, I visited a sugar estate

The CBF entrance

four times the size of Manhattan. It had a population of 10,000 and, like a postcard from a forgotten world, a private steam railway with a 1920s English locomotive. Most of the estate's inhabitants cut the cane with their hands and were earning about £10 for a seven-day week. Not slavery, but almost.

My research into the commercialisation of football was reminding me of the latifundos. Brazil is the world's largest exporter of sugar, coffee *and* footballers. I began to see the country like a big estate where the agricultural product is 'futebol'. The country is a sporting monoculture. And football mirrors the old hierarchies. The oligarchic powers are sustained by those at the bottom, who like the cane-cutters, live on almost nothing.

The offices of the Brazilian Football Confederation, the CBF, are situated in the Rua da Alfândega, a narrow side street in the centre of Rio. The frontage looks like the back-entrance to a block of flats. The door is a metal grille. Behind it sits a grumpy man who could be the janitor. His cubby-hole is lit by a neon horseshoe lamp on the ceiling. There is neither a welcome sign nor a plaque. The only way of knowing you are at the headquarters of the most glamorous football team in the world is three CBF crests in the gate and a battered CBF doormat. The entrance is so nondescript and run-down, in fact, that when Luiz Felipe Scolari went there for the first time after being made national coach he could not find it and had to be shown the way by journalists.

At the beginning of my research I visited the CBF library. I arrived at the offices and the janitor buzzed me in. I waited for several minutes as he chatted to a friend on the telephone, showing no concern in attending to me. He then told me to go upstairs. I took the lift and got out at the third floor. Behind a green metal door was a medium-sized room that looked like a second-hand bookshop. Along one wall shelves were clumsily stacked with books and files. In a corner sat the librarian, wearing a grey tanktop, maroon tie and a pair of glasses connected round the back of his head by string.

He looked up at me and pointed to a table, which was covered in books, papers, a small tree of garlic cloves, paper clips, a stapler and a packet of pork scratchings.

'Sit down there and research,' he barked, as if he was a prison warder and I a new internee.

I read a sign on the wall: 'If possible, please do not smoke.' *If possible?*

The CBF library was almost useless. The book collection was neither comprehensive nor catalogued. It was also difficult to concentrate since the librarian was listening to his radio at full volume.

I remember wondering at the time where all the CBF's Nike money had gone, since it had obviously not been spent on sprucing up their offices. Or on training personnel in the art of good manners. If I had wanted any proof that the CBF was run – at least superficially – like the worst type of state firm, then I had found it on my first day out.

Within Brazil, the CBF is seen in much the same way as all authority; untrustworthy, incompetent and corrupt. Its international nadir came at about 9pm on 19 December 1983. Two men entered the Rua da Alfândega offices. They bound, gagged and blindfolded the night watchman and took the lift to the ninth floor – where the Jules Rimet Cup was kept.

The World Cup's gold trophy had been given to Brazil for keeps after they won the tournament, in 1970, for the third time. To safeguard the prize, the CBF owned a replica cup and had a cabinet fronted with bullet-proof glass. Yet in its wisdom, the CBF kept the replica hidden in a cupboard and the bullet-proof cabinet was nailed into the wall – which meant that any half-brained thief only needed a crowbar to prise it open from the back. The robbery lasted twenty minutes and the Jules Rimet Cup was never seen again.

(Four people were eventually convicted for their part in the crime, although the details of what happened are still unclear. It is understood that the cup, made of 1.8kg of gold, was sawn into pieces and melted down into bars.)

One of the principal reasons the CBF is held in such low esteem is that it has proved incapable of organising a credible national league. In 1989, a new president took over with the promise that he would put football's house in order. Ricardo Teixeira, then aged forty-two, was a financier with no previous involvement in sports administration. Yet he had impeccable family connections. Teixeira was married to the only child of João Havelange.

Havelange is the spiritual figurehead of the Brazilian sporting establishment. A former athlete – he competed twice at the Olympic Games, as a swimmer in 1936 and in the water polo team in 1952 – he has dominated football for more than forty years. He was president of the CBF's precursor, the CBD, between 1958 and 1974. That year he became FIFA's president, a position he held until 1998. Havelange is still an imposing character; the strongest-looking eighty-four-year-old you have ever seen.

Brazil is unique in being represented by a football confederation rather than a federation. This is a consequence of the state-based way the sport originated. Each state has a federation, which votes on the CBF president. The system distorts power since all states have the same power of vote, even though, for example, São Paulo is more than a hundred times as populous as Roraima. Teixeira was elected after a campaign that involved paying some of the poorer federations with his own money. In power, he continued the nepotistic atmosphere started by his father-in-law, appointing his uncle, a chemist, and his cousin to prominent CBF positions.

It was not long before Teixeira became a widely despised figure. In 1993, Pelé gave a voice to the prevailing anti-Teixeira sentiment. In an interview to Brazilian *Playboy*, he claimed that the CBF was corrupt.

Havelange retaliated on behalf of the family and excluded Pelé from the launch ceremony of the 1994 World Cup – a move which attracted worldwide condemnation as a petty, dictatorial act.

The incident, however, that confirmed Teixeira's unpopularity occurred immediately after Brazil won the 1994 World Cup. When the squad arrived back from the United States, the plane was carrying fifteen tonnes of baggage, mostly of electronic goods bought by players and the CBF entourage. Teixeira demanded that the products pass through Rio airport customs without inspection, therefore avoiding tax. He argued that there were crowds of supporters waiting to see the team and there would be a safety risk if they delayed the planned victory procession. He made several threats to customs officers, encouraging players to do the same, saying that they would throw their medals away and refuse to parade if they were not let through immediately. The matter was only solved when the government in Brasília intervened and liberated the baggage without inspection. After public outrage, the CBF supplied a list of items afterwards for which they paid duty, although the list contained items that only weighed just over one tonne – leaving fourteen tonnes unaccounted for.

In 1996 Ricardo Teixeira signed the Nike deal. It might

have been for the good of Brazilian football, yet Teixeira's refusal to make the contract public aroused many doubts. Suspicions were vindicated when the clause guaranteeing an average of five 'Nike friendlies' a year became known.

A few weeks into the CPI investigations Teixeira told the press that he had already changed the 'Nike friendlies' clause. He admitted that he made a mistake because he forgot that if Brazil did not win the 1998 World Cup then its diary would be full of World Cup qualifiers. In 1996, when the contract came into effect, Brazil were exempt from qualifiers as champions.

Teixeira renegotiated to reduce the number of 'Nike friendlies' to two a year. He did this seven months previously, but, in keeping with the CBF's policy of non-transparency, did not make it public. Why such secrecy?

Ricardo Teixeira's arch enemy is Juca Kfouri, the journalist who interviewed Pelé for *Playboy* and to whom the Nike contract was first leaked. On the basis of these scoops alone, Juca is Brazil's most influential sportswriter. He is also the most prolific: he has a daily backpage column in *Lance!*, a daily weekday football show on national radio and a football television progamme on Sundays. What most sets him apart from his peers is that he is essentially a campaigning journalist. It is as if Paul Foot presents *Match of the Day*, commentates on Radio Five Live and has a football column in the *Sun*.

I travel to São Paulo to speak to Juca about the parliamentary investigations. I meet him in the studios of Rádio CBN shortly before he goes on air at 8pm. We walk into a soundproof studio and shut the door behind us. Juca is tall and professorial, with a big forehead and brushed-back black hair that shines in light curves. When he speaks he scowls slightly and leans forward with a learned nod. 'Brazil is in transition,' he begins. 'We only became a democracy recently – in 1985. But the last thing to change in this country will be the structure of football. It is reactionary. It is corrupt. It is profoundly corrupt.'

Juca's fight against the Brazilian football establishment has made him a distinguished national figure. His reputation goes beyond Brazil's borders. When, in 1998, he was refused a World Cup press pass, he became an international cause célèbre. After FIFA relented, he received messages that Ricardo Teixeira would send his son – a martial arts black belt – to beat him up. I tell him that I find it odd that the country's best-known sports journalist is so militantly against the footballing powers. 'Someone had to do it,' he replies. 'For a long time I felt very alone.'

If there is a weakness in Juca's position it is that Ricardo Teixeira, irrespective of whether he is corrupt or not, has presided over the Brazilian national team's best results in more than thirty years. Brazil were world champions in 1994 and were second in 1998. Not since 1958 and 1962 has Brazil played in two consecutive World Cup finals. Does he not deserve some credit?

'The victory in 1994 wasn't like the others,' Juca replies. 'Brazil won because Roberto Baggio missed a penalty. And you can't forget about the [controversial] performance of the Costa Rican ref against Holland [in the quarter-final].' Juca believes that Brazil have triumphed in spite of the cartolas. 'When the national team starts a game with Ricardo Teixeira in charge they are already losing 1–0.'

Juca adds that the good results have, if anything, made it easier for the CBF to get away with unacceptable behaviour. 'In Brazil there is still this ideology of 'rouba mas faz' – *it's OK to steal if you get things done*. In football this is stretched to the most far-reaching consequences. Everything is forgotten in the light of victory. I have always said that God put the best players here and the worst bosses to compensate.'

I ask what his opinion is of the football CPIs. I suggest that they are farcical. What is the benefit for democracy of directionless sessions asking Ronaldo who marked Zidane? He disagrees strongly. He believes the CPIs must be seen as part of Brazil's slow process of democratisation. 'Independent of their final results,' he argues, 'the simple fact that they have

submitted the cartolas to questioning is a service to the citizen.
These people were never submitted to any kind of interrogation. There is an absolute absence of laws.'

I sit through Juca's radio show. It is very good. He is not
a natural broadcaster, but he makes up for a somewhat
forced delivery by his intellectual weight and an unrivalled
contacts book. The evening I am there Pelé is in Rome being
presented with FIFA's award for 'Player of the Century'. Juca
calls Pelé up on his mobile and chats to him live. The two
men are very affectionate with each other.

Pelé says: 'So Juca, I have a question for you now. When
will you write my biography?'

Juca replies good-naturedly: 'When Pelé has time!'

Pelé and Juca have been strong allies since their *Playboy*
interview. Pelé suffered for taking on Teixeira. His sports
marketing companies were practically frozen out of business. Pelé's feud with Teixeira intensified when the ex-
footballer was made Extraordinary Sports Minister in 1995.
In trying to reform football legislation Pelé was attacking
the interests that kept Teixeira in power. Pelé became the
figurehead of football's 'modernisers' – and Juca Kfouri was
his most articulate mouthpiece and confidant.

In February 2001 Juca has another exclusive. It lands like
a bombshell. Pelé and Teixeira are calling a truce. The most
high profile vendetta in Brazilian football is over.

At first I am unsure what it means.

I call Aldo. He is very angry. He believes the pact is a
backroom deal to save both their skins, since Pelé's business
partner, Hélio Viana, is also being investigated by the Nike
CPI. Aldo is not the only one who is furious. The press is
unforgiving. It comes down harshly on Brazil's formerly
untouchable hero. 'The union of Pelé and Ricardo Teixeira
is the biggest stab in the back that those of us fighting for
ethics in sport could receive . . . Pelé has let us all down
. . . He has sold his soul to the devil,' writes José Trajano,
a respected sports journalist, in *Lance!*.

I go to see Juca again. He is clearly devastated. He tells

Ricardo Teixeira and Pelé: Friends again

me that 'the King' has been exposed as a commoner. 'It was a terrible let down. And a great surprise. For eight years Pelé had an essential role in the denouncing of corruption. When we were on our knees, without oxygen, he gave us his hand.'

I ask Juca if he has broken off his friendship. 'Personally it resulted in a distancing, and I have told him that I will not write his biography any more, for obvious reasons. How would I write this chapter?'

My sympathies are with Juca and the 'modernisers', but I am beginning to doubt all their accusations. If corruption is so widespread, I ask him, why is it so difficult to prove? 'This is typical of the democratic process, which is slow,' he replies. 'And it is also typical of Brazilian justice, where things are slower still. But when you read the CPI report it is stunning that these people are not arrested.'

*   *   *

In May 2001, Aldo's investigation into the Nike–CBF contract is completed, after fifty-nine separate hearings totalling 237 hours and involving 125 witnesses. Unable to pin any dirt on Nike, the original villain, the focus became the cartolas, principally at the CBF. Aldo may have wasted time on silly questions with Ronaldo and Roberto Carlos, but serious progress was made in less high-profile sessions. The 686-page report lists thirty-three people who it alleges have committed crimes. Ricardo Teixeira is accused of thirteen, including making bad loans, tax evasion, withholding information, giving misleading information, lying on his tax form, and using CBF money for his private needs. Pelé's partner Hélio Viana is accused of five.

Even though the trigger for the inquiry was whether or not Nike forced Ronaldo to play in the World Cup final, the report uncovered a different cover-up. The real scandal of the Nike deal was what Ricardo Teixeira did with the money. It may have been the largest contract signed with a national team, but accountants looking through the books said that the CBF was so badly managed that were it a business it would be declared insolvent.

From 1997 to 2000, the CBF's revenue quadrupled, but it did not pay off its debts. Ricardo Teixeira, however, did very well out of it. He and his directors received pay rises of more than 300 per cent. Meanwhile, spending on football decreased from a 55 per cent share of the budget to 37 per cent.

The report reveals how Teixeira used the CBF for his personal gain. He sold milk from his ranch to the CBF, and hosted CBF events at his restaurant and nightclub. The report also shows how the CBF shamelessly bought power and influence. In 1998, for example, the CBF gave all-expenses-paid trips for five senior judges to travel to the World Cup. But perhaps the most suspicious outlay was the travel budget. In 2000, the CBF spent $16 million on travel – enough for 1,663 first-class returns from Rio to Australia. Who were they paying for?

I read the document closely and find a mine of suspicious payments. In 2000, for example, the CBF paid £100,000 to a Brasília newspaper for an advert. The ad never appeared, but a fortnight later the paper printed an exclusive interview with Ricardo Teixeira.

A few weeks later I meet Aldo again. He is in Rio to give a talk at the Superior War School on 'Authoritarian and Totalitarian Experience in Republican Brazil'. We dine at the Hotel Glória, a classy 1920s building near the city centre. I order the vegetarian option. When it arrives, underneath a thick layer of mushrooms there are two large breasts of chicken.

I ask Aldo if he is happy with the conclusions of the CPI. I suggest that it failed in its primary objective, which was to find abuses of sovereignty in the Nike contract. The swoosh gets off scot-free. 'The report was very good,' Aldo insists. 'The report was a criticism of the entry of the market into football.'

He does not describe Teixeira as a villain, but as a victim of capitalism. I had almost forgotten that Aldo's motives were ideological. Marxist jargon is creeping into his patter. 'Corruption is a consequence of the shock of capitalism,' he says. 'Corruption is like a skin disease. It is the most visible, but it is not the fundamental problem.'

Ricardo Teixeira, he says, was in charge of the CBF when the world became globalised. 'He was in a position from where he could have preserved Brazilian football. But he didn't look after it. He used it to look after himself. The Nike contract was just the most visible sign of what was going on.'

As our meal progresses, Aldo tells me he is glad the investigation is over. He was exhausted by it. I ask him if he thinks that it will change the way football is run. He does not seem very hopeful. 'There will never be democracy in football. The best we can hope for is that the state will be able to oversee how it is run.' The CBF is a private organisation, so it can do what it likes, despite it being responsible for something as public as the national football team.

Aldo hopes for a change in the law to force the CBF to be more transparent. 'Apart from the top three people [at the CBF] no one has the faintest idea of what is going on.'

He adds again that the main problem isn't corruption. 'There's probably more corruption in Italy,' he says. 'The problem here is disorganisation and the lack of a coherent direction to deal with the money coming in. Brazil might not be in the first world in many things. But in football it is. We have the clubs, the style, the resources. So why are we losing all our stars to Europe? It doesn't make sense.' Despite his attempts to be upbeat, I sense that Aldo is frustrated and sad.

After the Copa América defeat against Honduras, Brazil continue to stumble. In World Cup qualifiers they lose 2–1 to Argentina in Buenos Aires and 3–1 to Bolivia in La Paz. Brazil only guarantee qualification after their last match, a 3–0 victory against Venezuela, thus maintaining – just – their record as the only country to have attended every World Cup.

There is much soul-searching about the national team's unconvincing performances. Some say Brazilians are deficient tactically because of their lack of education. Others that the joy of playing for their country has been overly diluted because of the large number of games the team plays. The *Folha de São Paulo* counts the FIFA-recognised matches that the world's main football nations have played between the 1994 World Cup and the end of the 2002 qualifiers. Brazil are way ahead – 138, compared to 99 for Argentina, 96 for France and 81 for England.

A prevalent view is that Brazil play a negative game. Brazil, argues the former player Tostão, is now the country whose players commit the most fouls. In one top-level match in 2000 there were more than a hundred. (The English Premiership has an average of about thirty). Tostão says this is an indication that Brazil has been left behind while the rest of the world has progressed in tactics and training methods, and also in players' emotional preparation.

Fernando Calazans, another columnist, goes further. He writes that there are so many fouls because there is no leadership within Brazilian football. The chaos and violence in the boardroom is reflected on the pitch.

If there is a unanimous opinion it is that the *sporting* crisis is really a *political* crisis. And that any solution must include a complete clear-out of the cartolas. The amateuristic rules that govern clubs must be modernised. There must be decent domestic leagues. The CBF needs a new, professional leadership. How will this happen? The best – maybe the only – chance is the CPIs.

Aldo Rebelo's CPI was made up of twenty-five federal deputies. They included Eurico Miranda, the president of Vasco. He saw no conflict of interest in being both investigator and investigated. In fact, Eurico was not the only football-linked Congressman on the CPI. So was José Mendonça, the president of Santa Cruz, Luicano Bivar, the president of Sport, Max Rosemann, a director of Paraná Clube, Nelo Rodolfo, a director of Palmeiras, Darcísio Perondi, brother of the president of the Rio Grande do Sul Football Federation, Olímpio Pires, a former president of Itabira and José Rocha, a former president of Vitória. These men – known as the 'football faction' – worked collectively to hinder Aldo Rebelo's inquiry. And they succeeded.

It is a formality that on the last day of a CPI its members vote to approve the commission's final report. Aldo realised that the football faction had managed to persuade enough 'neutral' deputies to vote against it. So he closed the session – reasoning that it was better for there to be no vote than to lose. (It's a common political shenanigan.) When he did this, the football faction shouted across the chamber: 'Stalinist coup!' Eurico stood up, called his sympathisers to his side and guffawed: 'They're using guerilla tactics – I've known what the left is like for a long time!' Eurico then presented his own 'alternative' report, which cleared the CBF. (Eurico and Darcísio Perondi, it should be noted, both received campaign donations from the CBF. They have no interest in the situation changing.)

In the last days of Aldo's CPI, Ricardo Teixeira was in Brasília, staying at the CBF's 'offical residence' – a house with rustic décor in the wealthiest neighbourhood, nicknamed the 'football embassy' and legendary for courting politicans over kickabouts. The CBF was frantically lobbying congressmen to vote against the report. Teixeira had even given a press conference in Brasília with the Brazil coach, Luiz Felipe Scolari, hoping to deflect attention from the allegations against him.

CPIs have no powers of prosecution. They simply make recommendations for investigation that are then passed over to the public prosecutor's office. Aldo delivers his report. The prosecutor's office says it will follow up the allegations against Ricardo Teixeira. Yet Aldo's failure to have his report rubber-stamped by the CPI results in a legal order stating that the information in it is *not* allowed to be followed up by the attorneys. Ricardo Teixeira has slipped through the net. Eight months of investigation, a stackload of accusations and . . . *nada*.

But all is not well for the regime at the CBF. Slowly, the country's institutions are turning against it. TV Globo – the main terrestrial football broadcaster – compiles a report claiming the evidence against Teixeira points strongly to money laundering and fraud. Carlos Melles, the Sports Minister, says publically that he wants Teixeira to resign. And the second CPI, in the Senate, is in full swing. The Senate CPI always had more teeth than Aldo's did, mainly because the 'football faction' has less influence in the upper house than in the lower. Teixeira is obviously worried. He is overheard at a meeting of federation presidents saying: 'If the Senate's [CPI] report . . . is approved, we're fucked.'

(For several months I tried to get an interview with Ricardo Teixeira. I met with his advisor, Mário Rosa, a former journalist who is Brazil's only 'crisis-management' consultant. Mário wanted to fix an interview, saying that

Teixeira's problem is one of poor communication skills, rather than of corruption. I even got to shake Teixeira's hand – Mário introduced us at a CBF press conference. But Teixeira did not look me in the eye. From that moment Mário never returned my calls.)

When Ricardo Teixeira is summonsed by the Senate CPI, he refuses to go. He announces that he is suffering from heart problems and is exempted on medical grounds. He hands over the CBF presidency temporarily to Alfredo Nunes, his deputy. Nunes is a colourful character. He is the mayor of a small town in Piauí, a state with a lower human development index than Papua New Guinea. Nunes is hardly a breath of fresh air. He is accused of fraud in the Piauí Electoral Court. He allegedly bought votes by distributing Brazil football shirts and CBF keyrings.

Yet I sense that the political climate seems to have changed. The cartolas look weaker than they have ever been before. They are now on the defensive. For me, the turning point comes during the interrogation of Edmundo Santos Silva, president of Flamengo, at the Senate CPI. He is suspected of fraud. At the end of his hearing Edmundo bursts into tears. 'I have dignity, and have to look in the face of my children,' he blubbers. 'I'm being treated like a common criminal.' That Edmundo humiliates himself there is no doubt. But he is also crying for others. The cartolas have always acted with impunity. No one thought that they would ever be called to account.

Eurico Miranda is in trouble too. At the beginning of the year he was all-powerful, openly courting politicians and judges. But allegations are mounting against him. TV Globo – retaliating against Eurico's gesture of putting the logo of rival TV station SBT on Vasco's shirts – ups the ante. It claims the cartola has a secret £300,000 house in Florida, yet another indication of crime against the financial system. The police report into the São Januário disaster is also incriminating. The stadium is judged to have a maximum capacity of 27,306. On the day of the 'human avalanche'

the official public figure was 32,537. Eurico is typically uncooperative, so police raid São Januário to impound documents – as if Vasco's antique stadium is the headquarters of
a criminal gang. The club has other problems. It is behind
in paying its players' wages. Romário alone is owed about
£4 million.

I call the Federal Prosecutor's Office to ask how many
actions are pending against Eurico. Within the hour I am
faxed back thirty-seven pages of allegations, all signed by
the Attorney General. Of course, all the actions are in limbo
because, as a federal deputy, Eurico is immune from prosecution.

In 2001 the Senate was snarled with other embezzlement
and corruption scandals. Yet there were signs that politicians were trying to clean up their acts. The two men at the
centre of the allegations – the outgoing and the incoming
Senate presidents – were forced to resign. Brazil's 'coronels',
it seems, are not as immune as they used to be.

In order to improve Congress's image, federal deputies
announce an historic vote to end parliamentary immunity.
The rule that stops politicians from being prosecuted from
common crimes is perhaps the single biggest reason for the
lack of faith that Brazilians have in their democracy. The
vote, in November, passes overwhelmingly. More than 400
vote in favour. Only nine are against. Including – *quelle
surprise!* – Eurico Miranda.

In December 2001, the chain of events that started with
Ronaldo's fit in the Château de Grande Romaine in July
1998 enters its endgame. The Senate CPI's 1,129-page report
is written. Summing up its conclusions, Senator Álvaro Dias
describes the CBF as 'a den of crime, revealing disoganisa-
tion, anarchy, incompetence and dishonesty'. The report
owes a great deal to Aldo Rebelo's Nike CPI and includes
almost all of Aldo's important discoveries. It recommends
that criminal investigations are launched against seventeen
men – including Ricardo Teixeira, Flamengo president

Edmundo Santos Silva, the São Paulo federation boss
Eduardo José Farah, Wanderley Luxemburgo (the report said
that his many incomes 'reinforced' the idea that he received
bungs) and Ronaldo's agent Reinaldo Pitta. The strongest
evidence is against Eurico. He is accused of electoral crime,
fraud, tax-evasion, theft and money-laundering – all arising
from claims that he looted Vasco's coffers for his personal
gain.

In 2001 the cartolas lived their *annus horribilis*. A year
ago they were unassailable and impune. The parliamentary
hearings have been their requiem. Now they are humiliated
and beaten. Almost. All that is left is for the report to be
approved by senators at the CPI's final session. The stakes
are high, since without approval all the prosecution service
will – as in Aldo's case – be unable to follow up the investigations.

Victory is very much up for grabs. A week before the vote
Lance! lists the thirteen senators on the CPI and their likely
decisions. Six are in favour of the report, four are against
and three are undecided. In the battle for the wavering senators' votes both sides play dirty. To mobilise public opinion
Senator Geraldo Althoff, who authored the report, appears
on the main evening television news bulletin to say that there
is clear evidence that Eurico Miranda is a criminal.
Information from the CPI report is leaked to the bestselling
weekly news magazine, *Veja*, which prints a cover story on
Ricardo Teixeira's alleged corruption.

The CBF fights back. Incapable of winning public opinion,
it instead concentrates on persuading the CPI's senators
personally. But this does not work. Geraldo Althoff tells the
police that he was contacted by a man claiming to be from
the CBF who offered him money to dilute the report. Álvaro
Dias says in the Congressional chamber that the CBF is
offering to fund senators' re-election campaigns in exchange
for votes. The CBF reacts by buying advertising space in
newspapers to deny the allegations – but the cartolas increasingly appear out-manoeuvered.

Two senators who had crossed my path researching this book are coincidentally involved. Senator Sebastião Rocha, the left-wing gynaecologist who I had met in an Amazonian nightclub, is reported to be in favour of approval. Then rumours circulate that CBF sympathisers have prepared a dossier against him and are using it to blackmail him to vote against. (A traditional method of political persuasion.)

Another senator in the spotlight is Bernardo Cabral, a confidant of Eurico Miranda. Less than a year before I had seen Cabral stand up at Eurico's inauguration as Vasco president and lovingly describe him as a 'jabuti', an indestructable Amazonian tortoise. I cannot imagine Cabral betraying Eurico and voting for the report, which recommends criminal proceedings against him. But I also cannot imagine him voting against it in the changing political climate. Is Carbal's loyalty to be to his friend or to his electorate? To avoid expressing an opinion, the senator resigns from the CPI.

When Cabral withdraws I become convinced that the CPI's momentum is unstoppable. If the cartolas' allies will not defend them who will?

Voting day arrives. The CPI report is approved 12-0. It is a crushing defeat for the CBF; and possibly the most important scoreline for Brazilian football all year.

Juca Kfouri is euphoric, describing the report's approval as evidence of a 'new Brazil, a new politics and a new football . . . victories of citizenship like this are rare.'

The CPI's triumphal end closes an ugly chapter in Brazilian football. Maybe such pains were necessary for it ever to improve again. Since there is no point clearing out one corrupt regime only for another to step in its place, the CPI includes proposals for a Law of Social Responsibility in Football. In this legislation lies the hope for a better future of the Brazilian game.

Chapter Fifteen

SOCRATIC DIALOGUE

If Brazilian football at its best is the game's Platonic ideal, then it is particularly appropriate that the last time Brazil played that way was when the team was captained by a man named after Plato's favourite thinker.

Sócrates captained the national team in the 1982 World Cup. With an aristocratic gait, wild black beard, head of unkempt hair and dark-eyed, pensive scowl, he really did look more like a philosopher than an athlete. His style of play also suggested a moral authority. He always kept his cool, hardly ever given to shows of 'Brazilian' exuberance, even when scoring goals. He was not about speed or strength (his feet, size nine, were tiny for his height, 6ft 3ins), but about vision, intelligent passes and tricks. His trademark was the back-heel. Pelé said that Sócrates played better backwards than most footballers did forwards.

Alongside him in 1982 were Zico and Falcão, a midfield line-up as strong as any that have worn Brazil's yellow shirts. The team was knocked out 3–2 by Italy, or, more precisely, Paolo Rossi, who scored all the Italians' goals. Yet despite its failure to win a title, the Class of '82 is remembered more fondly than any other since 1970 – much more, unquestionably, than the 1994 world champions, when victory was bittersweet since the team played defensively and won the final on penalties. In 1982, Brazil were *Braziiiil*; they looked

BRASIL

SOCRATES

Sócrates B.S. de Souza Vieira de Oliveira

like they played for pure enjoyment.

I remember Sócrates from the 1982 and 1986 World Cups, more vividly than any other Brazilian footballer. When I came to Brazil, I soon learnt that he was equally exceptional for his activities off the pitch. He became the footballer I most wanted to meet. Sócrates started his football career when he was at medical school. After retiring, he returned to his studies, qualified and then opened a multi-disciplinary sports clinic in his home town, Riberão Preto. His nickname in Brazil is O Doutor, *the Doctor*.

But most importantly, Sócrates was a social activist. He managed to politicise football in a way no one in Brazil has ever done. Footballers are generally working class, uneducated and poor. The Doctor was a bright middle-class kid who implanted his left-wing idealism on his colleagues and ended up playing a role in his country's unfolding political destiny.

Wanting to speak to an 'expert' about the state of Brazilian football, I reasoned that Sócrates would be an excellent oracle. There is probably no one more qualified. He has been a sports medic and a professional coach, he has studied sports administration and he writes newspaper columns. Most importantly, his heroic feet (and heels) were one of the last registered users of the 'beautiful game'. Maybe he could reveal where it had gone.

Sócrates is famously independent. He says what he likes when he likes. He never had an agent as a player and still doesn't. If you want to speak to him you phone his mobile, which he attends to personally. I call him. We arrange to go for lunch in a bar in São Paulo.

When I arrive the bar is almost empty. Sócrates is sitting alone, wearing a pair of reflective shades and with a cigarette in one hand. A sparkling tulip of beer is on the table in front of him. The impression is less of a once-great sportsman than it is of an ageing rocker or an ex-con. His hair is black and neatly cut short. His beard, although trimmed, is still resolutely scruffy and a hotchpotch of greys.

I introduce myself. Sócrates has a deep smoker's voice and the rural 'ooh-arr' accent of upstate São Paulo. He welcomes me, the way Brazilians do, like I am a long-lost friend. Once he starts talking he doesn't stop.

So, Doctor, I ask him, what is your diagnosis?

At the beginning of the twentieth century most Brazilians lived in the countryside. Industrialisation caused millions of poor rural workers to migrate to urban centres. Cities grew increasingly crowded, like São Paulo, now a mega-conurbation of eighteen million inhabitants. From our outdoor table you get a good sense of São Paulo's heat, pollution and concrete claustrophobia. The decade in which Brazil's rural population was outnumbered for the first time by the population of its cities and towns was the 1960s – the same decade that football was at its peak.

Futebol has changed, begins Sócrates, because Brazil has changed. 'We've become an urban country,' he says. 'Before, there were no limits for playing – you could play on the streets or wherever. Now it's difficult to find space. This means that whatever type of relationship you have these days with sport involves some kind of standardisation.'

I agree with what he says. The cliché about Brazil, that its happy football comes from childhood games played with unrestrained abandon, is false. The barefooted tykes kicking footballs on Rio's beaches are not doing so at liberty – they are members of 'escolinhas', Beach Soccer training clubs, which operate along the seafront. In São Paulo, children do not learn to play on patches of common land – because there is no common land any more. They learn in society football or futsal escolinhas. The freedom that let Brazilians reinvent the game decades ago is long gone.

But the new formality has developed informally. Escolinhas tend to be run by enthusiasts, rather than experienced coaches or sports teachers. 'The people who run escolinhas are usually very poorly qualified for the job. They create models which are limited to their capacities,' argues Sócrates. 'The pupil can never know more than the teacher, so if the teacher knows very little, the pupil will know even less. Of course, creativity is obviously a part of our culture. We don't lack it – but we are limiting the possibility for creativity. Our game is very bureaucratic now, and this is related to players' development.'

Sócrates believes the solution is education – of teachers. Children need to be allowed to create and have fun with the ball, rather than learning tactical systems from the age of two. The Brazilian Football Confederation has no nationally coordinated, long-term plan for its junior levels. 'These days if you want to be a football coach you can. There are no requirements. I think there has to be. To teach kids properly you need courses on pedagogy, fitness training, that sort of thing.'

The bar owner, a woman in her late thirties, comes over and Sócrates introduces us. She calls him Magrão, which means *Big Skinny Bloke*, an affectionate nickname for tall thin people. Sócrates is not that thin any more. Neither is he fat, yet. But Sócrates drinks and smokes like a *bon viveur*, and he is gaining the physique to accompany it. His face has filled out and his stomach is going the same way. After his third beer, I stop counting.

Sócrates says another structural problem is that Brazilian football has whitened. Blacks, he argues, have more natural aptitude.

But aren't you white? I say immediately.

'In reality, there's some black in me,' he teases. Sócrates laughs with his teeth closed. He is good-natured and sensitive all the way through the interview. He makes fun of himself without ever losing his seriousness.

Until the 1970s, he says, middle-class children did not often become professional footballers. The wages were too low and the social scene marginal. Then serious money started to come into the game and the middle-class whites who ran the clubs started to have an interest in putting their family and friends in the teams. 'Gradually a barrier formed against the poorer parts of the population and the quality of our football started to decline.

'Players are not always chosen on individual talent in our country. Privileges can help you at all levels. If you have a personal or political or family relation with a player, maybe you will favour him beyond his capacity.'

This provides an opportunity to start talking about what has happened to the national team. I ask why he thinks Brazil are playing so badly, when – even if overall quality is not what it once was – Brazil *still* has the highest concentration of talented footballers in the world.

Sócrates is clear in his response: 'Players get into the team to be negotiated to Europe. This puts them in the shop window. European clubs like to contract players who have already played for the Brazilian national team. I think the team is being used much more as a negotiating table rather than for professional reasons.'

Some figures: in his two years as national coach, Wanderley Luxemburgo called up ninety-one players. Emerson Leão, in six months, called up sixty-two. Luiz Felipe Scolari, who started off saying that what was needed was continuity, called up forty-two in his first three months. Admittedly any Brazilian coach is faced with an embarrassment of riches, and there are more international games than there used to be – but still? In total, sixty-two Brazilians played for their country during the eighteen World Cup qualifying games. Argentina, who won the group, used half that amount.

'In every game there is an absurdly large number of different players. The base changes every hour. The style changes every hour. There is no tactical planning. Of course the team is not going to do well. Now if you want to put together a team you could. You could win the World Cup. It's just putting together characteristics. Of course it's possible to create a good team. They just don't want to.'

Them. *Them.* The enemy within.

Brazilians who play for European clubs often fail to perform well when they play for the national team. They are invariably criticised for putting more passion into their clubs than their country. They are badmouthed as arrogant and greedy; derided as mercenaries. I find this hardly surprising. Brazilians who play abroad are known as the 'estrangeiros', or *foreigners*, when they return home. If you are called a 'foreigner' by your own countrymen, then how can you expect to build team unity based around national pride?

Sócrates believes that the 'foreigners' play badly for a simpler reason. They know that the team isn't chosen on merit. 'There is no bigger thrill for a footballer than playing with people from the same culture. So these players should come to the national team with complete pleasure. But they don't – because they feel more than anyone that individual talent is not valued. They know other interests are at play. Why would Rivaldo and Roberto Carlos come here and play with someone who is ten times worse than them?'

Sócrates says that this is not a new phenomenon. It has been going on for more than a decade. How, I then ask, did Brazil in this period manage to reach two World Cup finals?

'Of course, sometimes there are spells when more serious people are involved in the process . . . but we are now in a period between World Cups, which is a time when [having a good team] is not valued very much. Every area of football today is based around selling players. This occurs, either licitly or illicitly, at every team at every level. It has created the conditions for our football to go down the pan. If you don't have a long-term strategy or planning, of course the quality will fall a lot.'

I return to my question about why he played well, even though he is not black.

'I had to develop my game through necessity. First, I am impatient, always looking for new experiences. This is part of my character. Second, the more difficult things are, the more this stimulates you. I played football and studied medicine at the same time. I *had* to be more inventive than anyone else. If I hadn't studied medicine I would have been a more limited player than I was. Definitely.

'And of course it was another era. Our references were different. I played against Ademir da Guia, Rivelino, Pelé – My generation had this mirror that the current generation doesn't have. We were playing with exceptional players and we were always trying to catch up with them, learning from them, trying to get close to them. This already pulls you right up there.'

Interviewing Sócrates is a refreshing experience. In Brazil, footballers are usually shockingly underprivileged and uneducated. Yet Sócrates, while being atypical, is nevertheless distinctly and overwhelmingly Brazilian. His easygoing posture, his empathetic informality, his humour and the lilting music in his Portuguese are national traits, as well as an instinctive desire to expound strong convictions about football. He just approaches the subject in a more intellectual way.

Most reassuringly, he has internalised his role as the *futebol* philosopher. He tells me that he thinks there is another reason why Brazil do not play the way they used to.

'A football player in the 1970s ran an average distance each game of 4km. Today this has almost tripled. Which means that the spaces between players are relatively smaller. This causes a lot more physical contact, and makes it a lot more difficult for the player to create moves. Today, if you can't play with one touch you have little chance of playing at the top level. As a consequence football has become uglier.'

I tell him this sounds believable.

'So – the sport needs to change. It needs to take into account the physical evolution of the game. All other sports have adapted their rules because of human physical development. But football never has.'

To recreate the conditions for beautiful football he wants to reduce the number of players in each side.

To how many, I ask?

'Nine,' he replies. 'Nine-a-side. The theory is this: to improve the quality of football, to have less injuries and for the players to use their technical ability more – you need to compensate for the physical evolution of the athletes.'

His talk is not just bar chat. Sócrates is about to start a masters thesis at the São Paulo School of Medicine, arguing that football should become nine-a-side.

It seems to me that behind the dry rationale of Sócrates' analysis is the constant Brazilian urge to creatively transgress laws and rules. Brazil has already invented one-a-side (the keepie-uppie queens), two-a-side (footvolley), five-a-side (futsal) and seven-a-side (society football). Sócrates is filling in the gaps.

It is perhaps my most childish question. And with good reason. Ever since 1982, when I was twelve, I have wanted to ask Sócrates if his name had influenced the person he is. I tell him that I find it hard to disassociate the name from his style – both on and off the pitch.

I discover that the question was more insightful than I thought.

'The name in itself doesn't do anything,' he replies. 'But it's obvious that from the moment that you think "why did my father decide to give me that name?" you realise what kind of a man my father is. My father lived in his library. So I lived with him there. I read a hell of a lot. He passed this experience to me, especially because I was the oldest.'

Sócrates tells me he has brothers called Sófocles and

Sóstenes (the Portuguese transliterations of Sophocles and Sosthenes), which are also a reflection on his father's reading matter. (Sócrates has another brother, Raí, who played for Paris St Germain and the Brazilian national team in the 1994 World Cup.)

'My dad was from a very poor family. He wasn't able to study. He had to go to work young. He was a real self-learner. He gave me my name and he has a lot to do with who I am.'

Have you read Plato, I ask?

'Of course. I read loads of philosophers. I like Plato, I really like Machiavelli and I really like Hobbes. It depends on the time, on your head, on where you are going . . . I read a lot, not everything, but I really like philosophy, not formally, more out of curiosity.'

In 1964, the year of the military coup, Sócrates was ten years old. An incident that happened at home sparked off an interest in politics. On the day the army took power his father took a book from his library, on the Bolsheviks, and burnt it. 'I didn't even know what it was, I had an inkling it was something about the Russian Revolution, but what struck me was the act.'

It sowed the seed of Sócrates' left-wing views. 'I am the child of a dictatorial system,' he says. 'When I started college at sixteen, I started to live through the repression – there were colleagues who had to hide, who had to run away.' His ethical beliefs guided his football career. (Plato would have been so proud.) Two decades before Aldo Rebelo and the Brazilian Congress tried to change football, Sócrates did it from the inside. In what sounds more like a hidden chapter of ancient Greek history, Sócrates founded a player-movement called 'Corinthians Democracy'.

Sócrates started his career at Botafogo, the local team in Riberão Preto. In 1978 he transferred to Corinthians, in São Paulo. After a few years he started to tire of the way he and the players were treated by the management. Players were never consulted on decisions. It was an authoritarian atmosphere that paralleled the political situation of the country.

So, Sócrates – together with his team-mate Wladimir – rose up against the club hierarchy. They organised their footballing colleagues into a utopian socialist cell, called Corinthians Democracy, which took control of all the decisions that would affect them. 'We decided everything by consensus,' says Sócrates. 'It was simple things, like "what time will we have lunch". We would suggest, say, three options and we would vote on it. And the majority decision was accepted. Problems hardly existed. There are only problems if there are confrontations of opinion. And there weren't any. Everything was voted on.'

But it was not just 'simple things'. Corinthians Democracy voted to print 'vote on the fifteenth' on the backs of their shirts in the run-up to elections on 15 November 1982. The elections – for federal deputies, senators, governors and mayors – were one of the first steps towards ending the dictatorship.

Sócrates' comrades also challenged the 'concentração', which is the part of Brazilian footballing culture that is perhaps the greatest affront to players' liberties. The word means 'concentration' in the military sense, of 'bringing together troops'. It is usual for Brazilian clubs to insist that before every match – no matter how unimportant – the team must sleep in a hotel, often for several days at a time. The reasoning behind it is that players are not grown-up enough to look after themselves, and must be supervised. 'Footballers are not mature enough to behave themselves before games without anyone supervising them,' argues the national coach Luiz Felipe Scolari. 'It's been proved that sex before a game isn't bad for you. But, for our players, they don't do things by halves. At home they behave more normally. Away from home, with their other sexual partners, they want to prove that they are the best lovers in the world. So they go carousing and tire themselves more, to the point that their performance on the pitch is affected.' The concentração may

Corinthians: political football

be paternalistic, he says, but it is for the players' own good.

'It took us six months to change the rules about the concentração,' explains Sócrates. 'This was the trickiest one. There was a certain fear, which remains until today – that without the concentração some players feel exposed. But, ideologically speaking, concentração exists to lower a person's status. It's like: "You aren't worth anything. You are irresponsible. You need to be a prisoner." It's stupid. The better someone is feeling, the better he will play. It's obvious. And where do you feel better than in your own home?'

He smiles sincerely when he remembers the battles that were won. In 1982, Corinthians won the São Paulo state championship with 'Democracia' printed on their shirts.

'Perhaps it was the most perfect moment I ever lived. And I'm sure it was for 95 per cent of the others too.'

Because Sócrates' movement happened in football – at São Paulo's biggest club – it was very public, and it spilled out into the national political arena. Corinthians Democracy became a point of reference for the debate raging about the democratisation of the military regime. Sócrates became an important figure in the campaign for presidential elections.

In 1984, aged thirty, he spoke at a rally of one and a half million people. He made the crowd a pledge: if Congress passed a constitutional amendment to re-establish free presidential elections, which they were due to vote on a few days later, he would turn down an offer to play in Italy.

The vote did not pass, Sócrates went to Fiorentina, and the era of Corinthians Democracy was over. But the groundswell of momentum for political opening was unstoppable. A year later, a civilian, José Sarney, was made president, which started the transition to free presidential elections in 1989.

Nothing like Corinthians Democracy has ever happened again. I ask what he thinks its legacy is: 'In terms of working conditions we caused deep changes. Today the valuation of players' rights is a lot more than it was before, and we played a fundamental part.'

Sócrates' heroes are Che Guevara and John Lennon. 'The only people I would put a poster of on my wall,' he says. His political beliefs are well known in the most unexpected places.

For several years he has written a column for an Arab newspaper. In 1996, it invited him on a publicity tour of Egypt and Libya. When he arrived in Tripoli he was informed that Colonel Muammar al-Gadaffi wanted to meet him.

'I said: "Cool!",' Sócrates recounts. 'It was a fantastic saga.

'I asked at what time we were going to meet him. They said, "Look, we don't know what time, but we will leave at five in the morning."

'I got up. There was an embargo. You couldn't enter the country by plane. We were taken to the airport. I asked: "How come? You don't have any planes?" And there was Gadaffi's personal plane. It took us to a city where his government is based. We went to a hotel and waited the whole day. We waited and waited. Then, at 6pm, they said, "The time has come. Let's go!"

'We got in these Toyota Land Cruisers. The guy drove and drove. It got dark. We drove on to a trail. Then there was a gate, we opened it and entered a camp. It was a desert, or almost a desert. All the lights were switched off. We stayed maybe twenty minutes in the dark before we got to Gadaffi's tent.'

The Libyan leader and the Brazilian footballer then spent an hour chatting to each other. Gadaffi even had a suggestion.

'He proposed that I put myself forward for president of Brazil. He said he'd back me and finance my campaign, because he already knew my political opinions.'

Sócrates smiled at me and says he turned the offer down.

The Doctor has never hidden his smoking and drinking. I ask him if it has harmed his health as an athlete, or if he thinks it makes him a bad role model?

'This is what I am.' he replies. 'I've smoked since I was thirteen. The only philosophical issue for me is – "Why would I try to pretend I'm something that I'm not?" I smoke. I'll die of lung cancer or of emphysema. I can't stop smoking.'

Have you ever tried to give up, I ask?

He laughs out loud: 'Fifty thousand times. But I can't. Even today I tried to stop. But I had my first cigarette at 11am. This is what I am. I'm not that bothered about what other people think. The best thing that a man can have, in the society in which he lives, is independence. I'm not bothered what people think. They can even think I'm gay. So what? It doesn't change anything.'

When Pelé, to widespread disillusionment, made peace with Ricardo Teixeira, football's democracy movement lost its figurehead. Were there no good men? Sócrates answered the call, declaring himself the 'anticandidate' to the Brazilian Football Confederation.

'At that moment,' he says, 'it became clear that [Pelé and Ricardo Teixeira's] idea was to take the wind out of the sails of the parliamentary commissions. They were saying: "Let's smother it so things continue the same way." No. We need to discuss everything.'

I ask, then, if his candidacy is serious or rhetorical?

'It is a banner that I decided to wave to mobilise public opinion. Brazilian football was never discussed. Intrinsically there is no control over the command, and this is something you need to discuss, the CBF is a national entity. Football is our greatest identity, perhaps it's our greatest ambassador. And – dammit – the state has no control over this. They do as they want to and no one does anything.

'The repercussion was absurdly big. If there was an election I have no doubt I would get more than 95 per cent of the public's vote. I would have no adversary. But it's not like that, it's a closed shop, it's manipulated, economic power is very present. I will fight to be a candidate, but I do not see the viability yet, the structures aren't in place for it to happen. But in the way that my candidacy grew so much, it's impossible for me to retreat. I will never retreat.'

I tell him that I read in a newspaper that Pelé would support him.

'I don't know. I don't know. He always has dubious postures. I don't think so, not any more.'

Sócrates' manifesto contains many eminently sensible proposals, especially those about improving investment in children's education. Some, however, seem so excessively democratic they are downright loopy. He wants the national coach to be voted for by plebiscite.

He is absolutely serious, but adds: 'If this isn't possible you need to open the decision-making process to a big committee of journalists, coaches, athletes and others. And there should be votes of confidence like in a parliamentary system. If the coach is failing, then he should go back to the board for a new vote.'

I suggest that this is slightly bureaucratic.

'Not at all. It is exactly the opposite. There will be more people taking part in the decisions, you will decentralise it.

It should never be bureaucratic. Bureaucracy is the conduct of those who want to manipulate the nation. You want to be as democratic as possible. You need to get rid of the bureaucracy.'

I tell him that a plebiscite is unfeasible. No country in the world has a referendum for their national football coach.

He smiles again. 'Then we'll be the first.'

As the interview draws to a natural close, I close my notebook of prepared questions. I want to know if he is depressed by Brazil, if the constant struggle for democracy gets him down. In football too, the professional game is in disarray. Off the pitch it is corrupt, and on it, it's a sisyphean struggle to live up to past expectations. I ask if he is proud to be a Brazilian.

He says he most definitely is. 'Brazilian culture – this mix of races, this form of seeing the world and life – is possibly our greatest natural resource. Because it is a very happy culture, it is not discriminatory, it's free . . . it's a big disaster zone, really, but it is the essence of humanity. When humanity organised itself too much it lost its most basic characteristics, its instincts, its pleasures. I think this is what we have which is best, and that's why I'm absolutely in love with Brazil.'

Despite all its problems?

'We're a new, young nation, man. You've already had centuries of history. The Old World has had fifty years of stability. We are just being born.'

Appendix One

NOTES ON CHAPTERS

Chapter One

It is not easy flying to the Faroe Islands in April. I overnighted in Copenhagen. The following day I took a nearly empty plane that flew over beautifully clear Danish and Norwegian skies until reaching the islands, which were covered in thick, bumpy cloud. I am very grateful to Niclas Davidsen, who picked me up from the airport and gave me lodging. *Sosialurin*, the Faroese newspaper, was an informative resource. Statistics on foreign players are from the Brazilian Football Confederation's annual reports.

The prevalent view of the origin of the name Brazil is that it comes from Brazil-wood, a tree whose bark gave a red dye that was discovered in abundance by the first Portuguese navigators in South America. The country became known as 'terra de Brasil', or *Brazil-wood land*, later abbreviated to Brazil. The country, according to this explanation, was named after the tree, not – as is frequently assumed – the other way around.

Mitchell, A. and Cantarino, G., *Origins of Brazil, A Search for the Origins of the name Brazil*, unpublished, 2000

Chapter Two

Mário Filho's classic book is the basis of almost all serious analysis of Brazilian football's first half century. In recent years, however, academics have started to consider it a 'literary' rather than a 'historical' text, and one which colours the facts to fit his friend Gilberto Freyre's theories. I have used knowledge gleaned from interviews with the sociologist Antônio Jorge Soares and César Gordon and am much indebted to Leonardo Affonso Pereira's comprehensive study, *Footballmania*. Aidan Hamilton's history of the British in Brazil was my source for Charles Miller.

Filho, M., *O Negro no Futebol Brasileiro* (second edition), Civilização Brasileira, Rio de Janeiro, 1964

Freyre, G., *The Gilberto Freyre Reader*, Alfred A. Knopf, New York, 1974

Hamilton, A., *An Entirely Different Game, The British Influence on Brazilian Football*, Mainstream Publishing, Edinburgh, 1998

Pedrosa, M. (ed.), *Gol de letra: O futebol na literatura brasileira*, Livraria Editora Gol, Rio de Janeiro, 1967

Pereira, L. A. de M., *Footballmania, Uma História Social do Futebol no Rio de Janeiro, 1902–1938*, Editora Nova Fronteira, Rio de Janeiro, 2000

Ribeiro, A., *O Diamante Eterno, Biografia de Leônidas da Silva*, Gryphus, Rio de Janeiro, 1999

Toledo, L. H. de, *No País do Futebol*, Jorge Zahar Editor, 2000

Chapter Three

There is no shortage of literature about the 1950 World Cup. Paulo Perdigão's book is the best, both for its analytic rigour and its obsessive passion. Paulo also lent me his documentary 'Paradise Lost' that he made about the Fateful Final, from which I took the images of Gigghia's goal. I absorbed ideas from Roberto DaMatta's writings on football at several moments in the book, most of which can be found in the collection *Universo do Futebol*.

DaMatta, R. and others, *Universo do Futebol: Esporte e Sociedade Brasileira*, Edições Pinakotheke, Rio de Janeiro, 1982

Máximo, J., *Maracanã, Meio século de paixão*, Dórea Books and Art, São Paulo, 2000

Moraes Neto, G., *Dossiê 50. Os onze jogadores revelam os segredos da maior tragédia do futebol brasileiro*, Objetiva, 2000

Morales, F., *Maracaná, Los Laberintos del carácter*, Ediciones Santillana, Montevideo, 2000

Moura, G. de A., *O Rio corre para o Maracanã*, Editora Fundação Getúlio Vargas, Rio de Janeiro, 1988

Muylaert, R., *Barbosa. Um gol faz cinquenta anos*, RMC Editora, 2000

Noguiera, A., Soares, J. and Muylaert, R., *A Copa que ninguém viu e a que não queremos lembrar*, Companhia Das Letras, São Paulo, 1994

Perdigão, P., *Anatomia de uma Derrota, Edição revista e ampliada*, L&PM Editores, Porto Alegre, 2000

Schlee, A. G., *Contos de Futebol*, Mercardo Aberto, Porto Alegre, 1997. First published as *Cuentos de Futbol*, Ediciones de la Banda Oriental, Montevideo, Uruguay, 1995

Vieira, C., *Maracanã, Templo dos Deuses Brasileiros*, Mauad Editora, Rio de Janeiro, 2000

Chapter Four

I researched the Pareci at Rio's Indian Museum and at the National Library. Background about Índio's life was taken from a long article by Ricardo Kotscho in *Época*. Information about the Xikrin do Cateté was plundered from the standard reference book on Brazil's indigenous population:

Ricardo, C. A. (ed.), *Povos Indígenas do Brasil 1996–2000*, Instituto Socioambiental, São Paulo, 2000

Chapter Five

I chose João Pedro Stedile for the opening quote since he has nothing to do with football – the Landless Movement is a Marxist group that campaigns for land reform by squatting on disused land and demanding title. My comparisons with mythical creatures arose from conversations with the oral historian José Carlos Sebe Bom Meihy. According to the Portuguese dictionary *Aurélio*, a 'garrincha' is the nickname in Pernambuco and Sergipe of the 'garriça', which – after days of research and dozens of calls – an English-speaker in the ornithology department of Rio's National Museum told me was a bird from the same family as the common wren. Ruy Castro's terrific biography of Garrincha formed the basis of my description of the player's life.

Azevedo, R., *Armazém do Folclore*, Atica, São Paulo, 2000

Camara Cascudo, L. da, *Dicionário do Folclore Brasileiro*, Editora Itatiaia, Belo Horizonte, 1993

Castro, R., *Estrela Solitária, Um brasileiro chamado Garrincha*, Companhia Das Letras, São Paulo, 1995

Leite Lopes, J. S., *The 'People's Joy' Vanishes: Considerations on the Death of a Soccer Player*, Journal of Latin American Anthropology, 1999

Mendes Campos, P., *O gol é necessário, crônicas esportivas*, Civilização Brasileria, Rio de Janeiro, 2000

Monteiro Lobato, *O Sacy Perêrê: Resultado de um inquérito*, 1918, reproduced by Fundação Banco do Brasil, Rio de Janeiro, 1998

Various authors, *Para Entender O Brasil*, Editora Alegro, São Paulo, 2000

Chapter Six

There are no biographies of Mário Filho. I was reliant on conversations with Ruy Castro, who wrote the biography of his brother Nelson Rodrigues, for information on their family history.

It was difficult to decide which symbol-fans to write about since there are so many. I feel obliged to mention Salvador club Bahia, who have the most colourful supporters I came across. At one Bahia game I saw several women in superwoman leotards – superman is the team mascot – and a man rolled up entirely in toilet roll.

Castro, R., *O Anjo Pornográfico, A Vida de Nelson Rodrigues*, Companhia Das Letras, São Paulo, 1992

Filho, M., *Histórias do Flamengo* (second edition), Gernasa, Rio de Janeiro, date unknown

Filho, M., *O Sapo de Arubinha* (ed. Castro), Companhia Das Letras, São Paulo, 1994

Kfouri, J., *Corinthians, paixão e glória*, Dórea Books and Art, São Paulo, 1996

Rodrigues, N. and Filho, M., *Fla-Flu . . . e as Multidões Despertam*, Edição Europa, Rio de Janeiro, 1987

Toledo, L. H. de., *Torcidas Organizadas de Futebol*, Editora Autores Associados, Campinas, 1996

Chapter Seven

I first read about Brejinho in Mário Magalhães' insightful collection of football journalism. The book also revealed many other stories I followed up in other chapters.

Magalhães, M., *Viagem ao país do futebol*, Dórea Books and Art, São Paulo, 1998

Chapter Eight

As a result of my interview with Roza FC, local TV and press started to cover the team. New players became involved and Roza now intend to represent Brazil in the 2002 Gay Games in Sydney.

Décourt, G. C., *Aconteceu, sim!*, Pannartz, São Paulo, 1987

Chapter Nine

Padre Antonio Carlos Barreiro and his hardworking staff at the Room of Miracles helped me beyond their call of duty. My under-standing of the complicated theology of Brazilian faiths was aided with advice from Ralph dellaCava, of Columbia University, and Regina Novaes, of Rio's Institute for Religious Studies.

Rosenfeld, A., *O Futebol no Brasil*, 1956, in the journal *Argumento*, no. 4, Paz e Terra, São Paulo, 1974

Chapter Ten

Although compiling lists of curious Brazilian names is nearly a national hobby, there is almost no serious research into it. Max Gehringer, Mário Souto Maior and Marcos de Castro suggested some of the more revealing examples. The two 'futebol' dictionaries were also indispensable.

Amado, J., *A Bola e o Goleiro*, Editora Record, Rio de Janeiro, 1984

Buarque de Holanda, S., *Raízes do Brasil*, Companhia Das Letras, São Paulo, 1936

Cabral, S., *No Tempo de Ari Barroso*, Lumiar Editora, Rio de Janeiro, 1993

Castro, M. de., *A Imprensa e o Caos na Ortografia*, Editora Record, Rio de Janeiro, 1998

Maranhão, H., *Dicionário de Futebol*, Editora Record, Rio de Janeiro, 1998

Marques, J. C., *O Futebol em Nelson Rodrigues*, Educ, São Paulo, 2000

Penna, L., *Dicionário Popular de Futebol, O ABC das arquibancadas*, Editora Nova Fronteira, Rio de Janeiro, 1998

Proença, I. C., *Futebol e Palavra*, Livraria José Olympio Editora, Rio de Janeiro, 1981

Rodrigues, N., *A Pátria em Chuteiras, Novas Crônicas de Futebol* (ed. Castro), Companhia Das Letras, São Paulo, 1994

Rodrigues, N., *À Sombra das Chuteiras Imortais, Crônicas de Futebol* (ed. Castro), Companhia Das Letras, São Paulo, 1993

Rodrigues, N., *A Vida Como Ela É . . .* (ed. Castro), Companhia Das Letras, São Paulo, 1992

Soares, E., *A Bola no Ar, O Rádio Esportivo em São Paulo*, Summus, São Paulo, 1994

Souto Maior, M., *Nomes Próprios Pouco Comuns*, Bagaço, Recife, 1996

Verissimo, L. F., *A Eterna Privação do Zagueiro Absoluto, as melhoras crônicas de futebol, cinema e literatura*, Objetiva, Rio de Janeiro, 1999

Chapter Eleven

My stay in Manaus was made cheaper courtesy of the Amazonas tourist board, which paid for my accommodation. Sidney Netto kindly sent me his doctorate on the Big Kickabout from the University of Porto, Portugal. The freshness of the extracts from *A Crítica* is perhaps because they were among the first articles ever written by Márcia Guimarães, a twenty-year-old intern.

Filho. P., *Estudos de História do Amazonas*, Valer Editora, Manaus, 2000

Netto, S., *A Organização nas Estruturas Desportivas. Um Estudo De Caso Sobre O Campeonato De Peladas Do Amazonas – Peladão*, Universidade do Porto, 2001

Chapter Twelve

I mention that Amapá has no tourist industry. If tourists ever do decide to travel there I can recommend the recently-built Ceta Ecotel, where ecoball was invented. The hotel's Adriano Ferreira introduced me to Mundica, whose ball recipe is in the fourth appendix. The culinary high point was when Joaquim Neto invited me home to feed me a bowl of açaí – a delicious purple berry stacked full of protein. I predict that one day açaí will be available all around the world.

Chapter Thirteen

The Byzantine rules of the Brazilian leagues are explained in Marco Aurelio Klein's almanac. The book is an invaluable reference, since it also lists every player to have ever played for the national team, together with number of appearances and goals.

Klein, M. A., *Futebol Brasileiro 1894–2001*, Editora Escala, São Paulo, 2001

Chapter Fourteen

The Nike–CBF contract and the full texts of both CPIs were available on the internet. On other government websites you can see the legal actions against Ricardo Teixeira and Eurico Miranda.

Torres, S. (ed.), *Comissão Parlamentar de Inquérito Destinada a Apurar a Regularidade do Contrato Celebrado Entre a CBF e a Nike*, Brasília, 2001

Yallop, D., *How They Stole The Game*, Poetic Publishing, London, 1999

Chapter Fifteen

Shirts, M., *Sócrates, Corinthians, and Questions of Democracy and Citizenship*, journal and date unknown

General

It may not look like it judging from this list, but until the mid-1990s there were comparatively few books about Brazilian football. Studies on football's anthropological or sociological influences are also few and far between. The pioneer was an American, Janet Lever, in the 1970s. Since 1994 a group of anthropologists in Rio have been expanding research into football significantly.

The following all contributed in some way to my understanding of the subject.

Bruhns, H. T., *Futebol, Carnaval e Capoeira*, Papirus Editora, Campinas, 2000

Bussunda, *Bussunda na Copa*, Editora Record, Rio de Janeiro, 1994

Da Costa, M. R., Florenzano, J. P., Quintilho, E., D'Allevedo, S. C. and Santos, M. A. S. (eds.), *Futebol, espectáculo do século*, Musa Editora, São Paulo, 1999

Feijó, L. C. S., *A Linguagem dos Esportes de Massa e a Gíria no Futebol*, Tempo Brasileiro, Rio de Janeiro, 1994

Galeano, E., *Football in Sun and Shadow*, Fourth Estate, London, 1997

Gonçalves, M. A., and Mattos Jr, W de, (eds.), *Lance!'s Enciclopédia do Futebol Brasileiro*, Areté Editorial, Rio de Janeiro, 2001

Goussinsky, E. and Assumpção, J. C., *Deuses da Bola, Histórias da Seleção Brasileira de Futebol*, Dórea Books and Art, São Paulo, 1998

Jenkins, G., *The Beautiful Team: In Search of Péle and the 1970 Brazilians*, Simon and Schuster, London, 1998

Kuper, S., *Football Against The Enemy*, Orion Books, London, 1994

Lever, J., *Soccer Madness, Brazil's passion for the world's most popular sport*, Waveland Press, 1983 (1995 reissue)

Mason, T., *Passion of the People? Football in South America*, Verso, London, 1995

Mattos, C., *Cem Anos de Paixão, Uma mitologia carioca no futebol*, Rocco, Rio de Janeiro, 1997

Máximo, J., *João Saldanha*, Relume Dumará, Rio de Janeiro, 1996

Mendes, L., *7 mil horas de futebol*, Freitas Bastos, Rio de Janeiro, 1999

Milan, B., *O País da Bola*, Editora Record, Rio de Janeiro, 1998

Murad, M., *Dos pés à cabeça, Elementos Básicos de Sociologia do Futebol*, Irradiação Cultural, Rio de Janeiro, 1996

Proni, M. W., *A Metamorphose do Futebol*, Unicamp, Campinas, 2000

Ramos, R. (ed.), *A palavra é Futebol*, Editora Scipione, São Paulo, 1990

Saldanha, J., *Histórias do futebol*, Editora Revan, Rio de Janeiro, 1963

Sebe Bom Meihy, J. C. and Witter, J. S. (eds.), *Futebol e Cultura, Coletânea de estudos*, Imprensa Oficial do Estado, São Paulo, 1982

Souto, S. M., *Os Três Tempos do Jogo*, Graphia, Rio de Janeiro, 2000

Souza, J. de, Rito, L. and Sá Leitão, S., *Futebol-Arte, A cultura e o jeito brasileiro de jogar*, Editora Senac, São Paulo, 1998

Sussekind, H., *Futebol em dois tempos*, Relume Dumará, Rio de Janeiro, 1996

Taylor, C., *The Beautiful Game, A Journey Through Latin American Football*, Victor Gollancz, London, 1998

Journals

Pesquisa de Campo, Revista do Núcleo de Sociologia do Futebol, 1–5, Universidade Estadual do Rio de Janeiro

Revista USP, no. 22, June–August 1994, Dossiê Futebol, Universidade de São Paulo

Newspapers

Lance!, O Globo, Jornal do Brasil, Estado de São Paulo, Folha de São Paulo, Extra, O Dia

Magazines

Caros Amigos, Época, Istoë, Placar, Playboy, Realidade, Veja

Films

The Brazilian film industry has produced several interesting football movies. The difference between the Garrincha and Pelé biopics reflects the difference between the two players – Garrincha is only heard twice in his film; in Pelé's, the 'King' is constantly talking about himself. *Barbosa* is a short, and includes a moving interview with the 1950 keeper. While deeply sympathetic to him, it nevertheless reinforces his image as a national pariah. *Futebol* includes several interviews with old footballers – some who have since died – which I have quoted.

Barbosa, directed by Jorge Furtado, 1988

Boleiros, Era Uma Vez o Futebol, directed by Ugo Giorgetti, 1997

Futebol, documentary directed by Arthur Fontes and João Moreira Salles, GNT/Videofilmes, 1998

Garrincha, Alegria do Povo, directed by Joaquim Pedro de Andrade, 1963

Isto É Pelé, directed by Eduardo Escorel and Luiz Carlos Barreto, 1975

Appendix Two

THE CLUBS

It is impossible to say precisely how many professional clubs there are in Brazil, since they are endlessly being founded and shut down. The best that the Brazilian Football Confederation can say is that in 2000, the last year for which figures are available, it registered forty-eight new professional teams – almost one a week. *Lance!* lists 794 in its encyclopaedia, and *Placar* claims that 302 are operational. However, according to Marco Aurelio Klein's almanac *Futebol Brasileiro*, the twenty-seven professional state leagues (accounting for fifty-two divisions) contain 531 clubs. I have separated the major teams into their four states.

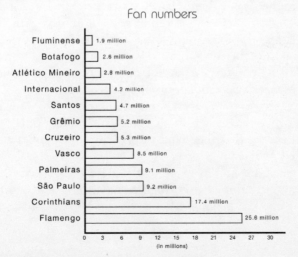

Fan numbers

Fluminense	1.9 million
Botafogo	2.6 million
Atlético Mineiro	2.8 million
Internacional	4.2 million
Santos	4.7 million
Grêmio	5.2 million
Cruzeiro	5.3 million
Vasco	8.5 million
Palmeiras	9.1 million
São Paulo	9.2 million
Corinthians	17.4 million
Flamengo	25.6 million

0 3 6 9 12 15 18 21 24 27 30
(in millions)

Rio de Janeiro

Fluminense, founded by the upper classes, were Rio's first football club. In 1911 a group of Fluminense players left to join Flamengo, already an established rowing club, where they formed its first football team. Botafogo started life as an idea that a fourteen-year-old had during his algebra class. He scribbled the suggestion down on a piece of paper. The teacher saw the note and enouraged his pupil to carry it through. Vasco da Gama are the club of the Portuguese community.

Flamengo soon established itself as the best-supported club in Rio. Many reasons are given, none conclusive. Some say it was because the club trained on public land in its formative years, others say its mass appeal comes from the late 1930s and early 1940s when the club won titles with the most famous black stars of the era – Domingos da Guia, Leônidas and Zizinho.

In many situations to call someone a 'Flamenguista' is akin to calling them a slum-dweller. There are middle-class Flamengo fans, sure, yet the percentage increases the lower you go down the social ladder. If Flamengo are losing, opposing fans chant: 'ela, ela, ela – silêncio na favela' – *silence in the favela*.

If Flamengo are the team of the masses, then, conversely, Fluminense are the team of the aristocracy. I have met Fluminense fans living in poverty who believe they are more socially refined than their Flamenguista neighbours – merely because of their choice of football club. Botafogo gained, in the 1950s and 1960s, a reputation as the team supported by intellectuals and the superstitious. Vasco, although still the club of the Portuguese, have a large black following too – linked to their pioneering introduction of black players.

Only Vasco has a proper home stadium, at São Januário. The other three have such small grounds – holding only a few thousand each – that they tend to play all home games at the city-owned Maracanã.

Fluminense means 'from or of the state of Rio', Vasco da Gama was the name of a Portuguese navigator, and Botafogo and Flamengo are neighbourhoods in Rio's South Zone.

Botafogo

Founded: 12 August 1904
Colours: Shirt with vertical black-and-white stripes, black shorts and grey socks.
Titles: Brazilian champions 1995. Seventeen state championships.
Famous Players: Garrincha, Nilton Santos, Didi, Zagalo, Gérson, Jairzinho.
Website: www.botafogo.com

Flamengo

Founded: 15 November 1895 (football department started on 24 December 1911)
Colours: Shirt with horizontal red and black stripes, white shorts with red vertical stripe on the side, striped red and black socks.
Titles: Brazilian champions 1980, 1982, 1983, 1987, 1992. Twenty-seven state championships. Libertadores Cup 1981. World Club Champions 1981.
Famous Players: Zico, Zizinho, Leônidas, Domingos da Guia, Júnior, Romário, Bebeto.
Website: www.flamengo.com.br

Fluminense

Founded: 21 July 1902
Colours: Shirts with thin white and thick green and grenadine-red vertical stripes. White shorts and white socks with green and grenadine-red stripes.
Titles: Brazilian champions 1984. Twenty-eight state championships.
Famous Players: Rivelino, Telê Santana, Didi.
Website: www.fluminense.com.br

Vasco da Gama

Founded: 21 August 1898 (football department started on 26 November 1915)
Colours: Black shirts with a white diagonal stripe that contains the Patée Cross. Black shorts and white socks.

Titles: Brazilian champions 1974, 1989, 1997, 2000. South American champions 1948. Libertadores Cup 1998. Twenty-one state championships.
Famous Players: Roberto Dinamite, Ademir, Barbosa, Bellini, Vavá, Edmundo, Romário.
Website: www.crvascodagama.com.br

São Paulo

Like in Rio, São Paulo's clubs are divided along social lines. São Paulo is the traditional club of the elite. It emerged from the ashes of Paulistano, who were runners-up in the first state championship in 1902 and, in 1930, shut down their football department in protest at professionalism. Corinthians are the team of the masses; the club was founded by members of the working class – a driver, a mason, a cobbler and two painters. They chose the name since in 1910 the British team Corinthians had toured Brazil. In 1976, 70,000 Corinthians fans went to Rio's Maracanã to see them play a semi-final of the Brazilian championship – the largest away crowd in Brazilian history.

Palmeiras – meaning *Palm Trees* – are the team of the Italian community. They were originally called Palestra Italia but changed their name in 1942 when the Justice Ministry ruled that, because of the Second World War, no sporting entity could contain the name of enemy countries. Santos are the only one of the state's big teams from outside the city of São Paulo. The club owes its fame and success largely to Pelé, who played there between 1956 and 1974, scoring 1091 goals.

Corinthians

Founded: 1 September 1910
Colours: White shirts, black shorts and white socks.
Titles: Brazilian champions 1990, 1998, 1999. FIFA World Club Champions 2000. Twenty-four state championships.
Famous Players: Sócrates, Rivelino, Gilmar.
Website: www.corinthians.com.br

Palmeiras

Founded: 26 August 1914 as Palestra Italia, changed name on 14 September 1942
Colours: Green shirt, white shorts and green socks.
Titles: Brazilian champions in 1972, 1973, 1993, 1994. Libertadores Cup in 1999. Twenty-one state championships.
Famous Players: Ademir da Guia, Djalma Santos, Rivaldo, Edmundo, Roberto Carlos.
Website: www.palmeiras.com.br

Santos

Founded: 14 April 1912
Colours: White shirts, shorts and socks.
Titles: Libertadores Cup 1962, 1963. World Club Champions 1962, 1963. Fifteen state championships.
Famous Players: Pelé, Pepe, Zito, Carlos Alberto, Clodoaldo, Coutinho.
Website: www.santosfc.com.br

São Paulo

Founded: 16 December 1935
Colours: White shirts with two horizontal stripes – one red, one black. White shorts and socks.
Titles: Brazilian champions 1977, 1986, 1991. Libertadores Cup 1992, 1993. World Club Champions 1992, 1993.
Famous Players: Raí, Leônidas, Careca, Müller.
Website: www.saopaulofc.com.br

Rio Grande do Sul

At the turn of the twentieth century, Germans were the dominant immigrant group in Porto Alegre. Grêmio – which means *Fraternity* – was founded by the man who owned the city's first football and, in its early years, only admitted Germans. Two Brazilians who had moved south from São Paulo were not allowed to join, so they founded Internacional.

Grêmio

Founded: 15 September 1903
Colours: Shirts with thin white and thick black and sky-blue vertical stripes. Black shorts and white socks.
Titles: Brazilian champions 1981, 1996. Libertadores Cup 1983, 1995. World Club Champions 1983. Thirty-three state championships.
Famous Players: Renato Gaúcho, Everaldo
Website: www.gremio.net

Internacional

Founded: 4 April 1909
Colours: Red shirts, white shorts and socks.
Titles: Brazilian champions 1975, 1976, 1979. Thirty-three state championships.
Famous Players: Falcão, Taffarel, Paulo César Carpegiani.
Website: www.netinter.com.br

Minas Gerais

Atlético acquired their first football by sending some beetles found in the streets of Belo Horizonte to an insect collector in Paris, who sent a ball back in return. Their local rivals were originally called Società Sportiva Palestra Italia, founded by the local *oriundi*. Its name changed during the Second World War for the same reason that Palmeiras's did. Cruzeiro is shorthand for Cruzeiro do Sul, the constellation Southern Cross – whose pattern is on the team's shirts.

Atlético Mineiro

Founded: 25 March 1908.
Colours: Shirts with black-and-white vertical stripes, black shorts and white socks.
Titles: Brazilian champions 1971. Thirty-eight state championships.
Famous Players: Reinaldo, Dario.
Website: www.atletico.com.br

Cruzeiro

Founded: 2 January 1921
Colours: Blue shirts, white shorts and blue socks.
Titles: Libertadores Cup 1976, 1997. Twenty-nine state championships.
Famous Players: Tostão, Piazza, Ronaldo.
Website: www.cruzeiro.com.br

The Other States

Flamengo's fans are referred to as the Nação Rubro-Negra, *the Ruby-and-Black Nation*. Justifiably, since the number of its supporters is the equivalent of the population of Peru. About 15 per cent of Brazilians are Flamenguistas – double the total number of fans of all Rio's other clubs combined. However distant you are from Rio you can guarantee that you will find a Flamengo fan wearing a replica shirt. In the swathe of land that stretches from the northeast and covers the entire Amazon region, there are more than three times more Flamenguistas than fans of the next most popular team, Corinthians. Since Flamengo is associated with the masses, there is a sense that a Flamengo shirt is more authentically Brazilian than even a Brazil shirt.

Brazil is also a nation of Flamengos. Six states have their own Flamengos, independent professional football clubs named in homage to the Rio original. Similarly there are four cloned Corinthians, three Vascos, three Fluminenses, two Botafogos, two São Paulos, two Santoses and one Palmeiras.

Radio spread the popularity of Flamengo during the peak of transmissions between the 1940s and 1960s. In most states more attention is paid to the Rio and São Paulo championships than to their own state leagues. With seven exceptions: the four mentioned above and Bahia, which has two big clubs – Bahia and Vitória; Pernambuco, which has three – Sport, Santa Cruz and Náutico; and Paraná, which has Coritiba, Atlético Paranaense and Paraná.

Appendix Three

BRAZIL IN WORLD CUPS

Brazil is the only country to have taken part in every World Cup. The line-up in each case is of Brazil's last game.

1930
Hosts: Uruguay
Winners: Uruguay

Brazil knocked out in first stage.

First Stage: Brazil 1 Yugoslavia 2, Brazil 4 Bolivia 0

Brazil: Velloso; Zé Luiz, Italia; Hermógenes, Fausto, Fernando; Benedicto, Russinho, Carvalho Leite, Preguinho, Moderato. Coach: Píndaro.

1934
Hosts: Italy
Winners: Italy

Brazil sail home after one game.

First round: Brazil 1 Spain 3

Brazil: Pedrosa; Sílvio Hoffman, Luiz Luz; Tinoco, Martim Silveira, Canalli; Luizinho, Waldemar de Brito, Armandinho, Leônidas da Silva, Patesko. Coach: Luiz Vinhaes.

1938
Hosts: France
Winners: Italy

Brazil win third place.

First round: Brazil 6 Poland 5
Quarter-final: Brazil 1 Czechoslovakia 1, Brazil 2
Czechoslovakia 1
Semi-final: Brazil 1 Italy 2

Third-place play-off: Brazil 4 Sweden 2

Brazil: Batatais; Domingos da Guia, Machado; Zezé Procópio,
Brandão, Afonsinho; Roberto, Romeu Pellicciari, Leônidas da
Silva, Perácio, Patesko.
Coach: Adhemar Pimenta.

1950
Hosts: Brazil
Winners: Uruguay

Brazil are runners-up.

First stage: Brazil 4 Mexico 0, Brazil 2 Switzerland 2, Brazil 2
Yugoslavia 0
Final stage: Brazil 7 Sweden 1, Brazil 6 Spain 1, Brazil 1
Uruguay 2

Brazil: Barbosa; Augusto, Juvenal; Bauer, Danilo, Bigode;
Friaça, Zizinho, Ademir, Jair da Rosa Pinto, Chico.
Coach: Flávio Costa.

1954
Hosts: Switzerland
Winners: West Germany

Brazil knocked out in the violent quarter-final 'Battle of Berne'.

First stage: Brazil 5 Mexico 0, Brazil 1 Yugoslavia 1
Quarter-final: Brazil 2 Hungary 4

Brazil: Castilho; Pinheiro, Nilton Santos; Djalma Santos, Bauer, Brandãozinho; Julinho, Didi, Índio, Humberto and Maurinho. Coach: Zezé Moreira.

1958
Hosts: Sweden
Winners: Brazil

First round: Brazil 3 Austria 0, Brazil 0 England 0, Brazil 2 USSR 0
Quarter-final: Brazil 1 Wales 0
Semi-final: Brazil 5 France 2
Final: Brazil 5 Sweden 2

Brazil: Gilmar; Djalma Santos, Bellini, Nilton Santos; Orlando, Zito; Garrincha, Didi, Vavá, Pelé, Zagalo.
Coach: Vicente Feola.

1962
Hosts: Chile
Winners: Brazil

First stage: Brazil 2 Mexico 0, Brazil 0 Czechoslovakia 0, Brazil 2 Spain 1
Quarter-final: Brazil 3 England 1
Semi-final: Brazil 4 Chile 2
Final: Brazil 3 Czechoslovakia 1

Brazil: Gilmar; Djalma Santos, Mauro, Zózimo, Nilton Santos; Zito, Didi; Garrincha, Vavá, Amarildo, Zagalo.
Coach: Aymoré Moreira.

1966
Hosts: England
Winners: England

Brazil knocked out in first round – their worst result in three decades.

First stage: Brazil 2 Bulgaria 0, Brazil 1 Hungary 3, Brazil 1 Portugal 3

Brazil: Manga; Fidélis, Brito, Orlando, Rildo; Denílson, Lima; Jairzinho, Silva, Pelé, Paraná.
Coach: Vicente Feola.

1970
Hosts: Mexico
Winners: Brazil

First stage: Brazil 4 Czechoslovakia 1, Brazil 1 England 0, Brazil 3 Romania 2
Quarter-final: Brazil 4 Peru 0
Semi-final: Brazil 3 Uruguay 1
Final: Brazil 4 Italy 1

Brazil: Félix; Carlos Alberto, Brito, Piazza, Everaldo; Clodoaldo, Gérson, Rivelino; Jairzinho, Tostão, Pelé.
Coach: Zagalo.

1974
Hosts: West Germany
Winners: West Germany

Brazil win fourth place.

First Stage: Brazil 0 Yugoslavia 0, Brazil 0 Scotland 0, Brazil 3 Zaire 0

Second Stage: Brazil 1 East Germany 0, Brazil 2 Argentina 1, Brazil 0 Holland 2
Third-place play-off: Brazil 0 Poland 1

Brazil: Leão; Zé Maria, Alfredo, Marinho Peres, Marinho Chagas; Carpegiani, Rivelino; Valdomiro, Jairzinho, Ademir da Guia (Mirandinha), Dirceu.
Coach: Zagalo.

1978
Hosts: Argentina
Winners: Argentina

Brazil win third place, without losing a game.

First Stage: Brazil 1 Sweden 1, Brazil 0 Spain 0, Brazil 1 Austria 0
Second Stage: Brazil 3 Peru 0, Brazil 0 Argentina 0, Brazil 3 Poland 1
Third-place play-off: Brazil 2 Italy 1

Brazil: Leão; Nelinho, Oscar, Amaral, Rodrigues Neto; Batista, Cerezo (Rivellino), J Mendonça; Gil (Reinaldo), Roberto Dinamite, Dirceu.
Coach: Cláudio Coutinho.

1982
Hosts: Spain
Winners: Italy

Brazil knocked out in second stage.

First Stage: Brazil 2 USSR 1, Brazil 4 Scotland 1, Brazil 4 New Zealand 0
Second Stage: Brazil 3 Argentina 1, Brazil 2 Italy 3

Brazil: Valdir Peres; Leandro, Oscar, Luizinho, Júnior; Falcão, Sócrates, Zico; Cerezo, Serginho, Éder.
Coach: Telê Santana.

1986
Hosts: Mexico
Winners: Argentina

Brazil knocked out on penalties in a dramatic quarter-final in which Zico misses a penalty in normal time.

First Stage: Brazil 1 Spain 0, Brazil 1 Algeria 0, Brazil 3 Northern Ireland 0
Second Stage, first round: Brazil 4 Poland 0
Quarter-final: Brazil 1 France 1 (France win 4–3 on penalties)

Brazil: Carlos; Josimar, Júlio César, Edinho, Branco; Elzo, Alemão, Júnior (Silas), Sócrates; Müller (Zico), Careca.
Coach: Telê Santana.

1990
Hosts: Italy
Winners: West Germany

Brazil surprised by losing to arch-rivals in the last 16.

First Stage: Brazil 2 Sweden 1, Brazil 1 Costa Rica 0, Brazil 1 Scotland 0
Second Stage, first round: Brazil 0 Argentina 1

Brazil: Taffarel; Ricardo Rocha, Mauro Galvão (Silas), Ricardo Gomes; Jorginho, Dunga, Alemão (Renato Gaúcho), Valdo, Branco; Müller, Careca.
Coach: Sebastião Lazaroni.

1994
Hosts: United States
Winners: Brazil

First Stage: Brazil 2 Russia 0, Brazil 3 Cameroon 0, Brazil 1 Sweden 1
Second Stage, first round: Brazil 1 United States 0
Quarter-final: Brazil 3 Holland 0
Semi-final: Brazil 1 Sweden 0
Final: Brazil 0 Italy 0 (Brazil win 3–2 on penalties)

Brazil: Taffarel; Jorginho (Cafu), Aldair, Márcio Santos, Branco; Mauro Silva, Dunga, Mazinho, Zinho (Viola); Bebeto, Romário.
Coach: Carlos Alberto Parreira.

1998
Hosts: France
Winners: France

Brazil are runners-up.

First Stage: Brazil 2 Scotland 1, Brazil 3 Morocco 0, Brazil 1 Norway 2

Second Stage, first round: Brazil 4 Chile 1
Quarter-final: Brazil 3 Denmark 2
Semi-final: Brazil 1 Holland 1 (Brazil win 4–2 on penalties)
Final: Brazil 0 France 3

Brazil: Taffarel; Cafu, Aldair, Júnior Baiano, Roberto Carlos; César Sampaio (Edmundo), Dunga, Rivaldo, Leonardo (Denílson); Bebeto, Ronaldo.
Coach: Zagallo.

Appendix Four

A BRAZILIAN FOOTBALL
IN FOUR STEPS

Even though footballs can be bought in Brazil for the equivalent of a few pounds, they are still out of many people's financial reach. Poor Brazilians in the Amazon often spend days making balls from the raw materials. When I was in Amapá, I met Mundica, a rubber-tapper who kindly gave me the following instructions – indispensable knowledge if you are stranded, ball-less in the jungle and feel like a kickabout.

Day One

Step One:
Find three rubber trees (*Hevea Brasiliensis*) that are between 15m and 30m high. Make eight cuts on each trunk in the shape of a 'V'. Attach a bowl to the tree underneath the cuts. As the day passes white latex spills out and gathers in the bowl. If you do this in the morning, by the afternoon there will be enough latex to transfer to a small bucket.

Step Two:
Light a small bonfire made of twigs and straw covered with a layer of earth. The fire should billow thick smoke. Take a cherry-sized clay ball and attach it to a stick. Holding the stick, dip the ball-end into the bowl so that the ball is covered with a thin film of latex. Put it in the smoke until the latex hardens. Repeat twelve times and then leave it to dry.

Day Two

Delicately squeeze the hardened rubber to remove the clay ball. You should be left with a small rubber sphere that has a small hole, from where the thin stick protruded. Blow through this hole like a balloon and tie a knot when the ball is football-sized.

Day Three

Collect more latex and put it in a bowl. Pour the latex into a second bowl over the smoke to give the liquid more consistency. Then cover the ball in a layer of latex and fumigate it until it is hard. Once this process has been repeated six times the football is ready.

Appendix Five

NOTES ON THE COVER

The image on the cover details the last sketches that, in 1953, nineteen-year-old Aldyr Garcia Schlee made before he designed the Brazilian football strip. Each of the figures is based on a famous footballer of the early 1950s. On the back cover, the man on the left is Claudio, who played on the right wing for Corinthians. To his right is Pinheiro, a Fluminense defender. Of his shirt, Aldyr says: 'That was a crazy suggestion. Really it was a windcheater, with a yellow belt tight around the waist and with an old-style collar, the kind you tie together with string . . . A kid thing.' On the front cover, the man in the green and yellow stripes is Ademir Meneses, of Vasco, who scored nine goals in the 1950 World Cup – still the country's record. The final figure is Baltazar, known as *Cabecinha de Ouro*, or 'Little Golden Head', since he scored outstanding headed goals.

After he had jotted down these examples Aldyr decided which combination he thought worked best. He took Baltazar's top, without the stars and the 'Brasil', and put them together with Ademir's collar and Pinheiro's shorts and socks. He painted this outfit in much more detail, put it on a background of the Maracanã, and sent it off to the Brazilian Sports Confederation (CBD). The copy has either been lost or destroyed. When I called up the Brazilian Football Confederation, which took over from the CBD, I was told by its library assistant that the picture was most probably incinerated. 'All public documents are incinerated after five years,' he said gruffly. 'It's the law. Paper doesn't keep in this climate.'

Aldyr stuffed the four moustachioed almost-weres inside a magazine and forgot about it. The quartet remained in the back of a drawer of his home in Pelotas for almost fifty years. In January 2001 Aldyr came across the magazine when he was preparing for my visit. The yellow and the green have held their colour, but the cobalt blue used has faded to sky-blue. He was surprised at how enchanted I was when he showed me the picture: 'It was a draft, a doodle, one of so many that I sketched without thinking anything.' A few months later we spoke about it being used on the cover. He said that Baltazar suggested to him 'the voodoo-esque figure of a drunken zombie: a lost gaze, his arms searching for balance with an old, flat, threadbare, useless ball at his feet'. Aldyr concluded wryly that considering Brazil's recent poor performances the image therefore had unforeseen relevance.

OBRIGADO

I was able to research and write this book together with my duties at the *Guardian* thanks to the generosity and patience of Ed Pilkington and the foreign desk.

Many friends offered help and encouragement. Especially Matt McAllester, David Bellos, Ilona Morison, Aidan Hamilton, Aldyr Garcia Schlee, João Carlos Assumpção at the *Folha de São Paulo*, Marcia Moreira, Alessandro Penna of *Guerin Sportivo*, Marcelo Senna at *Extra*, Aldo Rebelo, Matt Tench at *Observer Sports Monthly*, Bill Prince at *GQ*, Sérgio Xavier Filho and André Fontenelle at *Placar*, Marcelo Damato at *Lance!*, Max Gehringer, Simon Robinson, Gavin Pretor-Pinney, Simon Kuper, Geoff Dyer, Ed Baden Powell, Angus Mitchell, Ana Paula Pedroso, Roberto B. Dias da Silva, Francisco de Assis Alves, Silvia Rogar, Marcelo Carneiro, Luiz Cesar Saraiva Feijó, Luiz Gustavo Vieira de Castro, Hermano Vianna, Toby Calder, Matthew and Gay Kershaw, Grant Fleming, Michael Ende, Adriana Pavlova, Julian Smith, Gareth Chetwynd, Andrew Downie, Matt Butler, Tony Young, Annette MacKenzie, Sam Cartmell and Luis Nachbin.

At Bloomsbury thanks to Edward Faulkner and Liz Calder.

PICTURE CREDITS

Fon-Fon, National Library, Rio de Janeiro: p.78
Franco Cosimo Panini: p.358
Gazeta Press: p.109
Leônidas da Silva Archive: p.39
O Malho, National Library, Rio de Janeiro: p.31
Manchete: p.99, p.113
Nelson Rodrigues Archive: p.248
Pedro Martinelli: p.86
Ricardo Azevedo, *Armazém do Folclóre*: p.96
Roberto Porto Archive: p.200

Colour sections and maps designed by Richard Horne

Every reasonable effort has been made to trace copyright holders of material reproduced in this book, but if any have inadvertantly been overlooked the publishers would be glad to hear from them.

A Note on the Author

Alex Bellos is the correspondent for the *Guardian* and the *Observer* in Rio de Janerio where he has lived and worked for four years. This is his first book.

The CD 'Futebol' of Brazilian music inspired by football is available on Mr Bongo Records (mrbcd/lp24).